Racing with Rich Energy

Racing with Rich Energy

*How a Rogue Sponsor Took
Formula One for a Ride*

ELIZABETH BLACKSTOCK *and*
ALANIS KING

McFarland & Company, Inc., Publishers
Jefferson, North Carolina

LIBRARY OF CONGRESS CATALOGUING-IN-PUBLICATION DATA

Names: Blackstock, Elizabeth, 1996– author. | King, Alanis, 1995– author.
Title: Racing with rich energy : how a rogue sponsor took
Formula One for a ride / Elizabeth Blackstock and Alanis King.
Description: Jefferson, North Carolina : McFarland & Company,
Inc., Publishers, 2022. | Includes bibliographical references and index.
Identifiers: LCCN 2022029578 |
ISBN 9781476688800 (paperback : acid free paper) ∞
ISBN 9781476647920 (ebook)
Subjects: LCSH: Automobile racing—History. | FIA Formula
One World Championship—History. | Formula One automobiles—
History. | Storey, William (Rich Energy founder) | Sports
sponsorship. | BISAC: TRANSPORTATION / Automotive / History
Classification: LCC GV1029.15 .B52 2022 | DDC 796.7209—dc23/eng/20220630
LC record available at https://lccn.loc.gov/2022029578

BRITISH LIBRARY CATALOGUING DATA ARE AVAILABLE

ISBN (print) 978-1-4766-8880-0
ISBN (ebook) 978-1-4766-4792-0

Front cover image: Formula One race car
illustration © 2022 Alanis King

Printed in the United States of America

*McFarland & Company, Inc., Publishers
Box 611, Jefferson, North Carolina 28640
www.mcfarlandpub.com*

TABLE OF CONTENTS

Acknowledgments

From Elizabeth Blackstock

When we set out to write this book, I knew it would be a challenge, but I absolutely underestimated the amount of work it would require—long nights, weekend meetings, delirious editing sessions, and a truly absurd amount of planning. Because of that, above all, I want to thank my coauthor Alanis King, whose do-better work ethic inspired me to keep going long after I'd gotten totally fed up with this book. She was the ideal partner in writing, and without her, this book would be withering away in a drafts folder somewhere, just waiting to see the light of day.

In the same vein, I want to thank my husband Chris, whose infinite patience was absolutely tested every time I wrapped up a work day just to tell him I had to work on the book and who gave up asking if I was finished with this book because the definition of "finished" changed every time I hit a new milestone. Thank you.

And another massive thank you to my family—my mom and stepdad, my brother and sister, my mother-in-law and sister-in-law—for supporting me along the way. I appreciate the hot meals, the words of encouragement, and the comforting homes you provided me. This book couldn't have happened without you.

From Alanis King

I've done so many investigations throughout my journalism career, but none as long, tedious, and detailed as this book. Having Elizabeth by my side the whole time helped me through it—the organization, the creative direction, the editing, and every granular detail we had to cover—and I'm forever grateful for that and for her incredible writing talent. The book was a team effort, and Elizabeth was the perfect teammate to write it with.

It's also hard to imagine that we spent nearly two years on this book, and I want to thank my dear, sweet husband for his patience as I worked on it. There were so many nights when I stayed up later than I should have or closed myself off in a room to go over edits, and so many days when I told him we were almost done when we were, in fact, months from being done. Yet he supported me the whole way, letting me chase that final page because he knew how much it meant to me. I also have to thank my dear, sweet cat, Portia, who can't read but would be honored by this if she could.

So many people also supported me along the way—proofreading my drafts, cheering me along, and telling me their honest thoughts about the book: my mom, Kristen, Allie, Jason, Trish, Patrick, Bozi, and many others. I appreciate you all for your help with the book and help distracting me from it when I needed to take a break.

From Both of the Authors

We're eternally grateful to all the people who made this book possible, from the editors who trusted us to chase Rich Energy's story while we worked at *Jalopnik*, to the sources who spoke to us, to the readers who told us they couldn't wait to see how our book turned out, and to the people who promoted it on iRacing and on their race cars out of the kindness of their hearts. We appreciate all of you, and we hope the end product was everything you expected (and hopefully more). Thank you.

PREFACE

When we set out to write this book in March 2020, it's safe to say we couldn't have predicted what would befall the world between then and the day we finally published it. The COVID-19 pandemic shuttered life as we knew it, confining many to home offices and couches—and others to face the virus at work every day, even if it was the last thing they wanted to do. Both authors saw their job titles change multiple times as we took on and left behind work. It was both the perfect and the worst time to write a book.

But our story begins just before the 2019 Formula One season. At the time, Alanis King and Elizabeth Blackstock were staff writers at *Jalopnik*, an automotive and motorsport news site, and we were tasked with parsing out the mystery behind the Haas F1 Team's newest title sponsor, Rich Energy. The original 4,000-word story we wrote, titled "What You Find When You Look Into Rich Energy, the Mystery Sponsor of America's F1 Team," published on April 10, 2019. In it, we tried to parse out the origins of Rich Energy's money and spoke to company CEO William Storey on the phone. We didn't get all the answers we sought, but that article signaled one crucial milestone: We became the first two journalists to deeply question what was going on.

As the 2019 F1 season progressed, the authors of this book reported on the Rich Energy saga as it unfolded—from the company's Indianapolis 500 car sponsorship to well past its messy departure from F1. To say that we became motorsport journalism's resident Rich Energy experts wouldn't be much of a stretch.

In March 2020, a literary agent who had just watched the F1 Netflix documentary series *Drive to Survive* reached out to the authors to ask if we'd be interested in writing a full book on Rich Energy. We readily agreed and began our work in earnest, crafting a compelling proposal designed to attract the highest bidder and diving into writing our first book.

That agent, though, simply wasn't meant for this project. In a saga almost as compelling as the Rich Energy story itself (and one that, perhaps,

1

will be told in a different medium), we left that agent behind and turned to McFarland, a publisher that welcomed us with open arms and provided us with the freedom and resources we needed to complete this book.

In all, we reached out to more than 150 sources we believed would have information about Rich Energy or its CEO. We crafted lists of hundreds of questions to ask those sources. We referred to archived social media posts, long-forgotten websites, court documents, financial filings, and old newspaper pages. We dove into the history of F1, and we researched sponsorship structures for other motorsport series in order to situate Rich Energy within a larger context. (Because auto racing is a global sport, anonymous quotes have been lightly edited to avoid sources' sentence structures giving away their nationalities or identities. Anonymous sources' identities have been verified by the authors, and the meaning of their quotes has not been altered.)

We wanted to know how and why—besides the obvious—Rich Energy captivated everyone the way it did.

That's one of the questions we tried to answer in this book. What made Rich Energy such a potent force for chaos in a series with a long history of strange sponsors? Why did one man with a Twitter account become the story of a race season? What *was* Rich Energy?

We hope you'll enjoy this journey as much as we did.

1

As the Storey Goes

Williwilliam Storey is a classic salesperson: He won't just try to sell you the ground you're standing on—he'll try to sell you the world, all shined up with a bow on top.

But if you pay attention to him long enough, you'll start to wonder if he has a single square foot of that world to give.

Storey, who founded British energy-drink company Rich Energy in 2015, doesn't look like most CEOs, nor does he act like them. His coarse, wavy hair drapes midway down his chest alongside a beard of the same length. Both are a dark brown at the root and trickle to a near blonde at tips, with threads of gray woven in between. Storey regularly leaves both unkempt in a stereotypical biker ethos, styling only the roots of his fading hairline by smoothing them back past the crown of the head. He dons a signature velvet suit jacket for fancier occasions, and in less formal settings, he can be found in black-and-gold company swag and reflective, face-hugging sport sunglasses fit for a dad spending a day on the lake.

When Storey talks, his gray-blue eyes stare you straight down. His attention doesn't divert, and his tone almost never changes. The only thing that really moves, aside from an occasional demonstration with his hands, is his beard, which engulfs the calm motions of his mouth.

There's a hint of rasp in his voice; it's low but not deep, touched by a subtle British accent. He rarely emphasizes his words, perhaps because he rarely feels the need to. When he does, it comes with a raise of the eyebrow and a swish of the hand, and it is likely paired with one of his favorite words: "premium," "brand," "British," "strategy," "superb," "platform," "fantastic," "absolutely," "obviously." He has an "international business," he'll tell you, and the energy drink he's trying to sell you—and the rest of the world—is made with only "high-quality ingredients." He goes right into the next talking point instead of elaborating.

Storey's product is a "market leader," he'll say, and his small British startup is going up against the Red Bulls of the world like David taking on Goliath. The people who need to know his startup is legitimate do know, and they also know its products are "head and shoulders above the rest." Everyone else is just a doubter.

And, Storey will tell you, doubters will be proven wrong in due time. He just won't say how.

Storey doesn't want to focus on the now or on the hard questions. When something might possibly inconvenience him or his narrative— such as asking how his startup squirmed onto the world stage of motorsport with a $20 million annual sponsorship deal[1] just one year after it reported having a mere $770 in the bank,[2] or mentioning how he has a history of failed businesses—he'll quickly pivot the conversation to the future. It's a bright future, at that. A failure to also focus on that future will make you a doubter, and you know what happens to doubters, because Storey is convinced his company will come out of the other end in a better position than before. Somehow.

His product exudes the same energy he does: confident, perhaps overly so. Its original black can is accented only by one color, gold, with a sleek geometric deer head stretching nearly half of the can's height and the outline of a British flag slicing down its sides. The deer's antlers reach as sharp a point as its chin, with "RICH" spelled above and "ENERGY" below in one of those faux-futuristic fonts perfect for a movie staged on a space station 500 years from now.

William Storey knows he's great and knows he's destined for greatness. His truth might not be *the* truth, but that doesn't matter. He sees himself as the next big thing, the Elon Musk of energy drinks: so convinced of his vision that regardless of what reality says, he's going to make you convinced of it, too—so long as you don't put much focus on running the numbers or checking the facts for yourself.

And that, right there, is where the Haas Formula One Team went wrong.

*   *   *

The Formula One World Championship, also known as F1, had been around for nearly 70 years by the time Rich Energy became a sponsor of the Haas team for the 2019 season. The series was born from prewar grand prix racing and formally entered the motorsport scene in 1950, when a British Grand Prix roared through Silverstone Circuit in front of 120,000 spectators that May.[3] In the decades after, Formula One became what many saw as the pinnacle of auto racing, as well as a nearly unmatched spectacle in the sporting world: a series that rolled its red carpets out in dozens of countries, dressing its spectator suites in white tablecloths and serving their wealthy visitors four-course lobster lunches while multimillion-dollar race cars rolled onto the racing grid below.[4] When Rich Energy entered the series, Formula One was by far the highest and most recognizable discipline under the Fédération Internationale de l'Automobile, or the FIA—a motorsport governing organization founded in 1904 that oversaw dozens of renowned international racing championships.[5]

Even those unfamiliar with racing have likely heard of Formula One. It's the series with race cars that far surpass 200 mph and have enough downforce—the aerodynamic force that glues cars to the ground in order to make them faster—to make many onlookers search one thing online: "Can a Formula One car drive upside down?"[6]

The answer to that question, according to Mercedes F1 Technology Director Mike Elliott in April 2020, was yes. He advised that you don't try it at home.[7]

That's because those Formula One cars were painstakingly designed and purpose built for the pinnacle of racing. In the 2010s, the long, sleek machines had grown increasingly complex while regulations dictated that teams shave down weight. Unlike street vehicles or more conventional sports cars or stock cars, Formula One cars had both exposed wheels and a cockpit open to the sky, the latter of which was partially closed in 2018 with a V-shaped "halo" safety bar designed to deflect debris and prevent head injuries.[8]

Formula One shipped those cars to more than 20 global race circuits per year, from vintage tracks like Spa-Francorchamps that were designed to mimic the natural, hilly Belgian landscape to tight street circuits and newer, more manufactured tracks like the Circuit of The Americas in Austin, Texas. Drivers wound through both left- and right-hand turns, up steep hills, and down city streets for just under two hours in pursuit of championship points that could earn them millions throughout the year.[9]

Historically, the series' most famous race came on the streets of Monaco, where as of 2019, more than 32 percent of residents were millionaires[10] and where a one-bedroom apartment went for a minimum of $1.6 million.[11] Many Formula One drivers have been among those Monaco residents, and one of 2007 F1 champion Kimi Raikkonen's most iconic moments came when he retired early from the 2006 Monaco Grand Prix.[12] ("Retirement" is otherwise known as exiting a race before it ends, whether that be for a wreck or a terminal mechanical failure.) Raikkonen climbed out of his stationary car and walked straight across the track onto his yacht, still in his racing suit. The television broadcast caught a glimpse of Raikkonen soon after, with commentators pointing out that he hadn't even gone back to the paddock before taking off his shirt and getting into a hot tub.[13]

Formula One itself didn't fall far from Monaco's upscale aura: In 2019, the championship-winning Mercedes-AMG Formula One

Team—Mercedes-Benz's in-house effort, and unquestionably the most dominant team of the mid– to late 2010s—spent more than $438 million yet still turned a profit, while Storey's apparent annual spending on Haas represented less than 5 percent of that sum.[14]

Formula One had always been glitz, glamor, and a little bit goofy. But it was the last place, most would think, that a startup just three years into existence might have the money or name recognition to end up. Yet from the outside, a startup with no money or name recognition was exactly what William Storey's brand appeared to be.

✳   ✳   ✳

In 2010s-era Formula One, teams hosted fancy "launch" events every year where they showed off their new, upgraded race cars for the upcoming season. The February 7 launch for Haas' 2019 season, its first and only with Storey and Rich Energy, was a good indicator of what was to come.[15]

"William, what does it mean to now be title sponsor of the Haas F1 Team?" the *Motorsport Network*, one of the broadcast crews at the event, asked.[16]

"We're absolutely delighted," Storey said. Next to Haas' two meticulously groomed drivers, Romain Grosjean and Kevin Magnussen, he stood out like a caricature of a biker at a black-tie affair. "We think that Haas are absolutely our favorite team on the grid. They're brilliant people, and they're the perfect partner for Rich Energy as we move forward to challenge Red Bull on and off the track."[17]

By then, there were already doubts about Rich Energy's credibility as a company—and as a Formula One sponsor. But Storey insisted those concerns were unfounded. On the day of the car launch came another headline from the *Motorsport Network*, which read: "Haas title sponsor likens doubters to moon landing truthers."[18]

"The detractors are obviously not on the same planet as you and me," Storey told the *Motorsport Network*, adding that he welcomed scrutiny. "I think a lot of people have put two and two together and got five. I've heard these nonsense rumors, whatever, and it's just completely risible. I just ignore it.

"As far as I'm concerned, anyone who says it doesn't exist, it's like saying man never walked on the moon or Elvis is still alive. It's just fantasy."[19]

Some of the doubts stemmed from Rich Energy's financial statements and absence on store shelves. But Storey, the *Motorsport Network* wrote, said his company's lower profile was due to it being an "exclusive" product.

"Actions speak louder than words," Storey told the outlet. "At the end of the day when the tide goes out, we see who is swimming naked, don't we? Ultimately, I was very consistent from day one. Everything I've said has been the case. It's interesting that all these so-called detractors have never met me, and actually don't know us at all. It's speculation based on no information. Everyone who actually knew us, and knew what was going on, knew what we were about.

"All our detractors were not in possession of the facts."[20]

Storey could be described as a few things during his company's short foray into Formula One: unfiltered, inconsistent, and obsessed with Red Bull, an Austrian company valued at nearly $10 billion by Forbes at the time.[21] His entire campaign for Rich Energy hinged on the product being better than Red Bull, which was aggressively involved in sports sponsorships around the world and sold 6.8 billion cans across 171 countries in 2018, the year Rich Energy began its campaign to enter Formula One.[22]

Storey, for his part, insisted in February 2019 that Rich Energy had produced 90 million cans.[23] He told the authors of this book a month later that Rich Energy had sold "in excess of 100 million cans" since the company came onto the scene in 2015.[24] At the same time, one analytics company listed Rich Energy as only having sold 1,025 cans in the UK between March 2017 and February 2019—a period of nearly two years.[25]

Storey painted Red Bull out to be Rich Energy's arch rival, a sentiment that wasn't publicly reciprocated. Joining the Formula One grid was another way to get into Red Bull's orbit, where the company had purchased a race team in 2004, more than a decade before Rich Energy even existed.[26] In 2005, Red Bull bought a second, more junior team and named it Toro Rosso.[27]

In his first interview with the authors on March 14, 2019, Storey summed up Rich Energy's mission as "creating a competitor to Red Bull."[28]

"We're very proud of what we're doing," he said. "We're ignoring conventional wisdom. We're completely going against the grain within the traditional drinks industry, which I personally feel could be run much better, and I think we've got a brilliant business strategy. So, we're actually doing something I'm proud of."[29]

That interview, the authors would later learn, occurred the day after Rich Energy had gone to court in a copyright case filed by British company Whyte Bikes over its stag-head logo. Rich Energy's logo was nearly identical to that of Whyte Bikes, but the bicycle company had designed its version seven years before Storey incorporated Rich Energy. Rich Energy lost the case.[30]

The general obsession with Red Bull, which fueled many of Rich Energy's marketing decisions, eventually landed Rich Energy in court as well. There, both it and Storey were ordered to stop infringing upon Red Bull's trademarks on their company website, social media accounts, and just about everywhere else.[31]

But long before those legal disputes, and before Haas' black-and-gold Rich Energy car even made it to the grid for the 2019 season, Rich Energy became the talk of online posts and motorsport forums. Tweets sprang up about the company's apparent lack of money.[32] Questions emerged about its strange online presence. Onlookers wondered who Storey was and if he was full of revolutionary ideas or simply full of himself. The whole thing was one giant question—a question that the Haas F1 Team hadn't bothered publicly answering.

"What is 'Rich Energy'?" a December 2018 submission to the *Autosport* forum read.[33] Its writer, whose profile photo was a GIF of IndyCar champion Will Power stuffing his face with marshmallows, continued the question in a thread below.

"A drink that you cannot buy (unless you order a crate on Amazon. Yeah, no thanks...), yet they are sponsoring an F1 team," they wrote. "Their own marketing looks like it's just done by one bloke and phone, placing these mythical cans infront [sic] of things/places.

"So, it's obviously a scam or some sort of dodge."[34]

"I still very much doubt Haas will get any money from this," a user on the forum responded. Another said that "out of curiosity," they went to the location stated as Rich Energy's contact address on documents filed with the UK government.

"What a shock," they wrote. "It is a medium-sized building in Wandsworth that operates on a rent-a-desk-by-the-week basis. There is a single receptionist for all the various tenants." Independent research backed up the rent-a-space claim, and Storey told the authors in their March 2019 interview that the registered address was simply where Rich Energy's accountant was. He said the practice was "very common in the UK" and that Rich Energy had two other office locations it used in London.[35]

Another forum user linked to a later-deleted tweet in which Rich Energy posted a photo of its "HQ." It was a photo of the Bingham Riverhouse hotel in Richmond, London, England, which apparently served as Rich Energy's base.[36] When contacted by the authors for confirmation that the hotel was actually Rich Energy's headquarters, a phone operator for Bingham Riverhouse declined to comment, citing guest privacy.

"Is Rich Energy a scam?" headlined a Reddit thread from August 2018.[37] "My Spidey sense is tingling," the writer continued. "Can anyone from [the] UK confirm the popularity of Rich Energy and give a bit more information about the company?"[38]

"I had a look in the supermarket because I had the same question," one user responded. "Wasn't there."[39]

"What is Rich Energy?" another Reddit thread, this time from December 2018, read. "Can anyone explain the inside joke?"[40]

"They make energy drinks that no one has ever had," one user said.[41] Others discussed theories of money laundering. One user decided to explain the "joke."

"The joke is that they're massively obscure—nobody's ever heard of them, despite them having enough money to sponsor an F1 team," they wrote. "It's even difficult to get any of their product—it's on Amazon but only in bulk, and by all accounts, it's not exactly a bestseller.

"Basically, they're a load of apparent nobodies who have mysteriously bought their way into the F1 paddock without anyone knowing a thing about them."[42]

Rich Energy's online presence didn't help. The brand's social media pages were long believed to be run by Storey himself due to similarities between the bizarre, hashtag-laden tweets posted on both his personal account and company ones. The official Rich Energy Twitter account also had a habit of plucking the same pixelated stock photos from the internet without credit, over and over again—often claiming or insinuating that they had something to do with the company when those photos did, in fact, not.

When the topic of Formula One teams taking Rich Energy seriously came up during an interview with longtime Formula One journalist Peter Windsor, Storey provided vague reassurance for all of his doubters.

"We are a very fast-growing business," Storey said. "We have some unbelievably strong backers. We have a really compelling proposition in the marketplace, and our curve is very significant upwards.

"So in terms of that, to the people that need to know, we proved that bonafide-ness very early on in the process."[43]

*   *   *

Storey was in his late 30s when he founded Rich Energy, the fifth company he'd registered with the UK government. The first four were vastly different from his proclaimed energy-drink empire, as could be derived from their names: Tryfan Technologies Limited, Wise Guy Boxing, Danieli Style Limited, and Tryfan LED Limited. In all of them, including Rich Energy, Storey's occupation was listed as a "computer consultant." It was only with Rich Energy Racing, a company incorporated in the UK in December 2017 and dissolved in January 2020, that his listed occupation became "CEO." Rich Energy's racing endeavors continued after January 2020 despite the "Rich Energy Racing" UK business listing going kaput.

Business and financial documents filed for the first four companies painted them as bizarre failures, but with the fifth, Storey struck gold—or so he wanted everyone to think.

Rich Energy, despite being Storey's baby, wasn't even his own brainchild. The "Rich d.o.o." trademark that appeared on Rich Energy cans was first registered in Croatia in 2011 by an entrepreneur named Dražen Majstrović, and it was a private company registered as selling soft drinks.[44] It had a very quiet rollout on the world stage, appearing to debut on the nightlife scene in Zagreb, Croatia's capital, with the goal of promoting the country as a tourist attraction for young travelers.[45] An archived Rich Energy webpage from 2013, richenergydrink.com, showed an image of a black-and-gold can in front of a nightclub.[46] While not exactly the same as the design used by Storey's version of Rich Energy, the initial cues were there: a black can with a vertical "R-I-C-H," one letter on top of the other, spelled down its length. The gold, blocky letters were shaded to look three dimensional, all in a style somewhat reminiscent of the History Channel's "H." "ENERGY DRINK," in gold and all caps, appeared below the drink's name in horizontal, 3D-shaded letters, and a translucent gold strand of lettering that said "RICH RICH RICH" wrapped around the can diagonally like a bad photo watermark.

Somewhere along the way, Majstrović dipped off the map, and William Storey took over. Storey claimed his drink got its name from its British home base in Richmond, but the brand's international ties made that hard to believe.[47] When questioned about the inconsistencies in a 2019 interview with the authors, Storey called the original Rich trademark "sort of serendipitous" when paired with Richmond—a change from his previous story.[48] Storey also regularly championed Rich Energy's stag-head logo as paying homage to the deer living in a local park in Richmond, but the copyright case with Whyte Bikes threw doubt into that as well. Even the language used to describe the Croatian iteration of the drink, like the archived website's claim that it was "conceptualized in Croatia" but "manufactured in Austria," lined right up with rhetoric used by Storey, as did the promise that the drink was "poised to make a stunning debut on the energy drink market in the United States."[49]

In 2018, just three years into his tenure at the British take on Rich Energy, Storey set his sights on the world stage of auto racing. In an early example of Storey's tendency to overpromise and under-deliver, he said the records that showed his company having $770 in the bank were misleading and that he was backed by "sterling billionaires" able to fund his high-profile exploits.[50] His confidence in his ability to save Formula One from itself was intoxicating; right out of the gate, he promised much-needed financial injections to struggling teams. But it often seemed like empty rhetoric; he might have been smooth, but he was vague.

The need for a financial savior often stemmed from Formula One being such an expensive sport.[51] From 2008 to 2017, the championship-winning Formula One team spent an average of $285 million annually just to be competitive.[52] In 2017 alone, the Mercedes team spent $413.6 million on the way to win its fourth championship title in a row.[53] In 2019, that ballooned to nearly $440 million.[54]

Rising costs proved inhospitable to teams not backed by major companies like Mercedes and Ferrari, and even long-standing race teams like McLaren and Williams began to struggle as operation costs skyrocketed by 1,000 percent between 1990 and 2018.[55] While Williams was still operating when Rich Energy entered Formula One, its profit margins had been slowly decreasing for years.[56] A lack of funds meant performance suffered, and when performance suffered, no one wanted to invest.

In the late 2010s, Williams lost sponsors like Martini,[57] Rexona, Tata Communications, Omnitude, Symantec, PKN Orlen,[58] and Rokit.[59] The team teetered on the brink of extinction as it crawled into the 2020 race season, propped up by the multimillion-dollar cash injection from driver Nicholas Latifi's father.[60] That year, Williams found refuge when United States–based investment company Dorilton Capital bought it.[61] The team had been seeking a buyer for a while,[62] and although Rich Energy spoke about stepping in, nothing ever came of it.[63]

It was the struggling teams Storey targeted as he attempted to enter Formula One. In 2018, Storey first set his sights on what was then known as Force India, a team about to enter administration as driver Sergio Perez sued it over unpaid funds.[64] Positioning himself as mounting a "£100m takeover" of the team,[65] Storey claimed the deal had been in the making for six months, but the news came as a surprise to both journalists and onlookers in what was often a very loose-lipped community.[66] It was the fact that Force India's assets had been frozen, Storey said, that kept him from buying in.[67]

But he wasn't done yet. During the late October United States Grand Prix, Storey was seen courting Claire Williams, the deputy team principal of the Williams team. Reports later said Storey was poised to buy out the entire team, thus transforming it into Rich Energy Racing[68]—but, *ESPN* reported in July 2019, he never showed up to the dinner at which they were to finalize the deal.[69]

About four days later, on October 25, 2018, the Haas F1 Team announced that Rich Energy would join as a title sponsor for the 2019 season in a "multi-year agreement."[70] The Rich Energy Haas F1 Team was born.

"I think it might have been seen as this big sponsor was going to Williams, and now they're not—they're coming to us instead," a former Haas employee, who spoke on the condition of anonymity, told the authors in an August 2021 interview. "When actually, that was the worst thing they could have done. I wouldn't have wished it on Williams either."[71]

But the deal was great for Storey. "The reality was that the deal that I did with Haas was by a million miles the best deal available, because we took over the entire identity of the team," he said in a May 2020 appearance on a podcast called *Chasin' the Racin'*, which got about 600 views during its first few months on YouTube before it was later removed. "They were a team punching well above their weight, had a tremendous deal with Ferrari [to supply power units], and it just made sense.

"We created Rich Energy Haas F1. De facto, we had our own team, you know, in essence. We were the only energy drink in the world to have our own Formula One team apart from Red Bull, and don't forget, we were only, at the time, four years old. Basically, I felt that would position us against the market leader, which it did."[72]

∗   ∗   ∗

Haas made headlines when it entered Formula One in 2016 for two reasons: It was American, and it was fast.[73] In a sport as Eurocentric as Formula One, it was rare to find an American anywhere in the paddock, be they drivers, engineers, or the big bosses, known in Formula One as "team principals." The team's founder, Ohio-born businessman Gene Haas made a name for himself with his CNC machining company, Haas Automation. That led to his founding stake in the Stewart-Haas NASCAR Cup Series team, which began as Haas CNC Racing in 2002.[74] When he decided to introduce his brand to the world stage of racing with Haas F1, much of the initial marketing centered on it being America's team.

Haas was competitive from the start compared to other teams trying to break into the notoriously expensive Formula One grid, and that's because it was smart. It bought out the failed Marussia team's English headquarters in Banbury.[75] It partnered with veteran Italian race-car manufacturer Dallara to make its chassis—the framework of the car—and Ferrari to supply its power units, gearboxes, and technical support.[76] It took advantage of FIA regulations that allowed it to buy many of its car parts from established teams, thus reducing the risk of having to correct issues with parts developed in-house.[77] It hired former Jaguar managing director and Red Bull Racing technical director Guenther Steiner as its team principal.[78]

In its first year of racing, Haas F1 finished eighth in the overall standings for Formula One teams—called the "constructor championship"—ahead of Renault, Sauber, and Manor, all of whom had previous Formula One experience.[79] It was a promising start for a fledgling team, and one that only a few brand-new outfits had been able to achieve in that era. By 2018, Haas had finished fifth in the constructor championship.[80]

In debuting its 2019 race car, called the "VF19," Haas thus seemed optimistic. The team said its cars would wear the "resplendent black-and-gold colors of Rich Energy" for the upcoming season, unveiling them "before a throng of assembled guests" in February of that year. Haas said it looked to "build on the success of the VF18, which carried Haas F1 Team to a fifth-place finish in the 2018 constructors' standings," setting its goals even higher than before.[81]

But the car was a disaster. Plagued with so many problems that it seemed impossible to compete, drivers Kevin Magnussen and Romain Grosjean retired from nine of the 21 races in 2019. Across those 21 races, they only finished 10th or higher on track seven times between the two of them.[82] (Tenth was often seen as a marker of success in that era of Formula One, as only the top 10 out of 20 cars in each race scored points.)

"This is the worst experience I've ever had in any race car, ever," Magnussen said over the radio at one point during the season.

"For us, it's also not a nice experience," team principal Guenther Steiner responded. "Enough now."[83]

Magnussen and Grosjean—along with much of the rest of Haas— seemed distraught. As Magnussen described it in Netflix's Formula One documentary series, *Drive to Survive*: "Being overtaken all the time, it just feels so hopeless. You could do the lap of your life and then be 15th, still. You start questioning everything, including yourself."[84]

In 2019, Haas finished second to last in the final constructor standings. Only the flailing Williams team finished worse.[85]

If that wasn't bad enough, throughout what was arguably Haas' worst season yet in terms of on-track performance, the team had its own title sponsor to contend with. Just two months into the Formula One season, Rich Energy lost the copyright case over its logo with Whyte Bikes' parent company, ATB Sales, and was then ruled to owe the company roughly $45,000.[86] The company's logos had to be removed hastily from the Haas F1 cars during a race weekend, and at the time of the court-ordered payment deadline, Whyte Bikes told the authors Rich Energy failed to pay any of the $45,000 sum it owed.[87] Haas F1 faced a one-two punch of lackluster performance on track and increasingly embarrassing headlines about its main sponsor.

It only got worse. In July 2019, not long after the logo fiasco, Rich Energy tweeted that it was terminating its contract with Haas due to poor performance and the "politics and PC attitude" in Formula One.[88] "PC" was internet speak for "politically correct," a moniker that had risen in popularity at the time to condemn progressive actions and mindsets by those with extremist conservative ideals. Considering that Formula One was notoriously not politically correct, no one really knew what the tweet meant.

The following day, Rich Energy—a new, more corporate Rich Energy, one not governed by Storey—said a "rogue" individual posted the tweet and that it was not representative of the views of the company's shareholders.[89] That rogue individual was believed to be Storey. Not long after, Storey claimed to control more than 51 percent of the Rich Energy shares and said minority shareholders were attempting a "palace coup."[90]

The relationship between Haas and Rich Energy had almost entirely devolved by the midpoint of the 2019 season, but Steiner had other problems to worry about. In *Drive to Survive*, which condensed Formula One seasons into intense storylines with interviews from key players, he described the season as: "Fucking everything is fucked up at the moment."[91] Steiner quickly became one of the fan favorites on *Drive to Survive* due to just how honest he was, underscored by his regular profanity and thick accent that sometimes caused people to confuse him for German. He was, in fact, from the Italian province of South Tyrol near the Austrian border, where many locals spoke German.[92]

Steiner generally avoided talking about Rich Energy at length while it was a partner of the team, but he had plenty to say in *Drive to Survive*. He summed up his experience with the sponsor succinctly on the show: "I'm getting sick of answering these stupid fucking questions on a race weekend. I've never seen any fucking thing like this."[93]

So bountiful were his other comments that the Haas team's *Drive to Survive* episode from the 2019 season was almost entirely devoted to Rich Energy. It was a rare approach for *Drive to Survive*, which was known for focusing more on people than sponsors—especially sponsors that only paid a fraction of their bill.

"The Rich Energy deal was supposed to be worth $60 million," team owner Gene Haas said on the episode. "Other than the initial payment, that was the only money we ever received."[94]

*   *   *

By the time Rich Energy came around, questionable sponsorships were nothing new in motorsport. Costs were high, and teams and drivers could be easily tempted to latch onto the next promise of easy cash. Whether it be a mysterious supercomputer meant to predict the stock market or people pretending to be obscure royalty, onlookers didn't have to dig deep to find a race series getting involved with the sketchier side of marketing. If political scandals are a little more your flavor, consider high-level Formula One officers' penchant for tax evasion and blatant racism, sexism, and anti–Semitism. Much about Formula One wasn't pretty, but the series didn't let anyone look in its shadows for long.

Indeed, Formula One had a history of covering up even deeper scandals. Bernie Ecclestone, former CEO of the Formula One Group, frequently publicized his polarizing opinions on everything from Adolf Hitler[95] to women in sports.[96] Several names connected with Formula

One, including Ecclestone, Flavio Briatore, Jacques Villeneuve, Alain de Cadenet, Eddie Irvine, and Pedro Diniz, were listed in what was purportedly a copy of Jeffrey Epstein's "Little Black Book."[97] During Rich Energy's era and long before, Formula One was criticized for its leniency in scheduling races in countries known for human-rights violations, including Bahrain, Azerbaijan, and Russia, where protesters could be jailed, raped, or killed and where journalists were severely limited in what they could say.[98] The day before the 2016 Grand Prix of Europe in Azerbaijan's capital city of Baku, a *Guardian* headline read: "As F1 roars into Baku, activists tell drivers: Help our fight for human rights."[99]

"The asphalt has been laid over Baku's ancient cobbled streets, many residential buildings have been covered with false fronts for the cameras, and bling-built new ones are on proud display," the story read. "Well away from the limelight of this weekend's 3.7-mile grand prix circuit through the city are Azerbaijan's prisons—their populations swollen by activists, journalists, bloggers and opposition."[100] A Formula One race merely served as a distraction.

Even the sex life of Max Mosley, president of the FIA from 1993 through 2009, made headlines during his tenure.[101] A 2008 legal claim filed by Mosley against News Group Newspapers said a story appeared in tabloid newspaper *News of the World* on March 30 of that year, featuring the headline "F1 BOSS HAS SICK NAZI ORGY WITH 5 HOOKERS" and calling Mosley a "secret sado-masochist sex pervert."[102]

"It was claimed as an 'EXCLUSIVE' and accompanied by the subheading 'Son of Hitler-loving fascist in sex shame,'" the judgment in the case read, including the following quote from the front page::

> The son of infamous British wartime fascist leader Oswald Mosley is filmed romping with five hookers at a depraved NAZI-STYLE orgy in a torture dungeon. Mosley—a friend to F1 big names like Bernie Ecclestone and Lewis Hamilton—barks ORDERS in GERMAN as he lashes girls wearing mock DEATH CAMP uniforms and enjoys being whipped until he BLEEDS.[103]

The legal representation for Mosley, the judgment read, "submitted that what took place was simply a 'standard' S and M prison scenario"— not "anything to do with Nazism or concentration camps." The judge ordered in Mosley's favor, saying they found "no evidence" that the gathering was "intended to be an enactment of Nazi behaviour or adoption of any of its attitudes." Mosley was awarded 60,000 British pounds.[104]

"I am delighted with that judgment, which is devastating for the *News of the World*," Mosley said, as quoted by the *Guardian*. "It demonstrates that their Nazi lie was completely invented and had no justification."[105]

Mosley remained president of the FIA until October 2009, when he was replaced by Jean Todt. Images and video from the event published by *News of the World* no longer appear on internet searches, which return several images of the paper's suitable-for-work front page.

It wasn't just the off-track behavior of Formula One's elites that caused concern. In 2007, a high-ranking Ferrari F1 employee named Nigel Stepney went through a disgruntled breakup with the team.[106] Ferrari then accused multiple people of stealing 780 pages of its technical secrets: Mike Coughlan, a senior engineer from Ferrari's on-track rival McLaren, Coughlan's wife Trudy, and Stepney.[107] The scandal, known alternatively as "Stepneygate" or "Spygate," resulted in McLaren's exclusion from the 2007 World Constructor Championship and a fine of $100 million.[108] Stepney received a lifetime ban from working in Formula One, and Spygate remains one of the largest acts of intellectual theft in the sport's history.[109]

There was also the fondly named "Crashgate" scandal of 2008, where an FIA investigation found the Renault team guilty of instructing one of its drivers, Nelson Piquet, Jr., to intentionally crash in such a way that would give teammate Fernando Alonso an advantage at the Singapore Grand Prix—a meticulously calculated advantage that would lead to Alonso's victory in the race, despite his qualifying 15th.[110] Motorsport officials threatened to disqualify Renault from Formula One altogether if a similar incident happened between then and 2011, and high-ranking team personnel were banned from FIA-sanctioned events.[111] In a sport that prided itself on technological ingenuity and a fair—if not level—playing field, reports of cheating were almost more taboo than any off-track sexual escapades.

Outsiders often didn't hear much about these questionable behaviors or brands because Formula One did, and continued to do during Rich Energy's tenure, its damnedest to cover up anything that threatened its reputation as the only red-carpet racing series in the world—rolling that carpet over everything from the piles of sanctioning fees it accepted from oppressive regimes using its races as public-relations campaigns to the human-rights activists protesting them, and putting up facades in front of anything that might compromise its reputation. Even visual evidence of the Mosley saga, which dragged on for years across various legal actions, is nearly impossible to find unless you know what you're looking for. If you weren't reading the papers during its news cycle, you might not even know to look in the first place.

The red carpets and facades didn't fool those paying close attention, but that's not necessarily what mattered. What mattered was keeping the rest of the world in the dark and the enlightened ones complacent.

The one thing Formula One couldn't wall off with its red carpets and facades? Storey, who quickly and easily dismantled them with a loud mouth and an active Twitter account.

2

BAD GENES

In some ways, an unknown company wasn't much of an oddity in Formula One.

"You do get quite a lot of unheard-of sponsors," motorsport journalist Luke Smith told the authors in an August 2021 interview. Smith worked for the publication *Crash.net* during the Rich Energy saga before moving to *Autosport*, a division of the *Motorsport Network*. "But that's kind of the point of it. You come into F1 to get people to know about your product. Get an F1 sponsorship, and then you make it into something."[1]

Stuart Taylor, the motorsport mind behind popular Chain Bear You-Tube channel, added: "Billionaires turn up all the time in Formula One and will be like, 'Now we're a title sponsor.'"[2]

But Taylor said Rich Energy was different from the "dozens" of other energy drinks that have attempted a racing sponsorship—including companies like Red Bull and Monster, or even something like Rowdy Energy, a drink from NASCAR driver Kyle Busch. In other words: companies with products that were either readily available in stores, or ones race fans could easily source.

"It's funny now, because there was the whole thing where no one has ever seen a Rich Energy drink," Taylor said. "You have to open the holy grail to find it.

"But that's fine, the fact that you haven't heard of it. It'll be like, 'Oh, sure, it's probably big in America, or it's probably big in Australia.' It could be massive somewhere. So at the time, it wasn't a big deal."[3] The problem came when many people—no matter their home country—couldn't source the drink at all.

For a long time, Rich Energy's Wikipedia page said it was "a British beverage company that *claims to manufacture* the Rich Energy energy drink."[4] The "claims" part was edited out sometime around 2021, six years into its existence, to make the entry read: "Rich Energy Ltd. is a British beverage company that *manufactures* the Rich Energy energy drink."[5]

But even after the edit, the main photo on Rich Energy's Wikipedia sidebar in Google search results showed remnants of its past: its original logo paired with that of fellow British company Whyte Bikes, an ode to Rich Energy's trip to copyright court.

The mystery and confusion around the drink, though, could have been ignored. But the more Rich Energy CEO William Storey spoke, the more concerns came to the fore.

And once people started digging, they weren't inclined to stop.

*   *   *

Companies big and small typically have some form of public-relations team puppeteering their narrative, hired to both tout the brand and mitigate any kind of negative public image. That PR team often communicates with journalists and controls media interactions with executives and other major players at the company, especially when a critical story is on the horizon. It's all a coordinated attempt to keep the news story positive, even in the times when it isn't.

But Rich Energy didn't have that. As of March 2019, press emails to the Rich Energy information line were forwarded directly to Storey—if they didn't automatically land in his inbox to begin with.

Email statements from CEOs of larger companies almost entirely come by means of a PR representative, perfected to a near robotic tune and presented ready for publication. Storey handled his own press dealings—often writing out his real-time thoughts via email, with sporadic line and paragraph breaks instead of actual punctuation in between. Storey was his own PR person, and it often worked against him.

While very few PR people are willing to provide damning facts to the media, they will at least provide inquiring minds with either good or neutral information. Storey did that as well, but he seemed to speak in circles and was quick to deflect when questioned about his company's history, finances, and dealings.

With very little direction from the man behind the operation, it was up to onlookers and journalists to track down Rich Energy's origins. That required a deep dive into public records, where traces of the company were scattered across the UK, Croatia, and Austria, and where the same handful of names were knotted up in a circle of failed former businesses that never seemed to do much business at all.

Trademark information for Rich d.o.o.—Rich Energy's 2011 registration as a private company by businessman Dražen Majstrović—came courtesy of Poslovna.hr, a Croatian business portal that claimed to, in part, "enable entrepreneurs, managers and other businesspeople to check the reliability of existing and potential business partners."[6]

But traces of Majstrović's involvement with the company weren't easy to track down. His online presence included multiple Twitter accounts, where he really only interacted with Rich Energy–related content, and most of the media coverage of Majstrović centered on his goods exchange in the Croatian town of Osijek. But a brief 2011 blog from *Moj Zagreb,* a website dedicated to providing information about Croatia's capital, tied Majstrović with something called Party League Croatia, an initiative to promote Croatia as a hip tourist country with a lively nightlife scene. It was one of the first mentions of Rich's existence in a public context, along with confirmation that it was, in fact, an energy drink:

> At the Party League Croatia, a new energy drink Rich will be promoted, which were designed by Osijek entrepreneur Dražen Majstrović and famous athlete and caterer Alen Borbaš. Realizing that only foreign brands are present on our energy drink market, they, in cooperation with experts, set out to create an original Croatian recipe, but also a recognizable visual identity.[7]

The address on the Rich trademark was listed as Podravska ulica 20, Osijek, Croatia, which appeared to be residential.[8] While it wasn't uncommon to register a trademark to a residential address, Majstrović's various businesses and trademarks were registered in different locations.

Majstrović's medical-research organization, for one, was located in a nondescript older building in the Croatian city of Vukovar.[9] Google Maps photos from 2012 matched the date of the company's founding, and a March 2012 Google street view showed signs on the building that, translated from Croatian, appeared to advertise "doors and windows."[10] Majstrović's goods exchange was registered in an Osijek shopping center.[11]

Rich and Majstrović seemingly disappeared not long into Rich d.o.o.'s existence, only to be replaced a few years later by William Storey and his British take on the brand. But Majstrović still actively posted about Rich Energy and its new endeavors—such as sponsorships in Formula One and British Superbikes—online. When contacted by the authors in August 2021 to discuss creating the brand and working with it, Majstrović declined an interview.[12]

"In principle, I am not interested in talking about this topic," Majstrović said. "It was an extremely successful but also an extremely demanding time. In all of this, I was not directly involved in certain positions, so I would not be a relevant interlocutor. I am therefore focused exclusively on the future."

"Given that we then survived a very serious attack of enemy takeover, and in an ugly way, came out of the partnership with Haas F1, I believe that we have now become stronger and that in the future, we will avoid the problems we had in the past. Thank you very much for your interest in the Rich Energy topic."[13]

That "serious attack" wouldn't come until well into Storey's tenure at Rich Energy.

The version of Rich Energy that entered Formula One was incorporated in the UK on September 23, 2015, according to records filed with Companies House, the British registrar for businesses. Its directors at incorporation were: Storey; a man named Zoran Terzic, whose occupation was listed as a "Keep Fit Instructor" on the incorporation documents; and another man named Richard Fletcher. Storey held all 50 shares in the company at incorporation, and Fletcher was terminated as director in June 2017.[14]

"That was an administrative move at the time," Storey told the authors in early 2019. "In 2017, we had some slight restructuring in terms of the legal side. Richard is very much still working with us. He's a very good friend of mine, and he works with the company."[15]

Storey didn't elaborate, and Fletcher didn't respond to the authors' requests for an interview in August 2021. Fletcher continued to work with Storey at Rich Energy and elsewhere, and in August 2019, his LinkedIn account listed him as becoming a chairman at one of Storey's other companies, Wolf Data Systems.

Storey, for his own part, told British newspaper *The Telegraph* he stumbled into the drinks business after "meeting this mad beverage scientist" and then buying the rights to the drink.[16]

Consulting the records seemed to raise far more commercially sensitive questions than it answered. Companies House logged information on businesses like Rich Energy, requiring them to file financial data and records for each important event. When Rich Energy announced its partnership with Haas in 2018, its most recent balance sheet filed with Companies House showed that as of 2017, the company had a mere 581 pounds in the bank—about $770 in the U.S., and up from 103 pounds the year before. The balance sheet was in the black, meaning Rich Energy was, at the very least, not in debt.[17]

Add several zeros to that latter number and you get the Haas F1 Team's annual budget: roughly 100 million pounds, according to a 2018 Forbes report.[18] Rich Energy's 581-pound bank statements represented 0.000581 percent of that cost, yet the company still secured the deal.

Storey's promotion of Rich Energy was similar to that of Majstrović's: essentially, the creation of a highly nationalized energy drink—but this time in the UK, not in Croatia. As of early 2019, the company description on Rich Energy's website read as such:

> Rich Energy is a premium and innovative British energy drink painstakingly developed and optimised over the last 6 years with leading beverage experts and recently launched in the UK and US. [...]

We worked with leading experts around the world on all elements of this fantastic product and we are very proud to bring the elevated taste and experience of the UK's premium energy drink to the market. Get Rich and enjoy the experience![19]

That line about the UK and the U.S. was important. Despite the launch claims, one of the only places where a person could easily find the product was on Rich Energy's website, which only shipped to the company's home country of the UK at the time. When the U.S.-based authors of this book asked their acquaintances in the UK—many in the London area—to search for Rich Energy in early 2019, all were unable to find it in actual stores.[20]

There was, though, one potential link to the United States during Rich Energy's formative years: a listing with the Better Business Bureau for Rich Energy Drink, which was labeled a "food manufacturer" based in Lincoln, Nebraska. In this case, the branding appeared to be done through a bar called the Rich Lounge.[21]

The company's owner was listed as a man named Lawrence Chatters, who also owned a place called the Main St. Cafe in Lincoln.[22] Main St. Cafe was scheduled to host the Rich Energy Drink launch party on December 31, 2012, according to an archived version of the American Rich Energy Drink website at the time.[23]

In a 2014 interview with Chatters, the University of Nebraska–Lincoln's student news organization, the *Daily Nebraskan*, described Rich Energy Drink as "a Croatian product for which [Chatters] and a business partner owned the U.S. distribution rights."[24] Much like Storey, Chatters' sights were on a much larger rival.

"We were really looking for a way to continue the branding process for Rich Energy Drink, because if you look at Red Bull, they're not just an energy drink," Chatters told the outlet. "They have NASCAR, IndyCar racing, and other things like that, so we decided to open a club on one of the busiest corners in the city."[25]

In a December 2021 interview with the authors, Chatters said he initially discovered Rich Energy Drink while DJ'ing in Osijek, Croatia.

"During the night, there was this energy drink that I'd never seen there," Chatters said. "It was this can called Rich Energy Drink, and it had two silhouettes of naked people on it. It was very odd."[26]

Chatters said he then met Dražen Majstrović, who "was doing a promotion that night for his new energy drink that he had created earlier that year."

"[I] talked to him that night, and he said, 'Hey, I'm the owner of this drink, so if you guys want to talk more about it, maybe we can meet,'" Chatters said. "We met the next morning."

"Basically, he said: 'Hey, I just started this product this past summer. I was originally in the cell-phone business and did a lot of research for marketing purposes. As I was going through that process, I was looking at different industries, and the energy-drink industry is one. I found that there was a gap in the industry when it came to energy drinks, so I wanted to create my own, and this is what I came up with.'"[27] (Since Majstrović did not agree to an interview, the authors couldn't confirm these claims with him.)

Since he owned the bar in Nebraska, Chatters saw potential in distributing his own energy drink rather than purchasing that of a different manufacturer. He was impressed with "the fact that this guy had come up with his own energy drink and it actually tasted pretty good," he said, and after revamping the can to cater more to an American audience, Chatters and a business partner brought the drink stateside.

Where Red Bull sought the extreme-sports audience, Chatters said Rich Energy Drink belonged in nightclubs—hence the decision to open the Rich Lounge.

"What I realized was that Red Bull was a really amazing advertisement company that also happened to have an energy drink," Chatters told the authors. "And so, that's the way that I was looking at it."[28]

Unfortunately, Chatters said, large-scale distribution and finding a foothold in Nebraska proved to be difficult. Because Chatters was a bar owner as well as an energy-drink distributor, he said competing bars declined to stock the drink due to feeling like they were essentially promoting his business in their own.

Chatters said he and his business partner ultimately ceded the distribution agreement when Majstrović sold Rich Energy Drink to an undisclosed buyer who intended to revamp the brand. That was the last Chatters had to do with the company.[29]

But Chatters wasn't the only person with an early connection to Rich Energy in the United States. Extreme scooter rider Dakota Schuetz told the authors he got involved with Storey a few years before the brand entered Formula One.

"I owned the U.S. rights to Rich Energy, so any business that came to America if ever, I would have to manage and get royalties from this," Schuetz said in an August 2021 interview. "At one point, I owned a percentage of the parent company, which was based in England. Then I was supposed to also get a salary from Rich Energy per month."[30]

Schuetz said he met Storey around 2016, when he was at a party in Monaco during the F1 race weekend and a friend of his asked to take a photo with Storey because of his beard. During the exchange, Storey learned that Schuetz was an athlete—a champion scooter rider—and asked to meet with him the following day.

"At this time, he had maybe a small website, an Instagram page, and he also had a physical can," Schuetz said. "It was just a mock-up can."[31]

Before long, Schuetz had become a major player in the Rich Energy game—what little of it there was.

"The first contract, I owned equity in Rich Energy, a lot, and then obviously nothing happened," Schuetz said. "Then I switched it, because they were doing something [different] with the company, so I said: 'OK, pay me this percent of royalties per can.' Up till today, I think I've spent—I calculated it with William before it exploded—maybe $30,000, $40,000 flying around and meeting everybody with Rich Energy. I've made maybe $0."[32]

Even further, Schuetz used his 500,000-follower Instagram page to promote Rich Energy, which he said "could cost like $4,000 a post if I charged somebody." After "70 to 80 posts that tagged and were literally just for Rich Energy," Schuetz claimed he still hadn't been paid.[33] (The authors didn't see documentation of Schuetz's claimed expenditures. When asked about their relationship, Storey didn't respond.)

Schuetz said Storey isn't deceitful; he's just "a big dreamer with a lack of follow-through."

"The issue with these types of people ... they can talk about anything," Schuetz said. "But there's no follow-up. I would just physically meet him because you couldn't get anything on the phone, text message, email. He just disappeared into thin air."[34]

Schuetz was unable to provide an exact date for the end of his involvement with Rich Energy. The last time Schuetz remembers seeing Storey, he said, was in 2019, during or possibly just after the Monaco Grand Prix.

"At the end of the day, it didn't bring me any value," Schuetz said. "I was bringing more value to them than they brought me."[35]

Rich Energy, then, had a presence in the United States—albeit a very small one—for several years before entering Formula One. But its presence in the United Kingdom wasn't much greater.

Rich Energy's own registered address during its Formula One tenure was at Hyde Park House, 5 Manfred Road in London, which was the office equivalent of an apartment building.[36] The offices were available to rent by individuals and businesses, but Rich Energy wasn't listed as a tenant at the location, according to a database that pulled from Companies House. Attempts by the authors to contact Hyde Park House for confirmation of this in early 2019 were unsuccessful.

When the authors spoke to Storey in early 2019, he said Rich Energy had three offices in London.

"The office that you've mentioned, which is Manfred Road, is just a registered address," Storey said. "That's very common in the UK. We actually have an accountant there, and there are thousands of companies registered to that address. The way the company is set up is often, it has a registered address, which is usually an accountant's address, and that's the case in Manfred Road. Our head office is in Richmond."

Storey also claimed—including during the legal proceedings with Whyte Bikes—that Rich Energy got its name from its base in Richmond.[37] But since the company was actually trademarked and named in Croatia back in 2011, that story didn't quite fall into line. Neither did the one about the stag-head logo.

The inconsistencies about Rich Energy's name could be seen long before the company teamed up with Haas, including in a March 2018 story from the *Telegraph*:

> The name "Rich" is short for Richmond, the company's base from which it hopes to topple the giants that occupy the energy drinks world. The stag is an homage to the deer that live in the affluent south-west London district's park.
>   Cracking open a can, [Storey] makes himself comfortable in the bar area of the posh, boutique Bingham hotel in Richmond. "It's definitely better than Red Bull," he asserts matter of factly.[38]

The Bingham hotel in Richmond, remember, was the place Rich Energy called its "HQ" on Twitter. The tweet did not call the Bingham by name, nor did it note that the photo actually showed a hotel.

There were similar name discrepancies during the Whyte Bikes case. The judge, Melissa Clarke, wrote in her judgment:

> In the Amended Defence, which was signed by […] Mr Storey, the Defendants contend […] that the first word of the First Defendant's name:
>   "…was selected before the incorporation of the First Defendant to simultaneously refer to a number of things and concepts. One of the purposes of its selection was as an abbreviation of 'Richmond,' in order to give the brand a sense of geographical origin and to assist in the creation of a brand narrative."
>   […] In fact, as Mr Storey acknowledged in his witness statement and accepted in cross-examination, the name "Rich Energy" was selected by the Croatian creator of the energy drink formula, Drazen Majstrovic in 2013 […]. Mr Storey had no formal involvement with the brand until 2015. Accordingly the name of the drink was not selected by him to reflect his associations with Richmond, Surrey, as pleaded. By the time of his witness statement, Mr Storey's evidence was that he was from Richmond, Surrey and the connection between the word 'Rich' and 'Richmond' was why he kept the name Rich Energy, albeit not why it was originally chosen.[39]

In the early 2019 interview after the Whyte Bikes court appearance, Storey told the authors the name "was sort of serendipitous, really."

"I mean basically, they had a word mark 'Rich,' which has a slightly different meaning, shall we say," Storey said. "We said, 'Right, OK, we can work with that, but we want to completely change the whole brand.' I created the brand from scratch, but there had been that earlier word, and I was quite happy to work with that because it actually worked quite nicely with Richmond."[40]

Storey himself was notoriously tight-lipped when it came to revealing detailed information about his company. He declined to send current financial documentation to the authors in 2019, despite the fact that the data would eventually need to become public through Companies House anyway. Storey claimed the information was confidential, but he told the authors in March 2019 that he thought it would "very quickly become apparent that [Rich Energy was] very significantly bigger than one set of accounts from 2017 shows."

"We've sold now over 100 million cans, which is a very significant number which is growing rapidly by the day, and we now have considerably in excess of eight figures in our bank account at any one time," Storey said, after having admitted in court earlier that week that the company had only sold "circa 3 million cans" in 2018. Given the number he provided in court, total sales of "over 100 million" was a stretch.[41]

At the time, Rich Energy's website said it also had a "cutting-edge," roughly $65 million manufacturing facility and that its cans were made in the UK.[42] The can said the product itself was made in Austria.

"So that snapshot from 2016, which was effectively a startup company at that stage, that figure of 581 or whatever it is, is really completely meaningless," Storey continued. "That was almost before we were getting started. It's pretty irrelevant."[43]

But the numbers kept coming back to one central question: Where was all that money coming from, if there was any at all?

Due to Majstrović's lack of any substantial online presence, it wasn't clear where the initial backing for Rich came from. As for Storey, he claimed to have made money from a very unusual source: investing in and then selling shares of a Zimbabwean tobacco farm where he'd worked. A March 2018 story from the *Telegraph* posited that Storey was able to sell his shares to fund Rich Energy, reading:

> [Storey] spotted that a flood of Chinese businessmen were descending on the country and wondered why. He soon discovered that the value of land had been pushed artificially low because of political strife around controversial land reforms.
> "A farmer I knew had a farm which had been worth $30m but was only worth $2m even though the amount of money being earned from the sale of tobacco was vastly more than that," he remembers.[44]

In terms of money, developing a drink brand was one thing. Funding a Formula One team was entirely another—one that took steady, large amounts of income and the assurance that cash would always be available, even during a slow selling season. That was apparently where billionaire David Sullivan and millionaire David Gold came in.

Sullivan and Gold owned the West Ham United Football Club at the time, but their ties went back decades. Sullivan and Gold founded a pornography empire, beginning with mail-order soft-core porn photos.[45] The enterprise was so popular that the two men were able to open sex shops, publish adult magazines, and produce pornographic films. Sullivan was convicted of living off "immoral earnings" in 1982, but he was released after 71 days in jail and continued to amass his impressive fortune.[46]

In August 2018, Storey told the *Motorsport Network* that in attempting to buy the Force India Formula One Team, his consortium was backed by "four sterling billionaires," reported to include Sullivan and Gold.[47] Mere days before Rich Energy confirmed its Haas deal on October 12, 2018, the brand announced via LinkedIn that Sullivan had "acquired a significant stake in Rich Energy."[48] The funding from Sullivan, if real, might have allowed Storey to court both Williams and Haas around the time of the United States Grand Prix later that month. But it also fueled wild—and unproven—rumors in the Formula One paddock.

"As the season kicked in, the problems started," a person who worked for Haas F1 at the time told the authors. "Not problems, but everyone started to realize something was wrong. The product wasn't there; the rumors were going around: 'What are these people doing? They're trying to wash money they made in the porn industry or something?' Some weird shit."[49]

As for Rich Energy's involvement with West Ham, the company was listed online as the "Official Energy Drink of West Ham United Ladies" as of September 2020.[50] The West Ham website said Rich Energy took that title in summer 2017, and Monster Energy was also listed as a partner of the team.

When asked about Sullivan and Gold's apparent involvement with Rich Energy in March 2019, West Ham spokesperson Ben Campbell told the authors via email: "This isn't a club matter, I suggest you refer directly to the company."[51]

The authors did confirm that on the company's end and were looking to do so on behalf of Sullivan and Gold. The address on Gold's personal website at the time was the West Ham media line, which led to Campbell, and a request sent through a contact form was not returned. When informed of those things and asked to be redirected to a spokesperson for the team's owners, Campbell did not respond.

The authors reached back out to Campbell two years later in August 2021 with questions for Sullivan, Gold, and the West Ham clubs. They were as follows:

David Sullivan

- Do you have involvement with William Storey and Rich Energy? Have you ever?
- If so: How did you meet Storey and how did you get involved with his company?
- Mere days before Rich Energy confirmed its deal with the Haas Formula One team, the brand announced via LinkedIn on October 12, 2018, that you had "acquired a significant stake in Rich Energy." Did you? How big was the stake and how much did it cost? Are you still involved with the brand?
- What is your business experience with Storey?
- What is your opinion of him and of Rich Energy?

David Gold

- Do you have involvement with William Storey and Rich Energy? Have you ever?
- Both you and David Sullivan were reported to be backers of Rich Energy around 2018. Were you? Are you still? How much do or did you have invested in the company?
- If you ever have been involved with either: How did you meet Storey and how did you get involved with his company?
- What is your business experience with Storey?
- What is your opinion of him and of Rich Energy?

West Ham Women

- Rich Energy was listed as one of your team partners recently (they are no longer on the website). What were the details of that partnership?
- How long did the partnership last?
- Was the partnership monetary? Was the full bill paid?
- Do you have any further comments on your experience with Rich Energy?

West Ham Men

- William Storey claimed that he and Rich Energy signed a deal with the 2017 West Ham United player awards. Can you confirm that they were partnered with that event?
- What were the details of the partnership?
- Was the full sponsorship bill paid?

Campbell responded once, asking for a deadline extension and saying: "Your first email never reached me…. I know we've already spoken on this topic, but [it] would be good to know claims/what's been said so I know what I am being asked to respond to specifically."[52] The authors provided links and screenshots for every claim, then followed up three additional times via email. It's unclear if those messages reached Campbell, but we did not hear back again.

* * *

Very little, if anything, was known about Storey or Rich Energy when they officially announced their Formula One entrance on October 25, 2018. Despite dubious means and a lack of product, Storey claimed to manage, sponsor, or otherwise work with a variety of athletes. Rich Energy's early forays into motorsport came by sponsoring driver Toby Sowery[53] and British Superbike team True Heroes Racing,[54] but many of its various sponsorships faded away without any public fallout. Other sponsorships included unnamed fashion shows and festivals, although there was evidence that Rich Energy sponsored the Fort Wayne Music Festival in Indiana[55]—not the kind of "elite" event Storey claimed, but not nothing, either.

Few people spoke much about Rich Energy after their sponsorship, but it was possible to trace a rough timeline of relationships through articles posted to William Storey's LinkedIn page, where he posted much of his breaking news.

Beginning in February 2016, Storey's concern seemed to lie more with his own PR company, William Storey Management, than Rich Energy. He hosted professional boxer and middleweight world champion Gennadiy Golovkin in London, taking him on a trip to the West Ham United Football Club (which Storey thanked another company of his, Danieli Style, for assisting in).[56] In July of that year, Storey wrote that he signed a deal to represent boxer Jay "Kidd Dynamite" Carrigan-McFarlane, appearing to imply that a Rich Energy sponsorship would be part of it.[57] Days later, he advertised signing the aforementioned professional scooter rider Dakota Schuetz, who was "pictured this week with leading Conservative politician and cabinet minister for Brexit, David Davis" at the top of the LinkedIn post.[58]

Golovkin, who had nearly 600,000 followers on Twitter and 3.8 million on Instagram as of September 2020, was one of the few truly famous people Storey regularly boasted his ties with in the public sphere. When the authors contacted representatives for Golovkin in August 2021 to request an interview about Storey and Rich Energy, we did not hear back.

While few of those sponsorship announcements contained any real details, they at least included traceable names and dates. Some posts, such as one titled "William Storey luxury brands," contained next to no information at all. That particular post read, in full, with all original punctuation and wording left intact:

> Very pleased to announce a collaboration with four of the biggest luxury brands in the world where William Storey management have been exclusively commissioned to act as agent for brands across a raft of elite fashion, sports and cultural events to maximise media value for the brands and to enhance strategic growth in emerging markets.[59]

In another post titled "Rich Energy sign exclusive deal with multiple festivals for summer 2017," which featured a photo of Storey with the rock band Thin Lizzy, Storey claimed:

> Pleased to announce that Rich Energy have secured a prestigious deal with multiple leading festivals throughout the UK and Europe for summer 2017 to further cement status as the company to watch in 2017. Very pleased to work with a number of rock legends and some of the biggest bands in the world.[60]

The authors were unable to find evidence of any sponsored music festivals, with the exception of one U.S. event: the 2019 Fort Wayne Music Festival in Indiana. As of August 2020, the Facebook page for the Fort Wayne Music Festival had 10,700 followers.[61]

When asked in August 2021 about its relationship with Rich Energy—whether Rich Energy was, in fact, the official energy drink of the festival; how long the partnership lasted; whether it was monetary and whether the bill was paid in full; and if there was any relationship with William Storey—an administrator for the festival's Facebook page told the authors: "We will pass, thank you for reaching out."

Other posts on Storey's LinkedIn page were more specific to motorsport. One from December 2016 announced the introduction of William Storey Management into Formula One, which came the same year that American company Liberty Media acquired the series for $4.4 billion. The post included a grainy photo of Storey next to that year's Formula One champion, Nico Rosberg.[62]

It also illustrated the back-and-forth between Rich Energy and William Storey Management on Storey's LinkedIn page—a fluctuation that continued until early 2018:

> Very pleased to announce that William Storey Management have agreed a multi-year partnership in Formula One with a world leading brand who have exclusively commissioned us to be their bridge into the sport and advise on ongoing activations and maximising media value within the world of elite motor racing. Formula One has been the nadir of sports branding ever since Bernie Ecclestone took commercial control in the early 80's and we are delighted to be continuing our association within this arena and are very

confident that with new owners Liberty Media at the helm the sport will go from strength to strength internationally with particular emphasis on strong commercial revenue increases in the US.[63]

Storey provided no specific information about what that "multi-year partnership" would look like, but used a similarly vague tone for a post roughly six months later in June 2017:

Rich Energy commence international media campaign across motor racing, boxing, football and extreme sports
Thanks to significant institutional backing we are rolling out a strategic media campaign across multi media across all our international markets. With tens of thousands of outlets now selling we are taking a proactive approach to ongoing expansion and investing heavily in those areas we feel offer most value.[64]

Nowhere was the source of this institutional backing mentioned, nor did Storey say which sporting divisions, exactly, would be the focus of the marketing campaign. Claims like those were not uncommon for Storey.

There were also plenty of blogs on Storey's LinkedIn page about Rich Energy–sponsored boxers and their performance in important matches, alongside political commentary and brief posts with either no traceable information or categorically incorrect claims. Storey posted one, titled "Rich Energy beat Red Bull to corporate accounts," in June 2017:

Delighted to confirm that Rich Energy the UK's premium energy drink has secured notable international corporate distribution deals ahead of Red Bull. These are with hotel groups and multi national beverage makers who wish to partner with the best product on the market as a mixer and stand alone luxury energy drink. The largest network in the USA just signed[65]

Rich Energy's motorsport claims began to grow in frequency near the end of 2016. Storey claimed to be putting together an Isle of Man TT team after securing two unnamed sponsors, writing on LinkedIn in August 2016:

Pleased to confirm that I am putting a race team together for the famous Isle of Man TT races which is the blue riband event for road racing worldwide. The ultimate test of endurance, speed and daring for motorcyclists. I have secured two major sponsors for the team and am in negotiations with several manufacturers over supply of racebikes. This is a British team with British sponsors and we aim to be competitive in what is widely considered one of the greatest and most entertaining challenges in motorsport.[66]

In May 2017, Storey wrote that Rich Energy was partnering with a lifestyle event company called the Amber Lounge at the Monaco Grand Prix. After the event, Storey wrote:

In what turned out to be an eventful weekend with Ferrari asserting their advantage on the tight street circuit , Rich Energy was being consumed by the gallon by A listers, celebs, mechanics, drivers and F1 fans in the principality. Everyone absolutely loved the taste of a superior premium energy drink made with luxury ingredients and pure mineral water. We were particularly pleased to sponsor the charity drivers fashion show which raised alot of money for charity.[67]

In August 2021, a representative for the Amber Lounge declined to answer the authors' specific questions—the details and length of the Rich Energy partnership, whether the relationship was monetary and whether Rich Energy paid the full bill, and the overall experience with the company and Storey—but said: "Let's just say it wasn't a nice experience."[68]

In a post titled "Rich Energy sponsor British Superbikes," Storey explained that Rich Energy would not be sponsoring the entire motorsport category but instead just the True Heroes Racing team, which was "made up largely of injured ex-soldiers, sailors, and airmen who have sustained damage in the line of duty serving their country in places like Iraq and Afghanistan."[69]

That wouldn't be the first nor the only time Storey would affiliate his brand with the military. Storey wrote in November 2017 that Rich Energy sponsored a boxing event called "Remembrance Rumble 2," where he said proceeds went to charities for military veterans.[70] When asked for comment on Rich Energy's involvement four years later, an organizer for the event told the authors it was a "tricky subject" and declined to comment further.

Among other motorsport deals were: sponsorship of a "Lamborghini race series" that was unnamed and did not appear to have ever come to fruition,[71] as part of Rich Energy's "seven-figure investment in motorsport"[72]; the "support" of "many elite competitors" in the Dakar Rally off-road event[73]; "large scale activations at Monaco Grand Prix and TT races"[74]; and the sponsorship of several unnamed drivers at the 2018 Isle of Man TT motorcycle event, along with being "the exclusive drink at the coolest bars at the IOM TT."[75]

Rich Energy also claimed to have developed the world's "fastest road-legal car" as part of a partnership with Ultima Cars,[76] and Storey wrote that he collaborated on "a few projects" with British sports-car maker Noble Automotive.[77] There was, too, a claimed partnership with Castle Air, a company that specialized in charter aircraft.[78] Castle Air never appeared to acknowledge a partnership, and neither it, Noble Automotive, nor Ultima Cars responded to the authors' questions about their relationships with Rich Energy and Storey.

In other sponsorship arenas, Storey claimed on LinkedIn that he and

Rich Energy signed deals with sailing team Alex Thomson Racing,[79] the 2017 West Ham United player awards,[80] the "aviation industry,"[81] unnamed surfing events,[82] powerboat racers Sam and Daisy Coleman,[83] "a raft of current Premier League football stars,"[84] heavyweight boxer Lucas "Big Daddy" Browne,[85] unnamed casinos in Las Vegas,[86] and "key prestige accounts with Hilton and Marriot [sic] hotels."[87]

"With casinos in Macau and Vegas and significant UK on-trade presence Rich Energy continues its rapid ascent," an October 2017 post read. "With a significant acquisition fund in place watch this space."[88] (The post did not include commas, nor did it include a period after "space.")

The authors also reached out to countless other entities that Rich Energy sponsored at one time or another, including: race-car drivers Toby Sowery, Michael Crees, Rick Parfitt, Jr., and Daniel Lloyd; boat racers Alex Thomson, Sam Coleman, and Daisy Coleman; boxers Lucas Browne, Jay Carrigan-McFarlane, and Gennadiy Golovkin; and motorcycle racers James Hillier, Brad Ray, Kyle Ryde, Billy McConnell, and Álvaro Bautista. Most did not respond. Others agreed to speak but never responded to follow-up messages. Many also did not appear to be sponsored by Rich Energy as of November 2021.

While Toby Sowery did not respond to the authors' request for contact, he did answer a question about his Rich Energy sponsorship on an episode of the *Marshall Pruett Podcast*, which was published on September 4, 2019—five days before Rich Energy's Haas F1 partnership prematurely ended.[89]

"For me, I'd known the company way before they got into F1, so I've always been very much on the side of them despite the controversy they've sometimes had," Sowery said. "But for me, there wasn't any complications. I was informed that all the issues going on in the UK were a different set of issues for the U.S., so they didn't conflict.

"But no, I think there's not going to be many more complications. It's all going to change in the future, I'm sure. Whether or not that affects me, I wouldn't be able to tell you, sadly. I'd love to be able to. But, you know, we've still got the drinks, we've still got the contacts, and we're working with them to make sure that we get back in Indy Lights for 2020 and hopefully progress into IndyCar for the future years."[90]

Sowery competed for the Juncos Racing team for the first 14 of 20 Indy Lights races in 2021. His car did not appear to feature any significant Rich Energy branding, nor did his helmet.

Boxer Lucas Browne, who also did not respond to the authors, posted two Twitter videos in July 2019 about a canceled fight against fellow boxer Tom Little, saying: "Rich Energy basically dropped the ball in a big way, so we're now stuck in London and wondering how the fuck we're going to get home."[91] Three days later, Browne noted that he'd purchased his own flights for himself and his crew. He didn't mention specifically what happened, but said the fiasco cost him "15 grand." That was likely either 15,000 British pounds or 15,000 Australian dollars.[92]

British sports car racer Rick Parfitt, Jr., also did not respond to the authors' request for comment, but he did post a photo on Twitter in July 2019 showing Whyte Bikes had taken the place of Rich Energy on his car. The Whyte Bikes stag-head logo appeared in almost the exact position on the car as the old (and nearly identical) Rich Energy logo, and he included the hashtag #nomorenegativeenergy.[93]

West Ham spokesperson Ben Campbell, again, didn't confirm or deny the apparent partnership for the club's 2017 player awards. In photos posted by West Ham from the event, Rich Energy didn't appear among the logos on the "stand and repeat" wall[94]—otherwise known as the sponsor-patterned backdrop used for photos on red carpets—nor did the brand appear in an official recap video the club posted from the event.[95]

The question of money generally didn't pop up in Storey's LinkedIn blogs, but it did in a few circumstances: once, when he announced a "£100m takeover of Force India,"[96] and another time in March 2018:

Rich Energy chosen as trailblazing brand in city awards as company raises £220m

Delighted to be recognised by multiple financial institutions as a company at the forefront of innovation with a compelling proposition and business model as we take our international expansion to the next level. We now have the financial firepower to take on the established corporates. And win. Rich Energy is on the acquisition trail and moves further on trajectory of establishing a world class British performance brand.[97]

The city was not specified, nor were the financial institutions or sources of income. Aside from an undated photo of Storey in front of a presentation slide that read "Thrilling UK Energy Drink Looks to" before cutting out of the frame, there was very little other evidence backing this claim.

Storey's LinkedIn blog also seemed to be the ideal place to share his political opinions, including two successive stories about then–presidential candidate Donald Trump in September and November 2016. The first, titled "Why now is the time to bet on Trump," read in part:

As someone who has called the last 3 British and 2 American elections correctly (and who lumped on Brexit at odds of 7/1) I will now confidently predict in what appears to be entirely contrarian fashion that Donald J Trump is the going to be elected the next Commander in chief. [...]

He has also been a success in the real world which gives kudos over career politicians. Additionally he will carry the "anti politics" protest and reality tv votes. I have zero doubt that Bill Clinton would wipe the floor with Trump but Bill had charisma and the common touch. Hillary sadly is wooden and struggles to escape her haughty lawyer persona…. For every smoothie drinking, right on Californian yoga teacher, every noble thinking politically passionate college student and every liberal educated New York lawyer there are dozens of struggling farmers, disenchanted blue collar factory workers, poor unemployed , rednecks, ex cons on the scrapheap, Iraq war veterans feeling abandoned, NRA members, patriots , reality tv fans, tea party members and guess which candidate speaks to most of them…. M'lud I present to you the billionaire populist The Donald![98]

That was followed by a post titled "Congratulations President Trump," which read in part:

In an all too predictable presidential race, the "expert" pollsters, pundits and market makers were brutally exposed as utterly clueless. A fabulous result for the astute gambler at a widely available 6/1 on election day…. As with Bill Clinton, personal foibles will be Trumped by successful decision making. I suspect he will also avoid the sort of catastrophic interventions like Libya and Benghazi which really exposed Hillary's abysmal judgement and have left the world with significant problems as a result.[99]

Storey dropped hints in his posts that he was pro–Brexit, which he ultimately confirmed in an October 2017 post titled "Rich Energy enjoys international export boom post Brexit vote" that read in part:

Delighted to confirm our ninth major international trade deal since Brexit. We are now exporting to over 25 countries and have just concluded major deals in Australia and Singapore. The UK manufacturing sector is enjoying a renaissance post Brexit and we have found demand for our British premium drinks is growing ever stronger.[100]

Storey's political opinions also expanded into the realm of Formula One, particularly regarding its former CEO, Bernie Ecclestone. Ecclestone initially made a name for himself in motorsport by proving to be a savvy businessman, and he was the man Formula One had to thank for many of the lucrative television deals that made it rich.[101]

Ecclestone, though, was frequently surrounded by scandal. In 2009, he praised Adolf Hitler as a man who "was able to get things done."[102] He avoided paying taxes for years.[103] He was accused of bribery.[104] In 2016, he also denied that female Formula One drivers would be taken seriously due to his belief that women were "not physically" able to drive the cars fast.[105] When Formula One's first—and only, at the time—Black driver, Lewis Hamilton, faced racism online and spectators dressing up in Blackface, Ecclestone minimized it by claiming the situation was blown out of proportion, adding: "These things are people expressing themselves."[106] Indeed, in light of 2020's worldwide civil-rights demonstrations after

Minneapolis police officer Derek Chauvin killed a Black man named George Floyd—and as Hamilton, who would win his seventh championship that year, led demonstrations of his own on the Formula One grid—Ecclestone went so far as to posit that "in lots of cases, Black people are more racist than what white people are."[107]

For many forward-thinking Formula One fans, Ecclestone's replacement as CEO by Liberty Media's Chase Carey was a promising day for the sport, as was the series' decision to continue further distancing itself from Ecclestone.[108] In a January 2017 post titled "Lie with snakes and drink poison," however, Storey disagreed:

> In an outlandishly ironic move the brilliant dealmaker and de facto driving force of F1 for the last 40 years, Bernard Charles Ecclestone has been abjectly humiliated and forced out of the sport he has built up and been ringmaster of for decades. In a fascinating tale of greed, hubris and high stakes strategy he has lost and been betrayed by some of the men he has made so wealthy. A classic example of realpolitik and an example to any entrepreneur of the dangers of cashing in chips prematurely and believing in promises from investors. Ironically had he not sold majority stake he would be three times wealthier and still in charge. The hunter becomes the hunted. Meanwhile Liberty will almost certainly improve the sport whilst CVC partners run off with the loot![109]

Ecclestone was well into his 80s when he "cash[ed] in" his chips "prematurely." Ecclestone, for his own part, spent more than five decades in Formula One before Liberty Media bought it for $4.4 billion.[110]

Storey's behavior on LinkedIn mirrored that of the official Rich Energy social media accounts, and most infamously, the company's Twitter page. While Storey never admitted to being behind Rich Energy's tweets—when asked specifically by the authors in July 2019, Storey did not answer the question—they certainly fit his style.[111]

Twitter, where posts were capped at 140 characters until late 2017 and 280 characters for many languages after, didn't allow for the kind of verbosity Storey used on LinkedIn.[112] But the point came across.

The Rich Energy Twitter account was bizarre. Most of the tweets from its early days as a company, which oddly weren't deleted after a legal settlement with Red Bull like its other tweets were, had little to no engagement—be that shares, likes, or responses. Many tweets were accompanied by luxurious photographs that weren't taken by the brand, but were instead plucked from various corners of the internet and purported to have something to do with Rich Energy—sometimes by way of Photoshopping the brand's logo onto them, and sometimes by way of their captions. They had hashtags upon hashtags. They often tagged the account they came from, @rich_energy, which was the online equivalent of waving at yourself upon walking into a room.

But the tweets and photos were never one thing: convincing.

Rich Energy's tweets and often-poached photos had a few main themes: real estate, sporting activities, yachts, planes, motorcycles, women, and occasionally, women with large undomesticated cats. Perhaps the most notable example came on January 1, 2019. It was an image of a pool, the bottom of which was adorned with Rich Energy's logo, captioned: "A swim on New Year's day with @rich_energy #2019goals #lovelife #business #NewYearsDay #Swim."[113]

A reverse image search of that pool photo, however, revealed that the tweet was nothing more than a bad Photoshop job; whoever made the image had simply pulled it off of Google and edited a logo into it.

The photos of women were often provocative, and often either incredibly low quality or very obviously from somewhere other than Rich Energy's company archives. They included women on yachts, women who appeared to be from magazine makeup ads, women wearing low-cut outfits, and the like. One image from January 2017 featured a woman sitting topless on a beach, a bright-red helicopter behind her. The only thing covering her chest was her palms.

"You can enjoy @rich_energy all on your own on private beaches," the tweet read, along with the hashtags: #sun, #beach, #helicopter, #nature, #travel, #explore, #adventure, #new, and #landscapes.[114]

One regular image from Rich Energy's feed appeared to be a stock photo of a slender couple in black-tie attire, the man wearing a black bowtie and the woman in a black dress with a low-cut back. The man faced the camera and the woman away from it, both cropped at the neck to give a sense of mystery. One of the man's hands wrapped around her waist, and the other held the thin strap of her dress in a motion of taking it off. Her right shoulder featured a tattoo with the Rich Energy logo and name, just like the cans.

Rich Energy used the photo in multiple tweets during its early days, all with bizarre captions.

"Be Rich tonight," a tweet from November 2015 read.[115]

"Get the energy boost you need to get the job done," one from April 2016 said.[116] Eleven days later, Rich Energy used the photo yet again: "Get your energy boost this weekend!"[117]

The image was, in fact, a stock photo that appeared on at least three different romantic and erotic-fiction ebooks, including *Formal Fingering: Risk It All... (Becoming Naughty in Public Book 1)* by Jamie Fuchs. The Rich Energy tattoo had been Photoshopped in.

Another regular image from the Rich Energy account featured a blonde model bathing in an oversized cocktail glass, wearing all gold and lying with a "gold" rubber duck. The image was pulled from a video ad for a Paco Rabanne perfume, with a Rich Energy logo added to the top right corner. At least nine tweets from April 2016 featured the image with variations of the same caption, capitalization as such: "Premium Energy Drink—Take on your day with Confidence."[118]

Dozens of tweets featured other female models with Rich Energy logos either Photoshopped onto them or next to them, posted over and over again—including one image that returned results for an Estée Lauder ad[119] and one regularly associated with laser hair removal.[120] Then, there were the female models with large cats, all also pulled from random corners of the internet.

One from September 2016 pictured a woman in a cheetah-print swimsuit walking a cheetah on a leash. It came from a 2012 *Sports Illustrated* swimsuit edition and featured Russian model Irina Shayk. Neither the magazine, the model, nor the photographer were credited for the image, but the tweet did include the caption: "Live Rich and get some @rich_energy #premium #British #energydrink #high #performance #discerning #nolimits."[121]

Another, this time from December 2016, featured a woman wearing a short cheetah-print dress and running alongside a matching live cheetah. It featured the caption: "She drinks @rich_energy #nolimits #hardworkpaysoff #philosophy #speed #richenergy #africa #savannah #cheetah #athlete #nature #beauty."[122]

The photo was actually from a 2009 *Harper's Bazaar* magazine issue, featuring British supermodel Naomi Campbell.[123] No one involved in creating the image got credit in the tweet.

One of the most bizarrely sensual cat tweets from Rich Energy came in February 2017, when the account posted a photo of a model and a white tiger. The model wore only a burgundy bra, underwear, and heels, and sat mounted on the tiger with her hands gripped on its torso. The two were on a bed with satiny sheets, the model staring straight into the camera with her mouth slightly open and chin tilted down. The only context posted by Rich Energy was a short caption, which read: "Power, beauty and style #richenergy #power #beauty #style #tiger."[124]

Rich Energy took a similar approach with real estate, posting apparent stock photos of cities, islands, castles, lounges, pools, resorts, and large homes. Many were pixelated and low quality, and all featured vague captions.

"A great view enjoying a cool Vodka Rich cocktail," an April 2017 tweet read, accompanied by a fuzzy photo of a pool with a nighttime skyline view. "Elite performance with @rich_energy #premium #british #energydrink #city #cocktail."[125]

The photo was actually an "accommodations" image from the penthouse suite at the St. Regis Bangkok hotel. A much higher-quality version appeared on the Marriott website, meaning it was not, in fact, an original photo of Rich Energy's evening view.[126]

A February 2017 photo showed a plane in a hangar, along with the caption: "A night trip with @rich_energy #flying #aviation #pilot #jet #explore #adventure #new #landscapes #premium #performance #elite #richenergy."[127]

The photo hadn't been snapped on a night trip with Rich Energy in 2017, but was instead taken from a 2010 post on a U.S. government website. It featured a plane at the Yokota Air Base in Japan.[128]

An April 2017 tweet included a photo of a private jet and a Bentley at dawn. It read: "Early flight to Europe for @rich_energy management team this morning. Expansion in new markets #richenergy #premium #british #sales #business."[129]

That same photo often appeared on the photo-dominant social media site Pinterest, and it had been posted online as early as 2012—five years before Rich Energy's tweet.

"Thank you Santa," a December 28, 2016, tweet read. "@rich_energy now available in over 20 countries #richenergy #premium #british #energydrink #alpine #mineralwater #elite."[130]

A nighttime photo of a Ferrari Enzo, a roughly $3 million collector car as of 2020, accompanied the tweet.[131] The photo frequently appeared on websites to download computer wallpapers, some as early as May 2016—seven months before Rich Energy's tweet.

Other tweets weren't about apparent luxurious activities or items, but were just plain weird.

"Go ahead, tell me a joke," an April 2016 tweet said.[132]

"I was engaged to a contortionist, until she broke it off," a May 2016 tweet read. "Celebrate with @rich_energy."[133]

"#Abstinence is a good thing but only in moderation @rich_energy," a tweet from the same month said.[134] A June 2016 tweet included a photo of a dog with chew toys in its mouth. "How many balls can you get in your mouth ?" it read, with original punctuation intact. "I bet he drinks @rich_energy."[135]

Another post from that month had two photos of Tom Cruise side by side, with one featuring straight teeth and one crooked. "methinks #Tom has been drinking @rich_energy," the tweet said.[136]

A December 2016 tweet used a screenshot from a 2015 news story out of Florida, in which local television station NBC2 News reported that an "8- to 9-foot bull shark has been swimming very close" to a set of condos. Rich Energy captioned the image:

Not going for a swim today at the end of the garden. @rich_energy gunning for the competition #premium #british #energydrink #nolimits #elite[137]

The tweet received two likes.

It wasn't just Rich Energy's strange social media presence, though. There were also very few actual people publicly claiming to work for or with the company—both at its Richmond base and at distribution arms outside of the UK, such as Rich Energy USA.[138]

Rich Energy's United States website listed three members of its "executive team" as of September 2020: Jesse Gordon, creative director; Lance Henderson, vice president of branding and marketing; and Blake Farhoumand, CEO. Farhoumand was the only one with a bio listed:

> Blake began his career in the promotional entertainment industry at the age of 17. As his experience continued to develop, Blake began expanding his focus to include marketing and coordinating events and large productions including concerts and comedy shows around the country.
>
> Blake recently launched his own company, 400 Society, with the goal of connecting businesses, professionals and experts, small and large, around the world is involved with several companies both domestically and internationally as well as coordinating several events in the Midwest region of the US. He also assists certified Financial Consulting Firms by supporting executive level clientele with their personal travel and entertainment requirements.
>
> Blake, with his extremely diverse and vetted team, have created a sales/marketing strategy for 2019 and beyond that will not only guarantee success, but redefine what it means to be the most desired beverage and brand.[139]

The "partnerships" tab on the website said: "With an ever growing world of businesses, there are always ways to work together towards a common goal. Whether that be for strategic purposes, the greater good, to assist in the world's needs, or just to simply create an amazing event, we are always looking to team up with brands that share a similar vision." The "our partnerships" section below it was blank.[140]

What Rich Energy USA did appear to have, at least in 2019, was some amount of product. A Rich Energy USA Instagram post from that year showed Henderson standing in what appeared to be a warehouse, leaning against pallets containing thousands of Rich Energy cans with the company's original stag-head logo on them.[141] It wasn't clear when the photo was taken, but it was posted on June 18, 2019—more than a month after Rich Energy lost its UK copyright case over that logo.[142] The Rich Energy USA website, as of September 2020, also still used the original company logo, which Rich Energy's UK arm had to stop using more than a year earlier.

One person who briefly networked with Rich Energy's USA arm told the authors Farhoumand showed up to a 2019 meeting wearing sunglasses indoors and looking "ready for bottle service" at the club. That, they said, appeared to be the marketing approach for the USA arm. "They just seemed like they were going to go to the club and party, and that's how they were going to get their word out," the person said. "That's literally how it was."[143]

When contacted by the authors for an interview in August 2021, Farhoumand asked for an introductory call to talk about the authors' "goals and intentions prior to discussing anything in depth." The authors agreed to a preliminary conversation, and a person claiming to speak on Farhoumand's behalf—not Farhoumand—called during the scheduled time. After two minutes on the phone and the caller asking for a quick synopsis of the book, which had already been provided to Farhoumand, they said they'd pass the information along. Despite following up, the authors didn't hear back from Farhoumand again.[144]

The authors also reached out to Jesse Gordon, who didn't respond to multiple interview requests, and Lance Henderson, who declined to comment and said he didn't give permission for his name to be used in this book. Upon being told his involvement with Rich Energy had been public information on the Rich Energy USA website and thus his name could be used, Henderson asked for a contact number to touch base.[145] Henderson didn't call, nor did the authors hear back again. Read receipts showed that their unanswered messages had been seen.

Bernie Puz, listed as the director of Rich Energy Australasia on LinkedIn, was also reluctant to discuss the company. In response to a November 2021 LinkedIn message requesting a conversation, Puz requested that the authors "Tell me what you know 1st" before sharing a phone number. Puz did not answer when called.[146]

The authors did, however, receive an email with no subject line from a sender listed as "Bernard Puz" in August 2021. The sender's email account included references to Rich Energy in the imagery and actual address. Referring to one of the authors' last names, the email said: "Why does this surname King keep Reoccuring like herpes?"[147] It's unclear if this Bernard Puz was the same person.

While not listed as a Rich Energy employee, William Storey announced veteran financier Laurie Pinto as joining the Rich Energy management team via a December 2018 LinkedIn blog.[148] In February of that year, British tabloid the *Daily Mail* said it was "understood" that Pinto was advising Storey's attempted purchase of Force India.[149] Pinto didn't respond to a request for comment from the authors via LinkedIn despite viewing the message.

Five years, a tumultuous Formula One foray, and a few legal actions into his tenure at Rich Energy, Storey thought of himself as simply a misunderstood genius.

"Everyone said I was absolute bonkers, 'There's no way you can compete with anyone,'" Storey told the *Chasin' the Racin'* podcast in May 2020. "And to be honest with you, if I was less persistent, then they would have been right, because year one, I was basically getting told to fuck off by everybody. Nightclubs wouldn't stock it. Bars wouldn't take it. Supermarkets didn't want to know.

"For the first couple of years, I was basically just a glorified one-man band running around like a lunatic saying 'Rich Energy's amazing,' and very few people [were] buying into it."[150]

Storey said he "just kept on going" and "suddenly got some big names to help promote it" before reciting his usual vague list of ambassadors.

"They actually realized that I was onto something, we had a really good product and brand, and it went from there basically," Storey said. "We had a lot of detractors, and that's continued, but I think we're in danger of surprising a lot of people shortly."[151]

⋆   ⋆   ⋆

Rich Energy, of course, wasn't Storey's only attempt to develop a luxury brand. Companies House records listed him as an officer of six companies in the registry at the time of his Formula One arrival, showing that he'd been trying to hit it big for years. The businesses themselves were everything from a clothing brand to a technology company.

Only one of those six companies was still listed as active as of August 2020: Rich Energy. The others—Tryfan Technologies, Tryfan LED, Danieli Style, Rich Energy Racing, and Wise Guy Boxing, which had British boxer Frank "The Wise Guy" Buglioni as a director—were listed as dissolved. Many hadn't done well monetarily and all had been involuntarily removed from the registry. They often echoed Rich Energy in their strangeness.

During his time in Formula One, Storey apparently still headed William Storey Management, a company that strived "to offer … clients an unrivalled service geared towards maximising their success and commercial income." The agency, listed as established in 2010, was described as such—with formatting intact—on Storey's LinkedIn profile: "Agency looking after and promoting world leading footballers, bands, boxers, tennis players,artists , [sic] F1 drivers and international events."[152]

The business likely explained the connections Storey had elsewhere, such as with soccer players and other athletes. But Storey's apparent PR firm wasn't listed along with his other endeavors by Companies House, and Rich Energy's own LinkedIn page seemed to be connected to representatives from another PR firm.

The LinkedIn page for Rich Energy also listed the company as having a mere five employees as of early 2019—two were anonymous, while the other three were Richard Fletcher, listed as the distribution director, Jean-Eric Kies, listed as the "Director BeLux," and John Edward Morris, listed as "promotion" for Rich Energy.[153]

On LinkedIn, John Morris was listed as the company director at Morlee Leisure Limited. His profile described the business as such:

> Morlee Limited leisure is a company designed to maximise leisure opportunities through celebrity golf events abroad and in the UK. We also represent Rich Energy drink based out of London. Rich Energy looks and tastes as a superior brand should.[154]

The directors of Morlee were listed as Morris and a man named Robert Martin Lee—a former professional soccer player who also promoted Storey's Danieli Style brand and described himself as a brand ambassador for Rich Energy on Twitter.[155] The company was dissolved via compulsory strike-off in April 2017, and its most recent balance sheet before then, from February of 2015, listed its net current assets at just over 3,000 British pounds.[156]

Lee was just one example of the complex, intertwined nature of Storey's companies. Understanding them all required a deeper dive into the histories and financial situations of each.

The earliest of Storey's companies was "Tryfan Technologies Limited," which shared its name with a famous mountain in Wales.[157] Tryfan Technologies, incorporated in 2010, was listed by Companies House as the first company that named Storey as an officer.[158]

It was unclear what exactly Tryfan Technologies did. On its incorporation sheet, Storey's occupation was listed as a computer consultant. The company's nature of business was "information technology consultancy activities," which could include anything from software consultancy to computer planning services.[159] The only reference to Tryfan Technologies outside of miscellaneous company records occurred on the website for a company called Staxoweb, an IT services and web-design firm.

In the company's testimonials, Storey had only praise for Staxoweb, saying: "Our emails, our phones, and IT support are now where they should be."[160] Storey was still listed as the CEO of Tryfan Technologies on Staxoweb's website in September 2020, nearly two years after Tryfan was dissolved.[161]

There were only two other testimonials listed on the Staxoweb website: Ralph Buglioni and Terry Fletcher. For those aware of Storey's inner circles, their last names were oddly familiar.

Storey would later end up as a defendant in court alongside the founder of Staxoweb, his childhood friend Sean Kelly, when the two were sued by Whyte Bikes over Rich Energy's stag-head logo. Storey commissioned Kelly to design Rich Energy's brand identity the year it was incorporated in the UK, 2015, including that logo.

In the 2019 judgment against Storey, Rich Energy, and Staxoweb, a judge found it "more likely than not" that Storey and Kelly were familiar with Whyte Bikes' logo "and that they directly and knowingly copied" it.[162]

The William Storey Management website, williamstorey.com, also said it was "Powered by Staxoweb."[163] The website only had one page as of September 2020, which consisted of three things: two "about" paragraphs, a contact button, and a black-and-white background photo of a race car in the historic John Player Special Formula One livery. That iconic look, made famous by the Lotus squad in the 1970s and '80s, was entirely black and gold. In early 2019, Storey told the *Motorsport Network* that Rich Energy was "bringing that back" with its car design—pairing a borrowed paint scheme with an illegally borrowed company logo.[164]

Storey was the sole director of Tryfan Technologies throughout its nine years in existence, and the company was dissolved after liquidation in January 2019. By the time Tryfan was dissolved, its most recent balance sheet—a document detailing a company's financial standing and made public via Companies House—was from 2014. Tryfan's registered office became Hyde Park House in 2016, the same address as Rich Energy.[165]

Tryfan Technologies' other balance sheets—2011, 2012, and 2013— showed a company without much going for it. Its assets were listed as 280 British pounds in 2011 and 4,963 pounds in 2012. After three short years, Tryfan dipped into the red. Liabilities were 2,191 pounds in 2013 and a whopping 15,017 pounds in 2014. Tryfan rode it out on the registry without filing another balance sheet for its final five years.[166]

There were a lot of ways and reasons a company could be dissolved in the UK, such as if it was dormant or the directors wanted to retire without successors. There was also a compulsory strike-off, which was, according to business-recovery company Real Business Rescue, "typically initiated by Companies House due to non-filing of accounts or annual confirmation statement."[167]

In November 2015, Tryfan got a notice for compulsory strike-off. It was discontinued the next month.[168]

While the company wasn't struck off in 2015, its debts caught up to it the next year. A creditor could petition to have a company wound up by the British government—compulsory liquidation, in other words—if it couldn't pay its debts, and that's exactly what happened with Tryfan.[169] A court ordered the winding up of Tryfan Technologies in May 2016, and the action was finished in late 2018.[170]

The original winding-up notice in 2016 said that under the Insolvency Act of 1986, Tryfan Technologies would be wound up and that "costs of the petitioner" would "be paid out by the assets of the company." The creditor listed on the notice was Sky Deutschland Fernsehen GmbH & Co. KG, which translates to Sky Television Germany. Sky Sports, another division of Sky, would eventually broadcast the Formula One races that Storey's Rich Energy sponsored the Haas team in.[171]

While court documents from Sky Deutschland's claim couldn't be found, the October 2014 Companies House balance sheets from Tryfan listed 121,169 British pounds as falling due to creditors within a year.[172]

After Tryfan Technologies came Wise Guy Boxing, incorporated in late 2012, according to Companies House records. Its two original, and only, directors were Storey and the aforementioned boxer Frank Buglioni. Documents showed Buglioni was terminated as a director on April 30, 2015, and the company was dissolved via compulsory strike-off in March 2020.[173]

Wise Guy Boxing had received notices of compulsory strike-off twice before then, once in 2014 and again in 2017. Both were discontinued. No balance sheets or financial documents, aside from listed shareholders, were ever filed for the company.[174]

When asked about his experience with Storey, Buglioni said in a March 2019 email to the authors:

> Towards the end of William and I's business relationship it was evident we had differing plans and objectives for the businesses future. I didn't support William's business strategies.
>
> I elected to remove myself from association with William and concentrate my efforts on my successful boxing career and well respected boxing academy.
>
> Since retiring from boxing, Ive [sic] joined Herts Heritage Building & Roofing Ltd as managing Director. I'm proud to be part of a long standing, ethical construction company.[175]

When asked if Buglioni would like to elaborate on any of the email, including the mention of Storey's business strategies, the authors received no response. (The authors also reached out again in 2021 to see if Buglioni had more to say. Buglioni did not respond.)

About eight months after Wise Guy Boxing's incorporation came Danieli Style, where Storey was listed as a director alongside Buglioni and a person named Carlo Vagliasindi, who was listed as a "retailer" occupationally. They incorporated the company on June 5, 2013, according to Companies House documents.[176]

Dissolved about three years after its incorporation, Danieli Style had a Twitter account with 35 posts—13 of them being retweets from apparent ambassadors, and a handful of others being heavily filtered photos of boxers like Buglioni and Gennadiy Golovkin. The brand also mentioned two websites on its Twitter account, DanieliStyle.com and DanieliStyle.co.uk, both of which were defunct by the time the authors visited them in early 2019.[177]

Danieli Style appeared to be a clothing retailer, but whether it was meant to appeal to boxers or boxing fans was unclear. Its Twitter page displayed images of clothing and accessories that appeared to be for sale on its website, most of which were pricey. A snapshot of the website from the Wayback Machine internet archives captured "handmade shoes" as expensive as 480 pounds, along with "made-to-order" custom suits, swimwear, and Frank Buglioni apparel.[178]

The website also included Danieli Style's mission statement, which read:

Danieli is a brand built on hundreds of years of heritage and craftsmanship in Florence and the surrounding areas.

These rare skills have been perfected over centuries. We employ only the finest craftsmen, designers and shoe makers to manufacture to a peerless quality and give our customers access to extraordinary products.

We are proud to be stylish and tough in equal measure.[179]

The brand had five listed ambassadors, all of whom were boxers: Buglioni, George Groves, Mark Tibbs, Nathan Cleverly, and Tom Baker.[180] The authors reached out to Tibbs, Cleverly, and Baker in December 2021 and received no response. Contact information for Groves could not be found.

Danieli Style director Carlo Vagliasindi was listed by Companies House as having participated in eight different appointments as of September 2020, including serving as a director at Gelateria Danieli Limited, a gelato manufacturer incorporated in 2004, and a director at Lite Loafers Limited, a dormant company incorporated a few months after Danieli Style in October 2013.[181]

Danieli Style was listed by the Companies House as having 214 pounds in the bank in June 2014, and, less than a year later in April 2015, a "termination of appointment of director" form was filed for Buglioni. It was the same day Buglioni left Wise Guy Boxing.[182]

No other financial records were filed for Danieli Style. In June 2016, the Companies House sent a notice for compulsory strike-off, and the company was formally dissolved in August.[183]

In May 2015 came Tryfan LED Limited, with three officers listed by Companies House: Storey, listed occupationally as a computer consultant; Robin Day, listed as a technical engineer; and Chris Burbridge, listed as a financial director. They were also the three initial shareholders in the company.[184]

There are only two other Companies House documents listed under Tryfan LED: a notice of compulsory strike-off in August 2016 and documentation that the company was dissolved via compulsory strike-off in November 2016. No nature of business was ever listed.[185]

When asked about his previous businesses in early 2019, Storey simply told the authors: "I'm an entrepreneur."[186]

"I've had lots of different businesses in the past," Storey said. "Some have been successful, some have not. You know, when you're setting out, not everything's going to be a smash hit.

"I had an IT business, I had an LED-lighting business, I had an online-fashion business, I had a sports-management business, with varying degrees of success. For example, I had an IT company, and our biggest supplier effectively tried to take our client base, and we got into a legal dispute with them."[187]

Storey said that legal dispute arose as he was "moving into another business" and didn't expand much on what happened next.

"Ultimately, we had some scrapes along the way," Storey said. "But I've worked very hard. We've done some really good stuff, and clearly I started with absolutely nothing.

"I've worked very, very hard for 20 years, and Rich Energy is definitely my most successful business to date."[188]

∗   ∗   ∗

Mysterious funding, the same key players, minimal information, and compulsory strike-offs: Storey's previous businesses were a strange combination foreshadowing the enigma that would become Rich Energy.

Combined, those factors—the posts, the mysterious background, the apparent lack of funding to enter a series as financially prohibitive as Formula One—marked the beginning of a tale whose oddities never truly ended, and one that captivated those around it simply because it was more unpredictable than even the best of fiction.

As a wider audience began to follow that tale, Storey did two things: lean into the attention and try to steer the story his way. When the authors reached out to Storey in March 2019 about his and Rich Energy's early history, he was given a deadline of March 15 at noon Eastern Time to respond to a list of detailed questions—including how much the company was spending on the Haas F1 deal.

The reach-out would lead to the authors' phone interview with Storey the day after Rich Energy's court case against Whyte Bikes. But first, Storey responded via email:

> This was forwarded to me
> It appears your article a very inquisitive one
> It would be nice to disavow you of any fantastical notions
> Unfortunately because so little of our company information in the public domain you are reaching very inaccurate conclusions based upon extremely limited information

Perhaps you could have contacted us earlier so we can give you some real facts!![189]

Contrary to the final line of the email, Storey's response came more than 24 hours before the deadline he was given.

Haas had far less to say, with spokesperson Stuart Morrison responding as such via email—copying the questions sent by the authors and putting the team's official response in bold, red italics:

- The most recent Companies House balance sheet for Rich Energy (from September of 2017) shows 581 pounds in the bank, and that number (along with limited product availability, past failed companies run by CEO William Storey, etc.) has gotten a lot of attention online. Guenther Steiner has said Haas vetted the company, so can the team comment on the vetting process it used to confirm Rich Energy's legitimacy? *Our due diligence of potential partners is a confidential matter.*
- How did the findings of Haas' vetting differ from what people have found online? *Our due diligence of potential partners is a confidential matter.*
- What is the level of partnership Rich Energy has with Haas, considering that Haas is able to support itself and has in other seasons? How much of a stake does the company have in the team? *Rich Energy is Title Partner to Haas F1 Team (as announced 25th October 2018). Rich Energy has no stake in Haas F1 Team.*[190]

Storey's behavior and business history portrayed a serial exaggerator at the very least. While there was evidence that his company sponsored athletes and race teams, including Haas, Storey bragged of partnerships that could not be corroborated and very likely did not exist. In some cases, sponsorships existed, but they weren't the high-profile events Storey claimed. Meanwhile, Rich Energy's identity was built on low-quality, pixelated screenshots from the internet, Photoshopped to be relevant to the brand.

"I think the more that we kind of learned more about Rich Energy, it was all adding up that it wasn't a great partnership," one former Haas employee told the authors. "It wasn't a good thing to be involved with."[191] Yet Haas assured the world that it and its legal team had done their due diligence in making sure Rich Energy was legitimate.

"We did what we need to do," Steiner told the *Motorsport Network* right after the partnership was announced in October 2018. "Why do you doubt that?"[192]

3

DUBIOUS ENERGY

Even before Rich Energy, motorsport had seen its fair share of questionable and unconventional sponsors. While they weren't necessarily common, because most teams wanted legitimate sources of income to guarantee their survival, anything could happen with so much money at stake.

But even the sketchier sponsors, *Motorsport Network* journalist Luke Smith told the authors, maintained a very corporate relationship to teams.

"It's not just a guy with his phone," Smith said. "Nowadays, if you want to get your message out there in an instant, you can absolutely do that. And that's what William Storey did. It's similar ilk to Donald Trump in the way you can just get your message out there ASAP.

"There's never been a sponsor that's come in and been so vocal and noisy, and to have fractured so publicly with a team. We don't really do sponsorship stories [on the *Motorsport Network*], but it was the only story that anyone cared about."[1]

What made Rich Energy unique was its ability to puncture through the facade of elite legitimacy that Formula One curated for so long. William Storey brought financial concerns and power struggles to the fore through social media.

As Smith put it: "Nothing gets close to what's happened with Rich Energy."[2] But some sponsors certainly tried.

* * *

From 1979 to 1981, David Thieme, the American owner of Monaco-based Essex Overseas Petroleum Company, lived out a short stint in Formula One after striking a deal with Colin Chapman, the founder of British carmaker Lotus and boss of its iconic Formula One team.[3] Thieme encapsulated the early 1980s F1 type: If his black fedora, square sunglasses, and dark goatee didn't make an impression, his lavish parties and racetrack hospitality certainly did. At one point, he even hired Roger Vergé, who held the most Michelin stars of any chef in France in the mid–1970s, to cook for his party guests.[4]

Global news agency *United Press International* reported in 1981 that Thieme's Essex Overseas Petroleum paid Team Lotus somewhere around $4 million per year to be its principal sponsor.[5] The Lotus 88 race car Essex adorned was, naturally, black and gold—just like the Rich Energy Haas cars would be four decades later.[6]

An *ESPN* story from January 2014 described Thieme's theatrics:

> To be honest, the expected journalistic urge to investigate Mr. Thieme was diverted with remarkable and shameful ease when he threw launch parties that had to be seen to be believed. The first occurred in Paris in December 1979. An overnight stay in a posh hotel became small beer when we reached Paradis Latin, an upmarket nightclub that seemed to be decked from floor to ceiling in rich red velvet and frequented by strange people. [...]
>
> The following year, Thieme pushed the boat out even further when he hired no less than the Royal Albert Hall and engaged Shirley Bassey as the headline act. Just about anyone you have ever heard of in F1 was present and Roger Vergé, probably the first-ever Team Chef, managed to feed the entire ensemble with a very respectable three-course meal. Word had it that Thieme had chartered a Boeing 747 freighter to fly in enough bougainvillea to decorate the entire establishment and give the 'Riviera theme' that his chef had required.[7]

Thieme also sponsored Porsche in the 1979 24 Hours of Le Mans. The team hadn't planned to compete that year, but Thieme's money convinced it to try.[8] While one of the two Essex-backed cars was disqualified and the other retired due to engine issues, there was consolation in the fact that they were the quickest cars in the pack.[9]

But if Thieme's practice of throwing money at top-level race cars sounds too good to be true, that's because it was. In 1981, Thieme was arrested upon arrival at the Zurich airport in Switzerland for allegations of fraud. A warrant for Thieme's arrest came at the request of the Swiss Credit Bank, *United Press International* reported in April 1981, and police impounded his $7.6 million Mystere executive jet and the Lotus team's $761,000 double-decker bus.[10]

Thieme spent two weeks in jail while Swiss authorities investigated him, the *Associated Press* reported later that month, but he was soon released on what sources told the *AP* was a $150,000 bail.[11] Thieme and the Essex empire disappeared from the scene even more quickly than they'd entered it.

The Essex disaster and events surrounding it rocked the F1 paddock. The revolutionary Lotus 88 race car, which used lightweight carbon fiber, had been banned in 1981 for its "twin chassis" technology, where one chassis was nestled inside another.[12] The late 1970s had seen the introduction of cars using an aerodynamic principle known as ground effect, which drastically improved downforce—and speed—as the decade went on.

The Lotus team was the first to enact the technology, causing a massive change in the paddock. But safety improvements couldn't keep up with rising speeds, causing Formula One to step in with regulations to reduce the impact of ground effect—one being a mandated 60-millimeter ground clearance between the track and the bottom of the car.

Without that extra downforce, speeds were reduced, which left teams searching for other ways to negate the disadvantage. Lotus' answer was the 88.

"The key feature of the car is there was an outer, primary chassis, and then a secondary chassis, which was effectively inside the primary chassis," Colin Chapman's son, Clive Chapman, said in a 2016 interview with the motorsport-themed YouTube channel for Goodwood Road and Racing. "So the primary chassis, when the car left the pits, the downforce basically sucked it down such that the bottom edge of the primary chassis formed the all-important seal with the track, protecting the downforce under the car. And the Type 88 basically got around the rule that was trying to ban ground effect."[13]

The FIA initially declared the car legal, but not for long. Clive Chapman, standing by the car, pointed to a yellowing "PASSED" sticker on it. "This was applied to the car when it was presented in 88B form at the British Grand Prix in 1981," he said. "My father thought it was all thumbs up. Then overnight, the FIA ruled that the car was illegal and banned it. So, suddenly, Team Lotus didn't have any cars to race."[14]

The ban solidified the 88's legacy as the first and only twin-chassis Formula One car, while the 1981 season became one of the elder Chapman's last. He died of a heart attack in December of the following year at age 54.[15]

Lotus was one of the lucky ones. It was a team with a storied history of success dating back to the late 1950s, and its tenure lasted through 1994.[16] With seven constructor championships in its record books, all before 1979, the loss of a single sponsorship wasn't enough to kill the team at that juncture.[17] Others wouldn't have such good fortune.

One such group was the Onyx Formula One team. Perhaps one of the most obvious examples of sponsorship via a questionable product was the "groundbreaking" Moneytron machine, created by Belgian finance guru Jean-Pierre Van Rossem, who bought into Onyx in 1989. This supercomputer could supposedly forecast and accurately predict changes in the stock market, and according to the *Associated Press*, it caught on with investors.[18]

"Naturally, only Van Rossem had the key to the room in which the machine was kept at the offices of his company, Moneytron," British newspaper the *Sunday Times* wrote in a 2019 obituary for Van Rossem. "At the peak of his supposed fortune in the 1980s, Van Rossem was probably the most famous personality in Belgium besides its king."[19]

"For a time, the trick appeared to work," Irish news website the *Independent* wrote in December 2018. "It was rumoured that Moneytron clients included royalty and heads of states. In 1989, Van Rossem was reported by the *Financial Times* to have managed $7 billion from international investors."[20]

The story continued:

> Van Rossem amassed a personal fortune variously estimated at between $500m (€437m) and $860m (€752m). At his most successful he claimed to own a $4m (€3.5m) yacht, two Falcon 900 aircraft and no fewer than 108 Ferraris.[21]

Van Rossem was a character. The 1990 *AP* story said his "gray, straggly hair droop[ed] onto his chest" and that "in heated discussions—his usual style of conversing—white spittle form[ed] in the corners of his mouth."[22] The *Sunday Times* obituary said when one of Van Rossem's wives died, he "hinted darkly at murder and missing money" yet "spent years in the courts seeking permission to have [her] body stored in a cryonic chamber so that she might be brought back to life once science had advanced."

"The spark went out of the idea," the *Sunday Times* wrote, "when someone cut the electricity to the tomb."[23]

Van Rossem's funding promised great things, but nothing ever came to fruition. Out of 32 total race entries between three drivers in 1989, the Onyx cars only started a race 15 times and finished a mere five—with one early retirement being a disqualification.[24] Due to more drivers attempting to qualify than the grid could hold, Formula One implemented a pre-qualifying session to eliminate cars. Onyx failed to make it through pre-qualifying 17 times.[25]

Van Rossem's fortune dwindled almost as quickly as Onyx's season did. In 1990, the *Associated Press* reported that a French company accused him of not having the funds to cover a $54 million check, signaling the fall of an empire. But Van Rossem was always quick to change his tune.[26]

"Born into a Catholic family whose bourgeois lifestyle he said he despised, Van Rossem became a Marxist as a student," the *AP* wrote in 1990. "With his capitalist ventures in shambles, he now calls himself an anarchist."[27]

While the *AP* wrote that Van Rossem blamed his problems on an unnamed U.S. broker who owed him $362 million and didn't pay up, many critics argued that the whole Moneytron concept was a Ponzi scheme designed to benefit one person: Van Rossem.[28] He left the Onyx team high and dry, desperate for cash and unable to secure any long-term deals. Onyx folded just over halfway through the 1990 season.[29]

When Van Rossem's fortune fell apart and he went to jail, British investment magazine *MoneyWeek* quoted him as saying: "The good news is that there will be one capitalist less in the world, the bad news is that he is me."[30]

Also around the time of the Moneytron scandal came Leyton House Racing in 1990 and 1991. The Leyton House brand bought out the March Formula One team in 1990 after sponsoring it for several years.[31] Leyton House was also known for sponsoring endurance racing, and its promising Formula One roster included legendary designer and technical director Adrian Newey.[32]

The *New York Times Magazine* reported in 1988 that Leyton House began as a restaurant in 1986 before branching into sportswear, and that its boss Akira Akagi was moving into other areas as well—"a travel agency, country club, golf club and health club in Tokyo, and two resort hotels in Hokkaido."[33]

"When I first started sponsoring races, I didn't really have any product to sell," Akagi told the *Times*. "So I created the brand name and then followed it with a product. Most people do it the other way around."[34]

The car's bright blue livery was eye-catching, and its design pushed the envelope—something Newey was known for.[35] And while Leyton House struggled, it did so with the promise that success was on the horizon, if only the team could sort things out.

The problem came in the form of Akagi. In a *Motorsport Network* feature on Leyton House, Newey said Akagi began to borrow more and more money against the banks while slashing the team's operating budget.[36] Newey was fired in 1990 but said he knew he'd leave anyway, already concerned the team was headed for dire straits.[37]

Then, in 1991, the *Associated Press* reported that Akagi was arrested in connection with "questionable loans" from Japan's Fuji Bank.[38] The team was in trouble, but hope wasn't all gone—yet. Leyton House Racing reverted to its former March name and was sold to a consortium for 1992, according to British publication *Motor Sport Magazine*, but money was still tight. The operation finally folded the following year.[39]

Also in the late 1980s came Joachim Lüthi, a Swiss businessman who bought out Motor Racing Developments—better known as the iconic Brabham team—alongside Swiss millionaire Walter Brun.[40] What followed was a complex series of twists and turns that may be detailed best by Terry Lovell in the 2008 book *Bernie Ecclestone: King of Sport*.

Lovell wrote that Formula One journalist and management veteran Peter Windsor was "ambitious to run his own team," and attempted that alongside Brun and Lüthi. Windsor was confident Brabham would be back on the grid by November 1988, Lovell wrote, quitting his job at the Williams team to become managing director of Brabham. He was slated to "receive a 20 percent stake holding in the company."[41] But things went downhill quickly. From *Bernie Ecclestone: King of Sport*:

> [S]hortly after December 1988, when Brun and Lüthi were registered as directors of Motor Racing Developments, Brun decided to sell his interest in the company to Lüthi, who, according to High Court documents following subsequent litigation by Windsor, paid £5.5 million for the Brabham team. The sale by Brun of his interests in the company to Lüthi brought an abrupt end to Windsor's Formula One aspirations.[42]

One of Bernie Ecclestone's close associates told Lovell that Lüthi wanted Windsor out of the picture, and he ultimately succeeded. But the story got stranger. The book continued:

> [Windsor] successfully applied for a High Court injunction freezing his 20 per cent interest in the company. By then, however, Lüthi had already effectively removed ownership of the shares—and the company—out of the country. Retaining one ordinary share, he transferred the remaining 999 to the Lichtenstein-based Kingside Establishment.[43]

Lüthi owned a 50 percent share of Kingside Establishment, Lovell wrote, and the "transfer was all part and parcel of Lüthi's real interest in Motor Racing Developments—to use the company as a cover for major fraud."[44]

Lüthi was charged with embezzlement of $133 million from 1,700 different investors, according to the book. But before his case went to court, Lüthi fled to America, where he was finally arrested in California in 1995. He was living under a different name and ultimately ended up serving a seven-and-a-half-year jail sentence in Switzerland, Lovell wrote.[45]

His sudden disappearance proved disastrous for Brabham. The team scraped for sponsors, Lovell wrote, with the Japanese Middlebridge Group entity finally assuming control in 1990. The team eventually ran out of funds and collapsed in the middle of the 1992 season.[46]

Then there was French businessman and politician Cyril Bourlon de Rouvre,[47] who reentered Formula One in late 1992 when, according to the *Guardian*, Ligier F1 Team founder Guy Ligier "sold out" to him.[48] French newspaper *L'Humanité* wrote that upon his return to the series, de Rouvre was "already known to Formula One specialists for having taken over the AGS team in 1989, which was to file for bankruptcy a few months later."[49] Perhaps the second try would be the charm. (It wouldn't.)

Montreal's the *Gazette* newspaper wrote in 1993 that new Ligier boss de Rouvre "hired two British drivers for what was often looked upon as the quintessential French national team," and with money in its pocket, de Rouvre's era of Ligier began to look a bit hopeful—until his receipts got iffy.[50] The French magazine *L'Express* reported in 1994 that a company he sold, Cofragec, had an unexplained "hole" of hundreds of millions of dollars.[51] The entity that bought Cofragec asked de Rouvre for the missing money by the end of 1992, and when he didn't deliver, it filed a complaint against him. French newspaper *Libération* reported in 1994 that he'd gone to prison and sold his shares of Ligier to Flavio Briatore.[52]

In 1996 came a man named Sulaiman Al-Kehaimi, who claimed to be a Saudi Arabian prince but in reality was the son of an ambassador.[53] Al-Kehaimi claimed to own the Tyrrell Formula One team,[54] and, according to video evidence, entertained Cher and others in a 50-million-pound chateau at the 1996 Monaco Grand Prix.[55] The video evidence, given during a trial at Oxford Crown Court in the UK, apparently showed that Al-Kehaimi's Monaco guests truly believed he was "one of the richest men in the world."[56]

Of course, it was all a show. Al-Kehaimi had no intention of actually buying the team; he was more interested in living the glamorous Formula One lifestyle for a little while. And the chateau? The *BBC* reported in October 1999 that Simon Brown, prosecuting, said Al-Kehaimi "managed to rent the luxurious property in Monte Carlo by telling the owner that his friend, a Saudi prince, was interested in buying it."[57]

But Al-Kehaimi got off the hook—with Tyrrell and others. The *BBC* reported in November 1999:

> Sulaiman Al-Kehaimi was acquitted of five charges of obtaining property by deception, theft and attempting to obtain property by deception, at Oxford Crown Court. [...]
> He was also cleared of attempting to obtain £40,000 by deception from the commercial director of the Formula 1 Tyrrell Racing team. [...]
> Throughout the trial, Mr Al-Kehaimi [...] maintained that money given to him was for legitimate business transactions and he had every intention of paying back his creditors.[58]

Unfortunately for Tyrrell, no legitimate investor stepped in to sweep away its money problems.[59] The legendary championship-winning team folded two years later when team owner Ken Tyrrell, who the *New York Times* reported was 73 at the time, sold it to cigarette company British American Tobacco.[60] Tyrrell's last race was the 1998 Japanese Grand Prix.[61]

Then, just before the 1999 season, Formula One fell victim to a Nigerian prince scam.[62] Prince Malik Ado Ibrahim became co-owner of Arrows, a team that had existed for decades but failed to produce any tangible results. With a 20 percent share of the team, the *Motorsport Network* reported in 1999, Prince Malik became Formula One's first Black team owner.[63] Using the creation of his brand T-Minus as the vehicle, *Vice News* wrote in 2017 that Prince Malik promised to deliver $125 million to the cash-hungry team.[64] Mystery surrounded the unheard-of company and its branding, but money talks. *Vice* wrote that the main business plans for T-Minus were to sell rebranded products "such as clothing and motorcycles" and launch an energy drink.

Prince Malik made a lot of declarations that just couldn't be verified. As *Vice* wrote:

> Malik was educated privately in Britain, though no one is quite certain where, and claimed to be a prince of the Igbira people. It is likely that this was true, though given that there are at least 75 different royal families in his native Nigeria it's not quite the same as William Windsor showing up at the factory gates and promising to sink some of granny's money into your F1 team. Malik also claimed to have contested the Le Mans 24 Hours, which though not impossible lacks anything by way of proof.[65]

When $125 million is staring your broke team in the face, you take it and hope for the best. The best, though, turned out to be a single championship point scored during driver Pedro de la Rosa's debut race—good enough for last place in the constructor standings.[66]

As the season progressed, *Vice* wrote that the situation began to look dire. No one could locate Prince Malik, and no one could locate the money to complete the purchase of his shares. Team owner Tom Walkinshaw regained control of the shares, and Arrows eked out a Formula One career until 2002, but the funding issues proved to eventually turn fatal.[67] Walkinshaw died eight years later, his legacy including the reminder of his failed team.[68]

Prince Malik, though, seemed to be doing just fine. He popped back up about a decade later when he promised to fund a young NASCAR driver's team.[69] Even though he was accused of scamming the driver's family, local Texas paper the *McKinney Courier-Gazette* reported that a jury reached not-guilty verdicts for him in January 2008:

> The Collin County District Attorney's Special Crimes Unit accused Ibrahim of stealing approximately $750,000 from Robert Richardson Sr. of McKinney. Witnesses said Ibrahim claimed he would put Richardson Sr.'s money in a Bank of America account and use it to match corporate sponsorships to fund races for his son, NASCAR Busch Series driver Robert Richardson Jr.[70]

After posting the $35,000 bail required of him, Prince Malik managed to stay on the scene—promising electric cars for the Nigerian market, backing eco-friendly initiatives in Africa, and taking part in the Nigeria-based Youth Empowerment Solutions project, whose website listed him as being an "accomplished polo player and racing driver" who had "risen to the very top of the motor racing world in GT racing and For-mula One as an owner" and was "involved in high profile deals globally."[71]

Formula One also saw plenty of other people and entities who, while not outright deceptive with their money, proved to be disingenuous in other ways. Take, for example, Andrea Moda Formula, often referred to as one of the worst Formula One teams of all time.

The *AP* reported in January 1992 that Andrea Sassetti—sometimes called "Antonio Sassetti" by the papers—had bought out the remains of the oft-unheard-of Scuderia Coloni team for the upcoming season.[72] It quickly grew obvious that Sassetti had absolutely no idea what was required to run an F1 team: Andrea Moda Formula ran Coloni C4B cars with V10 Judd engines, despite the old Scuderia Coloni team being deeply uncompetitive in Formula One.

Andrea Moda Formula's problems started before the racing did. Prior to the 1992 season opener in South Africa, the *Guardian* wrote that "the need for pre-qualifying was eliminated when the Andrea Moda team were excluded from this race for irregularities concerning the way their new owner, the Italian shoe manufacturer Andrea Sassetti, acquired the team from the previous owner, Enzo Coloni."[73] Those irregularities, Miami-based newspaper *El Nuevo Herald* reported in February 1992, included the team not paying its $100,000 registration fee.[74]

The tone was set for the rest of the season. The *Guardian* reported in March 1992 that for the third round in Brazil, the team would replace both of its drivers.[75] One of the new drivers was Britain's Perry McCarthy, who the *Guardian* reported in April of that year "had his house repossessed last week and has now been disqualified from tomorrow's race."[76]

"He was hoping to make his Formula One debut after being signed recently by the Andrea Moda-Judd team, but the governing body has with-drawn his super license," the *Guardian* wrote. "Apparently there were doubts about his grand prix qualifications."

At the 1992 Spanish Grand Prix in May, the *Guardian* wrote: "The Essex driver Perry McCarthy failed to pre-qualify the uncompetitive Andrea Moda-Judd. He managed only about 10 yards in the pit lane before the engine cut out."[77]

The *AP* reported in September 1992 that an Andrea Moda car only managed to qualify for one race—the Monaco Grand Prix—but retired after a mere 11 laps.[78] In the first qualifying round at the Belgian Grand Prix in August, the leading Williams-Renault car of Nigel Mansell clocked a lap time of 1 minute and 50.545 seconds. The Andrea Moda cars were the slowest in the session, with driver Roberto Moreno clocking a 2:05.096 and McCar-thy a 2:15.050—an agonizing 15 and 25 seconds slower than Mansell's pace, respectively.[79] The *AP* reported in its September 1992 story that Sassetti was arrested in the paddock on charges of "forgery concerning payments of racing auto parts" that weekend.[80]

After that fiasco, the *AP* reported that the FIA suspended Andrea Moda Formula due to its "[failure] to operate ... in a manner compatible with the standards of the championship or in any way brings the championship into disrepute."[81] It was, after only a few months in existence, banned from competition for being an absolute disaster through and through. Sassetti then took his money to the CART paddock in America, acquiring a minor sponsorship of the Euromotorsport team in the 1993 season.[82]

Then, there was the strange case of Calisto Tanzi, who founded an Italian company called Parmalat in 1961.[83] Parmalat, a dairy and food company, began sponsoring many Formula One teams and drivers not long after its founding, including Brabham-Alfa Romeo and three-time champion Niki Lauda.

But there was another reality behind Parmalat, as described by the CFA Institute, an international organization for investment professionals:

> Parmalat's fraud apparently began in 1990 and lasted until 2003. In essence, when the company's financial performance began to slip in 1990, and rather than resolve its problems, management chose to disguise them through fraud and collusion. During this 13-year period, Parmalat executives used a wide range of unethical techniques to extend the fraud. They inflated revenues by creating fake transactions through a double-billing scheme. They used receivables from these fake sales as collateral to borrow more money from banks. They created fake assets thereby inflating reported assets. In some cases, they took on legitimate debt that they hid from investors (New York Times, 27 January 2004). They also eagerly worked with investment bankers to engage in financial engineering which moved debt off balance sheet or disguised it as equity on the balance sheet. They even colluded with third-party auditors and bankers to finance the fraud indefinitely.[84]

It was around the time Parmalat and Lauda ended their relationship, 2002, when the CFA Institute said the company's problems "began to emerge publicly."[85] In 2003, the *BBC* reported that while in custody, Tanzi was accused of "misappropriat[ing] as much as 800 million euros" during the prior decade.[86] Tanzi's fallout, therefore, had no real impact on Formula One—it simply showed how even sponsors that can pay the bills aren't always what they seem.

Time and time again, too, sponsors disappeared when it came time to pay up. There was the short-lived Super Aguri Formula One team and its sponsor United SS, a Hong Kong–based oil and gas company. Super Aguri took United SS to court in 2007, claiming it never made any installment payments after the initial one. The *Motorsport Network* reported in

August 2007 that the team was desperately seeking sponsorship,[87] and it announced the next year that it would be bought out by an automotive company called Magma Group.[88] The deal fell through, and Super Aguri pulled out of the championship four races into the 2008 season.[89]

There was also Mansoor Ijaz, who unsuccessfully attempted to buy a 35 percent stake in the Lotus Formula One team in 2013.[90] A year earlier, the *BBC* described Ijaz as the "charismatic businessman who has been at the heart of Pakistan's 'memogate' scandal, which threatened to derail the civilian government."[91]

These were certainly only the most high-profile cases—the ones that made the biggest splash and whose names will forever be carved into Formula One's history. They were joined by similar cases across other racing series.

* * *

American racing was its own beast, with a sports-car sanctioning body called the International Motor Sports Association—or IMSA—becoming the unofficial home of drug smugglers who used their money to fund lavish *Miami Vice*–like racing careers circa the 1980s. American open-wheel racing, such as the Indy car circles, saw some of the same.

In 1986, Florida newspaper the *Sun Sentinel* wrote:

> Just how widespread is drug money in sports-car racing? Fort Lauderdale car owner Preston Henn said: "I'd say, on a guesstimate, of the very top drivers in IMSA over the past four seasons, it's been a good percentage. If I had to, I'd say 15 percent."[92]

Five of the most infamous names to come out of it were Randy Lanier, Bill and Don Whittington, and the John Pauls.

Their stories are like movie plot lines. Randy Lanier won Rookie of the Year at the 1986 Indianapolis 500 and was an unknown name in motorsport at the time, all while making a reputation for himself in the world of drug smuggling.[93] The Whittington brothers were said to have shown up to the 1979 24 Hours of Le Mans—a race with multiple drivers per car due to its length—with a duffel bag full of cash, joking that they would buy their team's $200,000 car outright if they were allowed to drive it first. That money supposedly came from the hire-plane company the brothers owned, which they used to smuggle drugs into racetracks.[94] The Whittington brothers' car won the race.[95] John Paul, Jr., was accused of helping his father, who was also a racer, in a drug smuggling ring. He lost his chance to race in the 1986 Indy 500 when he was sentenced to five years in prison.[96]

As for his father, John Paul, Sr., the official website of the 24 Hours of Le Mans wrote of him in 2016:

Paul participated three times in the 24 Hours of Le Mans, between 1978 et [sic] 1982, with as [sic] best results fifth place and a class win in 1978 in Dick Barbour Racing's Porsche, along with owner Dick Barbour and Brian Redman. At the same time, he was involved in drug trafficking and was sentenced to 20 years behind bars for various crimes and offenses, eventually compounded by an escape attempt, but was finally released after a 15-year stint. After being interrogated about the disappearance of his girlfriend, he took off in his boat, which he then put up for sale before disappearing from radar screens in 2001. The file has never been closed....[97]

Later, drivers like Scott Tucker took up the racketeering throne. As *CNN* wrote in 2016:

[Tucker] was arrested on Wednesday, accused of running an illegal $2 billion payday lending enterprise and hit with federal RICO charges.

From 1997 until 2013, Tucker operated payday lending companies that gave 4.5 million Americans short-term, high-interest loans under "deceitful" circumstances, according to a federal indictment filed in New York City and unsealed Wednesday.[98]

American motorsport magazine *Racer* reported in 2020 that IndyCar and IMSA driver Ana Beatriz, who also raced under the name Bia Figueiredo, was believed to be tied to an embezzlement and money laundering scheme in her home country of Brazil. Her husband and father-in-law had already been arrested, *Racer* reported, and Beatriz was pinned as the direct recipient of an illicitly earned $250,000 channeled into her shell company B3Tres.[99] *Racer* wrote:

A complaint filed in Rio de Janeiro details a scheme to bilk vast sums of money from the state to operate a number of hospitals. The complaint lists a lack of certification to operate medical facilities, pre-arranged contracts with vendors to receive the government funds, and over-charging for medical services and materials. [...]

Over an eight-year span, the parent company led by Figueiredo's husband and father-in-law, Instituto dos Lagos Rio, is said to have taken in more than $118 million from the state, with payments made to shell companies like B3Tres.

According to the complaint, "[Instituto dos Lagos Rio] did not even have the ability to sign management contracts with the State, but forged its technical training thanks to obtaining false technical certificates." On the subject of embezzlement and money laundering, the complaint adds that Figueiredo and family have been "proven to have deviated a substantial part of the amounts."[100]

In 2013, six "prominent" unnamed Venezuelan car and motorcycle racers were accused of fraud. That year, car magazine *Road & Track* reported on its website:

Short on hard currency, Venezuela has very strict limits on the amount of foreign cash a private citizen can purchase. The government only allows $3000 per year for travel. This past week, the Venezuelan government froze all motorsport-related funds when the current Minister of Sport, 31-year-old former Olympic fencer Alejandra Benitez, discovered her signature had been forged on foreign currency requests to the tune of $66 million.[101]

Reuters reported at the time that these drivers were accused of making fraudulent requests for money, then offloading some of that money onto the black market, where they could get back about seven times the price. The fraudulent documents went unnoticed for so long due to the high cost of competing in motorsport, *Reuters* wrote. One specific racer was approved for $66 million to compete, Venezuelan Sports Minister Alejandra Benítez said, and two racers annually spent as much as it would cost for a team of more than 600 athletes to attend an event.[102]

The racers went unnamed because Benítez "wanted to respect them as fellow sportspeople," *Reuters* reported.

*   *   *

If Formula One seems to have a more deeply entrenched history of shady sponsors, that's because the business model almost encouraged it. In a deep dive of motorsport money conducted in 2018, automotive website *The Drive* found that Formula One's biggest source of income was its television rights—the series handled all of its TV logistics itself, then sold the global feed to local distributors. At the same time, teams themselves actively pursued sponsorships because the cost of running in the series was so high, and even "pay drivers"—those who paid their own money for a race seat, sometimes through sponsorship by a family company—still earned a salary from their teams.[103] Despite series-wide budget caps on the horizon, Formula One was still a massive operation. Even "poorer" teams needed hundreds of millions of dollars per year to operate in the late 2010s, making them prime targets for less-than-savvy sponsors.[104]

In other racing series like IndyCar, which mandated at the time that all teams have very similar chassis and aerodynamic kits in order to keep costs minimal, *The Drive* found that teams themselves did very little work when it came to seeking sponsors.[105] Each team also, as of 2018, started out with approximately $900,000 per car provided by the "Leaders Circle" program, which offered financial rewards to teams that participated full time.

But in that era of IndyCar, drivers generally brought the rest of the money. As described by *The Drive*:

> Paid drivers are another important source of income for some IndyCar teams. In fact, in the case of Dale Coyne Racing and others on that level, it's the *only* source of income. Extensive conversations with the likes of former

professional racing driver Alex Lloyd and half a dozen other active drivers have proven that some teams simply don't care to mine sponsorship opportunities on their own.

"Teams don't really actively look for sponsors because they've grown so used drivers coming in with a ton of personal money or a ton of sponsors," said a former IndyCar racer who now races at a different open-wheel series.[106]

IndyCar drivers made paltry sums compared to other top-level series—up to $30,000 for winning a race, not counting the crown jewel, big-money Indianapolis 500, part of which would immediately be given back to the team—and were required to cover things like their own health and life insurance. It made sense, then, why IndyCar drivers spent far more time looking for their own personal sponsors.[107] The teams took very little financial responsibility for them.

Many motorsport series shared that business model, and as such, it made sense that teams being destroyed by one shoddy sponsor was distinct to Formula One. Elsewhere, it was generally the drivers who suffered while the teams found someone new to take up the monetary mantle, leaving their operations relatively intact.

One example of that came around 2008, when sports car driver Ryan Dalziel was linked to Ponzi schemer and racer Henri Zogaib.[108] Dalziel said he ultimately lost his house in the ordeal, and *Road & Track*'s website chronicled the story in 2017:

> "It was a half million dollars all in. And it was one of those, your parents saved their whole life and there's pension money from them and I was, I guess, 25 at that time. 25, an Indy car driver, and life is amazing at the time. And you go from having a really bad ass apartment, penthouse driving a ... forced into a Smart car practically overnight. I did the right things and took the right steps and we knew it was bad. We pretty much got out of everything we were in with loans and cars and everything like that. Everything stopped overnight and you just have to reset. We were lucky."[109]

Motorsport news website *Sportscar365* reported in 2014 that for his endeavors, Zogaib was sentenced to 15 years in prison followed by 15 years of probation. Court documents obtained by the website showed that there were 33 investors in the Ponzi scheme, including Dalziel, NASCAR driver A.J. Allmendinger, and sports car driver J.C. France, the grandson of NASCAR founder Bill France.[110]

*   *   *

NASCAR itself—whose history included an unidentified man who went by L.W. Wright fraudulently posing as a driver to compete in the 1982 Winston 500 and then disappearing[111]—had multiple sponsors turn out to be something other than they seemed in the late 2010s alone. Five days after the 2018 Daytona 500, on February 23, a company called Earth-Water announced that it had become the official water of BK Racing, an underfunded team in the top-level NASCAR Cup Series.[112]

EarthWater, "an exclusives [sic] partner of Amazon.com" that worked with BK racing throughout 2017, called itself a "health and wellness company and manufacturer of Mineral Infused High-Alkaline Beverages" in the announcement, capitalization as such.[113]

"In another historic first, Amazon, one of the world's largest retail distribution Company's [sic] has agreed to join EarthWater as a co-sponsor and will appear on all the EarthWater Sponsored Races for the 2018 Season," the announcement continued. An "Available on Amazon" logo did appear on the car, but when asked by the authors whether it was actually a co-sponsor, Amazon did not respond.

EarthWater, in its company blurb at the bottom of the press release, described itself as:

> The FulHum and Zenful brands use a 100% natural, proprietary blend of organic Fulvic and Humic complexes mined from deep within the Earth's surface. Fulvic and Humic minerals are believed to have properties which detoxify free radicals, and improve absorption of key nutrients. EarthWater products are sold online, exclusively by Amazon. To engage with EarthWater online, you are encouraged to 'like,' 'follow' and 'share' on the brand's social media pages.[114]

The EarthWater name was, in a way, literal. The company made a water product that was dark brown.

"That looks disgusting," one YouTube reviewer said in a 2017 video, disconcertingly glancing back and forth between the camera and the glass of EarthWater they'd just poured. "It's a very similar color to, like, a very flat cola—almost caramelly at the bottom here. ... And it tastes like ... water. I cannot detect any flavor in that whatsoever. That is just water."[115]

The reviewer, whose channel went by the name of "Reviewy McReviewface," also had a brochure about EarthWater. They weren't impressed. "This thing has some of the worst, pseudo-science, phony-baloney marketing material that I have ever read," they said. "This thing has so many ifs, ands, or buts in it, it's incredible. Like, there is not a single scientific statement that is actually made as a statement. Everything in here is: 'Some people say,' 'Some speculate.'

"Like: 'Drinking [EarthWater] *can* assist in replacing *many* trace elements *often* missing from *some* modern-day diets. It has been *speculated* by *science* that a lack of *some* of these minerals *can* contribute to a weakened immune system, *often* enabling the body to become increasingly susceptible to *some* of the *many* chronic illnesses and diseases which are increasingly prevalent in today's society.'

"So, there wasn't an actual statement in any of that. It was just: 'Somebody said something about something.'"[116]

The reviewer said the pack of four EarthWater bottles they had cost $11.[117]

An account by the name of "EarthWater TV" commented on the video, saying it was "sorry to hear that you did not find our product to your liking." The comment continued:

> I assure you, this beverage has MANY more benefits than just drinking regular tap water; if you research our ingredients you will find countless scientific evidence of this. We take our claims very seriously and these ingredients have been proven, with scientific evidence, to do as such. In addition to this we have many consumer testimonies, some including professional athletes. You can find some of these stories on our website and our Amazon reviews from the U.S.[118]

NASCAR driver Ryan Ellis echoed the review, telling the authors in July 2020 that EarthWater "tasted like water, looked like poop water."[119]

"I had a case until last year and threw it out because I didn't trust it," he said.[120]

Others in the industry, like photographer Daylon Barr, soon concluded that EarthWater was a multi-level marketing scheme. Barr showed the authors screenshots of emails inviting him to join the pyramid.[121]

EarthWater CEO CJ Comu, a man with strong but likely unintentional "Dr. Phil meets Texas real-estate developer" vibes, had a similar Twitter ethic to William Storey: a lot of hashtags and a lot of weird posts. Comu, who had 82 Twitter followers as of early 2020, had a habit of pasting inspirational quotes over photos of himself, such as one blue-toned photo from 2018 with Comu giving the camera a peace sign. Just below that peace sign, a block of white text read: "If you don't learn to make money in your sleep, you will work until you die." Comu captioned the post as "A little Friday inspiration" and included 13 hashtags: #success; #quotes; #inspired; #inspiration; #business; #enrepreneur, which was spelled incorrectly; #ceo; #ceomillionaires; #ceolife; #ceomindset; #fridayfeeling; #instagood; and #inspires.[122]

Another post from 2018 featured a photo of Comu holding an EarthWater bottle in a strong sepia filter, with a quote attributed to 1800s essayist Henry David Thoreau: "Success usually comes to those who are too busy to be looking for it." It featured 14 hashtags—#dedicated, #success, #success again, #successquotes, #quotes, #motivation, #ceo, #ceolife, #ceomindset, #mindset, #dedication, #entrepreneur, #entrepreneurs, and #entrepreneurship—along with the caption: "Retweet if you agree!"[123] No one retweeted the post.

Comu announced on February 19, 2019, that he would run for city council in Addison, Texas, near Dallas.[124] Comu received 373 votes in the unofficial count from the May 4, 2019, election, while the highest vote-getter was incumbent Ivan Hughes with 1,026.[125]

Four days later, on May 8, came a new announcement—this time from the U.S. Department of Justice, which would later describe Earth-Water as a "multimillion-dollar, high-yield investment fraud scheme that targeted elderly victims." Its headline read: "Six Men Charged for Role in Five-Year High-Yield Investment Fraud Scheme."[126] Comu, who was 58 at the time, was one of the six men. He was arrested that day.[127]

The announcement from the Department of Justice said Comu and others "used EarthWater's investment account as a personal piggy bank, using victim investor funds for their own personal benefit and transferring victim investor funds to bank accounts controlled by them for their own personal use."[128] The DOJ continued:

> The indictment alleges that, beginning in 2013, Comu, [John] Price, [Harley] Barnes, [Richard] Kadish, [Richard] Green and [Daniel] Broyles [Sr.] conspired to sell stock in EarthWater, a United Kingdom company headquartered in Dallas County, Texas. EarthWater manufactured and sold bottled water that it claimed was infused with special minerals mined from an 80-million-year-old deposit hidden in a secret location.
>
> According to the indictment, Comu, who is EarthWater's founder, chairman and chief executive officer, falsely represented to victim investors that he was a successful Wall Street veteran with decades of experience and did not disclose to investors that, among other things, he was permanently barred from selling unregistered securities as a result of actions filed by state and federal securities regulators.[129]

On March 10, 2020, the DOJ said Comu pleaded guilty to one count of conspiracy to commit mail and wire fraud, 10 counts of mail fraud, 10 counts of wire fraud, and two counts of money laundering.[130] Later that month, Comu filed a request in *United States of America v. Comu* to be let out of jail as a result of the emerging COVID-19 pandemic.

He was not let out, with the representation for the U.S. arguing that Comu was a "danger to the community, particularly to the elderly population who are most at risk for contracting COVID-19."[131]

"Comu is an unrepentant and undeterred confidence man," the argument read. "Even after he was arrested and ordered to stop promoting securities, he continued to target the same elderly victims of the fraud for which he was indicted, using the same false and misleading statements, and the same modus operandi. Were he to be released amidst the COVID-19 pandemic, he would pose an even greater danger to his elderly victims and other vulnerable individuals.

"Comu previously promoted EarthWater as a 'magical' treatment for HIV and cancer. Comu could easily rebrand his EarthWater pitch to include COVID-19 among the list of serious diseases EarthWater purportedly cures and use his wife's email and telephone from the comfort of his home detention to continue the fraud."[132]

BK Racing eventually filed for bankruptcy, with *NBC Sports* reporting in March 2018 that the team's contract with EarthWater was valued at $3.6 million and could "be paid in cash, EarthWater stock, and product."[133]

But Comu implied that EarthWater wasn't paying in cash at all.[134] In an early 2018 post on LinkedIn, Comu shared a link to a *Business Insider* story headlined "Here's What It Costs to Sponsor NASCAR."[135] The story estimated costs for a main car sponsor to be between $5 million and $35 million per Cup Series season.[136]

"Cost of NASCAR Sponsorship!!" Comu wrote. "-OR- you can trade with EarthWater Products. Go Car 23."[137]

Also in the mid–2010s came a company called Zloop, which partnered with the Kyle Busch Motorsports team in the third-tier NASCAR Truck Series as a sponsor for driver Justin Boston.

Nine races into the 2015 season, Kyle Busch Motorsports said Boston was out and would be replaced by a new face: Christopher Bell, who would go on to win a Truck Series championship for the team in 2017. The abrupt parting, Kyle Busch Motorsports said, happened after Zloop breached its agreement with the team.[138]

Zloop, founded by Robert Boston and Robert LaBarge in 2012 as an electronic-waste recycling firm, adorned Boston's race cars for a few years before the whole thing went under—a case of father sponsoring son, which wasn't uncommon in motorsports. Racing costs money, and daddy's money makes it easier to get in the door.

But two years after Kyle Busch Motorsports split with Justin Boston, a May 2017 announcement from the U.S. Department of Justice gave more insight into what it believed the e-waste firm with a funny name really was: a big sham, according to an FBI investigation.[139]

"Federal Indictment Charges Founders of Defunct Hickory E-Waste Company with Defrauding Victims of at Least $25 Million," the DOJ headline read. The press release continued:

> Today, a criminal indictment was unsealed in federal court, charging Robert M. Boston, 53, and Robert S. LaBarge, 50, both of Hickory, N.C., with conspiracy relating to a fraud totaling at least $25 million, to include wire fraud, securities fraud, bank fraud, and money laundering, announced Jill Westmoreland Rose, U.S. Attorney for the Western District of North Carolina. [...]
> According to allegations contained in the indictment, Boston and LaBarge defrauded franchisees, investors, and lenders of their company, Zloop. The indictment alleges that, through their fraud, the defendants obtained millions

of dollars, much of which was spent on expensive personal real estate, a private plane, and the racing career of Boston's son.[140]

Drawing on lines of credit, Boston and LaBarge were said to have "spent hundreds of thousands of dollars on, among other things, a private plane, a new Corvette, and a new Grand Cherokee."[141]

"After Zloop subsequently drew an additional $1.3 million from the credit card line, the indictment alleges that more than $500,000 was spent on racing-related expenditures and approximately $79,808 on a suite at a professional football stadium," the DOJ announcement read.[142]

In October 2017, a North Carolina jury ruled that Justin Boston owed Kyle Busch Motorsports nearly $450,000 for breach of contract after his nine races.[143] The team had received more than $1.5 million from the Bostons. When asked by the authors if the team received the $450,000 or had any other comments on its time with Zloop, a representative for Kyle Busch Motorsports didn't respond.

Two months later in December, a federal jury convicted Robert Boston, who was 54 at the time, of conspiracy, wire fraud, securities fraud, and money laundering in the $25 million scheme.[144] Robert Boston was sentenced to 10 years in prison, the DOJ announced in October 2018, while LaBarge was sentenced to two. The announcement said Robert Boston was deemed liable for more than $27 million by the judge, and was ordered to "forfeit his interest in several properties."[145] It continued:

> Court records show that Boston concealed crucial information from franchisees, including that Boston's former company had filed bankruptcy, that Boston had filed personal bankruptcy, that Boston had a judgment against him for fraud, and that Boston had been held liable in an action alleging that he had knowingly submitted false financial documentation to a bank to obtain a $2.9 million line of credit. When Boston was warned that, according to the company's attorney, concealing this information from the franchisees of Zloop would be fraud, he wrote, "it is my decision how I want to move forward."[146]

"According to evidence presented at trial, while inquiring about the potential purchase of a private island, Boston wrote, 'My son is a NASCAR driver. I spend 5 Million [sic] a year so he can play race car driver,'" the announcement read.[147]

There was also California-based company DC Solar, which partnered with NASCAR team Chip Ganassi Racing in 2015 and expanded that partnership before the 2018 season.[148] When it broadened the deal again in November 2018, the Ganassi team said in an announcement that the company's investment in NASCAR "helped [it] to become one of the more recognizable brands both on and around the track."[149]

"DC Solar provides mobile solar lighting solutions, EV chargers, and power stations to numerous tracks, including Charlotte Motor Speedway, ISM Raceway (Phoenix), and Darlington Raceway, among many others," the announcement read. "DC Solar has powered nighttime construction throughout [a $178 million modernization project] at ISM Raceway, for what is sure to be one of the most exciting new venues in motorsports."[150]

The company's name recognition would soon take a turn. The month after the November 2018 announcement, the FBI raided the Martinez, California, home of DC Solar founders Jeff and Paulette Carpoff. Local outlet the *Mercury News* reported that "multiple" witnesses "watched the agents tow away vehicles" during the week of the raid.[151]

"FBI officials would not discuss what they seized from the home," the story read. "A source with close knowledge of the investigation said agents also removed computers, cell phones, and receipts."[152]

Soon after that report came out, *NBC Sports* reached out to the lawyer for the Carpoffs, Armando Gomez. Gomez told the outlet the Carpoffs were "surprised and disappointed with the actions taken by the government earlier [that] week, which appear[ed] to relate to an ongoing tax dispute."[153] The statement continued:

> They are long-time residents and supporters of the Martinez community who believe in our country and all that it stands for. The Carpoffs are grateful for the support of their friends and family, and have trust in the system to resolve this matter in a fair and just manner at the earliest opportunity so that they can continue to grow their business, which brings clean, reliable, renewable power to first responders and others whenever and wherever needed. Until that time, they will have no further comment on this matter.[154]

The statement from Chip Ganassi Racing to *NBC Sports* was a bit shorter: "Although we have received little in the way of facts, we are aware of the situation with DC Solar and are monitoring it closely," the team said.[155] NASCAR declined to comment to the outlet.

In January 2019, the month after the raid and the month before the start of the new NASCAR season, Chip Ganassi Racing announced that it would be shutting down its efforts in what was then known as the second-tier NASCAR Xfinity Series "due to a lack of sponsorship funding."[156] Much of that funding was supposed to come from DC Solar.

The team posted a statement from owner Chip Ganassi, which read:

> This was a difficult decision for me to make and it comes with much anguish as this is a championship caliber team (having won six races and finished second in the owners championship) and more importantly because it affects a number of good people's livelihoods. Running a car without funding is difficult to do.[157]

DC Solar had a heavy presence in the Phoenix area when the company existed, including a 2017 deal that, according to local outlet the

Phoenix New Times, had Phoenix pay $1 per year for each of the $150,000 mobile solar generators provided by DC Solar—totaling $500 across five years.[158]

"So what's in it for DC Solar Freedom?" the story read. "For one thing, they get to sell advertising space on their trailers."

But around the time of the FBI raid, the *Phoenix New Times* reported that the Carpoffs' finances "raise questions. ... court records from Contra Costa County, in California, show the Carpoffs have cycled through multiple tax liens and releases from both the state of California and the IRS," the story read. "In March 2016, the state of California filed a lien against the couple for $3.4 million; it was released in July that year.

"More recently, on November 6, the IRS released a lien of $2,441,500 that it filed on August 3 against the Carpoffs. The state of California also filed a lien against the Carpoffs in August, for about $1 million. As of this writing, that lien had not been released. In response to a message seeking comment, Jeff Carpoff asked for time to set up a phone call, then failed to pick up or reply to a follow-up email."[159]

Just a few months after the raid, in February 2019, DC Solar filed for bankruptcy.[160]

Nearly a year later in January 2020, the big headline came courtesy of the U.S. Department of Justice: "Top Executives Plead Guilty to Participating in a Billion Dollar Ponzi Scheme—the Biggest Criminal Fraud Scheme in the History of the Eastern District of California." Those top executives were Jeff and Paulette Carpoff, both nearing 50 years old at the time. Others involved had previously pleaded guilty.[161]

The DOJ said the investigation resulted in "the largest criminal forfeiture" in the history of the Eastern District of California, with more than $120 million in forfeited assets going to victims and $500 million returned to the U.S. Treasury. There was "more to come," the announcement said.[162] It said Jeff Carpoff pleaded guilty to conspiracy to commit wire fraud and money laundering, while Paulette Carpoff pleaded guilty to conspiracy to commit an offense against the U.S. and money laundering.[163]

The DOJ cited court documents in saying that between 2011 and 2018, DC Solar made mobile solar-generator units—units promoted as "able to provide emergency power to cell-phone towers and lighting at sporting events," the DOJ said. Some of the main investor incentives were the huge federal tax credits for using solar power.[164]

But DC Solar pulled off its scheme by selling nonexistent solar generators to its investors, the DOJ said, and made it look like generators existed in areas they did not.[165] "In reality, at least half of the approximately 17,000 solar generators claimed to have been manufactured by DC Solar did not exist," the DOJ said, adding that false financial statements and lease contracts were "among [the] efforts to conceal the fraud."[166]

The Carpoffs' Ponzi scheme eventually ended with 148 of their "luxury and collector vehicles" being seized[167] and auctioned for more than $8.2 million.[168] NASCAR Xfinity Series cars bearing the names of drivers Kyle Larson and Brennan Poole also went to new homes.[169]

The DOJ announcement also mentioned other things the Carpoffs spent their fortune on: a minor-league professional baseball team; luxury real estate in California, Nevada, the Caribbean, Mexico, and other places; a private-jet subscription service; a suite at a professional football stadium; jewelry; and the NASCAR endeavors.[170] Pitbull even performed at one of their holiday parties, according to a *Reuters* story from January 2020.[171]

The *Reuters* story continued, emphasis added:

> Malcolm Segal, a lawyer for Jeff Carpoff, said in an interview that **his client "feels terrible that this business started out intending to provide clean energy and tax benefits to many large corporations, but unfortunately failed and resulted in his committing a number of illegal acts."**
> Paulette Carpoff's lawyer Bill Portanova said in an interview: "She regrets absolutely what she did, and is looking forward to the difficult job of making amends."[172]

Perhaps the only appropriate response to getting caught in a $1 billion Ponzi scheme is, in fact, "We had really good intentions but then unfortunately, crime happened?"

In November 2021, Jeff Carpoff was sentenced to 30 years in prison—the maximum statutory penalty he faced. Paulette Carpoff faced a maximum of 15 years at the time, but had yet to be sentenced.

FBI agent Sean Ragan said the Carpoffs and their co-conspirators "wove a web of lies and deceit in [the] massive fraud scheme," according to the DOJ.[173] The criminal investigation agent with the U.S. Internal Revenue Service, Kareem Carter, added that from the outside, DC Solar "was a legitimate and successful company."

"But in reality," Carter said, "it was all just smoke and mirrors—a Ponzi scheme touting tax benefits to the tune of over $900 million."[174]

* * *

Given the history of Formula One—and motorsport as a whole—suspicion was natural with sponsors that were hard to pin down, even when they were paired with the most successful teams. In 2019, tobacco company Philip Morris tried to play coy with its "Mission Winnow" brand sponsorship of the Ferrari team, promoting a vague allusion to vaping.[175] The team pulled the livery off of the cars before that year's opening race, the Australian Grand Prix, due to tobacco advertising restrictions in Australia.[176]

Even Rokit, a telecommunications company that sponsored the then-back-marker Williams team in 2019,[177] sold what *Wired* magazine's UK publication called a "strange, pointless zombie of a phone"—one that few people actually owned in an era dominated by iPhones and Samsungs.[178] The Williams-Rokit deal came to a years-premature end in 2020 amid the team's streak of poor performance, but no reason was given for the split at the time.[179]

Williams, though, said it had met all of its contractual obligations to its sponsor.[180] From a May 2020 story on the Formula One website:

> In Williams' 2019 annual report, it said "at the balance sheet date an amount of $1m was owed by Rokit and carried within trade debtors relating to the 2019 season. There is an additional £9m within both trade debtors and deferred income at 31 December 2019 relating to Rokit sponsorship of the 2020 season."[181]

Williams staggered into the 2020 race season, saved only by the influx of cash that came with driver Nicholas Latifi and the team's eventual sale to investment company Dorilton Capital. The legendary team didn't disappear from the grid that year—although many thought it easily could—but the Williams family did. They had been with the team since Frank Williams cofounded it in 1977, but Williams F1's then-deputy team principal Claire Williams said the family decided to step away after 43 years to "allow Dorilton a fresh start as the new owners."[182]

Dorilton decided to keep the Williams name upon buying the team, but Claire Williams still said of the changeover: "It feels like grieving for us."[183] (Before Claire Williams stepped down from her role following the 2020 Italian Grand Prix—the same race after which Haas announced the end of its partnership with Rich Energy a year earlier—Storey tweeted that her departure would bring "an end to a catastrophic tenure." He added: "The woman couldn't run a bath," let alone a race team.[184])

No two sponsors were alike, which meant no two questionable sponsors followed the same path to ultimate destruction. But if there was one thing Formula One had beyond all other racing series, it was the shiny veneer of luxury and legitimacy. It was very easy for the series to sweep problems under the rug and cover up scandal, focusing instead on the brightest points of its history.

Yes, there had been quite a few notorious scandals leading up to Rich Energy's time in the series. Crashgate. Spygate. Max Mosley's sex life. Bernie Ecclestone's entire existence. And, of course, Formula One fans were all familiar with the accusations of Ferrari favoritism at the

FIA—sometimes derisively called the "Ferrari International Assistance" in place of its proper name, the Fédération Internationale de l'Automobile.[185]

The relationship between Ferrari, the FIA, and Formula One had been in question for years by the time the 2019 season rolled around, and rightfully so. In addition to its longtime ability to veto series rules that weren't in its interest,[186] Ferrari received a $100 million bonus each year simply for participating[187]—a sum dependent, in part, on how long the team had competed in the sport.[188] Controversy continued in early 2020 when Ferrari and the FIA reached a confidential settlement after the FIA's investigation of a potentially illegal Ferrari power unit from 2019.[189] Seven other Formula One teams issued a statement that requested information about the settlement, noting that "an international sporting regulator has the responsibility to act with the highest standards of governance, integrity and transparency." The *BBC* reported at the time that the only two Formula One teams aside from Ferrari that didn't sign the statement were Haas and Alfa Romeo, which both used Ferrari engines. In response to the teams' statement, the FIA later explained the settlement.[190]

"The extensive and thorough investigations undertaken during the 2019 season raised suspicions that the Scuderia Ferrari [power unit] could be considered as not operating within the limits of the FIA regulations at all times," an FIA statement read. "Scuderia Ferrari firmly opposed the suspicions and reiterated that its [power unit] always operated in compliance with the regulations.

"The FIA was not fully satisfied, but decided that further action would not necessarily result in a conclusive case due to the complexity of the matter and the material impossibility to provide the unequivocal evidence of a breach."[191]

And yet all of those teams, and all of their fans, could have seen the entire saga coming. Former Formula One CEO Bernie Ecclestone said in 2017 that Ferrari favoritism was an undisputed fact, noting that "helping Ferrari" was "always the smartest thing to do" because "F1 is Ferrari, and Ferrari is F1."[192]

But in a certain light, these scandals and questionable relationships are stories of Formula One's triumph—often portrayed as a "one and done" sort of deal, where a problem arises and is either taken care of before it reaches the media or is caught and mostly buried before the end of a season. In both Crashgate and Spygate, the FIA was able to step in and put an end to the issues before they grew truly insidious. Formula One was able to sweep those headaches under the rug once they were taken care of, relegating them to the margins of history. It did the same with its more questionable sponsors; casual racing fans likely wouldn't have known about Leyton

House or T-Minus unless they lived during their eras or discovered them through research.

The same often went for Formula One and its personalities' more serious transgressions. While viewers could generally recite Formula One's driver hierarchy at any given time, knowing how many of its historical stars appeared to grace the Little Black Book was far less common. While many knew the COVID-19 pandemic canceled Formula One's iconic Monaco Grand Prix in 2020 for the first time since 1954, far fewer knew about—or, rather, paid much attention to—the series' complacency in sportswashing schemes by countries known for human-rights violations.[193]

Those more insidious scandals were the ones Formula One didn't want people to know about, and members of the motorsport press often stayed away from such topics in order to preserve their access to events. (The key to access in sports, often, is not making any stakeholders mad.) After all, readers and viewers of sports often want to read about and view *sports*—their idols, their hobbies, their *break from politics or the outside world*—without admitting that sports are entwined with the outside world and its politics. Sticking to sports isn't possible because sports don't exist in a vacuum.

But pretending like they did was a favor to Formula One, as it was far easier to control a narrative about illegal engines or faulty sponsors than one that focused on the systemic dehumanization of entire peoples. So, Formula One remained with its shiny veneer of extravagance well intact. It was a sport of privilege—one where the tendrils of corruption might have lingered just beneath the surface but were consistently ignored.

It was easy to see, then, how unsavory people and brands could be attracted to the legitimacy Formula One could lend them.

4

A FORMULA FOR DISASTER

Heading into its 2019 season with Rich Energy, Haas F1 was running on a high. The team had just completed its best season since entering the series in 2016, finishing fifth of 10 in the constructor standings. It was a big deal, both for Haas and for American representation on the world's biggest open-wheel stage.

That's because as soon as Haas expanded from its big-name Stewart-Haas Racing NASCAR operation into Formula One, it became something the series had lacked for three decades.[1] It became America's F1 team.

Peter Habicht, a writer and event promoter who grew up in New York State and specialized in Formula One's American footprint, attended Haas F1's first race as a team: the March 2016 season opener in Melbourne held on a temporary circuit around the local Albert Park Lake. It was autumn in Australia, spring in America, and the atmosphere was triumphant in the Haas garage.

"It was a culmination of a lot of hopes, dreams, and expectations," Habicht told the authors, with a shrug and a proud sigh. "And possibility.

"Formula One is not an easy undertaking. I think there's a natural underdog story that comes out of that, and I, like most Americans, love an underdog story."[2]

Haas had mixed results at its debut weekend in Australia, with one car wrecking out early in the race and the other finishing sixth—an accomplishment that, in Formula One, few teams took for granted.[3] For Habicht, Haas' first race was "something not to miss."[4]

"So much of Formula One technology today can trace its roots back to either aircraft or racing or automotive development or defense technology that's come out of the United States," Habicht said. "For me, it was a very important event to see America return to the grid for the first time in 30 years."[5]

Habicht said Haas F1 was so new at the Australian Grand Prix, a few fans had designed their own team shirts and were showing them off to the team:

plain white T-shirts decorated in black marker, with one featuring a hand-drawn Haas F1 logo where the breast pocket would have been and "#NiceHaas" scrawled across the back.

"They're a world away, they're not in America, they've designed their own Haas F1 T-shirts and were showing everybody," Habicht said. "The love was there from day one."[6]

But Haas' debut wasn't just about love, pride, patriotism, or proving a point. It was about getting to work to build a future for the organization.

"They were not wasting any moves," Habicht said. "They were there, they knew what the job was, they knew what they had to do, and they fit in as any team would have been required to do.

"They looked, communicated, operated, and ran as a Formula One team, without a doubt. No one can take that away from them. It was an incredible debut. It could have been an opportunity for people to sort of look for weaknesses in the armor or fragility in the organization, and there was none of that."[7]

Still, as Habicht sat in the media center that weekend, he thought about how strangely impressive it was to see team owner Gene Haas—a NASCAR guy—"drop[ped] in the middle" of a panel of Formula One team bosses during a press conference. He posed a simple question to Haas' new peers: "Do you have any words of advice for Gene?"

"I think it's fantastic to have Haas join Formula One as an independent team—as a really credible independent team," Red Bull Racing team principal Christian Horner said in response. "Formula One's a big challenge. It's great to have an American, and a true American presence in Formula One. Words of advice: Get a good lawyer."[8] Haas would have to take that advice to heart once Rich Energy arrived.

*   *   *

Formula One had always been short on Americans, even if it gained the U.S.–based Haas team in 2016. When Haas joined Formula One, the most recent win by an American was Mario Andretti in 1978.[9] The only two Americans to compete in the series after the turn of the century were Scott Speed, who ran for Red Bull Racing junior team Toro Rosso in 2006 and 2007,[10] and Alexander Rossi, who ran five races for the Manor Marussia team in 2015.[11] Before them, the most recent American in the series was Mario Andretti's son, Michael Andretti, in 1993.[12]

But neither Speed nor Rossi had much luck making it in Formula One. Midway through the 2007 season, Toro Rosso replaced Speed with German driver Sebastian Vettel.[13] Speed hadn't scored a single point across his two seasons in the series, while Vettel went on to win four championships in a row with the big-kid Red Bull Racing team in 2010, 2011, 2012, and 2013.[14] With the 2010 title, Vettel became the youngest-ever world champion at 23 years old.[15] Then, he became the youngest double world champion. Then, the youngest triple champion, and finally, the youngest quadruple champion.

Vettel's streak ended after 2013, roughly coinciding with two major shake-ups in the realm of Formula One: The series entering a new generation of race car for the 2014 season, when it traded a V8 power unit for a turbocharged V6 hybrid and ushered in an era of dominance by the Mercedes-AMG Formula One team,[16] and Vettel moving to the famous Ferrari team for 2015. Speed, meanwhile, never returned to Formula One.[17]

Rossi's five starts during the 2015 Formula One season were more like a tryout for the Manor Marussia team, in which he replaced Roberto Merhi for a few races in order to help the team decide what its driver lineup would be the next year. Marussia team principal John Booth said at the time of Rossi's short run that "no decision" had been made about the team's driver lineup for 2016, and that Marussia would "continue to evaluate [its] options during the remainder of the season."[18]

Rossi wasn't chosen for 2016 and went to American open-wheel series IndyCar instead.[19]

Haas, even, wasn't as American as it seemed. While the team arrived in 2016 with an American base and headquarters alongside its NASCAR team in Kannapolis, North Carolina, those roots didn't extend to the people behind the wheel. Haas' driver lineup had been void of Americans from the start, and that caused plenty of controversy among open-wheel drivers in the U.S. early on in the team's existence.

As the *Motorsport Network* wrote in 2018, former F1 driver and four-time Champ Car title winner Sébastien Bourdais was not pleased:

"Clearly, there is just no consideration," Bourdais told the IndyCar website. "They [F1] are in their little bubble on their own island.

"Either you play their game and are rated on their game or you are just not rated at all.

"I completely understand that the American drivers take it personal because it's not fair, but since when is F1 fair? It's never been fair."[20]

Haas' debut lineup consisted of Mexico native Esteban Gutiérrez and Romain Grosjean, who was from Switzerland.[21] Haas replaced Gutiérrez with Danish driver Kevin Magnussen for 2017, keeping the Magnussen-Grosjean lineup through Rich Energy's season in 2019.[22]

Those unfamiliar with Formula One, though, might not understand the hype behind Haas' triumphant fifth-place championship finish in 2018. Is fifth of 10, after all, anything to be proud of?

In 2010s-era Formula One, it was. In the years before and during Rich Energy's involvement, Formula One was a sport of two tiers: the best—Mercedes, Ferrari, and Red Bull—and all of the rest. Haas was one of the rest, and far from the top of that list. When Haas entered the series in 2016, it finished eighth of 11 teams in the points standings. The grid then moved to 10 teams, with Haas finishing eighth in 2017, a bright spot of fifth in 2018, and a miserable ninth with the Rich Energy badging in 2019. Formula One only gave championship points to drivers who finished in the top 10 in each race, and in 2019, Haas scored a mere 28 points to the title-winning Mercedes team's 739. The team that finished last in the constructor standings, Williams, only scored one point across 21 races.

But longtime F1 fan Bex Foot was impressed by the team's debut. She'd counted Romain Grosjean among her favorite drivers since 2012, and she'd seen some of the highest and lowest points of his career. She thought the Haas era could be a good one.

"I remember those first couple of races," Foot said in an interview with the authors. "[Grosjean] was finishing really high, like fourth or fifth or something like that, in those first two races. I was like, 'Yeah, this is going to be great. He's made the right choice.' But then it all went downhill."[23]

*   *   *

With a new sponsor and a new black-and-gold look, Haas was ready to top the standings among "the rest" once again. But little did the team know that the February debut of its 2019 Rich Energy livery would arguably be its highest point of the year.[24]

That debut took place in an ornate, atrium-style room with ivory bricks and columns at the London clubhouse for the Royal Automobile Club, which had been around for more than 100 years.[25] The room was antique-chic, a symbol of old money. Its intricate blue-and-gold carpet shone under warm lighting from gold, candle-style wall sconces and a matching lantern-shaped chandelier—the kind of design features that retain their glitz even as time marches on, because envy is a beast and markers of wealth never truly go out of style. Haas' race car sat under a black Rich Energy-branded sheet as onlookers lined the show floor and a second level above it for the reveal, Storey beaming proudly alongside the race team that would soon wear his company's colors.[26]

"When we saw the livery, bloody hell, that was the best looking car, I can tell you that," one former Haas employee told the authors. "The car was amazing."[27]

Many people agreed. Netflix documentary series *Drive to Survive* caught a conversation during the 2019 car launch where Storey told Steiner:

"It's a good-looking car. If it goes as good as it looks, then we should be all right."[28]

"Yeah, we should be all right," Steiner responded. "But it doesn't always work like this."[29]

Another former Haas employee, though, told the authors the car launch was "really out of character"—both for Formula One's digital era and for team owner Gene Haas.[30]

"Back in the day in the '90s, F1 launches were a big deal," they said. "You'd have fireworks and the Spice Girls and all that kind of stuff. In this era, [teams] do an online thing. You roll out in the pit lane [at preseason testing] in Barcelona, and you've already done your digital launch.

"One thing we didn't do was big, emotional pomp and circumstance. That wasn't Gene at all."[31]

Yet there the car was in Rich Energy's home base of London, crowds gathered around as its fresh gold logos glistened in the room's warm glow.

"This is the time of the season when you hope you've got designs right and you can be competitive straight away," Gene Haas said of the February debut. "The new car looks distinctive, not only in terms of its color scheme, but also with the new regulations in play. Hopefully those design changes brought in for 2019 will improve the racing on track, and more importantly, give us a shot at making more of an impact at each Grand Prix."[32]

Steiner added that the goal was to keep improving, and that the Rich Energy deal was "another positive example of moving forward as an organization."

"We're pleased to see their colors on the [car]," Steiner said during the debut. "We welcome them as they join our valued partner group in utilizing Formula One as a global marketing platform. While 2018 delivered our best season to date, the year showed, sometimes sharply, that we still have areas to improve on as a team."[33]

Storey additionally told the Haas PR team that he was "naturally delighted to finally see the Rich Energy colors and stag logo in Formula One with Haas F1 Team" and that the partnership had "already significantly raised the profile" of the brand.[34]

But right away, Storey and the Haas team weren't quite on the same message. As British sports network *Sky Sports* described it, Storey was prepared to beat Red Bull right out of the gate while Steiner was more subdued:

> [S]teiner added: "You have to try hard. If you have no targets, you never achieve anything.
>
> "It's an ambition. In racing they are very good, but you never know. Last year we had the fourth-fastest car and finished fifth, but the next one up was Red Bull.
>
> "We can try. If you don't try, you don't achieve it."[35]

Despite the fancy, out-of-character launch treatment, one former Haas employee told the authors Storey "just turned up in his velvet suit and started goading Red Bull."

"I think that continued that worrisome time from October," they said. "We were all going, 'Really?'"[36]

Foot felt similarly about the lavish display. "I was a big fan of the black-and-gold color scheme because I've been there before," she said, referring to the fact that Grosjean drove for the iconic black-and-gold Lotus team from 2012 to 2015. Foot's old Lotus merchandise would look current again—but she wasn't sure if Rich Energy would be worth the convenience.

"I was just a bit cautious because no one knew who they were, and [it] all seemed dodgy as fuck," she said.[37]

For Haas, the problems didn't take long to start in. Formula One was a sport of hardware in the 2010s—those with the best cars often won, hence the starkly two-tiered competition and the dominance of certain race teams depending on the regulations of the era. Teams debuted their cars for the upcoming season before the opening race, revealing performance upgrades and appearance changes in hopes of inching closer to the cars that had outshone them the year before.

Ferrari, for example, debuted its 2019 car with matte paint, which was a change from the gloss look it ran in prior years. But the change wasn't for looks; it was for performance, Ferrari said, because a matte livery provided weight savings over a shiny one.[38]

Haas' 2019 car, the VF19, was a disaster, and that disaster started early. Formula One introduced new, simplified aerodynamic regulations for the 2019 season, aimed to produce closer racing and more passing—something the series desperately lacked at the time, since cars had entire zip codes between each other on track as they zipped around in a Mercedes-led conga line.

The regulations involved a wider, more simplified front wing for all teams, as well as other changes to allow drivers to get closer to the car in front of them. Front brake ducts were simplified to lessen teams' ability to manipulate aerodynamics, and alterations further back on the car—like a heightened rear wing—were meant to achieve the series' goal of bringing its conga line closer together.[39]

The regulation changes weren't kind to Haas, nor to the VF19. The car was volatile. It would sometimes be fast in qualifying and almost always be slow in the race, and Haas would regularly show up to the track with new upgrades meant to alleviate some of the team's problems. Often, those upgrades made the car worse than it was before, leading the team to run a mishmash of different car setups on different race weekends.

"In some senses, coming fifth in the championship that year was the worst thing that could have happened to us," one former Haas employee told the authors. "There were a few of us who were going, 'This isn't good, because next year, [some people are] going to want fourth, and we don't have the resources and the people to do it.' I think that's only natural, though. As a competitive sports team, whether it's soccer or Formula One or whatever it is, everyone wants to succeed. That's why we're there."[40]

The pressure to improve, they said, led to a divide among some employees: the ones who were just happy to have done well and the ones who pushed "for more new parts, more development, more aero, more people."[41]

The team had neither the budget nor the personnel to do that, the employee said.[42] A 2018 budget analysis by *RaceFans* calculated that compared to Mercedes and Ferrari's roughly 1,000 employees each, Haas had about 250—paltry even among teams alongside it in the mid-pack, like Renault's 625, Williams' 630, Toro Rosso's 460, Force India's 405, and Alfa Romeo's 400.[43] Former employees told the authors Haas' lean staff made the Rich Energy days, and the team's performance downfall, even harder to handle in 2019.

"I think there's quite a big misconception and misunderstanding about just how small it was," one former employee said. "Not a lot of people know, because there's this massive facility in Kannapolis, there's a facility in Banbury, and a facility in Italy. It was quite a good job by whoever— the marketing team, Gene, whoever—the smoke and mirrors thing.

"This is why we all took it so personally and took it to heart, because all the stuff we're reading, going, 'Why aren't they performing more?' Well, we can't. There are 20 of us."[44]

But things seemed good at first. Haas was fast in preseason testing at the 2.9-mile Circuit de Barcelona-Catalunya in Spain, with Romain Grosjean logging the third-fastest lap of anyone on the opening day and Kevin Magnussen doing the same on the next.[45]

"I don't recall through that preseason testing looking at Haas and being particularly like, 'Ooh, they're in big trouble,'" journalist Luke Smith told the authors. "I think the expectations going into that year would always be that, 'OK, well they're going to be fifth probably again, at best. They're not going to be taking the step up to be frontrunners or anything.'"[46]

Rich Energy even tweeted its excitement about topping Red Bull on the speed board.[47]

But that didn't tell the whole tale of Haas' trip to Spain. Instead, Formula One's own staff writers categorized the Haas team as one of the losers in Barcelona testing. That's because technical issues took the team off of the track for much of testing, with Haas logging only 384 laps—more than 200 laps short of the Mercedes team's tally. The VF19 spent much of its time either stopped on track or on the back of a truck, meaning the fast laps Haas did log weren't as positive a development as they should have been.[48]

Haas cars were the reason for four red flags over the three days of preseason testing in Barcelona that February, with three occurring in one day.[49] (Flags in racing are just like streetlights, with green meaning "go," yellow meaning "take caution," and red meaning "stop." When a car or group of cars causes a red flag, they've temporarily put the entire track out of commission.)

On the first day of testing, Grosjean had a fuel-pressure issue. When the third day came around, there were multiple incidents: Test diver Pietro Fittipaldi, who was on track due to a seating issue in Magnussen's car, had an ignition problem. Then, Grosjean had an ignition problem. Then, Grosjean had electronic issues that "influenced the working of the engine," team principal Guenther Steiner said at the time.[50]

"The engine couldn't run safely anymore, so we had to stop it," Steiner said, thankful that the breakage wasn't something major like the engine itself. "We just need to find what causes [the problems], and then we'll get to grips with it. But we are still good in time, in my opinion, to find it, so that's why I'm not too desperate about it."[51]

Steiner added that Haas' testing problems were "annoying more than frustrating," because the team knew the car was "OK," it had "good potential," and the drivers liked it. "We just need now to sort out these little gremlins," Steiner said.[52]

Those little gremlins wouldn't be the worst the Haas team faced. At the second race of the season in Bahrain, the team made it to the fastest round of qualifying before showing up on Sunday without the ability to produce any results in the race. While Grosjean was out of the Bahrain Grand Prix early due to contact, Magnussen finished 13th in a gradual, race-long downward slide.[53]

"We just don't know what happened," Steiner said during media availability that weekend. "We have no idea what happened. I'm not even upset because I'm just amazed, more amazed than upset. After having the qualifying we had and then ending up with the race and not knowing why the pace was just lost overnight, it's so weird to have no idea."[54]

Steiner blamed the Bahrain performance woes on top speed and tire performance—something that would haunt the team over and over again in 2019. Steiner said at the time that Haas "couldn't get the tire to work for more than one lap."[55]

Before the next race in China on April 14, Haas felt as if it had the pace to run with Rich Energy's longtime, one-sided arch rival Red Bull during qualifying.[56] Qualifying had been Haas' strong suit early on, with it being the only team aside from Mercedes and Ferrari to qualify both of its cars in the top 10 for all three races so far that season. Mercedes and Ferrari, of course, would go on to finish first and second in the championship—Mercedes with a large gap on Ferrari, and Ferrari with a large gap on everyone else.[57]

But tires struck again at Shanghai International Circuit, with both Grosjean and Magnussen immediately dropping back.[58] They finished 11th and 13th out of 20 cars, respectively.[59]

"The problem is getting the tires in the heat range so that the tires work," Steiner said that weekend. "It's high-speed tracks with long straights and low-energy corners where we can't get the heat into the tires."[60]

Steiner thought Haas had an understanding of the issue, but Grosjean wasn't as optimistic. "The car's amazing over one lap, but as soon as we go two laps on the tires, we're not there anymore," he said at the time. "We need to understand exactly what happened."[61]

Haas brought a major upgrade to the fifth race of the season in Spain on May 12, with the goal of landing its cars in the top 10.[62] That's exactly what it did: Magnussen finished seventh and Grosjean finished 10th.[63]

The high didn't last long. After more issues in the seventh race of the season in Canada on June 9, Steiner told the press that there "must be an end" to how badly the team was performing.

"What can you do?" Steiner said. "There's a point where you cannot get more annoyed. I wouldn't say I'm depressed, but there must be an end. There must be an upward trend somewhere, because it cannot get worse. I hope this point comes soon."[64] This is when the narrator would say that it didn't.

In the eighth race of the season in France later that month, Grosjean retired early and Magnussen finished 17th.[65] Both hung around the back of the field most of the day, and Steiner called the French Grand Prix the "worst weekend" by the Haas team in its four-year history.[66]

"In the race we still struggled," Steiner told the press at the time. "I don't know why. Don't ask me what it is. I don't know, so don't even ask me, please, because I couldn't answer it. We need to find out. It's very disappointing, to be honest. Ending up in this situation, but not having an understanding of it, is the worst of all."[67]

Team owner Gene Haas was similarly unimpressed with the car. Netflix's *Drive to Survive* filmed the team during the ninth and 10th rounds of 2019 in Austria and Britain, dedicating the second episode of the show's second season—aptly named "Boiling Point"—to Haas. In it, Netflix captured a conversation between Gene Haas and Steiner. "It seems like our biggest problem is keeping the cars with their initial speed, because it seems like it falls off way too fast," Haas said. "The drivers just kind of wave to everybody as they go by."[68]

"You have to rely too much on the data," Steiner responded.

"Well, you know, we have a lot of data, but we still run like dog shit," Haas said. "It can't get any slower than what we're going."

"We just need to figure out a few things—not to make mistakes—and we're good," Steiner replied.

Haas then leaned forward across the table toward Steiner. "I hope you get it fixed," he said.[69]

During the ninth-round Austrian Grand Prix, Grosjean finished 16th and Magnussen 19th. On his radio to the team, Magnussen said: "Fucking hell, I cannot do this."[70]

Drive to Survive caught Steiner in a similar mood, saying: "The car was a fucking rocket before. There's something fucking gone badly wrong."

"It was painful," Grosjean told Steiner after the race.

"I wasn't even watching anymore," he responded. "I couldn't give a fuck."[71]

Midway through the race season, Haas started running two setups.[72] For the 10th-round British Grand Prix, Grosjean went back to the car the team was running at the season opener while Magnussen continued to get aerodynamic upgrades.[73] Formula One's staff writers described it perfectly at the time: Haas was trying to "search for answers as to why their upgrades [were]n't working."[74]

Neither Magnussen nor Grosjean finished the British Grand Prix. The two hit each other on the first lap of the race, resulting in punctured tires and early pit stops for replacements. They both went back out on track, but Magnussen only made it six laps and Grosjean only made it nine before they were called into the pits to retire from the race.[75]

Setting up the explosive final scenes of Haas' *Drive to Survive* episode, Steiner gave the orders to retire over the radio, saying: "End this fucking pain." Steiner then brought Magnussen and Grosjean, still feuding from their contact on track, in for a closed-door conversation.

"I've fucking had enough of both of you," Steiner said, as captured by *Drive to Survive*. "You let the fucking team down, me down—which, I protected you all the time—and I'm not fucking going into who is right and who is wrong. I don't want to hear, 'He moved, he shouldn't have moved,' and all that fucking wank, you know. Gene spends a hundred fucking million a year of his own fucking money, which [*inaudible*] wants to pull the plug and let everybody down because you are two fucking idiots? I've not more to fucking say to you guys, and if you don't like it, I don't need you here. Do not come back, please."[76]

Steiner, still angry, said later on in the show: "We've got two fucking idiots driving for us. This is not acceptable. We will make changes. If it would be my decision now, I would sack them both."[77] He didn't.

By July 26, two days before the German Grand Prix, things weren't looking good. Haas hadn't finished in the top 10, thus hadn't scored any championship points, in four races, and the German Grand Prix upgrades didn't appear to be the hope the team needed. Grosjean, still running the spec from the opening race of the season, had a blistering second practice session before the German round, finishing sixth overall—just seventenths of a second slower than the lead car, Ferrari's Sebastian Vettel.

With the updates, Magnussen finished that same session in 18th, nearly 1.3 seconds off of his own teammate. In Formula One, 1.3 seconds was the equivalent of about 1.3 years.[78]

Magnussen ran another updated spec for the first practice session and still finished behind Grosjean by nearly seven-tenths of a second. He told the press at the time that he would "love" to revert to the season-opener spec Grosjean was running, and that the team should look at going back to square one with both cars to "make the best of this season and try and get as many points" as possible.[79]

When asked what he was hoping for that weekend, Magnussen provided a list of things that could scrap the race entirely. "Rain," he said. "Tornadoes, earthquakes, hailstones. Any stuff like that."[80]

Luckily for Haas, Grosjean finished the German Grand Prix in seventh and Magnussen in eighth.[81]

In the 12th round of the season on August 4, the Hungarian Grand Prix, neither driver scored points. Grosjean retired early due to water-pressure issues, while tire problems continued to plague the team. Magnussen at least finished the race, although out of the points in 13th place.[82]

Haas still didn't know what the deal with the tires was, and Steiner said the team would try to figure it out in the few weeks between Hungary and the next race in Belgium.[83] Haas had scored 26 championship points by then, and the team would only add two more across the remaining nine races.[84]

The problems had gotten so bad by then that despite clashes between Grosjean and Magnussen on track throughout the year, Steiner said the team was unlikely to bring on any younger drivers for the 2020 season. Fixing the car was the focus for the Haas team, not nurturing rookie talent—even if the conflict between the team's current drivers were a sideshow to the rest of its issues that year.[85]

Again shuffling to make anything work, Haas decided both of its drivers would run a newly updated aero spec when the season returned from its month-long break for the Belgian Grand Prix at Circuit de Spa-Francorchamps.[86] Since the 2020 regulations would be similar to the ones that season, Haas decided to focus not necessarily on salvaging 2019, but on trying to figure out its car for the next year. Running the updated spec would hopefully help.

The race came several days after the announcement that both cars would be on the updated spec. Not much changed, with Magnussen finishing 12th and Grosjean 13th. Steiner told the press at the time that the race was "nothing encouraging," and Grosjean said he was "very, very upset at the minute. Not against anyone, just the situation."[87]

Round 14 in Italy came a week later and was more of the same. Grosjean finished 16th, which was second to last among the drivers who actually finished the race. Magnussen didn't finish the race at all, retiring early with hydraulic problems.

Steiner said at the time that the car "was just difficult to drive."

"We were slow," Steiner told the press. "It's a disappointing weekend for the whole team. We just need to regroup and keep on going until we find a solution to our lack of performance."[88]

Adding to Haas' 2019 woes at the 16th-round Russian Grand Prix on September 29, Steiner left the track $7,500 poorer after calling a race official a "stupid idiotic steward" who "does not get any more intelligent."[89]

For once, at least, something other than the car was the focus for Haas after a race.

The 18th-round Mexican Grand Prix on October 27 was the sixth time in seven grands prix in which neither Haas driver scored a championship point. Steiner told the press at the time that "the best news" coming out of Mexico was that there were only three more races left in the season. "I'm not disappointed, because my hopes were always very low," he said.[90]

Looking back, journalist Luke Smith told the authors the team "just seemed to lose their way a little bit on the car-development front."

"The car form was so, so peaky and would go up and down so, so much," Smith said. "They did seem to come down to Earth, I think, even without all the Rich Energy shenanigans off-track."[91]

Haas' home race, the U.S. Grand Prix, came the next weekend on November 3. It extended the team's scoreless streak, with Grosjean finishing 15th in the race and Magnussen retiring early from 16th. Tire-overheating issues sent Magnussen tumbling down the running order, and a brake problem made him drive straight through the track's 12th turn on lap 52 of 56, coming to a halt in the runoff gravel. Just like his brakes, Magnussen's race came to an end there.[92]

Magnussen called the race a "tough day at the office," and when the press mentioned there were only two races left in the season, Steiner responded: "Thank God! I would be happy with one to go." He added that the team had "nothing" and every strategy Haas attempted was wrong because the team still fell back.

"It's like having a football team with 11 defenders and nobody in attack, and everybody attacks you, and you cannot do anything," Steiner said. "We just try to do damage limitation, and if everybody else does a good job, then that doesn't work because we cannot do anything."[93]

In an interview two years after the Rich Energy season, a former Haas employee described feeling similarly. "It was like, 'Just end it now. Please,'" they said.[94]

In the 21st and final race weekend of the season, the Abu Dhabi Grand Prix, Magnussen qualified 15th and Grosjean 16th. They each started one spot higher due to penalties for Mercedes driver Valtteri Bottas, which forced him to start in the last grid position after qualifying second to teammate and 2019 champion Lewis Hamilton. Fourteenth and 15th is exactly where they finished, respectively.[95]

When asked by the press after qualifying if he was glad that the season was almost over, Grosjean said he was "kind of happy, to be fair."

"I've been positive all year," he said. "Let's just say we're looking forward to getting rid of that [car], and it won't go into a museum."[96]

Haas' team total of 28 points in 2019 was its lowest since it entered Formula One in 2016, and ninth was its worst finishing position in the constructor championship.[97] Things would unfortunately get worse for Haas in 2020 and 2021.

Haas wasn't alone in its struggles. Once 2020 rolled around, the Ferrari team's performance was similarly dismal. Ferrari wound up sixth in the constructor standings that year—uncharacteristically bad for a long-time powerhouse accustomed to finishing in the top three.[98] Mid-pack teams Ferrari would have scoffed at in years prior finished ahead of it in the final points tally.

But "even Ferrari, to a certain extent, was just able to get on with it," Stuart Taylor of the Chain Bear YouTube channel told the authors.

"It's embarrassing, but you get on with it," he said. "But with Haas, they were having a bad year, but also, this guy was making this into a thing. He wouldn't shut up about it. There was this sub-story of: Who the hell is this sponsor? What's going on? What have Haas done? Are they a clown show?"[99]

There were also budget concerns, caused by both the loss of Rich Energy as a title sponsor and by the team chipping away at its own prize money due to poor performance. Those concerns were exacerbated by Haas' consistent car issues. In running so many different—and unsuccessful—car specs, often in the same race weekend, Steiner told *Autosport* near the end of 2019 that Haas had run up its development bill.

"It's very expensive, and if you don't gain anything, it's wasted,"

Steiner said. "But at least we know the problem. That's the starting point of any improvement. It's knowing what not to do, what caused the lack of performance."[100]

With the Abu Dhabi Grand Prix finale not offering a positive end to the year, the highest race finish recorded by Haas in 2019 was eighth.[101] There was still hope that the in-season development work would help the team in 2020, but it certainly didn't pay off in 2019.

"Hopefully, next year is a much better story," Grosjean said after the race. As if reading from the same script, Magnussen said that "hopefully" 2020 would be "a much better year. I think we're all happy to get out of this year and completely shift our focus to 2020."[102]

Steiner added that the season "ended as we expected."

"We got the most out of the car today," he said. "We're glad the season is over, and now we can focus on next year. We got a little bit bruised this year, but we're not broken. We will come back. The aim is to forget 2019 and start next season as we left off 2018."[103]

For all of Steiner's F-bombs during Haas' 2019 *Drive to Survive* episode, he struck a somber tone at the end. Haas F1 might have been his job, but it was also a major part of his life.

"The Haas F1 team means a lot to me," Steiner said with a shake in his voice. "I think if it is a failure, I would have no idea what to do next."[104]

Gene Haas, with a loud sigh, added: "I think we have a good team. Everybody shows up, but then, when we can't get the cars to perform, the question is: What the heck happened? What's going on here? What are we doing this for? We're here to race competitors—drivers and race strategies—and we don't do any of that. So where do we go in the future? It's a very, very expensive sport. If we're doomed to run in the back, I don't think I'm going to be part of that."[105]

*   *   *

While the Haas F1 Team bore Gene Haas' name alone, team principal Guenther Steiner had a lot to do with its creation. Steiner told the *Motorsport Network* in a retrospective 2021 story that he was tossing around an idea for a Formula One team when he found someone connected to Gene Haas, who co-owned the Stewart-Haas Racing NASCAR team at the time.

"We met and started talking about it, first distantly and then in detail," Steiner told the *Motorsport Network*. "The negotiations lasted a year, and eventually Gene was convinced to join, so he asked me to get him an entry. It's always difficult at the beginning, but once you find someone to finance the project, then it's just a matter of working on it to make it happen, doing it well, and using the knowledge you have."[106]

Netflix's *Drive to Survive* portrayed Steiner as a crudely honest leader, and his infamous on-camera quotes included everything from "Why did we develop a car that fucking goes slower?" and "Now we are a fucking bunch of wankers, a bunch of fucking clowns" to "Obviously, it was a little bit of a clown show today again" and "If I have to remind you to do your job every day, you're in the wrong fucking place. This is not a fucking kindergarten here."[107]

But in conversations with the authors, multiple former Haas employees described Steiner as the right team principal for the job. In a sport centered on sneaky politics and sly jabs, a direct boss worked for them.

"He is the best team boss I've ever worked with, and I've worked with a lot," one former employee said. "With Guenther, there's no question. You always know what's going on. He's not hiding, he's always telling you the truth. If I was fucking up something, if I fucked up, he came to me: 'What the fuck are you doing? Pull yourself together.'

"People in this kind of industry or environment, we love this, because if I make a mistake, I know that. I made a mistake, and I don't need someone trying to explain why I made a mistake in a language that I don't understand. I need someone to come here and tell me, 'You made a mistake.' But on the other hand, if you did well, he was always there tapping your shoulder like, 'Mate, that's it. Good work.'

"I think if Guenther had the resources, he could make a winning team easily."[108]

Another former employee said they figured Steiner was at least a little embarrassed about the Rich Energy deal, but that as a leader, he knew when to step in and when to let team members deal with hiccups on their own—even when they asked for help.

"Steiner is a great guy," they said. "He didn't micromanage, but he oversaw everything. He didn't have to come and talk to all the different employees and departments, but he did, because he wanted to know what was going on. Some stuff, he'd just bat away: 'Just go fucking fix it.' That's how he was. Other stuff, he would say, 'OK mate, let's have a chat. What do we need to do to sort this out?'"[109]

That dedication—and the straight-to-the-point behavior—didn't translate so easily to those on the outside, though. As Chain Bear's Stuart Taylor said of the team: "I've never understood Haas, I guess, as a character."

"You know who Williams are," Taylor said. "You know who McLaren are. Even teams like AlphaTauri and Alfa Romeo, you understand their ambition. Their goal isn't necessarily to win world titles and win races regularly. They'll try to be as good as they are, but they're a feeder team.

"But I just don't get Haas. I don't know what Haas are. I don't know what their goals are. I have no sense of who they are. There's nothing to them. They're this empty space.

"Some people associate [Haas] with Guenther Steiner, who is a character in his own way. But I don't.

"I'm glad they're there. I want them to do well. I don't want them to collapse, for the sake of Formula One and for the sake of the fact that there are hundreds of people tied to the team. But I have no feeling about them."[110]

The authors contacted more than 40 people employed by Haas during the 2019 season to discuss their time at the team—before, during, and after Rich Energy, if applicable—and offered anonymity to all. Only five agreed to talk. But when presented with the same set of questions in individual conversations, their answers were often similar.

All five employees spoke on the condition of anonymity in mid–2021, two years after the Rich Energy sponsorship ended. Their employment with Haas was verified by the authors.

The former Haas employees who spoke with the authors said they learned about the team's 2019 title sponsor, Rich Energy, right before the official announcement in late 2018. That was a common practice in Formula One to prevent leaks to journalists or other people, they said. What was less common was the sponsor itself.

"October, when it was announced, we had a feeling something was going on," one former employee told the authors, adding that they found out about the team's new title sponsor about an hour before the official announcement. "[The team] was small enough that you could pick up on certain stuff. It was almost, there was an air of excitement. The email came out, and then came the press release. Then there was this kind of lull. You could see people Googling."[111]

The atmosphere quickly went from "Who are these people?" to "Oh," the employee said. Their forehead wrinkled and their brows furrowed as they spoke, showing raw concern even years later. "Obviously, the first thing that comes up is a failed Force India purchase," they said.[112]

Another former employee said they weren't immediately concerned because on the surface, an energy drink in motorsports "was quite straightforward." It was true; at the time, all kinds of energy drinks had major presences in motorsport—in addition to Red Bull's longtime Formula One team, for example, Monster Energy was the title sponsor of NASCAR's top-level Cup Series.

"We did Google it," they said. "We had the idea that it must be a new energy-drink manufacturer, which it was. We were expecting something—all right, he's the manufacturer of the drink, he's going to the market, he's going to use F1 to advertise it. Then we realized it didn't exist. Well, it did, but the product was not there."[113]

Then, the former employee said, their reaction became: "What the fuck do they want?"

"But they brought money," they said. "So as long as they're paying, who cares."[114]

Another former employee said the reaction around them was similar: Employees wanted to know what Rich Energy was, Googled it, then realized there was "not a lot out there other than they're an energy drink."

"We had no idea," they said. "I couldn't find a can to find out what they looked like or what they potentially tasted like. It was a UK company, and we were like, 'Is this just something that hasn't made it to other markets? Do they just have a lot of money over there and are they popular over there?' Then we talked to people over there, and they were like, 'We've never heard of this company.'"[115]

Still, they didn't put much thought into it. "I've read up on F1 history in interest, and this happens," they said. "There's a random person who has money and says, 'Here you go.' You get a billionaire who does CNC machines and he wants to run a Formula One team. I don't know, maybe I used that experience unjustifiably to justify why I was staying. I never really thought about it until further down when other things started to hit the fan. Then, he started tweeting everything."[116]

"You know, we've all had dodgy sponsors," another former employee said. "We've all had dodgy money men. But you have to get your salary at the end of the month. You have to give it the benefit of the doubt, and you just get on with it. And that's just what we did."[117]

Former employees assumed the Rich Energy deal was an extension of Haas F1's efforts in years prior: acquiring small sponsors here and there to cover some of the costs of running the team, which primarily promoted Gene Haas' CNC company, Haas Automation, during its first few years. The difference between Rich Energy and those sponsors, which got minor placements on the cars, was that despite only agreeing to pay about 15 million British pounds per year toward Haas' annual budget of more than 100 million pounds, the brand took over the entire identity of the team.[118]

"Everything went black and gold," a former employee said—email signatures, equipment, clothing, accessories, race cars. "Everything. It felt very much like a takeover in that sense, because it was all-encompassing. To rebrand a Formula One team is a big project. It's not a cheap, five-minute deal. If anything, [Rich Energy] was more involved in the livery than Haas Automation. It felt disproportionate to the title sponsor and to what we believed—we never really knew, but what we believed—the actual amount [of money] to be."[119]

Much like Steiner and his drivers, former Haas employees who spoke with the authors couldn't exactly pinpoint what, mechanically, went so wrong with the Rich Energy–branded race car in 2019. One blamed it on disparities between the engineering and aerodynamics teams. Another blamed it on disparities within the aerodynamics team itself. Another blamed it on the performance of the engines Haas got from Ferrari.

But they all agreed on two things. First, Haas' breakthrough fifth-place finish in the 2018 championship led to pressure—from both Haas team members and management—to keep performing just as well or better, and second, Haas just didn't have the same resources bigger teams did to deal with issues it ran into along the way.

Despite the pressure that came after, the former Haas employees who spoke with the authors were proud of their 2018 finish. "It was on merit," one said. "We were quick. Everyone was working hard. We deserved to be there."[120]

"In the team, of course, we were happy with the results," another said. "But it wasn't a surprise. Grosjean and Magnussen were good drivers, [we had a] good car, and Ferrari was good. As Guenther said, we were like David and Goliath—a small team kicking the asses of the big teams. It was such a good feeling."[121]

"We'd just finished fifth in the world championship, [new] rules were coming out, we were doing well, we got a brand new title sponsor," another said. "We probably could have done a little more research on that, in hindsight."[122] Still, they had a lot of hope for 2019.

Then the environment started to shift: the growing division between those who were happy with fifth and those who wanted to finish even better; the push for more, more, more; and the entrance of the team's new, chaotic title sponsor. "You could almost feel the environment and the feeling around the team was changing, not necessarily for the better," one former employee said. "Then we get to the end of 2018 and into 2019, and even in my years of racing, I've never seen anything like it."[123]

Another former employee described post–2018 optimism morphing into near 17-hour workdays as Haas' 2019 race car continued to perform poorly. They said the grueling environment—and Rich Energy drama—ultimately factored into their decision to leave the team.

"It was just: 'Nothing we can do is right or good,'" they said. "I was trying to improve my career and like, everything just kept getting shot down and shot down and shot down." When they tried to take a break from their workday to exercise, they said, they started getting work notifications on their smartwatch. "There was a point when I would stop my workout. It got to the point that I stopped 10 minutes into the workout, and [others] were like, 'Are you OK? Do you need to call 9 - 1 - 1?' And I was like, 'No, I need to go to work.'"[124]

The employee said there was a lot of pressure on staying in fifth, and while they enjoyed pressure and thrived in that kind of environment, Haas' Rich Energy era "was just overwhelming."

"The expectation was that we would stay fifth or go to fourth, or be able to compete with the Force Indias, the McLarens—that echelon of teams, the higher mid-tier," they said. "We're not the Red Bulls, we're not the Mercedes, we're not the Ferraris. So we knew we would be second-tier to our engine supplier, [Ferrari], but that was the goal: to be the best of the rest.

"That's just what it was, to be fourth. There was no getting higher than that. You'd have to spend an order of magnitude more money just to get close to the top three."[125]

With Gene Haas, the employee got the impression that there was "only a linear progression forward, no decline." But decline the team did in 2019—and continued to do, no matter what—compared to its 2018 performance. "It was just like, 'Work harder and we'll dig our way out of it,'" they said. "But we just never did."[126]

"We were throwing carbon fiber at it," another former employee said. "Some people were like, 'This is crazy. We're not Red Bull. We're on version four of the front wing and it's race five. What are we doing here?' I'm generalizing, but the pressure ramps up."[127]

"With a team like Haas, there were significantly less opportunities that gave you that gauge of, 'Is this better or worse?'" another said. "A Ferrari or Mercedes, they'd put parts on the car every weekend and test setups. They had the flexibility and ability to do that, whereas we as a smaller team didn't. We needed to hope that when we did have an upgrade, it worked."[128]

The upgrades largely didn't work, and some former employees partly blamed the constant nature of the upgrades themselves. "To use an old racing phrase: We engineered ourselves into a problem we couldn't get out of," one former employee said. "Somebody like Red Bull or Ferrari, they get into a problem like that and they throw money at it and they throw people at it, and they work 24/7 until it's fixed. You can't do that when you've got a small amount of people."[129]

Another former employee said struggling race teams "can definitely over-engineer anything," but they can also lose sight of what they're engineering in the first place.

"You can get so far down a path and then forget about what actually matters," they said. "It's the main features of a car that make it work, so if you remember that and make sure the basics still work and are an improvement, then everything else just stacks on top. But you can definitely get down a path—and we kind of did—where it can get so complex that none of it works."[130]

The car was complex, as were its problems. But to former Haas employees, the reason behind its strange new sponsorship wasn't.

"I think Gene just saw the opportunity, because at the end of the day, you don't really care what your sponsor is doing as long as they're paying the money," one said. "It's the same everywhere in motorsport, and it's just business. Then they signed the contract and rumors started."[131]

* * *

Given Rich Energy's history and avid pursuit of continually higher-profile athletes—along with the whole "Red Bull" thing—a Formula One sponsorship was a natural next step. In 2018, the opportunity arose.

Rich Energy made its first big wave in F1 after the Force India team, which would soon become "Racing Point," went into administration in 2018 when driver Sergio Perez sued it for unpaid funds.[132] The *Motorsport Network* reported in July 2018 that Mercedes, the team's longtime engine supplier, claimed Force India owed it more than $12 million.[133]

In June 2018, Storey published a LinkedIn post titled "Rich Energy launch official £100m takeover of Force India."[134] In typical William Storey fashion, it made a variety of spectacular claims:

> In light of ill informed media speculation and certain external moves to destabilize the team I can confirm that Rich Energy made an official offer to buy Force India Formula One team at the end of April. This offer was accepted in principle and we are close to finalising purchase with SPA. We have deposited funds considerably in excess of the purchase price and will invest an additional 8 figure amount in the team. We have a long term business plan that not only involves our beverage brand but two multi national corporate sponsors who are not currently in Formula One.
>
> We have found the current shareholders to be excellent people who have the team's and employees best interests at heart. We aim to conclude deal as soon as practicable and the lawyers approve.[135]

Despite the *Motorsport Network* separately reporting in August 2018 that Storey said the deal was six months in the making, Rich Energy seemed to come out of nowhere with an offer to save the team.[136] In a July 2018 interview with Formula One journalist Peter Windsor, Storey said he had a contract to purchase the team in May—months before the team went into administration.[137]

For "largely" legal reasons, Storey claimed, he was "prevented from so doing by the lawyers on their side." Storey told Windsor that Force India's shares being frozen killed the deal.[138]

Windsor rarely challenged Storey during interviews, often moving to the next topic despite Storey's either vague or combative claims about the one they were on. During the July 2018 interview, Windsor brought up the topic of funding Force India's future. Instead of probing deeper, Windsor repeated Storey's claims: "You've got this purchase money and you believe you've got the sponsorship you need for the team to carry forward and grow."[139]

"It's probably worth mentioning, a lot of people have said: 'Rich Energy is quite a new business ... how on Earth are they in a position to buy a Formula One team?'" Storey said in response. "I think there's been quite a lot of commentators within the sport and the wider world who've queried that. There's an awful lot of very senior people in the sport who've seen our money and are well aware that we are more than capable of buying the team, and we're certainly ready to do so."[140]

Who were those people? What were their qualifications? Why were they looking at Rich Energy's money? Windsor never asked.

Windsor, it should be noted, had a relationship with Rich Energy. At least 15 of Windsor's YouTube videos from December 20, 2018, through May 9, 2019, featured either a Rich Energy logo in the video, a link to Rich Energy in the video description, a note in the description that "Peter Windsor's YouTube channel brought to you in association with Rich Energy," or some combination of all three. The videos ranged from a deep dive into the creation of Pirelli's tires to interviews with professional racers like Sam Posey.[141]

When the authors requested an interview about Windsor's relationship with Rich Energy via email, Windsor said: "Sorry. No. Not interested."[142]

The *Motorsport Network* reported in July 2018 that Rich Energy said it pitched a sponsorship agreement with Force India for 30 million pounds, but it didn't work out.[143] Storey posed himself as the team's savior, claiming he was the only person independent of the team to show up to Force India's court date and that he was ready to advance the money to keep the team out of administration.[144] The *Motorsport Network* wrote:

> This offer was dismissed and the team was placed in administration, which Rich Energy called a "tragic and avoidable outcome" and labelled the involvement of Perez, Mercedes and [creditor and team sponsor] BWT "disgraceful."
> *Autosport* understands the offer from Rich Energy, which had previously been dismissed by the team as a credible outright buyer, involved two £15million installments and was viewed as insufficient to guarantee the long-term future of the team.[145]

The *Motorsport Network* reported in early August 2018 that Storey said his consortium—backed by "four sterling billionaires," reportedly including West Ham owners David Sullivan and David Gold—had only been trying to help. He added that Rich Energy would be in Formula One "sooner or later" because it had "the money to do so, the business model, and the reasons to do it."[146]

In a July 2018 interview with Windsor, Storey described a "malaise afflicting the sport" in the sense that teams as promising as Force India or as legendary as McLaren could struggle so publicly to garner the necessary funding to mount a challenge for the title.[147] He was right, too; the massive amounts of money required to compete with the likes of Mercedes made it impossible for a mid-field team to challenge for a championship. Force India's lack of results could be pinned on its finances, but financiers were also looking for good results to justify investing in the team—an unending negative cycle that had long plagued the sport.

In that sense, Storey came across as the good guy. Introduced by Windsor as an "ultra-successful businessman [and] a mathematician by training" who "just might become Formula One's latest team owner," Storey said he recognized talent and wanted to provide it with the funding necessary to advance. It was the kind of thing many fans hoped for, but that kind of vulnerability also allowed companies to enter the sport with promises of money and no checkbook to back them up.[148]

Force India owner Vijay Mallya, a serial fraudster wanted in his home country of India for defaulting on more than $1 billion in loans, also came up in conversation.[149] Mallya ultimately lost control of the Force India team after it went into administration, all while trying to fight extradition to India by seeking asylum in the UK on humanitarian grounds.[150]

Storey told Windsor he thought Mallya, whom he described as having a "kamikaze" approach to running things financially, was likely not guilty of anything but "believing his lawyers and trusting those closest to him." Windsor laughed and opted not to question that reasoning.[151]

When Windsor asked Storey how he dealt with people who didn't take him seriously due to his looks or background, Storey said people were "entitled to their opinion."

"Never judge a book by its cover," he said. The more you know, the less you have to show. But I mean, if people want to be superficial and judge it, that's entirely their prerogative. Obviously we have a wonderful drink that we hope people will try and prefer to Red Bull and Monster. That's our No. 1 objective. In terms of an erratic hairstyle or whatever, quite frankly, it's absolutely irrelevant."[152]

Storey's attempts to take over Mallya's former team didn't work, and Force India was eventually bought by driver Lance Stroll's billionaire father, Lawrence Stroll, in late 2018.[153] *Reuters* reported in October of that year that Lawrence Stroll led a consortium that paid $117 million, or 90 million pounds, for Force India—three times Rich Energy's reported offer of 30 million pounds.[154]

Lance Stroll, whose father also spent a reported $80 million to help get him into a Williams F1 seat in 2017, became a driver for the team the year after the purchase.[155]

Then came Rich Energy's pursuit of Williams, a team that first hit the grid in 1977 and had competed ever since. That effort concluded during the 2018 United States Grand Prix, according to an *ESPN* story from the next year:

> It is understood Claire Williams and several senior team members were left waiting for Storey at an Austin restaurant on the evening of the race to finalise the terms of their deal. He never showed up, and a few days later the Haas partnership was announced. It has never been clear how much of this Haas was aware of at the time.[156]

The authors reached out to Williams about its relationship with Storey in August 2021. The team never responded.

It wasn't clear why Storey would leave a potential sponsorship opportunity hanging, but it might have been because he'd moved onto a bigger target. By *ESPN*'s timing, he stood up Williams on October 20 or 21, 2018. Rich Energy announced its partnership with Haas on October 25.[157]

An October 27 report from automotive news site *The Drive* noted that the Haas title sponsorship cost "reportedly ... as little as half" of what Williams was asking to become Rich Energy Racing.[158] The source for that information wasn't cited by *The Drive*, nor could it be corroborated by the authors. Team principal Guenther Steiner, though, told independent motorsport website *RaceFans* that the deal came together quickly.[159]

"It was before Austin that we started to talk," Steiner said. "We talked [about] what we can do, what we will do and what they will do, and then it came together."[160] The deal was announced mere days after the Austin race Steiner mentioned.

The detailed financial aspects of the partnership, though, were kept under wraps until July 2019, when Haas went after Rich Energy for the sums it owed through the end of 2021—35 million pounds—as the multi-year partnership fell apart midway through their first and only season together.[161]

The deal was a perplexing one from the start, since Haas didn't really need outside sponsorship to operate. The whole point of the Formula One team during its first three years, according to the *Motorsport Network*, was to promote team owner Gene Haas' CNC business, and many found it odd for the team to suddenly take on a third-party brand.[162]

"I was thinking, like, maybe they are struggling for money," said Romain Grosjean fan Bex Foot. "I don't know how much money Gene Haas has, but has he spent it all already in a couple of years? Does he need more money coming in from outside? As long as Ro' still had a drive, I guess."[163]

But Steiner soon explained why the team opted for the deal, as quoted by the *Motorsport Network* not long after the sponsorship announcement: "If a partner comes along which contributes enough that you do something together and it gives you opportunities as well, because this gives us opportunities, why not do it? I think it will help the team."[164]

It certainly made sense: more money and more opportunities, on top of an already opportunistic 2018 season for Haas. But was any money really there? Haas would soon find out.

*   *   *

Discussions about Rich Energy's money and viability as a title sponsor came immediately. In his July 2018 interview with Peter Windsor about the failed Force India purchase, even Storey noted that it was a little strange that a "three-and-a-half year old" company should have the funding available for such a big monetary commitment—especially with so many other sponsorship deals on the table.[165] It was even stranger that Haas would entertain accepting money from an untested brand.

Guenther Steiner, though, initially rejected the skepticism. In a *Motorsport Network* story from the week of the sponsorship announcement, he claimed Haas had done its due diligence looking into Rich Energy and that the team's legal advisors "were content" with it.[166] More money, Steiner implied, was always worth having in a sport as expensive as Formula One, even if the team wasn't in a place to share plans about what it aimed to do with that money.

"This is not like, we've got more money, let's go big now, let's employ 200 people, let's buy a new big building, let's buy five dyno [machines to measure engine output]," Steiner told the *Motorsport Network*. "Nothing like this. We are well grounded. I think we show that our business model is working quite well. It's not perfect by any means. We can get better, but we want to grow it where we think we are weak."[167]

As the mystery of Rich Energy grew, more and more people began to seek out the drink. For Formula One fans, it had become a talisman of sorts, something to wield with pride. But for many people, the only way to actually acquire Rich Energy was through wholesale distributors, Rich Energy's website, or, for a time, retailers like Amazon or Walmart.[168] In the latter cases, it was rare to see a single can for sale; if you wanted to purchase the drink, you had to buy a pack of at least 12.

In the March 2019 interview with the authors near the start of Rich Energy's first Formula One season, Storey was eager to hype his young brand as innovative and creative, utilizing unorthodox marketing to attract attention. But he wasn't eager to dive into the tangible reality of his business. Storey said he wanted to "give as much information … as possible" without getting "commercially sensitive," but he wasn't able to clarify questions around Rich Energy's financials and business model—both pertinent discussions, given that all most people knew about the company at the time was that it apparently had 581 pounds in the bank in 2017 and its products were all but absent from store shelves.[169]

"I'm trying to strike a balance between being as helpful to you as possible and give as much information to you as possible, without necessarily advertising anything that's commercially sensitive to us," Storey said in the 2019 interview. "But I think it will very quickly become apparent that we are very significantly bigger than one set of accounts from 2017 shows."[170]

Yet numbers were an area where Storey was known to exaggerate. During the Whyte Bikes copyright trial on March 12 and 13, 2019, Storey was asked about his claims that Rich Energy had "produced 90 million cans." According to the judgment, he then clarified that Rich Energy "had produced 90 million cans, but had not yet filled and sold them." Instead, he estimated that Rich Energy actually filled and sold "circa 3 million cans" in 2018.[171]

The day after trial, March 14, was Storey's first interview with the authors. We asked: "Since this data will become public regardless, do you have estimates that show how quickly you've grown since 2015? Do you have monetary estimates that—"

"We've now, we've now, we've now—" Storey interjected. "We've now sold in excess of 100 million cans, and we're just getting started." He later doubled down on the number.[172] It was the same incorrect claim Storey had been called on, and made to correct, in court during the two days before the interview. Yet there it was again.

"So you could sort of work back from those figures," Storey continued. "But ultimately, people are sort of scratching their heads: 'Who are Rich Energy? How are they doing these things?' In a way, that's a compliment to us."[173]

Storey told the authors in 2019 that buyers of Rich Energy included nightclubs, bars, hotels, and high-end wine shops—"places that energy drinks normally wouldn't sell," he said.[174]

"Our business strategy is to be very lean and mean—to approach the drinks industry from a very common-sense, innovative standpoint, not from the usual conventions," Storey said. "And while I'm obviously not going to tell you my confidential plans, ultimately, we think we have some pretty smart ideas on how to do things better, and we are demonstrating that. And that's why we're growing so quickly.

"The conventional approach is all about competitors—working with

wholesalers and retailers in a traditional way, building business in a traditional way. All of the advice I was given in the beginning by experts was complete rubbish. It was total nonsense. We've ignored that, we've done our own
thing, and people don't like it. People don't like that we're getting very big,
and, dare I say, starting to make some of our competitors look very stupid."[175]

Storey didn't go into many details. "We've completely changed the
whole framework of the market," he said. "There's been a race to the bottom
with energy drinks—everyone's accepted that Red Bull is the dominant party
and that they need to find a niche in this market. We haven't done that."[176]

Rich Energy's business model relied on how much better it was than
Red Bull, despite Red Bull selling nearly 7 billion cans in 2018—a mam-
moth number even when tallied against Rich Energy's debunked claim of
more than 100 million over four years.[177] Compared to Red Bull's market
of 171 countries in 2018, Storey told the authors as of the March 2019 interview that Rich Energy had distribution partners in 37 countries. "Every
single one of them has a company, which is effectively a Rich Energy business, so clearly we're operating internationally," Storey said.[178]

Rich Energy remained on a mission, even if it only had four years of
market experience compared to Red Bull's more than three decades. The
company regularly played up its #BetterThanRedBull social media campaign, and the main page of its website proudly instructed visitors at the
time to "Forget the wings, Rich Energy gives you horns." Storey described
Rich Energy as a "very fast-growing company," and throughout the
39-minute interview from early 2019, painted Rich Energy's doubters as
the ones who needed to get their facts straight.[179]

"I've been rather puzzled as to why people have been suggesting that
there's anything wrong with us or anything like that," Storey said at one
point. "It's quite the opposite. We've worked incredibly hard, we're very
proud of what we're doing, we think we've got a great product and brand,
and we're growing very quickly.[180]

"Some people are thinking, 'How on earth is this small company able
to do these things?' Well, we've worked incredibly hard, we've been very
creative, very innovative, and I would say we're unorthodox. We've just
been very successful in a very quick period of time, we've made some very
smart moves, we've grown really quickly, and I think people are looking
for something that doesn't exist.

"That's why I'm very happy to speak to people, because actually we're
very proud of what we're doing, which is creating a competitor to Red Bull,
and we're ignoring conventional wisdom. We're completely going against
the grain within the traditional drinks industry, which I personally feel
could be run much better, and I think we've got a brilliant business strategy. So, we're actually doing something I'm proud of.

"It's puzzling that people are seeing a company that's growing very quickly, that's working very hard, that's got nice people involved, and rather than applauding us, there are some people who want to criticize us or find fault with us. It is unreasonable, but I'm sure in the fullness of time, people will change their opinions."[181]

Yet the reluctance to share any substantial funding information, paired with financial reports of a few hundred pounds in the bank and inaccurate claims about sales of 100 million cans, made a very perplexing case. It was possible that Formula One had finally attracted Moneytron 2.0.

Despite the hints that Rich Energy would enter Formula One, many were surprised to not only see the company actually sponsor an entire race team but to see so much media coverage right off the bat—particularly, so much media coverage that allowed Storey to craft his own narrative while the rest of the internet was still trying to figure out who he was. The *Motorsport Network* seemed to have the news first, reporting on both the upcoming Rich Energy Haas F1 livery reveal and the energy-drinks business overall—as well as conducting several of the first in-depth interviews with William Storey, which posited him as a hero-type savior for Formula One. The *Network* also gave credence to Storey's claim that Rich Energy was set to challenge Red Bull both on and off the track, despite driver Kevin Magnussen reminding everyone that Haas still had a long way to go before it could beat the longstanding team. *Autosport* lauded the "bravado" of Haas' title-sponsor makeover, noting that Storey had "not just avoid[ed] the usual script. He tore it to shreds."[182–187]

Indeed, it was the #BetterThanRedBull campaign that became Rich Energy's rallying cry for the season. It was a bold approach, given that Red Bull was one of the top teams in the paddock at the time, and it was a slogan that attracted attention from fans and media alike. In the decade before Rich Energy entered Formula One, Red Bull's finishes in the constructor standings consisted of: four championships, three second-place finishes, and two third-place finishes. During those 10 years, the team's worst finish in the constructor standings was fourth in 2015. Red Bull also acted as a landing place for legendary drivers like four-time champion Sebastian Vettel, up-and-coming competitors like Daniel Ricciardo and 2021 champion Max Verstappen, and big names across motorsport as a whole, such as David Coulthard and Mark Webber.

Formula One was a sport of empires at the time, and significant rule changes—switching from V8 engines to turbocharged V6 units, for example—often led to one team outperforming the others. Many Formula One fans thus grew tired of Red Bull from 2010 to 2013—the stretch of Vettel's four championships during Formula One's V8 era, when it was almost guaranteed Red Bull would dominate. A similar process happened with the Mercedes team during the V6 turbo reign that began in 2014, and with Ferrari during the days of seven-time champion Michael Schumacher. Years of major rule or design modifications became the main bastion of light for some fans, as those were often the only opportunities for one team to usurp another.

Having one team so dramatically present a challenge to another was a welcome change, and with Haas' growing performance in the sport, there really did seem to be an opportunity for Rich Energy to close in on Red Bull. Some fans latched onto the #BetterThanRedBull hashtag, both for its promise and its humor. Many stuck around for the latter.

*   *   *

As social media became more popular during the 2010s, Formula One seemed to lag behind the times under CEO Bernie Ecclestone, often being criticized for its lack of engagement and interaction. In 2014, Ecclestone said Formula One wouldn't embrace social media like all other sports.[188] Later that year, he made a stink about bloggers setting up websites to get into races "for free."[189] In 2016, he personally banned multi-time champion Lewis Hamilton from using a service called Snapchat to share videos from the paddock—a rule Hamilton immediately broke.[190] Formula One also long shunned YouTube under Ecclestone's rule, and clips of F1 broadcasts posted by third parties were swiftly taken down.

After Liberty Media took over Formula One in 2016 and began its embrace of the internet, the American company let race teams post videos of preseason testing, historically ending the blackout from Ecclestone's rule.[191] Formula One also finally embraced YouTube, posting both historic and modern clips from the series—a welcome arrival to the 21st century.[192]

Ecclestone went public with his disagreement about Liberty Media's choices, saying the American company was running Formula One "like a Starbucks."[193] It wasn't clear what this meant.

Formula One wasn't just late to the internet. It was also accused, with merit, of being rather bland in the 2010s. Like many sports, auto racing suffered from a very corporate presence at the time, and viewers often compared their rose-tinted memories of the golden years with the worst aspects of the modern times. Gone were the days of NASCAR's moonshine running or Formula One's glorified embrace of danger and potential death; in their place came competitors with a strict sponsor script and a whole lot of bosses to please.

This, of course, was an extreme exaggeration, and many of motorsports' faults—such as its atmosphere often dominated by white hypermasculinity—continued to mend with the passing of time and presence of more progressive voices at the highest level. Yet there was a small truth to the idea: the truth of everything being a little more straitlaced, and a little more boring, with so much corporate interest. If you were looking for World Wrestling Entertainment personalities in auto racing, you wouldn't find them unless the idea went over well in sponsors' corporate offices.

For years, then, two teams responding to one another's tweets was the pinnacle of online excitement when it came to a series that often lacked it on and off the track. Many interviews felt scripted; journalists asked the same kind of questions, and drivers were coached on providing the same style of answers across the board.

So, Rich Energy's online presence was something different—something exciting, even if in a bad way. It was cheeky and amusing, if not factually accurate. It was an approach to public relations—if you could even call it "public relations"—that few had attempted in F1 since the turn of the century.

The #BetterThanRedBull campaign started to get more personal as the season approached. A cheeky hashtag began to morph into pointed challenges, with Storey claiming, according to news site *PlanetF1*, that Haas was "vastly superior" to its rivals "by every metric."[194] Indeed, more than a month before the 2019 season began, a February 7 tabloid story in the *Sun* quoted Storey as saying:

> We are confident we will beat Red Bull in many races this year. That is holy grail marketing but sometimes you get a bit of serendipity and right timing.
> Red Bull have spent £250 billion in F1 and last year across Toro Rosso and Red Bull, there or there abouts, £400 million.
> Ultimately, we are going to have a better-looking car.[195]

Storey's estimation of the combined Red Bull and Toro Rosso junior team budgets from 2018—400 million pounds—was fairly accurate, according to independent motorsports website *RaceFans*.[196] It was unclear where he got the figure of 250 billion, and neither Storey nor Red Bull commented on its accuracy.

No 2019 race cars had been on track yet at the time of the story in the *Sun*, so Storey had no clear-cut metrics by which to prove his claims about performance.[197] But the initial rounds of preseason testing came not long after, and they seemed fruitful. After its first day on track in 2019, February 18, Rich Energy tweeted:

> A superb effort today in testing by @HaasF1Team & the tremendously talented @RGrosjean. Our 1st day in @F1 & we are faster than @redbullracing. Superior performance fuelled by @rich_energy #worldclass #RichEnergy #HaasF1 #betterthanredbull #F1 #F1Testing #Barcelona #Elite #fuel[198]

But in that era of Formula One, testing didn't mean much. It was simply an opportunity for teams to work out any kinks and see, finally, what their cars could do when they hit the asphalt. It was, as evidenced by Haas, by no means a reliable predictor of the ultimate championship standings. Red Bull and Haas might have been neck-and-neck on the lap-time leaderboard,[199] but Haas' disastrous number of off-track excursions became a fitting prequel to the team's year. (Plus, Romain Grosjean's Haas ride ended as the second-slowest car of the day on the first day of testing.[200])

For the next several weeks, rather than engage in Twitter spats, the Rich Energy account opted to tweet factual comments on its performance during the first races of the season.[201] Rich Energy's attitude came back in full force in May 2019, largely due to publicity about the accusations that its logo looked stunningly similar to that of British bicycle company Whyte Bikes. After losing its copyright case to Whyte, Rich Energy took to Twitter to lament:

> Today the judgement was released in the claim brought by @WhyteBikes against us in respect of our stag logo. We are disappointed with the judgement & the findings of the judge which run counter to our submissions. We are considering all of our legal options including appeal[202]

Rich Energy did try to appeal, and failed. All the while, it grew punchier on Twitter. Whyte Bikes also joined in, tweeting an image of then–Haas Formula One driver Romain Grosjean riding one of its products.[203] In a video that later became private, longtime Formula One journalist Peter Windsor once again jumped into the ring, allowing Storey to defend the logo in an interview.[204]

With another hearing scheduled for June 27, Rich Energy found solace in tweeting. The brand posted photos of Storey with celebrities and images of Rich Energy–branded Croc sneakers, as well as a video of a Renault F1 car—not a Haas—turning laps at Circuit Paul Ricard in France, captioned: "Premium performance with @rich_energy."[205-207] It claimed Whyte Bikes' case was "baseless" and posted a few taunting messages directed, once again, at Red Bull Racing:

> @KevinMagnussen pushing the limits hits the wall and knocks out @Max33Verstappen
>
> Oh deer! @redbullracing #denmark #eliteperformance #viking #warrior #f1 #richenergy #betterthanredbull
> —Rich Energy (@rich_energy) June 8, 2019[208]
>
> @redbullracing get on yer bike!!
>
> @Max33Verstappen should drink the world's premium energy drink @rich_energy and he would be a bit happier #givesyouhorns #richenergy #BetterThanRedBull #F1 #CanadianGP #kevinmagnussen #viking #Warrior
> —Rich Energy (@rich_energy) June 8, 2019[209]

For Foot, Rich Energy's social media was "so embarrassing."

"That's the main thing," Foot said. "I was embarrassed to be a fan of [Grosjean] and therefore the team. I kept having to justify my support. It's not fun."[210]

It wasn't always easy to be a Grosjean fan. Back in 2012, he was banned from a race after causing a multi-car pileup at the Belgian Grand Prix.[211] Foot still stood by his side. "But then you get through the Rich Energy year, and I'm trying to really say I'm not a fan of the team, I'm a fan of the driver," Foot said. "Like, really trying to separate the two."[212]

The Twitter saga continued with a spat between Rich Energy and *MsportXtra*, a website for racing updates, when the *MsportXtra* account tweeted the brand on June 12, 2019, with formatting as such: "Goodmorning. Few weeks ago William said in an interview that RE was available in supermarkets in Holland. Which supermarkets ? I like to get some. Thanks."[213] The exchange continued:

Hundreds of Dutch supermarkets
Contact Rich Energy Netherlands
—**Rich Energy (@rich_energy) June 12, 2019**[214]

Hundreds ??? Which one ? Just give me a name. Is it the Jumbo supermarket, the Albert Heijn, the Spar ? Which chain of supermarkets so I know where to go ? I never use webshops.
—**#MsportXtra (@MsportXtra) June 12, 2019**[215]

Contact Rich Energy Netherlands
Or email richenergy.com and Web team will answer query
Thanks
—**Rich Energy (@rich_energy) June 12, 2019**[216]

I contacted you guys to give me a straight and simple answer. Why do I need to email web team ? You're not a websteam ? Just the name of the store, nothing else. You said hundreds of stores available but you don't know which ? That's a bit strange.
—**#MsportXtra (@MsportXtra) June 12, 2019**[217]

We will get list to you later today
Feel free to share
—**Rich Energy (@rich_energy) June 12, 2019**[218]

Just wondering… "later today," would that be this afternoon or evening ? That way I can have an idea on when to go to the store.
—**#MsportXtra (@MsportXtra) June 12, 2019**[219]

It has been 9 hours. Did you forget to send the list ? Please let me know.
—**#MsportXtra (@MsportXtra) June 12, 2019**[220]

Rich Energy never appeared to provide a straight answer. Instead, days later on June 18, 2019, the brand tweeted an image of a Rich Energy can lined up next to a Red Bull can and a Monster can, captioning it: "Delighted with feedback from the beverage industry. A quiet revolution happening with @rich_energy #richenergy #britishbrand #EnergyDrink #business #F1 #RoyalAscot @redbull @redbullracing @Monster Energy."[221]

It was an interesting choice, considering how difficult the drink was for many buyers to find. Coincidentally, a product-testing Instagram account called "livingproof" with 5,000 followers at the time had posted an informal review of Rich Energy that same day, saying: "Rich Energy is much better than Red Bull in terms of taste."[222]

The *MsportXtra* account, following up on its earlier questions, pointed out the strange timing in a June 18 tweet: "Feedback from beverage industry ??? It was done by Dutch 'Livingproof' who are a mum and dad with a few kids that try out stuff."[223]

(The team behind the "livingproof" account described themselves as simply "BFFs for eternity."[224] When asked by the authors multiple times about their relationship with Storey and Rich Energy in August 2021, the duo behind the account did not respond.)

Many of Rich Energy's tweets at the time followed a similar pattern: People asked the company where they could purchase the drink, and Rich Energy either did not respond or merely directed users to its website. Yet Storey claimed to be baffled by his critics.

"People are looking at us the wrong way," Storey told the authors in their March 2019 interview. "Rather than saying, 'Blimey, this company has, in under four years, grown this quickly; well done,' they're saying, 'Oh, there must be something wrong.'

"Well, there's nothing wrong at all."[225]

5

WHYTE COLLAR CRIME

O n May 14, 2019, Rich Energy was the talk of the Formula One paddock once again—this time because its branding came back to haunt it.

That day, Whyte Bikes announced Rich Energy lost a copyright case that its owner, ATB Sales, filed over the companies' logos—one of which adorned the Haas cars on the world stage of motorsport.[1] In the announcement, Whyte Bikes called the similarity between its logo and Rich Energy's "staggering."[2] Rich Energy's featured just two extra points on the stag's antlers and slight angular differences.

The announcement continued:

> "We only use the finest ingredients," boasts the Rich Energy website. Unfortunately, until now, those ingredients have included an un-authorised copy of the Whyte Bikes' Stag's head logo, used without permission and against the wishes of the Hastings-based cycle brand. The result is that Rich Energy's logo has been held to infringe the copyright in the Whyte logo, entitling ATB to an injunction and damages or an account of Rich Energy's profits.
>
> Whilst the Rich Energy drink has proved almost impossible to find or purchase, the visibility of the Rich Energy brand has recently increased, coming to the attention of F1 viewers as a result of their sponsorship of the Rich Energy Haas F1 Team, whose cars both feature multiple applications of the copied Whyte Bikes logo.[3]

Judge Melissa Clarke of the Business and Property Courts of England and Wales accompanied her decision in the Whyte Bikes logo case with a scathing 58-page judgment, much of which described the ways in which Clarke found the Rich Energy camp, Storey included, to be "poor witnesses" whose evidence she treated with a "high degree of caution."[4] Clarke added that she found some of Storey's evidence to be "incorrect or misleading," and that she deemed he was "involved in the manufacture of documents during the course of litigation to provide additional support of the Defendants' case."[5]

Whyte Bikes, whose design team was formed in 1994 and poetically led by a former Formula One design engineer, took Rich Energy to court

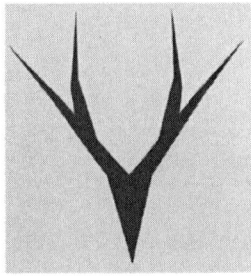  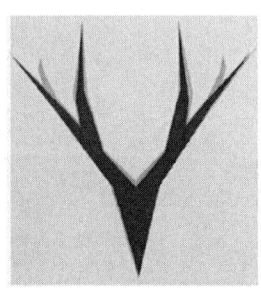

Whyte Bikes' logo (left), Rich Energy's logo (middle), and Rich Energy's logo over Whyte Bikes' logo (right). The judgment in the copyright case over the logos detailed their exact differences: a two-degree difference in angles, 6.8 percent taller antlers, two small tines on the outer antlers, and a thickening of the inner ones (The Business and Property Courts of England and Wales).

seeking an injunction that would require the company to remove the logo from Haas' race cars and website, "amongst other things." The claim was that Rich Energy copied its logo, which was designed in late 2008 by two of its employees, Guy Farrant and Mark Morgan, and had been on the Whyte Bikes website as early as 2010.[6]

"At trial," the judgment said, "the Defendants abandoned their pleaded challenge of these points and now accept them."[7] But it was a long road to get there. Also involved in the case was a digital-marketing company called Staxoweb Limited, founded by Storey's childhood friend Sean Kelly. The defendants said Storey commissioned Kelly to design a brand identity for Rich Energy in May 2015, according to the judgment, and Kelly gave Storey an invoice of 50,000 British pounds for the work—which included the logo and a wider marketing strategy, such as developing, launching, and maintaining the Rich Energy website—at the end of that month.[8] Rich Energy Limited was incorporated in the UK just four months later.

The defendants in the case—Rich Energy, Storey, and Kelly's Staxoweb Limited—denied copyright infringement, saying Rich Energy's logo was designed independently, without knowledge of or reference to Whyte Bikes' nearly identical one.[9]

Judge Melissa Clarke heard from four witnesses during the course of the trial: Farrant, then the managing director of Whyte Bikes' owner, ATB Sales; Morgan, a graphic designer for the company; Kelly; and Storey.[10] (Kelly didn't respond when contacted by the authors multiple times for an interview.)

"I found Mr. Farrant and Mr. Morgan to be straightforward, credible, and reliable witnesses who came to court to assist it to the best of their abilities," Clarke wrote. "Conversely, I found both Mr. Storey and Mr. Kelly to be poor witnesses."[11]

Storey argued that both Rich Energy and Whyte Bikes' logos were very simple, according to the judgment, and the use of geometric stag designs was "commonplace."[12] Storey provided two examples from fellow UK businesses: one from a restaurant called Moor Hall, and one from The Wild Beer Company brewery. "Both are very different" from the logos of Whyte Bikes and Rich Energy, Clarke wrote.[13] Indeed they were.

The judgment also included the exact measurements of the Rich Energy and Whyte Bikes logos, saying, on Rich Energy's part, that the "differences relied upon are minimal and only serve to highlight the similarities" between them. The differences, according to the judgment, consisted of: a two-degree difference in angles, 6.8 percent taller antlers, two small tines on the outer antlers, and a thickening of the inner ones.[14]

Adding to the suspicion about whether the logo was directly copied, Clarke said, was the "unreasonable unwillingness" of both Kelly and Storey "to even countenance the possibility that they might have seen, but forgotten" Whyte Bikes' logo during the course of their "extensive" research into brands with stag-head logos.[15]

Clarke described Storey as having an "apparently natural tendency to exaggerate," and as providing "different and inconsistent accounts" of the development of the Rich Energy logo, "which also conflicted to a large extent with the evidence of Mr. Kelly."[16]

"He often did not answer questions directly, preferring to make speeches about his vision for his business or alternatively seeking to evade questions by speaking in generalities or in the third-person plural," Clarke wrote. "He only answered several questions when I intervened. He had a

The logos of Moor Hall (left), Rich Energy (middle) and The Wild Beer Company (The Business and Property Courts of England and Wales, Moor Hall, The Wild Beer Company).

tendency to make impressive statements, which on further investigation or consideration were not quite what they seemed."[17]

Clarke then cited an example that came up in court, in which ATB Sales' legal representation, Roger Wyand, asked Storey about sales figures in cross examination. Storey had been quoted in February 2019, the month before the trial, as saying Rich Energy had produced 90 million cans.[18] Storey gave that tally to the *Motorsport Network* that month, during the same interview in which he said claiming Rich Energy didn't exist was "like saying man never walked on the moon, or Elvis is still alive." The story's headline was: "Haas title sponsor likens doubters to moon landing truthers."[19]

When presented with the question about producing 90 million cans, Clarke wrote: "Mr. Storey explained that [Rich Energy] had produced 90 million cans, but had not yet filled and sold them."[20]

"He said he would have to check the figures, but in 2018 he thought the First Defendant had filled and sold 'circa 3 million cans' of Rich Energy drink," the judgment read. "In another example, he stated in an impassioned fashion that he was 'not in the business of trying to create a world-class business by taking any inspiration from anybody else whatsoever,' but his own written evidence was that his starting point when thinking about developing a logo was to carry out logo research on what other drinks companies were doing, and to carry out internet searches on stag head logos used by other companies."[21]

The day after the court case, of course, Storey told the authors in a phone interview that Rich Energy had sold "in excess of 100 million cans" since its 2015 inception—a hard number to reach if the company only sold 3 million in 2018.[22] The court documents weren't available at the time of the interview, so there was no way to compare his claims in court versus during the phone call until after the documents became public.

There was also the topic of Kelly's 50,000-pound compensation for brand work and the logo that landed them in court, which the defendants used as evidence of actions that were "inconsistent with copying."[23] But Clarke described Storey's evidence about whether he'd actually paid Kelly to be "characteristically somewhat evasive."[24]

"It was settled, so, yes, it was settled ..." the judgment quoted Storey as saying, with that exact punctuation. "Sean and I do a lot of business together in terms of I have had different IT businesses and sports management companies that he does web development for and design so, yes, it was settled ... yes, it was settled, yes, it was paid.... I cannot recall exactly, but I know that it was paid."[25]

No documentary evidence of the payment was disclosed, Clarke wrote.[26] Clarke also found Kelly to have "manufactured documentation to provide additional support for the Defendants' case," and said the manufacturing was a "joint endeavor" between Kelly and Storey. Clarke said Kelly's oral evidence was inconsistent with other elements of his evidence, which he'd signed, and that she found Kelly to be "evasive in some aspects of his evidence."[27]

She admitted that Kelly made admissions against Rich Energy's case but that some of the admissions were "unwillingly made in the face of incontrovertible evidence" presented by ATB Sales' legal representation, Roger Wyand. Kelly also said, according to the judgment, that he was "personally proud of the design of the logo, especially now [that] it is becoming internationally recognized."[28]

"He would not make other, obvious admissions, for example that [the two logos] are closely similar," Clarke wrote. "For those reasons, I do not accept either Mr. Storey or Mr. Kelly as credible or reliable witnesses, and I treat all of their evidence with a high degree of caution."[29]

Clarke called Kelly and Storey's evidence that they designed the logo independently to be "at best … confused and contradictory and purports to be supported by documents which are not what they seem."[30] As a reminder, Clarke found the same when it came to Rich Energy's name and branding. She wrote:

> Pursuant to the procedural rules which apply to IPEC, pleadings stand as evidence. In the Amended Defence, which was signed by both Mr Kelly and Mr Storey, the Defendants contend in para 22(b)(ii) that the first word of the First Defendant's name:
> "…was selected before the incorporation of the First Defendant to simultaneously refer to a number of things and concepts. One of the purposes of its selection was as an abbreviation of 'Richmond,' in order to give the brand a sense of geographical origin and to assist in the creation of a brand narrative." […]
> In fact, as Mr Storey acknowledged in his witness statement and accepted in cross-examination, the name "Rich Energy" was selected by the Croatian creator of the energy drink formula, Drazen Majstrovic in 2013, when Mr Majstrovic founded a Croatian company, Rich Energy C.O.O, to market his new drink. Mr Storey had no formal involvement with the brand until 2015. Accordingly the name of the drink was not selected by him to reflect his associations with Richmond, Surrey, as pleaded. By the time of his witness statement, Mr Storey's evidence was that he was from Richmond, Surrey and the connection between the word 'Rich' and 'Richmond' was why he kept the name Rich Energy, albeit not why it was originally chosen.[31]

The judgment came out on May 9, 2019, and the trial took place on March 12 and 13. The authors' initial *Jalopnik* investigation into Rich Energy, which published on April 10, read:

> Storey has claimed in the past that Rich Energy gained its name due to its base in Richmond, London, England, but told *Jalopnik* the name was, in reality,

"sort of serendipitous"—it was trademarked as "Rich" in Croatia back in 2011, and Storey picked it up and rebranded it all "from scratch."

"I bought a liquid and a drink from which I then created the brand," Storey said. "They had a word mark 'Rich,' which has a slightly different meaning, shall we say, and we said, 'Right, okay, we can work with that, but we want to completely change the whole brand.'"

The stag logo is also said to reflect the deer that live in a park in Richmond, according to the *Daily Telegraph*—interesting, considering reports of Whyte Bikes suing Rich Energy over its logo in February.[32]

Kelly brought a document to trial created specifically for the litigation, the judgment said, and it was meant to show some of the creative process from the design of the logo. The document was called the "Logo Research page" in the judgment, and it apparently showcased the early logos that inspired the final Rich Energy one.[33]

But the defense admitted to creating the document in 2018, when the actual research and creation was done in 2015. It contained the label: "The final row are logos which could be a starting point for Rich Energy's identity." Wyand asked about that label in cross examination: basically, why a document "manufactured for the purposes of this litigation in 2018 using logos selected from internet searches also carried out in 2018" conveyed that this was a starting point for a logo created three years earlier.[34]

"To effectively portray how we went about coming to the Rich logo, the original concepting and ideas," Kelly responded. "Again, there was a lot of documentation that we did not keep. There is some that we did, which we submitted to the court. Some of it was paper, some of it was electronic. So, most of this document—bar the sketches and the black geometric shapes—we effectively recreated just to tell the story and put it all together."[35]

Wyand then suggested that someone reading the document would think that the logos shown were the ones Kelly and Storey actually used to create theirs in 2015, not logos they'd later gathered to artistically portray what happened. Kelly said the document was "effectively meant to say: 'This is what we could have done, this is what we did do, here is the whole story, here is how we put it together,' and that is making the best use of what originals we had."[36]

"Mr. Kelly agreed in cross-examination that the statement in the [request for information] response, which he had signed—that 'the documents have been created by, or were in the possession of, the third defendant prior to that compilation'—was not correct," Clarke wrote.[37]

But Storey's statements didn't align with that. When he was questioned about the document Kelly claimed was entirely created in 2018 to put the story from 2015 "together," the judgment read, Storey said the photos were found in 2015 and then compiled into the document in 2018.

"So, this document was produced in 2018 and was a selection of some of the research results that you had from 2015?" Wyand asked, according to the judgment.[38]

"Correct," Storey said. "In order to answer the questions raised, we put together a summary in 2018 of the work that we had done, which was based on the sketches and the work that we had done in 2015. We could have created a 300-page document, but chose to raise the most pertinent points which is, you know, the work that we did."[39]

The judgment broke down the difference between Storey and Kelly's admissions as such:

> This contradicts the admissions made by Mr Kelly in his oral evidence, that he had not carried out internet searches in 2015, had not saved any internet searches that Mr Storey carried out in 2015, and the pictures and images were obtained in July 2018. It is also difficult to understand how Mr Storey could say that "we could have created a 300-page document" when:
> i) his evidence was that Mr Kelly kept all the documents from 2015 (or at least that only Mr Kelly knew where any saved documents were kept); and
> ii) Mr Kelly's evidence was that he only had the pencil sketches and some computer-aided renderings from 2015. No further documentation has been disclosed.[40]

But Storey's evidence wasn't only inconsistent with Kelly's, in Clarke's view—it was inconsistent with his own. Clarke wrote:

> Although Mr Storey's witness statement stated clearly that he had conducted research and attached the Logo Research page to evidence that research, in cross-examination he gave confused and contradictory evidence. He originally said that *"we"* i.e. he and Mr Kelly, had carried out *"an awful lot of research.... We looked at dozens and dozens of the stag-inspired logos."* He said, *"we were doing a lot of research and brainstorming" "we looked at lots and lots of designs."* He later increased this estimate to *"hundreds and hundreds"* of logos.
> When asked if he personally carried out internet searches (and I had to intervene before he would answer Mr Wyand's question), Mr Storey answered *"You will have to ask the designer that question. I personally did not."* He said Mr Kelly showed him *"hundreds of things which I would pass an opinion on to give him some steer on how we should be moving towards our design."*
> Mr Wyand asked Mr Storey why he had said in his witness statement that he carried out the internet research, if it was Mr Kelly. Mr Storey then said: *"We both conducted the research. Mr Kelly did an awful lot of perhaps the donkey work in actually exploring different things that were out there, and together we worked on the design. So, Mr Kelly did do an awful lot of the leg work, but we obviously did a lot of research and looking around to give us, you know, as*

comprehensive an understanding of the market as possible." I note that Mr Kelly's oral evidence was that he did not carry out this research, and that it was Mr Storey who did it.

When asked in cross-examination how the logos which were included in the Brand Document had been picked out of all of the hundreds and hundreds of logos he said he had looked at, Mr Storey originally said: "*it would have been the designer."* He then amended his position again, saying: "*No, we were both, if I can say that, researching, both together and independently, and this is some of the research that I did, and we then worked on it together.... And obviously, this is a, you know, quite frankly, this was months and months of work, so a lot of this is a snapshot of the research that we were doing."* [...]

Again, when asked who had picked the Example Geometric Stag Designs for inclusion in his witness statement, Mr Storey said "*Myself in conjunction with my legal team."* He said: "*I would have picked them from the original work that we had."* When asked if he had selected them from a document that he still had in his possession, relating to searches carried out in 2015, he said that they were picked from "*assorted paperwork that we would have held.... I believe you have seen a lot of the information that we hold and that these were picked out as examples...."*

Again, this contradicts Mr Kelly's oral evidence that he didn't believe he had found those Example Geometric Stag Designs, but thought they were picked by Mr Storey. He originally said "*I'm not sure whether these came from the original research [in 2015] or recently as examples [in 2018],"* but on further questioning confirmed that he did not save any documentary evidence of searches carried out in 2015. Certainly, none have been disclosed.

Mr Storey's oral evidence was that the "Design Research" moodboard collage of photographs was created in 2015. Mr Kelly said it was in 2018, from images which he obtained in 2018. Mr Wyand showed Mr Kelly that Mr Storey had appended that Design Research page to his witness statement with the description: "*Sean put together a collage of images of stags which he could use as inspiration when designing the logo.... Exhibited at page 28 of WS1."* Mr Kelly said he "*didn't believe that Mr Storey meant that is the original. I believe he is saying that is effectively the example."* Of course, that is not Mr Storey's evidence.[41]

Clarke came to the conclusion that "only one of them [could] be telling the truth about how, when, and from what materials" the document was created, and found it "highly improbable" that Kelly would lie to the court about manufacturing it in 2018 if it had actually been created in 2015—even if both Kelly and Storey submitted an "incorrect and misleading description of the document" that they both signed. Clarke also wrote that she didn't believe Storey could have been mistaken about where the information in the document came from, given that it was created in mid–2018 for use in litigation in early 2019.[42]

"For those reasons, in relation to this evidence, I prefer Mr. Kelly's account, and I am driven to the conclusion that Mr. Storey's evidence was untruthfully given," Clarke wrote.[43]

Clarke also found issues with the pencil sketches and design renderings submitted by Kelly and Storey, and said the "the high degree of inconsistency and contradiction between the differing accounts of the role each of Mr. Storey and Mr. Kelly played in the design process" was, in her opinion, "inconsistent with a truthful case of independent creation."[44]

But that alone might not have meant much to the defendants. Clarke wrote that she found it "clear" from oral evidence that Storey had "very little idea of what copyright is and no idea of the difference between copyright and trademarks, even after going through this litigation process." A trademark, as defined by the British government, was "a sign which can distinguish your goods and services from those of your competitors"—differing from a copyright, which the government described as "protect[ing] your work and stop[ping] others from using it without your permission."[45]

Basically, a copyrighted piece of original work could be used as a trademark, but that didn't make a copyright and a trademark the same thing.

"I have no doubt his state of knowledge was worse, not better, in 2015," Clarke wrote. "It may be that he and Mr. Kelly simply thought that [Whyte Bikes' imagery] was a great logo, and that it was one from a company sufficiently removed from their own business not to notice or complain about their copying, or that it did not attract copyright protection. Perhaps they thought that trademark clearance was all that mattered. I cannot know."[46]

Thus, in a storm of confusion, evidence found to be manufactured, and anecdotal accounts deemed untruthful by the court, Rich Energy lost the case.

"I am satisfied on the balance of probabilities that both Mr. Kelly and Mr. Storey have lied about not being familiar with [Whyte Bikes' logo]," Clarke wrote. "I find it more likely than not that they were familiar with it, and that they directly and knowingly copied [it] in designing [the Rich Energy logo]."[47]

When asked for comment about the case outcome by the authors for a *Jalopnik* story, Storey responded via email on May 14:

> We are disappointed with the judgment as we felt the evidence strongly supported us and I know we designed independently
> We intend to appeal
> Unfortunately any case like this is about an opinion of a third party
> Legal matters for our lawyers
> We are focused on growing the business and this will not impact that one bit[48]

The official statement from Rich Energy, which seemed to be written by another person or group of people entirely, was more organized. It read:

Rich Energy are considering to appeal a decision to change their existing logo after a United Kingdom court ruling declared its need to change. The now well-known branding of Rich Energy has been under scrutiny since the brand launched itself as a title sponsor within the global platform of Formula One.

With over a billion people now watching the Rich Energy brand, the potential requirement to change its logo will not change the company's future programs. Whilst the initial judgement is disappointing, and only applies to the United Kingdom, Rich Energy will now focus on its strong sales growth and commitment to delivering its premium product to current and new markets.[49]

Not long after the May 9 ruling became public, Rich Energy tweeted on May 16 that it was ready to return to court for an appeal the next month.

"We are looking forward to meeting @WhyteBikes again in court on the 27th June," the tweet said. "Premium British performance with @rich_energy #business #KO #sport #Competition #richenergy #justice #victory."[50] It was accompanied by a homemade boxing meme, hence the "KO" hashtag.

"Perhaps @WhyteBikes can answer a few questions," a tweet from later that day said. "Truth will emerge #truth #richenergy #performance."[51]

When it was mentioned by a user that Rich Energy did, indeed, lose the court case, the account responded: "Did we? Feel free to review June 27."[52]

The idea of the "truth" emerging ended up being somewhat of a pattern, with Storey actively using it roughly a year later in Twitter arguments about the severity of the COVID-19 pandemic. He discussed the pandemic as a whole and the respective lockdowns put in place to slow the spread of the fatal virus, which infected and killed millions of people worldwide. Some of those arguments, which Storey tweeted from his personal account, included:

@piersmorgan I fully agree the incompetence of #government is staggering. However this is not and never has been a #pandemic. Even despite the gerrymandering of death numbers. Everything about this fiasco a disgrace

Hell to pay when the #truth emerges
—William Storey (@richenergyceo) April 28, 2020[53]

Now the British people are waking up to the fact that @BorisJohnson is a dishonest charlatan, the #truth about the #COVID19 fiasco may yet emerge.

People have been unable to visit dying relatives because of #lockdown policy yet @10DowningStreet staff can flout rules! #facts #UK
—William Storey (@richenergyceo) May 24, 2020[54]

When the truth emerges about the payments from #BigPharma & #BillGates you & @BorisJohnson will need immunity from prosecution not #COVID—19
—William Storey (@richenergyceo) May 25, 2020[55]

Fancy that. Any opinion @piersmorgan and @SadiqKhan ? You have advocated destroying #CivilLiberties #jobs and #freedom over an illness that is actually killing vastly less people than #flu. Imbeciles.

#truth starting to emerge at last. #lockdown is the killer! @maitlis @afneil
—William Storey (@richenergyceo) July 6, 2020[56]

The above are just a small selection of Storey's tweets throughout 2020 about the pandemic, which he often referred to as a "scamdemic" or "coronabollocks." Some of his other tweets about the virus were more sensational. One from August 26, 2021, said: "Women who are smart enough to have avoided the jab will be in high demand!"[57] Another from August 31, 2021, added, with original formatting intact: "In 1945 millions of Germans retrospectively claimed they did not support Nazi policies. How long will it be before millions in the U.K. sheepishly claim they never really supported experimental medicine & lockdown restrictions Spineless & brainless sheep are facilitating fascism."[58] Interestingly, neither of these two tweets contained any hashtags.

Haas, as it often did, declined to comment on the situation with Whyte Bikes. But while Haas always remained quiet, Rich Energy always remained the exact opposite. The company Twitter account was still on the subject of Whyte Bikes on May 24, 2019, when it tweeted a photo of Theresa May, then the Leader of the Conservative Party and Prime Minister of the United Kingdom. May announced her resignation that day, saying: "It is, and will always remain, a matter of deep regret to me that I have not been able to deliver Brexit."[59] May, who served as Prime Minister from July 2016 through July 2019, was in tears, her face drooped into a painful frown.

Rich Energy was in more of a laughing mood. Its resignation-day tweet, accompanied by the photo of May, read:

@theresa_may after finding out her next role is running small UK bike company @WhyteBikes

We feel her skill set perfectly suited to the role and will improve the business!#TheresaMay #farewell #newjob #PM[60]

"Boating in Cannes with @rich_energy #Cannes2019 #richenergy #yacht," Rich Energy tweeted a few days later on May 28. Attached was a video of a boat with a large yacht in the background.[61]

The company Twitter account was still talking about the court case on June 1, tweeting: "[Whyte Bikes] admitted they knew about us for 2 years before saying anything and we registered exclusively around the world and in UK [sic] with no objections including all trademarks. We would not invest in a copied logo. Saw us become big and now want money. Disgraceful but let's see the outcome!"[62]

One of the outcomes was that less than a month after Clarke's May 9 judgment, the infringing Rich Energy logo was gone from the Haas F1 race cars ahead of the Canadian Grand Prix. But it wasn't because of the court case, Rich Energy tweeted on June 6, 2019—it was because Rich Energy wanted the team to be able to avoid the extra media attention that weekend.

"We have asked our partners @HaasF1Team to remove stag element from car this weekend," the tweet said. "Whilst we own the stag trademarks & registrations worldwide Inc [sic] Canada we don't want any media circus for team whilst we contest baseless case with @WhyteBikes & win. #richenergy #CanadianGP #F1."[63] Rich Energy never beat that so-called baseless case in court.

A report from the *Motorsport Network* at the time said while the Rich Energy logos appeared on the Haas F1 cars on the Thursday before the Canadian Grand Prix, set to take place on Sunday, June 9, they were removed overnight.[64]

The cars thus appeared on track without the stag head for the opening Canadian Grand Prix practice session on Friday. The quick fix left a gaping black hole down the slender front nose of the car—a gap obvious enough that anyone seeing the car for the first time would know something was off, but they wouldn't be able to pinpoint just what. The "Rich Energy" branding, in word form, remained.

"We were told [that] when we need to change something, they will tell us," Steiner was quoted by the *Motorsport Network* and other outlets as saying. "For sure, we check that everything is OK, and we are doing everything they tell us. We don't have a problem with the logo, Rich Energy has a problem with the logo. So, I don't know if they need to change it or if there is another solution."[65]

Former Haas employees told the authors anyone who's worked in Formula One—or motorsport—long enough has done last-minute sponsor erasure, whether it be taping over logos on team clothing or removing them from the cars like the Haas team did.

The order to remove the logos from the car at the Canadian Grand Prix "was weird," one former Haas employee said. "But when we're at the race, we don't really have time to think about these kinds of things."[66]

"We have to finish the car, and that's quite a busy thing," they continued. "So we're just told to peel it off, and we peel it off. We didn't ask why. Of course, there was talk about it after the session, but we'd been told to peel it off so we did. If they want to tell us, they will tell us."[67]

Luckily for Rich Energy, the logo removal wasn't the biggest event at the 2019 Canadian Grand Prix. Ferrari driver Sebastian Vettel crossed the finish line first that weekend, marking the first time that season that a

Mercedes driver hadn't won the race. (Before then, Valtteri Bottas won two of the first six races, while Lewis Hamilton claimed the other four.)

But Vettel didn't keep that win. In the back half of the race, he exited the track surface in a turn and came back on as Hamilton closed in on his lead, squeezing Hamilton toward the wall as he did.

"He just came on the track so dangerously," Hamilton radioed to his team afterward.

"Yeah, copy, Lewis, we're on it," the team radioed back.

The stewards—Formula One's term for "officials" or "referees"—took nearly 10 laps to decide what to do, but they eventually handed Vettel a controversial five-second penalty to be added to his finish at the end of the race. The penalty was enough to knock him below Hamilton, who crossed the line roughly 1.4 seconds back. Vettel wound up second in the final finishing order despite the opposite being true on track.[68]

Afterward came the real drama, overshadowing anything Rich Energy could have stirred up that day: In a show of protest so often missing in Formula One, Vettel ran in and swapped the first- and second-place signs in front of his and Hamilton's race cars in the parc fermé after the race.[69] Vettel's car wasn't even parked there at the time of the switch, since the *Motorsport Network* quoted him as saying he "didn't really want to join anything that was happening" out of anger.[70]

The iconic display of pettiness was later immortalized in a "diecast" featuring an empty parking spot and the sign with the "1" on it, along with the shadow of Hamilton's winning car stretching across the ground.[71] Thus, Rich Energy didn't get its normal spotlight that weekend—even if it would have during one with less drama.

"Fly high with @rich_energy and @castleairltd," a tweet from the Rich Energy account read the day of the race. "Premium British performance #givesyouhorns #richenergy #FLYHIGHER #F1."[72]

The tweet featured a photo of a black helicopter with a gold Rich Energy logo. The photo was the same one the account had used in at least one other tweet, dated nearly two years earlier on November 22, 2017. Given that most of Rich Energy's other tweets were deleted, it was impossible to tell how many more times it might have been used.

⋆　⋆　⋆

The day after the Canadian Grand Prix—the first of several races without the stag head on the Haas F1 race cars—Rich Energy was back on Twitter. This time, the company was tweeting directly at Whyte Bikes.

"Enjoy the free PR while you can guys," the June 10, 2019, tweet said. "Those with an IQ higher than their age realise you are Mickey Mouse. Oh how we will laugh in due course. We are actually investing money in

F1 whilst you are investing zero. Total parasites who knew about us for 2 years before piping up #F1."[73]

By that point, Rich Energy's feud with Whyte Bikes had become widely public. It was then when *Top Gear* presenter Chris Harris got involved in the discussion—conveniently on Rich Energy's favorite platform. Harris quote-tweeted Rich Energy's "Mickey Mouse" post, offering some advice: "Hmmm @HaasF1Team You might want to disassociate from this bunch."[74]

"You do low rent videos in your bio," the account spat back, referencing Harris' Twitter biography section describing himself as doing "low-rent videos" about cars. "Analysis on a similar level. In the way your show does not support UK car companies like @UltimaCars (faster than @Porsche that you fawn over) it is entirely in keeping that you would disparage us. #F1 #ultima #TopGear #richenergy #FactCheck."[75]

"If I did ever see a can of @rich_energy in real life, which does seem unlikely, I think I'd probably not buy it," Harris tweeted. "I will however buy an @WhyteBikes this summer. Don't like bullies."[76]

Storey would go on to tweet Harris rather compulsively from his personal account. Sometimes he tagged Harris in random "news" updates, such as one from April 12, 2020: "The Rich Energy Haas F1 car at #MonacoGP in 2019. Shame 2020 cancelled but we expect to be there in 2021. #RichEnergy #F1 #British #energydrink @harrismonkey @JeremyClarkson @tiff_tv @GoodwoodRRC."[77]

Sometimes he responded to Harris' tweets, such as one where Harris wore a protective face mask during the height of the COVID-19 pandemic in 2020:

> Embarrassing on many levels. What a poodle to propaganda. I doubt you have even looked at the numbers to realise that not only is the risk infinitesimal but masks don't work either! Thanks for vindicating my analysis last summer. @simondolan @hughosmond @ClarkeMicah @mattletiss7[78]

Or one where Harris posted a photo of his Porsche in January 2021:

> Buy something much faster & connected to the road that is #British.I suggest an #Akula from @GinettaCars or even latest offerings from @Noblecars or @UltimaCars all of which absolutely destroy the poseur machine from Stuttgart. More fun, faster & not a ubiquitous banker chariot[79]

And sometimes Storey, unprompted, posted photos of other cars and tagged Harris in them:

> 600 BHP & under 1200 Kg. Unlike the modern idiot proof sports cars driven by bankers these are a little lairy on the limit. The likes of @harrismonkey & @jasonplato could learn a thing or two. A can of #RichEnergy could rev them up #Supercar #SundayMorning #Driving #MAGA #200mph
> —William Storey (@richenergyceo) Nov. 29, 2020[80]

British owned. And made in Leicester. Phenomenal. Isn't that right @harrismonkey
#British #Manufacturing #UK #UltimaRS #Supercars #200mph #Elite
—**William Storey (@richenergyceo) Jan. 2, 2021**[81]

In the November tweet with the "MAGA" hashtag, Storey posed in the photo he posted while wearing one of U.S. president Donald Trump's "Make America Great Again" campaign hats.[82] Before Trump's November 2016 election victory over Hillary Clinton, remember, Storey bet on him winning in a LinkedIn blog but claimed not to be cheering him on:

> As of tonight you can get odds of 5/2 with British bookmakers on a Trump win which is a staggering return for something that even pollsters would put at a minimum 45% chance. I would also like to clarify that this is what I think will happen not necessarily what I want to happen and I make no judgement on who is the best candidate merely that neither are particularly good.[83]

In just a few years, Storey had evolved from a mere spectator into an all-out fanboy of a politician from a country he did not live in.

* * *

Again on June 10, the Rich Energy account tweeted a photo of a two-page spread titled "Rich Pickings" in British car magazine *Evo*. One full page featured a photo of a sunglass-wearing Storey from the chest up, beard and hair both extending outside of the frame. The other had a roughly 1,050-word article with the tagline: "Upstart energy drink producer and Haas F1 sponsor Rich Energy is rattling cans on the shelves and sensibilities in the paddock. Company founder and CEO William Storey explains why that's a good thing."[84]

The story called Rich Energy a "new kid on the block" that "arrived out of nowhere" with its "enigmatic company founder and CEO, William Storey … stoking a firestorm of criticism, bewilderment, and disbelief from rivals, sections of the media, and from the cynical." It said Storey was "nonplussed by the negative reaction" and "motivated by our detractors."[85] (The story also described Storey as owning "about 100 different cars" over the previous two decades, including a "couple" of original Honda NSX models and a Ferrari F355 that "brimmed with character and remained a work of art at 150 mph."[86] Neither of those were cheap cars.)

In the article, Storey explained his claimed business model: deals with casinos, sports clubs, and independent supermarkets, as well as selling through Amazon. Through "the dogged persistence that the naysayers triggered inside" him, Storey said, Rich Energy was about to expand into two major supermarket chains.[87]

The story described "the deafening sound of feathers ruffling and noses snapping out of joint" in F1 as a result of Storey's nontraditional looks and his crew of "outsiders, non-establishment people."[88] It said Storey's past was "confound[ing] rivals and detractors," but that Storey simply called himself a "serial entrepreneur."[89]

"For the Haas deal, I invested some of my own capital but was joined by several other wealthy individuals who understand the potential of what we're doing with Rich Energy," Storey was quoted as saying. "These are very shrewd guys—otherwise they couldn't have amassed the fortunes that they have—so they have done extreme due diligence on our business proposition and concluded that the risk is worthwhile. The same is true of Haas; their lawyers have examined every fine detail and green-lighted the deal."[90]

"Will doubters remain?" the story in *Evo* concluded. "Of course they will. Yet Storey remains upbeat: 'Watch this space' is his calm appraisal of the situation."[91]

Rich Energy's tweet captioned the photo of the magazine spread: "Interesting article in @evomagazine about @rich_energy growth story taking on @redbull & @MonsterEnergy #richenergy #BetterThanRedBull #f1 #business #BritishGT #givesyouhorns #williamstorey #Boxing #extremesports #entrepreneurlife @Jalopnik @SkySportsF1 @westhamwomen @7RobLee."[92]

In the upper right-hand corner of the two-page spread, just above Storey's head, a disclaimer appeared in all caps but a thin enough font to gloss over if you weren't looking closely: "ADVERTISING FEATURE."[93]

The whole thing was an ad—but not necessarily one to encourage people to buy energy drinks. It was an ad to hammer into readers' minds that, yes, Rich Energy and its CEO were completely and totally legitimate. They had cars and lawyer examinations and big supermarket deals to prove it.

*   *   *

On June 11, the day after the Chris Harris spat, Rich Energy tweeted a video of several yachts. "Boating with @rich_energy #yachts #adventure #ocean #richenergy," the caption read.[94]

Rich Energy and Whyte Bikes returned to court on June 27, 2019, where Rich Energy was sure things would begin to turn around—at least, according to the person behind its Twitter account. But that's not what happened.

Clarke denied Rich Energy's request to appeal the decision, saying the company could further apply with the Court of Appeal by July 18, 2019, if it chose to do so. July 18 was the magic date for a lot of things in regard to the case—most notably, the kill date for the infringing logo, and the date on which that logo would no longer be a valid UK trademark.[95]

Rich Energy was also ordered to: either deliver any infringing products to Whyte Bikes, destroy them, or render them not infringing by August 1,

2019; pay Whyte Bikes 35,416 pounds for the costs of the legal action, not including copyright damages, within two weeks of the order; produce figures for Whyte Bikes showing the full details of money paid or payable to the Haas F1 Team in regards to the Rich Energy sponsorship; and disclose to Whyte Bikes' parent company, ATB Sales, the total number of UK and global sales of Rich Energy the drink, along with the total monetary sums received from those sales.[96] At the time, 35,416 pounds was equivalent to about $45,000 in the United States.

When reached for comment for a *Jalopnik* story regarding the orders via email, Storey responded on June 28, 2019:

> We are pleased with developments in court and are looking forward to the denouement of process which is some way away
> The latest hearing involved the same judge.
> Positive developments
> Rich Energy continues to go from strength to strength[97]

Storey was also asked about how Rich Energy would approach the order to remove its logos from items by July 18 and what the plan would be going forward. He didn't address those questions.

On July 2, 2019, four days after Storey's email, Rich Energy applied for a new UK trademark to replace its former logo.[98] The new image was a set of stag horns with no head.

Despite communicating with the authors regularly during its copyright dispute with Rich Energy in 2019, representatives for Whyte Bikes and ATB Sales did not respond to numerous calls and emails from the authors requesting an interview in mid–2021. Whyte Bikes Managing Director Guy Farrant, who had also been in contact with the authors in 2019, didn't respond to a mid–2021 interview request either. Earlier that year, though, Formula One journalist Thomas Maher reported that Farrant said Rich Energy had not yet paid the 35,416 British pounds it owed in court damages.[99]

Rich Energy was ordered to pay the sum within 14 days of the court order, which was stamped on July 1, 2019. Maher's report about the lack of payment published on January 18, 2021, about a year and a half later.

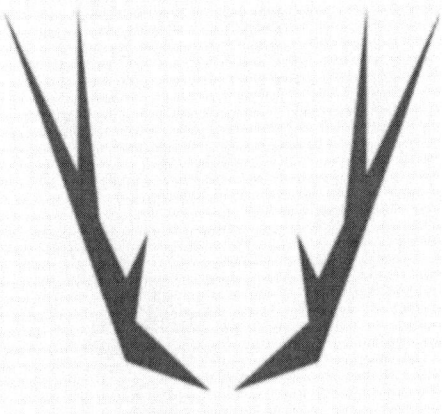

The new Rich Energy logo (UK Intellectual Property Office, trademark No. UK00003411114).

6

A PAIN IN THE HAAS

In a video interview with longtime Formula One journalist Peter Windsor from December 2018, months before Rich Energy's first and only season with Haas, Storey said he and Rich Energy needed "to be very respectful of the way the sport works."

"Obviously, a learning curve for us," Storey told Windsor. "We know what we don't know. We're going to go in and be very keen to be educated within the sport, and we're going to be hopefully as supportive as possible of a team, Haas F1, that we're really, really delighted to be working with."[1]

At the end of the interview, which took place in Rich Energy's home base of Richmond, the screen faded to black. It read: "With thanks to: the Bingham hotel"—the same hotel Rich Energy claimed to be its HQ.

"I wouldn't call them respectful," journalist Luke Smith said in an August 2021 interview with the authors. "I don't think [Storey] was respectful towards Haas at all, particularly with the way it ended. It was very poor form."[2]

* * *

On July 10, 2019, fewer than nine months after the Haas F1 partnership was announced, Rich Energy said it had terminated its contract with Haas "for poor performance."

"We aim to beat @redbullracing & being behind @WilliamsRacing in Austria is unacceptable," the company account tweeted. "The politics and PC attitude in @F1 is also inhibiting our business. We wish the team well #F1 #richenergy."[3]

The notion that Haas would beat Red Bull at the time, or any time in the near term, was something even casual viewers of Formula One would find preposterous. Red Bull was one of the best, while Haas was one of the rest—the latter finishing eighth of 11 in the team standings in 2016, eighth of 10 in 2017, and fifth of 10 in 2018. Haas would go on to finish ninth of 10 at the end of 2019, its cars featuring a gaping black hole where the Rich Energy branding used to be.

Meanwhile, Red Bull finished second in 2016 and third every year that followed through 2019. Each finish was among the best, not the rest, because the best almost always finished amongst each other in Formula One.

The notion of Formula One as "PC," or politically correct, was equally preposterous, given Formula One's historic willful ignorance to the damage its actions caused. On top of that, the contract wasn't even legally terminated. Rich Energy's announcement was apparently news to the Haas team, whose account remained plastered with Rich Energy branding and had, several hours before Rich Energy's tweet, posted photos and videos of team members and drivers in Rich Energy gear. Afterward, Haas' account remained silent.

The day after the original tweet, on July 11, Haas responded with its own Twitter statement. At the time of the tweet, neither Haas nor Rich Energy had responded to the authors' request for comment about the situation. "Rich Energy is currently the title partner of Haas F1 Team," the statement quoted team principal Guenther Steiner as saying. "I cannot comment further on the contractual relationship between our two parties due to commercial confidentiality."[4]

Afterward, the team finally responded to the authors. "We will be issuing no further statements or commenting further following on from the team statement attributed to Guenther Steiner yesterday—posted on our social channels," spokesperson Stuart Morrison said via email.[5]

That same day, Rich Energy spoke out again. But this new statement would become the first notion that Rich Energy, with investors apparently rising in power, was an entity no longer entwined with its bombastic founding CEO William Storey—a Rich Energy with a calmer head, a less knee-jerk approach to everyday situations, and a less politicized existence. As first reported at the time by Thomas Maher of Ireland-based motorsport website *Formula Spy*, Rich Energy—this new, separate Rich Energy—blamed the Haas F1 tweet on "the rogue actions of one individual" in a company statement.[6]

Formula Spy separately reported on July 11 that the July 10 tweet was made by "an employee who was released from the company prior to the tweet," but that it remained on the Rich Energy Twitter page because the company's new majority investors didn't have control over the account. Rich Energy the entity, the statement from July 11 said, was "in the process of legally removing the individual [who posted the tweet] from all executive responsibilities."[7] The statement read:

> The shareholders who own the majority of Rich Energy would like to clarify certain statements that have been circulated in the media from an unauthorised source. We wholeheartedly believe in the Haas F1 Team, its performance,

and the organisation as a whole and we are fully committed to the current sponsorship agreement in place. We also completely believe in the product of Formula One and the platform it offers our brand.

Clearly, the rogue actions of one individual have caused great embarrassment. They may speak for themselves, but their views are not those of the company. The incident is very regrettable; we will not be making further comment on this commercially sensitive matter and will be concluding it behind closed doors. We wish to confirm our commitment to the Haas F1 Team, Formula One, and to thank the Haas F1 Team for their support and patience whilst this matter is dealt with internally.[8]

The individual behind those rogue actions was not named, but both the executive moniker and prior events gave onlookers a good guess at whom it could have been. A report from the *Motorsport Network* that same day backed up the assumption, with unnamed sources describing the tweet as "either written by or authorized by" Storey "without the knowledge of Rich's investors after an apparent difference of opinion."

"The deal is not terminated, and William has no authority to do so," one unnamed source told the *Motorsport Network*. "The investors are trying to clear up the PR mess, but it's business as usual."[9]

The shareholders of Rich Energy UK at the time, as listed by the *Motorsport Network* report, were: Storey; Brandsellers Holdings Limited, listed as an investment-holding company by Companies House as of April 2019; Robert Lee, the soccer player affiliated with both Rich Energy and Storey's former Danieli Style brand; people named Charlie Simpson and Lloyd Tunicliffe; and Neville Weston.[10] The report continued:

It's believed that the same investors are also involved in a separate holding company which is in effect where the power lies.

Former Sainsbury [supermarket]'s boss Justin King, appointed as advisor to Storey and Rich's board of directors in April, is believed to be involved in sorting out the situation.

King's son Jordan, an IndyCar and F2 racer, had announced a sponsorship tie-in with Rich back in April.[11]

Another *Motorsport Network* report from that day, July 11, quoted Steiner as saying that the Rich Energy branding would stick around on the Haas car for that weekend's British Grand Prix at Silverstone Circuit— what would have been considered Rich Energy's "home race."

"They will be on the car this weekend, and then the rest we need to sort out going forward what we're doing," Steiner said. "The commercial agreement doesn't let me talk about it, and I don't want to stir it up any more."[12]

Steiner further added, according to a July 11 story from indie motorsport news site *RaceFans*, that Rich Energy's "surprise" tweet about the contract termination wouldn't draw him into a "war of words."

"It's part of the job," Steiner said about off-track distractions, as quoted by *RaceFans*. "You can do without it, but it's not like I'm staying up at night thinking about it. We get on with our job."[13]

Getting the car right was more important, Steiner said.

"We are being professional about it, and I think I'm known to be professional," *RaceFans* quoted Steiner as saying. "When I can speak, I speak. When I cannot, I don't speak. It's no point to go into a war of words about something. It doesn't upset me. It's just something I need to deal with next week, and I will."[14]

That didn't stop the press from trying to gain answers that weekend. "I remember in that initial press session, we got about halfway through the allotted time, and obviously every single question had been about Rich Energy," *Motorsport Network* journalist Luke Smith told the authors. "The communications manager was like, 'Anyone want to talk about this weekend? We've got Silverstone with Romain and Kevin.'"[15] As had been true for much of the Rich Energy saga, racing came second to the off-track spectacle.

* * *

But the spectacle didn't end there. Also during the 2019 British Grand Prix, Rich Energy shareholder Neville Weston—who received an apparent letter from Haas saying the team understood Weston was "seeking to take control of the company away from Mr. Storey"—spoke to *Racer* about the situation. Weston was on site to meet with Haas, *Racer* reported.[16]

"We were in the process of stepping in as shareholders to take better control of the company," Weston told *Racer*. "We weren't very happy with how things were being managed, handled, and financial reporting—things that William and the other director were personally responsible for." The other director at the time was listed by Companies House as Zoran Terzic.

"We were working amicably with William to say, 'Look, you need to move out, you're not doing this well, you're not doing that well,'" Weston added. "He *was* playing ball. We were on a shareholder call on Wednesday, he didn't show up on the call to discuss these items, and then during the call, [he] sent out this thing saying: 'I'm terminating the Haas contract.' We knew straight away that was him going rogue, so we then had to deal with that situation."[17]

Weston told *Racer* that Storey hadn't started the process of terminating the deal with Haas, and that his reasons for ending it—performance, mainly—weren't part of the contract. Weston called it "lunacy."

"There's facts and there's what he says," Weston told *Racer*. "I want to be really clear: Until we get an injunction or get him shut out of those social media accounts that he's set up and has the passwords to, he's probably going to keep doing this stuff for a while, and they are not the views of Rich Energy and the majority shareholders, which is why we made that statement. [Haas] just want[s] to run a race team. They don't need this. It's embarrassing. They've been a class act, is the only way I can describe it—including Gene, who just says: 'I get it, sort it out.'"[18]

Weston also reminded *Racer* that Rich Energy and Haas were "only six months into … a long-term arrangement."

"It started really well and then it went a bit wobbly, but we've just got to get it back on track," Weston said. "As you can see, it's not canceled. We are still on the side of the car. I am sat here today in a very amicable relationship with Haas, which will be continuing. All that's happened is we took steps to remove a CEO who didn't like it and has gone nuts."[19]

After the publication of a story about the investors' condemnation of this rogue employee, Storey, apparently acting on his own at that point, responded to a request for comment from *Jalopnik* via email. The response read, with all applicable formatting and grammar, as such:

> I am the CEO and founder of Rich Energy and control the board of directors and all assets.
> I also control more than 51% of the shares
> There has been an attempted coup of my position by a handful of shareholders who have a cosy relationship with Red Bull and Whyte bikes.
> These shareholders led by Neville Weston and Charlie Simpson have failed in their efforts.
> All key stakeholders support the current strategy of the UK's premium energy drink Rich Energy[20]

Rounding out that particular Thursday was yet another tweet from the official Rich Energy account, which called the events of the day an "attempted palace coup." The tweet, seemingly written by Storey, was a quote from Storey:

> @rich_energy CEO @_williamstorey has commented "The ludicrous statement by minority shareholders cosy with @redbull & @WhyteBikes is risible. Their attempted palace coup has failed. I control all of the assets of @rich_energy & have support of all key stakeholders" #RichEnergy[21]

On July 12, 2019, the Rich Energy Twitter account—which seemed to be under Storey's control, as it had the whole time—gave more insight into what might be going on by posting a screenshot that appeared to show a letter from a legal firm representing the Haas F1 Team. The apparent letter was from the Ebury Partnership on behalf of Haas, and it was addressed to Neville Weston, listed by Companies House as a minority shareholder in Rich Energy. The most recent Companies House documentation available at the time, which was from 2018, listed Storey as holding 64 of 100 shares in Rich Energy while Weston held two.[22]

The apparent letter to Weston from Haas' legal representation, Jeremy Courtenay-Stamp, referenced an email from Weston to Steiner but didn't mention what the email was about. It continued:

> Our clients' position vis a vis Rich Energy Limited and Mr Storey is as set out in the open letters, copies of which are attached.
>
> We understand that you are seeking to take control of the company away from Mr Storey, the current CEO. If that comes to pass, then our client will be happy to engage in without prejudice conversations with you but they will need to see clear and unambiguous evidence that Mr Storey has been removed as a director of the company and that a new CEO has been validly appointed in his place.
>
> Given the information available at Companies House on Rich Energy Limited, including its shareholder base, we are somewhat at a loss as to how you will be able to wrestle control of the company from Mr Storey.
>
> Furthermore there is the outstanding claim for damages against the company for copyright infringement in relation to its logo so that our clients are rightly concerned about the solvency/ongoing viability of the company.[23]

"The actual situation..." the July 12 tweet from the Rich Energy account read, hashtagging "#f1," "#RichEnergy," "#williamstorey," and "#nobull." The tweet also tagged accounts for: the Haas F1 Team; Formula One; the Goodwood Road and Racing enthusiast channel; military-operations veteran Phil Campion; Scottish company Kynoch Boxing; another boxing entity whose account was later deleted; Australian professional boxer Lucas Browne; and *Top Gear's* Chris Harris.[24]

Haas, when asked about the apparent letter posted to the Rich Energy Twitter account for a *Jalopnik* story—if it was legitimate, if the team would send copies of the "open letters" relating to Haas' position toward Rich Energy and Storey or summarize what was in them, and whether the team sought legal counsel in relation to the Twitter termination claim from the Rich Energy account—responded as usual.

"We will be issuing no further statements or commenting further following on from the team statement attributed to Guenther Steiner yesterday—posted on our social channels," Haas' head of communications, Stuart Morrison, wrote via email.[25]

But that was just the tip of Rich Energy's troubles on that particular Friday. On July 12, just over two weeks after Rich Energy was ordered to pay Whyte Bikes more than 35,000 pounds in court, Whyte spokesperson Ross Patterson shared an update from the company with the authors via email.

"On 27 June 2019 the High Court in London made various orders against the Defendants, Rich Energy, William Storey and Staxoweb," the update read. It continued:

> One of the orders was that they should pay to Whyte (ATB Sales) costs total-ling £35,416 by 11 July 2019. The Defendants have failed to pay any of the costs award[ed]. Each of the Defendants is jointly liable for the whole amount of costs awarded. ATB will now be forced to take appropriate action to recover the costs that they have been awarded. This may include applications to the Court to wind up both Rich Energy and Staxoweb and to petition for the bank-ruptcy of Mr. Storey.[26]

Storey already had plenty of experience with potentially being wound up, as evidenced by his previous business endeavors. When asked across multiple emails on July 12 about owing Whyte Bikes roughly $45,000, the apparent letter posted to the Rich Energy Twitter account, and whether he was running the account, Storey didn't respond.

That same day, Haas driver Romain Grosjean tore the Rich Energy–stamped front wing off of his race car in a bizarre crash while exiting pit lane during the first practice session of the British Grand Prix weekend.

"This, by the way, officially, is Romain Grosjean's worst season in For-mula One," one commentator said on the broadcast. "Just two 10th-place finishes in the opening nine races to show for his troubles. And this, prob-ably a new low in this worst season."

"How did he allow that to happen?" another responded. "This is the kind of stuff you'd see in Formula Ford, or not even."[27] (Formula Ford, an entry-level open-wheel division for young drivers, was often seen as a step up from go-karting.)

On July 13, Rich Energy got back into the conversation on its favorite platform, tweeting a photo of a Haas F1 car with the caption:

> @HaasF1Team love @rich_energy so much (we don't blame them as #betterthanredbull) they have kept our brand livery on the car even after we sacked them for poor performance! #RichEnergy #F1 #BritishGP2019 #business #worldclass #onyerbike #nobull[28]

Then came July 14, when the world learned that Haas F1 had finally fought back against Rich Energy. It happened just a few days earlier behind the scenes, where Haas seemed to prefer to keep things. But it didn't stay behind the scenes for long.

"Just to disavow people of lies from @HaasF1Team please see below," the Rich Energy account tweeted that day, posting an apparent letter from Haas' legal representation, Courtenay-Stamp, to Storey. "@rich_energy terminated the agreement as we said. The team have accepted contrary to their public denial. They were complicit in trying to oust CEO William Storey who even gave them a £35m personal guarantee #truth."[29]

The apparent letter was dated July 11, 2019. It read:

Dear Sirs

Sponsorship Agreement dated 21 October 2018 as amended by first amendment Agreement dated as of 6 February 2019 ("the Sponsorship Agreement") between Haas Formula LLC ("Haas") and Rich Energy Limited ("Rich Energy")

We act on behalf of Haas who have forwarded to us a copy of an email from William Storey, the CEO of Rich Energy, to Guenther Steiner, the Team Principal of our client.

For your ease of reference we are attaching a copy of that email.

In this email Mr Storey purports to terminate the Sponsorship Agreement with immediate effect. This amounts to a repudiatory breach of the Sponsorship Agreement by Rich Energy.

Our client has elected to accept this repudiatory breach and claim damages.

The first date on which Rich Energy would have been entitled to terminate the Sponsorship Agreement lawfully is 1 December 2022. Our client is therefore entitled to recover by way of damages from Rich Energy the £6m currently outstanding (for which an invoice has already been issued) as well as the sums due for the "Term Year" 2020, £14m and for the "Term Year" 2021, £15m thus a total of £35m.

For the sake of completeness, we deal with two points raised by Mr Storey in his email. The first is that he alleges "major issues with our agreement and the performance of the team." There is no basis in the Sponsorship Agreement on which Rich Energy are entitled to terminate the Agreement based on any performance criteria of the Haas F1 team.

Mr Storey also refers to the Rich Energy stag logo being removed for the F1 race in Canada. As Rich Energy and Mr Storey are well aware, the stag device was removed following a decision in the High Court in London that Rich Energy and Mr Storey had breached the copyright in this logo belonging to ATB Sales Limited. The suggestion that our client wrongly removed the infringing logo is therefore wholly unsupportable.

We are instructed that if payment of the sum of £35m is not received by way of cleared funds within 14 days of the date of this letter, our client will consider itself at liberty to issue proceedings without further notice.

In the view of the fact that the British Grand Prix is imminent, our client is not proposing to remove the Rich Energy branding from, inter alia, its cars unless instructed so to do and only then to the extent reasonably practicable. For the avoidance of any doubt, out [sic] client's not removing the Rich Energy branding shall in no matter constitute an affirmation of the Sponsorship Agreement subsequent to Rich Energy's repudiatory breach referred to above.

Given the seriousness of this matter, we would urge you to take appropriate legal advice at the earliest opportunity.[30]

When asked for confirmation of the letter's legitimacy by the authors for a *Jalopnik* story, Storey responded via email:

Yes it is from Haas lawyers
100 percent
Their complicity in seeking to remove me as CEO (a position I of course still hold) is wholly unacceptable conduct given I did the deal with them and I gave personal guarantee.
It is like me seeking the removal of Gene Haas! Disgraceful
For the record I remain CEO , the largest shareholder and have the support of the board of Rich Energy.[31]

Storey directly forwarded the authors the email from Courtenay-Stamp and the Ebury Partnership to show its legitimacy, and the PDF with the letter on behalf of Haas—as the letter mentioned—included Storey's original email to Steiner. Storey forwarded his email to Steiner individually as well.

It was dated July 10, which was the same day that the Rich Energy Twitter account announced its termination of the Haas partnership. The email recapped what the Rich Energy account said earlier in the week: that the company would terminate the Haas deal due to poor performance, and, in a reason that wasn't tweeted, for removing its stag logo from the Haas cars after the Whyte Bikes ruling. The email from Storey appeared to have an empty subject line. It read:

Dear Guenther
I am very sorry to be writing this and I do so with a heavy heart.
There are some major issues with our agreement and the performance of the team.
Further as you are aware I am facing internal issues from a number of shareholders who advocate a more corporate approach to the business rather than the buccaneering spirit with which I have created it.
They seek to remove me as CEO from my own company.
They will fail.
They are overplaying their hand but unfortunately are the sort of more corporate folk welcomed in F1.
I understand you support this move and that I am persona non grata with the team. This saddens me
Obviously we want to beat Red Bull so being behind Williams was a bit embarrassing at the home of Red Bull.
Further removing our stag logo unilaterally in Canada when not required undermined us to the world's media.
We have paid for 10 races and Silverstone is the 10th.
I understand I am unwelcome.
I genuinely think you are a great guy but I am in an invidious position with my agitating shareholders using F1 as the gun to my head.
I will not be threatened in my own business.
As such as the largest shareholder, founder and CEO of the company and

speaking for 100% of the board of directors I am terminating our contract as
title sponsor with the team.

I wish you the very best for the future[32]

"For sure, he wasn't welcome in Formula One, because Formula One
is quiet," one former Haas employee told the authors. "There is some shady
business. Always was, always will be. But they try to keep the picture of
professionalism—top level of motorsport, we are pros, we are gentlemen."[33]

A minute after being thanked for forwarding the letter from
Courtenay-Stamp and the Ebury Partnership along, Storey emailed the
authors back.

"Maybe you can credit that I am consistently telling it as it is and
Haas and the minority shareholders are not!" he said.[34]

* * *

Haas' letter and Storey's email detailed a side of the Haas-Rich Energy
partnership that had been a mystery since it was announced in October
2018—both in terms of the financials and the working relationship the two
had. Those financials were something neither Haas nor Rich Energy would
discuss over the course of their partnership, even if the uncertainty of how
much Rich Energy was actually paying to be a "title partner" for the team
created even more doubt about the legitimacy of the pairing.

Rich Energy, you'll remember, was shown on official Companies
House documents as having 581 pounds in the bank in 2017, and many
watching the Formula One partnership unfold questioned its very existence.[35] Storey, you'll also remember, called that figure of 581 pounds
"irrelevant" during a phone interview with the authors[36]—adamant as
ever that his brand was legitimate and its financials were strong enough
to play on the world stage, where teams operated on budgets ranging from
$44 million to $500 million per year.[37] It was hard to see how those numbers added up, and neither Haas nor Rich Energy would help the public do
the math.

But once the legal letter from Haas became public, less than a year
into their partnership, that all changed. The letter said this energy-drink
company from Britain—whose past was so murky, distribution so limited, and financials so perplexing that it became hard to come up with
synonyms for "mysterious" just a few months into reporting on its jaunt
on open-wheel racing's biggest stage—agreed to give the Haas F1 Team 14
million pounds, or $17.6 million, for the brand placement during the 2020
race season, and 15 million pounds, or roughly $18.9 million, for 2021.[38]
(Rich Energy never made it to those seasons.)

That was a fraction of the sponsorship money powering the bigger teams at the time—such as the Mercedes-AMG Petronas deal estimated at $75 million each year by *Forbes* and *Formula Money*, an outlet covering the business of Formula One, or the Ferrari-Philip Morris relationship, said to be around $50 million annually at the time.[39] But roughly $20 million per year was still a lot of cash to throw at two race cars, especially for a young and mysterious company like Rich Energy.

Then, there were the peeks behind the PR facade Haas tried to build as Rich Energy tore it down tweet by tweet, courtesy of the brief legal exchange between the two.

In addition to the spiral of Storey's email illegitimately terminating the partnership—from the empty subject line to the performance claims, the discussion of "internal issues" with shareholders going against his "buccaneering spirit," and the insistence that those seeking to remove him as CEO would fail—there were the seemingly false claims about the stag logo at the Canadian Grand Prix earlier that year. "Further removing our stag logo unilaterally in Canada when not required undermined us to the world's media," Storey wrote, referring to the overnight logo removal during the race weekend as a result of the Whyte Bikes court judgment.[40]

After mentioning the court loss, the letter from Haas' legal representation pushed back: "The suggestion that our client wrongly removed the infringing logo is therefore wholly unsupportable."[41]

Haas had a point. Storey's email didn't sync with the narrative from Rich Energy during the race weekend, which was that it was the company's decision—not Haas'—to remove the logo. If we revisit Rich Energy's verbatim tweet from June 6, three days before the race, it read: "We have asked our partners @HaasF1Team to remove stag element from car this weekend. Whilst we own the stag trademarks & registrations worldwide Inc [sic] Canada we don't want any media circus for team [sic] whilst we contest baseless case with @WhyteBikes & win. #richenergy #CanadianGP #F1."[42]

Storey, whose reputation for exaggerations and mistruths on the record had already been established, could be telling the truth in only one of these instances: either when the Rich Energy account said the removal of the logo was the company's decision, or when he claimed in the termination email that it was Haas' decision. The latter would mean that the person behind the account, always believed to be Storey, simply posted that the removal was to avoid a "media circus" in an attempt to partially save face. The former would mean that Storey and Rich Energy were under Haas' orders.

The apparent letter from Haas claimed Rich Energy's "termination" to be a breach of contract between the two entities, as Rich Energy wasn't contractually allowed to end the deal until December 1, 2022. It also said performance expectations weren't in the sponsorship agreement, thus weren't a basis for terminating the partnership.

But the July 11 letter said Haas accepted the breach and wanted to collect 35 million pounds in damages, or $44 million, within two weeks.[43] That made Rich Energy's $45,000 debt to Whyte Bikes—which wasn't paid by its deadline, according to Whyte Bikes, and which Storey didn't respond to a request for comment about—look minuscule.

* * *

Just as the letter from Haas' legal representation about Rich Energy's "repudiatory breach" of the partnership said, Haas ran the Rich Energy paint scheme and branding at the British Grand Prix on Sunday, July 14—the same day the Rich Energy account posted the photo of the letter for all of Twitter to see.

On the first lap of the race, Haas drivers Romain Grosjean and Kevin Magnussen went through the fifth turn at Silverstone Circuit side by side, making contact with each other and puncturing their tires. They both staggered back to the pits for new tires and returned to the track in the final two running positions, but the new shoes ultimately didn't make much of a difference. "Magnussen was called back to the pits after completing six laps and Grosjean after completing nine laps, and both were subsequently retired with accident damage," the official Haas race recap said.[44]

Grosjean and Magnussen were two of the three drivers who retired from that race, all of whom were listed at the bottom of the final finishing order.[45] The ordeal served as the backdrop for team principal Guenther Steiner's assertion that his drivers were "fucking idiots" in Netflix's *Drive to Survive*.[46]

Rich Energy was quick to comment on the situation with another homemade meme—this one featuring Storey, and likely made by him as well.[47] It pictured him driving a milk float designed to look like a Haas car.

A milk float is, by the British definition, a small electric vehicle used for delivering milk to people's homes—the last thing anyone would want their race car in the world's most prestigious open-wheel series to be called, let alone by the CEO of a company whose name was all over that race car.

With the meme, Storey was building on his own running joke. Just days earlier, the *Sun* said it "tracked down Storey" for his take on the Rich Energy–spurred contract termination.[48]

"We terminated them," Storey said, as quoted by the *Sun* on July 11. "Unfortunate but logical decision in light of events."[49]

He then got his signature Red Bull mention into the conversation, telling the *Sun*: "Haas [are] nice people, but the car is going backwards. We are a superior product to Red Bull. A milkfloat at [the] back of [the] grid [is] a disaster for us. End of."[50]

Rich Energy
@rich_energy

Follow

Great start boys
@HaasF1Team #BritishGP #HaasF1
#richenergy #milkfloat

6:22 AM - 14 Jul 2019

1,197 Retweets 4,900 Likes

Storey's infamous milk float tweet (Twitter).

Steiner called the British Grand Prix "a very disappointing race for us," adding: "I'm just stating the obvious here. The best that our drivers could bring to the battle was a shovel—to dig the hole we're in even deeper. We need to go back, regroup, and see what we do in [the] future."[51]

When asked for comment on the latest letter and given the opportunity to verify its legitimacy or illegitimacy for a story, Haas spokesperson Morrison responded even more succinctly than usual on July 15:

Hi Alanis

No comment.

Regards,
Stuart M.[52]

Steiner, though, had plenty to say to reporters. When asked by the *Motorsport Network* during the 2019 British Grand Prix weekend if he thought the Rich Energy saga hurt the Haas' team's image, Steiner basically said what he always had: that Rich Energy's drama wasn't Haas' drama, even if it was.

"What have we done wrong?" multiple outlets, including the *Motorsport Network,* quoted Steiner as saying on July 13 during the race weekend.

"How can you damage something if we don't do anything wrong? You can think [it's] damage, but I don't think we are damaged. It's not our fight."[53] Steiner went on, as quoted by the *Motorsport Network*:

> "There is a clear line. They pay us for advertising, and we do our job, so therefore I don't think we are damaged as a team, because we have not done anything wrong. We have done everything to the book, so actually it gives us a good reputation, because we didn't react, because we cannot. [...]"
>
> "We are keeping our line, like you do in professional life. If they've got a problem, so be it."[54]

Steiner said during the interview that Haas was "awaiting developments" about the control and ownership of Rich Energy, and alluded to the fact that the deal could end.

"We are discussing now," Steiner said, as quoted by the *Motorsport Network*. "As you can imagine, we are not in control of what they do internally—and neither do we want to be, just to mention that. I don't want any part of that one. Our hands are full."[55]

Steiner mentioned that Rich Energy was "sorting out what is happening there," and that the team of investors who wanted to take over also wanted to continue with the Haas partnership. "That is what we [will] be talking in the next weeks about: how and if we continue with them," Steiner said. "They know they need to agree between them how it is going forward. I have no comment and no knowledge about what is going on there, and I do not need to know anything."[56]

When asked if things were uncomfortable amid the critical tweets from the Rich Energy account, the *Motorsport Network* quoted Steiner as saying it was "not even uncomfortable, because I don't know what is coming next."

"I'm not in control, it's nothing about us," Steiner said. "Well, it is about us. I wouldn't say I don't care, but it is what it is. We will work at it, we will do our best, and what comes out, comes out. We cannot control, and don't want control, as I said before, of what is happening there."[57]

A *RaceFans* report after the British Grand Prix described Steiner as "not interested in the stream of tweets critical of the team posted on title sponsor Rich Energy's social media account."

"I don't really care about that stuff," Steiner was quoted as saying. "If somebody gets on Twitter, you know, there is a point where it's like: I'm over 50 years old, I'm not in kindergarten anymore. There is more problems than that for him [presumably referring to Storey], to be honest. He should focus on that and not on how we start."[58]

On July 16, two days after the British Grand Prix, Rich Energy was gone—apparently. That day, industry site *Formula Money* reported that

Rich Energy had become "Lightning Volt Limited" on Companies House and that Storey was no longer a director or controlling shareholder. The newest controlling shareholder and director was, according to Companies House documents, a man named Matthew Bruce Kell, listed as a resident of England born in 1956.[59]

The documents, dated July 16, confirmed the name change and new power structure. Storey was listed as terminated from his position that same day.[60]

Not long after news stories began to come out about the switch, the Rich Energy Twitter account was back: "William Storey founder of @rich_ energy has sold his majority stake in the legal entity of Rich Energy Ltd to a third party. This was in disgust at conduct of duplicitous minority stakeholders. In the words of @Schwarzenegger he'll be back! #richenergy #F1 #nobull #williamstorey."[61]

Because no story is truly complete without a Terminator quote or tagging oneself in a tweet.

*   *   *

As Rich Energy publicly spiraled, the former Haas F1 employees who spoke to the authors were split on how they felt about their place and future on the team. "No one was really worried about whether we were going to lose Rich Energy," one former employee said. "We knew the team was there without Rich, so we knew it was safe and we were going to carry on without Rich. We never felt like our jobs were at risk, because their contribution wasn't that big."[62]

"There were a few of us going, 'Well, maybe we're being cynical and maybe he has got $100 million tucked away on an offshore account somewhere, or he's got these business partners who we'll never know who they are, funding all of this, and everything's going to be OK,'" another said. "You kind of have to take that stance as an employee: Stop questioning what the people four levels above you are doing, and go, 'Hang on, you've got to trust these guys, and trust that they know what they're doing with this company and that we're still going to get paid every month.' Because that was the biggest thing for us. You do a quick look and you go: 'Are we still going to get paid?' That was one thing that Haas was always very, very good at. We would always pay the invoice, we would always pay the bills."[63]

"We'd hear things and we'd be like, 'Should we worry?'" another said. "Then emails would come rolling in where we'd have to hustle to do our job. It was good that we had our job to distract us, but ultimately it didn't help."[64]

Some of that might have been due to how quickly—and deeply—Rich Energy and Storey intertwined themselves with the Haas team. Whether

Haas wanted it or not, Storey had successfully handcuffed the two together in a synchronized spiral out of control.

YouTuber Stuart Taylor said most sponsors reap the benefits of a partnership with an F1 team without pushing to become a "living, breathing part" of that team. But that wasn't the case with Storey and Rich Energy. "The entire brand was funneled through this one bizarre character, who just seems to be one of the increasing embodiments of this weird post-truth thing that we seem to be living in, where it doesn't matter what you say as long as you have this big personality," Taylor said. "You just say it and stir shit up—let it go into the world, and hope that there is a group of people that clicks with."[65]

Motorsport Network journalist Luke Smith had a similar reaction. "Most title sponsors, they'll write the check, and they get the ads, and it's very obvious what the deal is," he said. "Whereas with Rich Energy, I think Storey maybe expected more from it."[66]

Haas continued to struggle after the end of its Rich Energy era, both on and off the track. The team scored a mere three championship points in 2020 and none at all in 2021, all while bringing in a widely criticized new title sponsor.[67-69] Taylor pegged the chaotic departure of Rich Energy as the moment when Haas began to fall apart.

"I feel like Rich Energy was the beginning of the complete destruction of Haas," Taylor said. "Now [Haas] just seem like people who will chase any dollar on a hook in front of them. I feel like they're going to have to do a lot of work to get themselves back, and it all started with, essentially, partnering up with Rich Energy and seemingly not doing any due diligence."[70]

Smith struck a more somber tone: "Ultimately, there are hundreds of people working for that team, and it's their livelihood. I think that it was a shame to see it end as it did. No matter how skeptical we were, it shouldn't have ended like that."[71]

* * *

This entire chapter happened over the course of seven days: July 10 through July 16. When dealing with Rich Energy, a lot could happen in a week.

7

WHEN YOU MESS
WITH THE BULL

From its 1984 founding onward, Red Bull embedded itself in the international public consciousness.[1]

Many attributed its success to one key factor: marketing.[2] While the full scope of Red Bull's marketing budget was unknown, the brand became effectively entrenched in the world of extreme sports thanks to sponsorships of everything from high-profile Formula One teams to Turkish taekwondo stars, tying Red Bull's name to the adrenaline rush of competition throughout the world.[3] The brand paired that with a popular media house including writers, social media gurus, and videographers worldwide.[4]

Rich Energy, by contrast, appeared to have little more than a website, a Formula One sponsorship, a few social media pages, and a marketing strategy that attempted to capitalize on Red Bull's already-established name—something that became all the more apparent midway through its Formula One season with Haas in 2019.

"Now @redbull are taking William Storey to court," a July 18, 2019, tweet from the Rich Energy account said. "A cynic might see a pattern emerging! #richenergy #betterthanredbull #williamstorey #BusinessIntelligence."[5] The tweet even used one of the trademark infringements Storey and Rich Energy were being sued over: #BetterThanRedBull.

The tweet again included a photo of what appeared to be a legal document with the letterhead of the Business and Property Courts of England and Wales, where Rich Energy had been less than a month earlier for the appeal hearing in the Whyte Bikes case. Upon being sent a screenshot of what the Rich Energy account posted by the authors, a representative from the court confirmed its legitimacy. The photo of the document only had a brief summary of the claim filed by Red Bull against Rich Energy and Storey. It read:

Brief Summary of Dispute

1. The Claimant alleges trademark infringement against the Defendants in relation to their use of signs identical and similar to the Claimant's well known trademarks RED BULL and GIVES YOU WINGS in advertising for energy drinks. The Second Defendant is the CEO and a director of the First Defendant.

Anticipated Issues

1. Subject to any issues being raised by the Defendants, it is anticipated that the following issues will arise in the dispute:

2. Identification of the signs complained of;

3. Whether the Defendants' use of the signs in issue takes unfair advantage of the repute of the Claimant's trademarks; and

4. Joint tortfeasorship.[6]

A "joint tortfeasor" was any of two or more parties being held liable for the same tort, and in this claim, it applied to joint liability between Storey and Rich Energy.

Throughout their long-held "rivalry," Red Bull didn't acknowledge Rich Energy publicly, nor did it have a reason to do so. While Storey said Rich Energy sold "circa 3 million cans" in 2018, *Forbes* reported Red Bull to have sold 6.8 billion cans across 171 countries that year.[7] The company also, according to *Forbes*, had a brand value of $9.9 billion and 12,239 employees as of May 2019.[8] Accordingly, Red Bull had the same approach to branding and social media as any other major company: on its best behavior, with a strict message and adherence to maintaining the brand's image.

Meanwhile, Rich Energy had meager sales and a mystery tweeter behind its bombastic official account—believed to be none other than its CEO, who used that account to battle everyone from his own shareholders to the big-name Formula One team he'd signed a partnership with.

But Rich Energy and Storey always had an obsession with beating their "equal" competitor. The trademark-infringement claim appeared to be the first time Red Bull actually acknowledged their obsession in a way that would eventually become public, either by journalists discovering the paperwork in the court system or by the Rich Energy account immediately posting that paperwork to Twitter. Of course, it was the latter.

The authors asked both Rich Energy and Red Bull for comment for a July 18, 2019, story about Red Bull's trademark claim, and we also asked Red Bull why its claim came in 2019 when Rich Energy had been a Red Bull–fighting Formula One partner since October 2018. Neither responded.[9]

But court documents usually become available eventually, and they

can tell a story even when the parties involved won't. And in the case of
Red Bull and Rich Energy, there was certainly a story to tell. The document
posted by Rich Energy on July 18, 2019, was dated June 11 in the court system. In it, Red Bull accused Rich Energy of infringing upon two of its UK
trademarks regularly: "Red Bull" and "Gives you wings." Those violations,
Red Bull claimed, came from Rich Energy's use of hashtags and slogans
along the lines of: "Forget the wings, Rich Energy gives you horns"; "No
Bull"; "No Bull with Rich Energy"; and #BetterThanRedBull.[10]

The claim came with eight attached exhibits, called annexes, all of
which were deemed confidential by the UK court system. One annex was
mentioned in the claim as such: "The Claimant wrote a letter before action
to the Defendants on 21 March 2019. A copy of this letter is attached at
Annex 8."[11]

No more details about that letter were mentioned in the body of the
claim, but the mere mention of it gave more insight into Rich Energy's
Twitter tactics: Red Bull originally wrote a letter to Rich Energy and Storey on March 21, according to the claim, but the company acted as if the
court case was a new development in its tweet four months later in July.

The claim also said Rich Energy admitted a couple of things in discussions with Red Bull long before the official court action: that the Red
Bull trademarks it was using had a reputation, and that anyone reading
the #BetterThanRedBull hashtag would read it as "Better than Red Bull."[12]
With those admissions, Rich Energy's tweet appeared to be a strange
attempt to control a narrative it had little chance of reeling in.

The full version of the image posted by the Rich Energy Twitter
account was a "Particulars of Claim" document dated June 11, of which
copies were available to purchase through the court system.[13] The document got much deeper into the details of Red Bull's argument—details
Rich Energy never publicized. In it, Red Bull didn't hesitate to point out
how odd a company Rich Energy was.

On the second page, the document described the parties: Rich
Energy, Red Bull, and Storey. The description of Rich Energy began as
such, emphasis added:

> The First Defendant is a company registered in England and Wales under com-
> pany number 09791667. It was incorporated by **the Second Defendant, who
> has described himself as the CEO of the First Defendant on his LinkedIn
> profile**, and who is a director of the First Defendant and has asserted to Com-
> panies House that he is the person with significant control of the First Defen-
> dant, with ownership of more than 50% but less than 75% of the shares of the
> First Defendant.[14]

The second defendant was William Storey.[15] The description of Rich
Energy in Red Bull's claim continued, emphasis added:

The Defendant's Energy Drink appears to be a recent entrant to the energy drinks market and is **not apparently available in shops and has made few sales in the UK. The Claimant has been unable to discover when or where the Defendant's Energy Drink was first available for retail sale in the UK.** Only one of the Claimant's sources of retailer EPOS (electronic point-of-sale) data reports any UK sales of the Defendant's Energy Drink. IRI's Temple Marketplace service, which has a deep coverage within the convenience channel, indicates that **between March 2017 and February 2019 approximately 1,025 cans of the Defendant's Energy Drink were sold with a value of £836.** The total UK Sports & Energy Drink sector unit sales figures from IRI Infoscan for the past 12 were [sic] months were just under 1.3 billion cans, with a value of just over £1.4 billion.[16]

The UK data cited by Red Bull in the case came from IRI Worldwide, an analytics and insights company with a global headquarters in Chicago and locations in more than a dozen other countries. The numbers—that Rich Energy had sold 1,025 cans and made 836 pounds in nearly two years—didn't exactly add up alongside its nearly $20 million annual deal with the Haas team. It also didn't add up to Storey's admissions in court during the Whyte Bikes case, in which he said he believed Rich Energy to have sold "circa 3 million cans" of its drink in 2018 alone.[17] When asked for more details about the data by the authors in June 2020, IRI Worldwide did not provide any.

Red Bull claimed that Rich Energy and Storey infringed upon its "Red Bull" trademark "from a date unknown." That date was at least midway through 2016, according to Red Bull's findings on social media and the few #BetterThanRedBull tweets that weren't deleted by the Rich Energy account after the case. Red Bull also discovered the #BetterThanRedBull hashtag used in "at least" 66 other posts online, all of which were included in a bulleted list in the claim.[18]

Red Bull argued that Rich Energy's use of its trademarks took an unfair advantage of Red Bull's reputation without its permission, given that the "Red Bull" trademark had been "used extensively" since its introduction in 1987—including with the Red Bull Racing and Scuderia Toro Rosso teams in Formula One. In addition, Red Bull claimed, the "Wings" trademark Rich Energy was incorporating into its own marketing had been used extensively by Red Bull in the UK since 1993.[19]

Red Bull claimed the unfair advantage came through the fact that Rich Energy and Storey were trying to "create a link" between their brand and Red Bull "in the mind of the average consumer seeing the phrases complained of." A reputation like Red Bull's "is achieved through extensive investment in marketing," the company said.[20]

The claim said that for Red Bull, marketing costs totaled about 34.4

million euros in 2018 in the UK alone. In 2020 exchange rates, that equaled nearly $39 million in the United States.[21]

Red Bull also listed out when Rich Energy had used variations of "Forget the wings, Rich Energy gives you horns" and "No Bull" on its social media and website, including a time in March 2019 when Rich Energy posted a graphic on Twitter and Facebook. Red Bull claimed that the graphic, which read "No Bull…" in red and blue writing on a black background, was "depicted in the same shades of red and blue and the same font as are used on the original version" of the Red Bull drink can. The claim included a photo of each, where the colors and fonts appeared to match up almost exactly.[22]

That was when Red Bull brought up memories of Rich Energy's trip to court with Whyte Bikes' parent company, which occurred just a few months prior to its claim:

> The Second Defendant is involved as a defendant in Case no. IP-2017-000235, in which proceedings the Defendants were found to have infringed the copyright of ATB Sales Ltd, the claimant in that case, in relation to the stag's head device which forms part of the logo for the Defendants' Energy Drink. In paragraph 22 of his witness statement (as recorded in [42] of the Judgment therein), and his oral evidence, the Second Defendant admitted that he had researched the energy drinks market and cans. This would necessarily have involved the Second Defendant researching the RED BULL Energy Drink, and the Claimant.[23]

In addition to all of its other evidence, Red Bull added another factor into the mix: "On a date unknown to the Claimant but prior to January 2019, the Defendants elected to promote the Defendants' Energy Drink by the sponsorship of a Formula One Team, Haas Formula LLC."[24] Red Bull Racing, one recalls, officially entered Formula One for the 2005 season.

Red Bull said in its claim that it wasn't aware of "every act of trademark infringement committed by the defendants," but that it would "seek relief in respect of each and every such act" at trial. The company had "suffered loss and damage" due to Rich Energy and Storey's acts, the claim said, and allowing them to continue meant Red Bull would "continue to suffer loss and damage."[25]

It's not as if Rich Energy and Storey were unaware of what they were doing, either, Red Bull said. The acts were "carried out knowingly, or with reasonable grounds to know, that they engaged in an infringing activity."

"[Red Bull's trademarks] are well known, and it is inconceivable that the defendants were not aware of them prior to adoption and use of the signs in the manner complained of above—particularly given the research carried out into the energy-drinks market," the claim said. "The use of the [Red Bull trademarks] by the Red Bull Racing and Scuderia Toro Rosso teams would have been apparent to the Defendants when considering whether to become involved with Formula One."[26]

Red Bull's asks in the claim were simple, and not all that different from the requests of Whyte Bikes just a few months earlier: an end to the claimed infringement; the delivery up or destruction of infringing products, materials, articles, and documents in possession or control of Rich Energy and Storey; the deletion of the trademarks from packaging and Rich Energy's website and social media; the disclosure of sums received or receivable by Rich Energy and Storey "as a direct or indirect result of the infringement" of Red Bull's trademarks; the disclosure of the costs incurred by Rich Energy and Storey "in respect to the infringement of" Red Bull's trademarks; and "an order that judgment in this action be publicised at the Defendants' expense, interest, further or other relief, and costs." Red Bull didn't suggest any potential damages.[27]

On July 16, 2019, another document in the Red Bull case was filed—this time, somewhat on behalf of Rich Energy.[28] The document was a three-page order from the court that had to do with the legal firm that advised Rich Energy during the Whyte Bikes trial, Brandsmiths.

Brandsmiths described itself as "one of the UK's leading boutique law firms, specialising in advising brands and entrepreneurs."[29] British chef Gordon Ramsay was included in a testimonial video for the firm, and trial lawyer Thomas St. Quintin was listed as representing Rich Energy as instructed by Brandsmiths in the Whyte Bikes case.[30] No specific lawyer working with Rich Energy during the Red Bull dispute was listed in the document—only Brandsmiths. Brandsmiths also isn't to be confused with Brandsellers Holdings Limited, listed as a shareholder in Rich Energy at the time of the case.

The filed document had to do with the UK's Civil Procedure Rules, and read as such:

UPON READING the Application of the First and Second Defendant's Solicitors, Brandsmiths ("Applicant") made by notice dated 16th July 2019

AND UPON Brandsmiths undertaking forthwith to serve this application on the first and second Defendants in accordance with CPR 42.3(2)(a)

THE COURT DECLARES THAT:

1. The applicant has ceased to be the solicitors of the First and Second Defendants

AND IT IS ORDERED THAT

2. The Application Notice and all evidence filed in support of the Application shall not be released to any other party or any Non-party

3. There be no order for costs

4. The Applicant shall serve a copy of this order on the claimant and pursuant to CPR 42.3the [sic] Applicant shall file Certificates of Service of the order[31]

On its own, that likely sounds very boring, as most legal documents do. But it's the underlying message that brings some intrigue: On July 16, just over a month after Red Bull's claim against Rich Energy got a stamp from the court on June 11, Brandsmiths submitted an application to no longer be the legal representation of Rich Energy and Storey.

Civil Procedure Rule 42.3(2)(a), as mentioned in the order, was categorized by UK law as an "order that a solicitor has ceased to act." It read as such: "A solicitor may apply for an order declaring that he has ceased to be the solicitor acting for a party. Where an application is made under this rule—notice of the application must be given to the party for whom the solicitor is acting, unless the court directs otherwise."[32]

Lexology, a legal-insights website boasting contributors from more than 800 global law firms, called terminating a retainer "an exceptional course of action" and said a solicitor "should think carefully before doing so" in a May 2010 story out of the UK.[33] The story noted a few situations in which a solicitor would want to stop working on behalf of a client, but that they would need to have "reasonable grounds for refusing to act further" such as "if fees are unpaid or instructions cannot be obtained."[34]

As of the story's 2010 writing, it listed several examples of good reasoning for terminating a retainer, including: a "breakdown in confidence," an inability "to obtain proper instructions," a construction of facts that the solicitor does "not consider to be properly arguable," and a "failure by a client … to pay a reasonable sum." Specifically, it said:

> Under Rule 2.01(2) of the code, a solicitor "must not cease acting for a client except for good reason and on reasonable notice." Paragraph 8 of the guidance to Rule 2 provides examples of good reasons: "where there is a breakdown in confidence" or where the solicitor is "unable to obtain proper instructions."
>
> Rule 11(3)(a) of the code informs solicitors that "you must not construct facts supporting your client's case or draft any documents relating to any proceedings containing any contention which you do not consider to be properly arguable." […]
>
> Under Section 65(2) of the Solicitors Act 1974, a failure by a client within reasonable time to pay a reasonable sum on account of costs of contentious business is a "good cause whereby the solicitor may, upon giving reasonable notice to the client, withdraw from the retainer."[35]

The story said the application notice and its evidence should be served to the client, not everyone involved in the legal action, "as this may injure the client." The order granting that termination is then served to every party and filed, it said—hence why the order from the court said that "the Application Notice and all evidence filed in support of the Application shall not be released to any other party or any non-party," and why the order was publicly available but not the application by Brandsmiths.[36]

The authors contacted Brandsmiths multiple times in 2021 to ask about the situation, but the firm never responded.

Nearly four months after Red Bull's claim was submitted to the Business and Property Courts of England and Wales, a Tomlin order—essentially, a settlement—got an official stamp from the court on October 3, 2019.[37] It was the fourth and final public document from the case between Red Bull and Rich Energy, and it opened as such, with emphasis added:

UPON the Application of the Claimant dated 27 August 2019 for Judgment in Default of Service and Filing of the Defence

AND UPON **the Defendants failing to file at Court and to serve on the Claimant a Defence**

AND UPON the Parties reaching an agreed settlement in relation to these proceedings set out in the agreement identified in the schedule hereto

AND UPON hearing **Jacqueline Reid, Counsel for the Claimant** and **William John Storey representative for the Defendants**[38]

Storey, it appeared, had represented himself.

As of July 2020, the UK government's website listed potential reasons for representing oneself as: "you think it's better to talk directly to the judge, jury, or magistrates yourself" or "you cannot afford to pay legal fees."[39]

The five-page Tomlin order said that by 4 p.m. on October 15, 2019, Rich Energy and Storey would be ordered to cease the infringement of both trademarks that Red Bull filed its claim about, particularly the phrases and hashtags: "Forget the wings, Rich Energy gives you horns"; "No Bull…"; "No Bull with Rich Energy"; and #BetterThanRedBull.[40] By that same time and date, Rich Energy and Storey were required to destroy all advertising or promotional material in their possession that was deemed infringing, as well as delete every infringing element on their website and social media accounts.[41]

Rich Energy also owed Red Bull money, according to the Tomlin order—25,000 British pounds. The first 5,000 pounds was due on October 21, 2019, another 10,000 pounds was due on January 2, 2020, and the final 10,000 pounds was due on February 1, 2020.[42] That was small change for Red Bull, a nearly $10 billion company at the time.[43]

*   *   *

By the middle of October, all of Rich Energy's tweets were gone.[44] The company joined Twitter in November of 2015, meaning four years of stolen images and stolen phrases appeared to have been canned in one swift movement.

"For those asking we have deleted all tweets up to beginning [sic] of October due to a legal agreement with a competitor," the account wrote on October 16, the day after Rich Energy's deadline to get rid of all of its infringing posts and marketing materials. "We look forward to continued growth in the market for @rich_energy #business #competition #aheadofthepack #richenergy."[45] The tweet was accompanied by a photo of a Haas F1 car's front wing with Rich Energy branding on it, even though the partnership was already over.

At some point, "Forget the wings, Rich Energy gives you horns"—once prominently on display on the Rich Energy homepage—also disappeared from its website. The logos had already been edited due to the ruling from the company's prior trip to court with Whyte Bikes, resulting in a slow whittling of Rich Energy's former brand.

Rich Energy never specified that the "legal agreement with a competitor" was actually the claim from Red Bull, which it had publicly mocked just months earlier on Twitter with its "Now @redbull are taking William Storey to court. A cynic might see a pattern emerging!" post.[46] The pattern was turning out to be one made up of court orders against Rich Energy.

Because of the randomness of Rich Energy's account, no one gave much of a thought to the October 16 announcement that it had deleted all of its tweets. It seemed at the time that perhaps Rich Energy decided those political rants, homemade memes, errant hashtags, and random account taggings weren't the best brand strategy after all, but that was far from the case. The Red Bull claim had been months earlier, after all, giving everyone the time to forget that it even happened. Thus, no major news outlets covering Formula One—or minor ones—appeared to make the connection. It wasn't even until the authors of this book began piecing together the timeline day by day that we realized it.

But if Storey was fazed by the court trips, he didn't want anyone to know. A year later in September 2020, he tweeted:

> My first foray into #Formula1 annoyed the energy drink competition so much that I'm on first name terms with their lawyers! Our product is peerless & we are just getting started in elite motorsport
> #RichEnergy #Elite #Performance #UK #EnergyDrink #SundayMorning #TuscanGP #F1[47]

(Storey was fond of tweeting about Formula One long after he and his brand left.)

After Rich Energy's October 16, 2019, announcement about deleting all of its prior tweets, the company stopped using its once-regular hashtags: #GivesYouHorns, #BetterThanRedBull, and #NoBull. But a few straggler tweets from 2016 remained, and they were all bizarre—some more than others.

One, dated October 21, 2016, featured a grainy photo of the Monaco coast. The photo was from a trip.com search of "Monte Carlo," part of the Principality of Monaco, continuing Rich Energy's habit of plucking photos from random corners of the internet without any credit to the source or photographer.

"@rich_energy secured multiple new outlets in the principality #richenergy #monaco #cotedazur #premium #beverage #luxury #betterthanredbull," the tweet read.[48]

Two others featured variations of the exact same script: "@rich_energy #betterthanRedBull—just saying." They were tweeted on the same day.[49]

Another post, dated December 4, 2016, was the most bizarre of the bunch: It featured a photo of two people diving off of a cliff. One was base jumping, while the other was wingsuit flying—an activity similar to skydiving, except while wearing a piece of clothing with webbing between the limbs in order to catch air. The person in the regular base-jumping getup was facing toward the sky, a plume of fire erupting in front of their face. "Fire breathing while wingsuit flying #fire #flying #aviation #fuel #nolimits #richenergy #premium #betterthanredbull #speed #ontheedge," Rich Energy tweeted.[50] A reverse image search showed the image appearing in several videos online, as was typical of Rich Energy's photo usage.

The original video appeared to feature stunt performer and base jumper JP de Kam, who was wearing a white bear suit when he hopped off the cliff to film it.[51] Much like the other photos Rich Energy grabbed from random corners of the internet, de Kam told the authors: "They do not have permission to use this picture. They did not have anything to do with it."[52]

But Rich Energy's desire to emulate Red Bull didn't die out, even if the infringement was ordered to stop. On June 17, 2020, sports reporter Adam Stern tweeted a chart from games-market insight company Newzoo showing the top five non-endemic sponsorship categories in esports—-non-endemic sponsors being those with products and services not directly related to the activity of esports.[53] Since the majority of in-person sports in 2020 were on hold due to the COVID-19 pandemic, esports was one of the few outlets that sporting sponsors had at the time. The chart was a way to show just how deep advertising went in the realm of gaming while the rest of the world was on pause.

Energy drinks led the non-endemic sponsorship charge in esports with 42 deals, followed by: telecommunications, 24 deals; automotive manufacturers, also 24 deals; athletic wear and sportswear, 17 deals; and soda, 14 deals. The company with the most deals in the leading category, energy drinks, was Red Bull.[54]

Perhaps by chance, perhaps not, Rich Energy tweeted a photo of a black-and-gold Forza 7 car just over a week later on June 26, 2020. The company's name was plastered diagonally across the side of the car, and its new "stag horns without the head" logo appeared just over the rear tire. The company captioned the photo: "Rich Energy becoming a very popular choice in esports and gaming #Esports #Gaming #RichEnergy #British #energy #beverage."[55]

The name under the car window was "Iredale," belonging to an esports competitor named Azzy Iredale—an avid member of both the esports community and furry fandom at the time. Iredale's social media pages mentioned previous ties to Red Bull in their racing career.

Iredale's Rich Energy deal had just come together in the past month, and it came together rather publicly. Iredale tweeted a photo of one of their esports rides: a car nearly identical to the former Rich Energy Haas F1 Team entries.

"Throwing this beauty of a car around the streets of Monaco, Lovely Black and Gold design of @weareRichEnergy's 2019 challenger," Iredale, who had 136 Twitter followers at the time, tweeted on May 25, 2020. "Hope to see this back on the grid soon with @richenergyceo leading the charge." The tweet included the #RichEnergy hashtag, along with two matching heart emojis: a black one and a yellow one.[56] Storey, who had just over 1,100 Twitter followers himself, liked and retweeted the tweet.

"No clue how much that means, wow, just shocked honestly!" Iredale tweeted 32 minutes after the original post. "Feel massively honoured to even have had my tweet seen by @richenergyceo Mr. Storey! Hopefully one day ill [sic] be able to represent the amazing Rich Energy brand in the Esports [sic] scene! That is the goal." The tweet ended in a biceps emoji.[57]

Two minutes later, Iredale posted a screenshot showing Storey following his Twitter account. "Oh my god ob [sic] my god oh my god," the post read.[58] By the next day, Iredale tweeted a photo of the Forza 7 car that the Rich Energy account would later use for its "becoming a very popular choice in esports" post.

On May 28, just a few days after their original interaction, Storey tweeted a photo of Iredale's Haas Rich Energy lookalike car that prominently featured the Haas branding, despite Haas having cut its ties with the brand about a year earlier. The post read:

> Pleased that Rich Energy a very popular livery in #F1 games
>   Looking forward to returning to the sport #MonacoGP #eSports
> #RichEnergy #British #EnergyDrink[59]

The post before that one on Storey's profile was a retweet from a user named Simon Dolan, described in their Twitter bio as "Taking the UK

Government to Court to end the illegal lockdown and bring those responsible to account." Dolan was referring to the government lockdowns put in place to slow the spread of the COVID-19 pandemic. The tweet read:

> A deluge of laws must regulate the conduct of everyday life, including the words that may be spoken, so that it is impossible for a person to walk through a day without committing an offense. The special police thus can proceed on the assumption that people are guilty
> Nazi Germany[60]

Iredale added "Rich Energy partner" to their profile bio at some point, and on June 9, tweeted a video of a taste test between—you guessed it—Rich Energy and Red Bull. It wasn't anything fancy; Iredale, wearing a black T-shirt with what appeared to be a duck on it and sitting at a small table in the corner of a room, had one can of each in front of them. Iredale had already tried the two, they said in the portrait-oriented video, and they were passing along their thoughts.

"We have a can of Rich Energy here," Iredale said. The Rich Energy can was closer to the camera, and its logo was directly facing it while Red Bull's was partially turned away. "And we also have a leading rival brand—'leading rival brand' being Red Bull here.

"I will say, straight away, from the get-go … the Red Bull can does have quite the more sugary and acidic taste to it, which, it's OK, but, you know, it can be a bit too much at times. Whilst with the can of Rich Energy, it has a much more smoother, toned down—it's just all around, to me, it's better, because Red Bull has a very fizzy—it just explodes in your mouth. Rich Energy is just completely smooth, very nice flavors, more fruity as well, and it tastes just more natural compared to the leading rival brand, and I will definitely be sticking with Rich Energy from now on."[61]

Iredale went on to say they get their energy drinks locally and that it "would be great to see this in there on the shelves being sold, because [they] would be in there every day basically."

"Thanks to Rich Energy for providing the cans," Iredale said. "I've got another one in the fridge at the moment which I can't wait to get into, and I hope that this review was useful to them as well. Thanks for the opportunity, lads, and hopefully I'll get another crate soon. Take care."[62]

In an August 2021 interview with the authors, Iredale said the Rich Energy sponsorship was something of a joke—a challenge amongst friends that, because Iredale had a beard like Storey, they should secure a follow from him on Twitter. Iredale made "the cheesy post" for that reason, they said, and Storey quickly followed their account.[63]

"You were just joking and he bought into it?" the authors asked.

"Yeah," Iredale said. "Then my friends were like, 'Take it one step further and see if you can get sponsored by him.' I sent him a message like, 'Hey, I'm a sim racer and racing driver. Would you like to sponsor me?'"[64]

Just like that, Iredale had a sponsor—but it didn't entail much, Iredale said. "I got a 24 crate of Rich Energy," they told the authors. "Then after that, it was a lot of, 'Oh, we'll send you support this week,' 'We'll send you support this week.' It has been one and a half years. I've not received anything."[65]

Iredale was perhaps the perfect sponsee. They maintained a Rich Energy logo on their car for several months, they said, and filmed the aforementioned comparison video upon Storey's request. But Iredale found the video uncomfortable. "I wanted to just say, 'My honest opinion was this tastes like fucking Red Bull,'" Iredale said. "It tastes like energy drink. There's no difference. And I'm just there, 'Oh, it's got more of a fruity flavor,' and I'm just thinking to myself, 'I don't want to fucking do this.'"[66]

Iredale said when they raised concerns that they weren't receiving anything in return for the sponsorship, they emailed Kay Johnson, Rich Energy's head of commercial partnerships and global sales. Iredale said Johnson told them she was unaware of any sponsorship deal, and that when Iredale informed Storey of the conflict, Storey said: "I'll be in touch tomorrow. Noted."[67] Johnson didn't respond to an August 2021 interview request from the authors.

"There was a lot of miscommunication between the company and Mr. Storey himself," Iredale told the authors. "First he told me to email in and just say, 'Hey, [I'm] supported by [Storey] and this and this, and we'll get them to send you stuff.' It was a three-month back and forth between me and the management of the company saying to me, 'We're not sponsoring you.' I'm just there like, 'But your CEO is telling you that you're sponsoring me.' Then they're like, 'Yeah, but we're not interested.' And I'm just there like, 'Well, he's telling me another thing, so what is going on here?'"[68]

A motorsport employee connected to Storey and Johnson told the authors this was a normal occurrence.[69] They requested anonymity to protect their career, but their employment and ties to Rich Energy were verified by the authors.

"There were a lot of instances where people would talk to William on Twitter and be like, 'I'm a massive fan of the brand. I really want to be a part of the sponsorship,'" they said. "Then [William] might say, 'Oh, I'm happy with this, but you need to speak to Kay.' Kay was the one who licensed out that kind of thing, and she was the one who said yay or nay on things."[70] But people would still receive a personal sponsorship from Storey, the person said—something other members of the company had no idea about.

Iredale publicly dropped Rich Energy in December 2020. It wasn't the ghosting that encouraged them to dissociate from the Rich Energy brand; rather, it was Storey's anti-vaccination stance amidst the COVID-19 pandemic. As Iredale tweeted that month:

> Little announcement, from now onwards I will no longer be representing the Rich Energy brand. I just cannot support a company which its CEO throws Anti-Mask and "Covid is a hoax" claims. Its dangerous, I will be looking for more sponsors for the new year
> Thank you all, stay safe[71]

But Storey didn't seem to be aware that one of his sponsored drivers had severed ties. During their interview with the authors, Iredale said they got a Twitter message from Storey about a care package they were supposed to receive with sponsored clothing and merchandise.[72] At the time of writing, Iredale said they still hadn't received a package.

For Iredale, Rich Energy was unlike any sponsor they'd worked with—and not in a good way. "Red Bull, they were straight to the point, got it done," they said. "Every other sponsor I've had has been very straightforward, to the point, we got it done. Rich Energy is like, 'I don't know what they're doing, and they don't know what they're doing.'"[73]

*   *   *

In a podcast published on May 25, 2020, Storey brought up Red Bull all on his own accord. When discussing why he chose to become a Formula One sponsor in particular, Storey called it a "very, very privileged area that didn't have much competition."[74]

"If we could get in it, we'd have an opportunity to make people look very stupid," Storey said. "Of course, we did. I mean, I'm biased, I think we had the best looking car on the grid, and we obviously had—again, I'm very biased—a cool brand. But one of the problems was, we really pissed off Red Bull. The reason for that is that they spent 4 billion pounds in Formula One and they were thinking, 'Who on Earth is this hairy bloke walking around the paddock taking the piss out of us?' and they just really didn't like it. But, you know, that's a bit of fun, isn't it? As far as I'm concerned, we had a better product, a better brand, and why not?"[75]

Outside of four DNFs—the motorsport abbreviation for "did not finish"—by the Red Bull team in 2019, a Haas car only beat a Red Bull car on track twice during the 21-race calendar: in the Australian season opener, when Magnussen finished sixth and Red Bull driver Pierre Gasly 11th, and late in the season in Brazil, when Alex Albon was on track for a podium but was spun out by Lewis Hamilton at the end of the race. That spin landed Albon, who replaced Gasly midway through the season, 14th behind Magnussen in 11th and Grosjean in 13th. Afterward, Hamilton described the spin as: "Completely my fault."[76] (Red Bull also, again, finished third in the 2019 constructor standings with 417 points, while Haas logged a mere 28 points for ninth place out of 10.[77]) Because of that, it's hard to know what Storey meant by "taking the piss out of" Red Bull.

The coronavirus-delayed first race of the 2020 Formula One season, which began nine months after the Red Bull court decision, was also a perfect storm of Storey's interests: COVID-19, carnage, and crummy luck among both the Red Bull and Haas teams, all wrapped up in a nice blanket of the pandemic's season opener at the Red Bull Ring. Red Bull co-founder Dietrich Mateschitz bought the track, formerly named the Österreichring and located in the Austrian town of Spielberg, in 2004—the same year Mateschitz's company bought the Jaguar Formula One team.[78]

The team was renamed Red Bull Racing for 2005, while the track was renamed the Red Bull Ring. It was a fitting track for Red Bull to buy, given the company's home base in Austria and its huge investment into the Formula One paddock. Formula One had previously left the track after its 2003 Austrian Grand Prix, and it sat idle to all racing until 2011.[79]

The old Österreichring was accustomed to a pattern of Formula One coming and going, for reasons such as safety and advertising issues. But by the time Mateschitz was done with it, the Red Bull Ring would be a nearly 2.7-mile racetrack overlooked by a massive statue of a charging bull. Ten years and a full makeover later, Formula One returned to the circuit for the 2014 Austrian Grand Prix—Red Bull branding and all.

While most 2010s-era Formula One seasons saw the Austrian Grand Prix occur in the middle of the race calendar, its July 5 running in 2020 made the Red Bull Ring the site of the pandemic-delayed season's opening round. No fans were in attendance, and face coverings were mandatory to help slow the spread of the virus, with then–Mercedes team principal Toto Wolff donning a large, clear face shield.[80] Mercedes drivers Valtteri Bottas and Lewis Hamilton swept the top two positions in qualifying, while the Ferrari team surprised everyone in the wrong way by turning its usual runner-up performance into a qualifying effort of seventh place for Charles Leclerc and 11th place for Sebastian Vettel, who had announced just two months earlier that 2020 would be his final season with the team. Red Bull claimed the third starting position for Max Verstappen and the fifth for Alex Albon, while Haas started the year right where the team left off in 2019. Romain Grosjean qualified 15th and Kevin Magnussen 16th.[81]

When Haas tweeted its poor qualifying results on July 3, Storey was quick to respond, posting from his personal account: "The #Friday Feeling when you know you made the right decision #AustrianGP #F1

#RichEnergy #Business #entrepreneurlife #FormulaOne #ارحل_يا_فاشل
#HamiltonFilm #sport."[82]

Hamilton the film had been released on Disney's streaming service that day.[83] Tweets about the topic were dominating the platform, which meant using the #HamiltonFilm hashtag had the potential to get Storey more views on the tweet. *Hamilton* the film was the at-home version of the popular Broadway show, not anything to do with Lewis Hamilton—who was, as Formula One's first and only Black driver at the time, leading the series' demonstrations against racism and police brutality in the wake of George Floyd's May 2020 killing at the hands of white Minneapolis police officer Derek Chauvin.[84]

Bottas won the Austrian Grand Prix, while both Haas and Red Bull were wiped out entirely before it could end. They weren't the only ones, either—only 11 of the 20 cars finished the race.[85]

Red Bull driver Max Verstappen told the press after the race that he was on track for an "easy podium" before losing power, and his teammate Albon went from podium hopeful to the DNF ranks as well after colliding with Hamilton, who got a five-second penalty after race stewards deemed that he caused the wreck. Both Haas drivers retired early with brake issues, and Steiner picked up right where he left his post-race interviews in 2019, saying that "if you're not running at the front, it's difficult times all the way."

"You try to do your best and get yourselves prepared so that you do better than last weekend," Steiner said. "But until you win everything, you will always be doing that."[86]

You could also say Storey picked up right where his 2019 form left off, but he never really stopped. Upon seeing how the Haas team performed at Red Bull Ring with its double DNF, Storey tweeted from his personal account:

> Another million dollars saved.
>   Serendipity for #RichEnergy
>   #F1 #AustrianGP #HaasF1 #serendipity #Business #Decisions #British #EnergyDrink #verstappen[87]

Storey created this new, personal Twitter account in March 2020, perhaps to differentiate his words from those posted by the corporate Rich Energy account. Instead, it provided two different spaces to share the same sentiments.

About an hour and a half before that, Storey had retweeted a photo of the podium originally posted by the official Formula One account. The photo featured a celebration unlike most: the top three finishers—Valtteri Bottas, Charles Leclerc, and Lando Norris—standing on platforms spaced out for the era of social distancing. Each wore a mask matching their fire suit, hands behind their backs and champagne bottles at their feet. Podium finishers were handed their trophies like normal that weekend; by the next weekend, Formula One had deployed "trophy robots"—square carts navigated by radio control in order to deliver the awards in a "contactless" manner, which was the name of the game during the COVID-19 pandemic.[88]

Storey had a lot to say about the scene, tweeting: "Apart from looking like total prats wearing stupid #Masks that do nothing apart from perpetuate the #Coronabollocks it is good to see #FormulaOne back even amid the virtue signalling. It's a shame @Max33Verstappen & @alex_albon retired!! #F1 #AustriaGP #NoMaskOnMe #sundayvibes."[89]

During the first year of the pandemic, masks and social distancing were widely upheld by medical professionals and organizations as the best ways to slow the spread of the coronavirus outside of staying home in quarantine. Storey wasn't quite on board with that.

Weighing in further on Formula One's coronavirus precautions, Storey tweeted, tagging the series' official account: "Why are they ignoring the clear #Science that #Masks are a total waste of time & don't work & instructing drivers & teams to wear them? Why are they perpetuating falsehoods & #propaganda? Embarrassing. #AustrianGP #4thofJuly #F1 #NoMasks #CovidHoax."[90]

Storey also shared an illustration of a person wearing a mask that said, "You can use anything for a mask, because it's not about safety; it's about compliance," with the hashtags: #propaganda, #NoMasks, #AustrianGP, #F1, #globalreset, #climatechange, and #lemmings.[91]

Storey continued his regular beat of tweeting coronavirus misinformation and conspiracy theories on July 6. Simon Dolan, the account he engaged with regularly during the pandemic, tweeted that day that a judge had "refused permission" for them to challenge the UK lockdown. "The most draconian laws ever introduced in England, with no Parliamentary scrutiny and they are seen to be fit and proper by the Courts," Dolan wrote. "England 2020."[92]

Quoting-tweeting a later tweet by Dolan encouraging supporters to help "continue the war," Storey wrote, with formatting intact: "The most astonishing thing about the #judgement today is that it is based on a clear falsehood ie that we are in a global #pandemic. We are not & never have been. The #historical definition never close to being met. Pure #propaganda. As such the decision unsafe. #COVID19 #Freedom."[93]

The World Health Organization determined the spread of the coronavirus to be a pandemic nearly four months earlier on March 11, 2020. By Storey's above tweet on July 6, the WHO had recorded more than 11 million COVID-19 cases globally, including more than 500,000 deaths.[94]

One of Storey's earlier shares from Dolan came on July 1, when Dolan responded to the official account of the UK Prime Minister—Boris Johnson at the time—instructing the public: "You must wear a mask on public transport. It will protect you and others."

Dolan's response, as retweeted by Storey in a strong endorsement, was as follows: "If you don't feel comfortable wearing a mask on public transport, simply don't wear it and if challenged say that under Part 1 Section 4 (a) of The Health Protection (CV, Wearing of Face Coverings on Public Transport) you are exempt as they cause you severe anxiety."[95]

Storey never quite gave up the "coronabollocks" thing. On December 26, 2020, long before vaccines were widely available, he tweeted: "Shopping today & seemed to be the only one not wearing a #mask. Honestly embarrassing that people this gullible. Any bloke under 60 wearing a mask is an innumerate bed wetter. More chance of being struck by lightning than dying of #COVID19. Pathetic. Deluxe morons. #NoMasks #UK."[96]

In March 2021, Storey posted a screenshot of Guenther Steiner in his Haas gear and a face mask. In the caption, he made fun of both the pandemic and Steiner's accent:

> "Fucking hell Gene, vis ze gimp masks ve look like a bunch of vankers."
> #BahrainGP #F1 #Motorsport #NoNewNormal #NoMasks #Qualifying #Truth.[97]

Formula One returned to Red Bull Ring on July 12, 2020, for yet another grand prix in Austria, and the *Sky Sports* broadcast opened by underscoring just how rare it was for Formula One to return to a track two weeks in a row instead of traveling across the globe for the next round. The two opening races of the 2020 season at Red Bull Ring marked the first time since 1995 that Formula One ran back-to-back races in the same country, the broadcast said. COVID-19 made that not just an anomaly, but a necessity—not only had the season been delayed by four months because of the pandemic, but the stringent safety protocols made it smarter and safer to move around the globe less. At the time, in fact, only 10 of the 22 grands prix originally planned for that season were confirmed to still go ahead.[98]

Hamilton won the second Austrian race of the year, the Styrian Grand Prix, ahead of Mercedes teammate Bottas. Red Bull drivers Max Verstappen and Alex Albon finished third and fourth, respectively. Ferrari took itself out of the race almost immediately with a collision between Charles Leclerc and Sebastian Vettel, with the former logging four laps and the latter only one. Haas drivers Kevin Magnussen and Romain Grosjean finished an unremarkable 12th and 13th, respectively, but that wasn't as bad as the team's qualifying run.

After neither Haas car had finished the first race of the year the week before, Grosjean failed to set a time during the qualifying session, hitting the gravel on his first lap out and then coming back into the pits with other problems. Magnussen qualified 15th.[99]

Storey was quick to jump on it, tweeting about another "poor performance" from Haas and attaching a photo of the team's former Rich Energy livery. His account and the one for the Rich Energy brand had been capitalizing on their former Formula One involvement all weekend, with the official company account tweeting a photo of its old race car on the day of the race: "Rich Energy in the #AustrianGP last year. Let's hope for a great race today #F1 #sundayvibes."[100]

Nearly an hour later on the same day, July 12, the account tweeted what appeared to be a rendering of a Rich Energy–branded open-wheel car with Honda logos on it—a departure from the Haas cars, which ran Ferrari power units at the time. Red Bull, however, was running Hondas. The tweet read: "Now this is a beautiful car. We can't wait to beat the competition in #F1. #RichEnergy #AustrianGP #Ferrari #sundayvibes #Formula1 #British #EnergyDrink."[101]

The tweet received a couple dozen responses within the first few hours of being posted—almost all of them confused, exasperated, or mocking toward the idea of the brand ever returning to Formula One. Some even pointed out that the image did not feature a Formula One car at all, but instead, one from Super Formula, a Japanese open-wheel racing series. The responses read:

> You should give up the daytime drinking.[102]
> Don't you have to be in F1 to beat the F1 competition?[103]
> You are a joke.[104]
> No team wants to work with your fake company.[105]
> But.... That's a Super Formula car....[106]

Another hour later, the Rich Energy account tweeted a photo of its logo with no caption, hashtagging "#RichEnergy," "#sundayvibes," and "#StyrianGP." The reaction was similar.[107]

The Rich Energy account posted the rendering of the Super Formula car once again on July 18, the weekend of the Hungarian Grand Prix. The tweet read:

> Powering premium with Rich Energy
> #F1 #HungarianGP #SkyF1 #RichEnergy[108]

Rich Energy, again, was not sponsoring an F1 car, nor was it posting photos of one—only a car that looked vaguely similar. The post was simply to capitalize on hashtags related to an event the company wasn't involved in.

*   *   *

Much of Rich Energy's very existence, it seemed—its former logo, its slogan, its posts online, and even its name—was borrowed from or inspired by something or someone else. Putting itself on the big stage simply enlightened the world to that.

Before Storey shared his legal issues with Red Bull on Twitter, former Haas employees told the authors they weren't aware of Red Bull or its race team being particularly bothered by Rich Energy. If anything, they said, Rich Energy's insistence on beating Red Bull was more of a burden to the Haas team.

"I do remember [Storey's public challenges to Red Bull] being talked about," one former Haas employee said. "My bosses being like, 'That's the last thing we need him to say. Where is he going with this? It makes us look stupid.' Especially as we'd just come off of a good year, and it fueled that fire of: You finished fifth last year, you now don't have any points at all, and your main money man is saying that you're going to beat Red Bull."[109]

In separate interviews, former employees agreed: It all became "a bit of a joke."[110]

"Guenther's not going to go against him and say, 'Well, that's not true, we've got a long way to go before we beat Red Bull,'" another said. "But he was trying to sort of temper expectations, I guess. It was added pressure internally, but also, it showed [Storey's] lack of knowledge and his lack of understanding of how Formula One works. The majority of us were like, 'What are you saying that for?' I think with us, as a coping mechanism, we just laughed it off."[111]

"This shows another good example of his personality: You don't put these things in public," another said. "These tweets against Red Bull, we'd see them and be like, 'What the hell is this bloke talking about? Beating Red Bull?' It was like a joke."[112]

"We'd be doing something and it would be like, 'Come on mate, we've got to beat Red Bull this week! Come on! Hurry up!'" another said. "It would turn into that kind of joke, but then it would just fizzle out, and from my side, it was never really a thing. It was a thing of comedy, more than anything. It was a thing of concern to start with, then it became a thing of comedy."[113]

For Red Bull, one former employee said, publicly ignoring Storey and Rich Energy was the right move. "I think they knew what was going on, and they knew that this guy was just trying to get into a fight," they said. "Because if he's getting into a fight with Red Bull, that's going to end up being everywhere, and he's going to be on the 'same level' as Red Bull."[114]

Red Bull would take a similar approach with this book. In September 2021, two years after the demise of the Rich Energy-Haas partnership, the authors reached out to Red Bull the drink company and Red Bull the race team about their relationships with Rich Energy. The questions asked of the drink company were:

- Red Bull's copyright case against Rich Energy centered on a few things, including its use of "Forget the wings, Rich Energy gives you horns"; "No Bull"; "No Bull with Rich Energy"; and #BetterThanRedBull.
    - o When did Red Bull become aware of this usage?
    - o Was it before or after Rich Energy announced it was entering F1 with Haas?
- Did Red Bull inform Haas about this usage? When?
- Red Bull never really publicly engaged with Rich Energy; the only time we had an indication that Red Bull engaged with the brand was through the copyright claim. Were there talks behind the scenes?
- Why did Red Bull take action in June 2019? Rich Energy officially entered F1 in October 2018 and was around before then, complete with that branding. Why wait?
- Red Bull originally wrote a letter to Rich Energy on March 21, 2019, before the legal action. Can you share a copy of this letter and what it said?
- Did Rich Energy, Storey, or any other party respond to the letter?
- Red Bull's claim against Rich Energy said the brand took unfair advantage of its marketing by creating "a link" between its brand and Red Bull "in the mind of the average consumer seeing the phrases complained of." Does Red Bull feel Rich Energy succeeded or had a threat to succeed in that?
- Red Bull settled with Rich Energy, and damages totaled 25,000 pounds from the company. The first 5,000 pounds was due on October 21, 2019, another 10,000 pounds was due on January 2, 2020, and the final 10,000 pounds was due on February 1, 2020. Were these sums paid to Red Bull?
- In early 2019, Storey was quoted by the *Sun* as saying: "Red Bull have spent £250 billion in F1, and last year across Toro Rosso and Red Bull, there or thereabouts, £400 million." The £400 million figure was in the right ballpark, but it's unclear where he got £250 billion, or over what time period he meant—presumably, he meant over the lifetime of Red Bull's involvement in Formula One.
    - o How much had Red Bull actually spent in F1 between its entrance into the series as a team, 2005, and early 2019?
    - o How much had it spent on the team itself during that time, and how much had it spent on general sponsorships and activities outside of the team, over the course of its involvement?

- After Rich Energy tweeted that it was terminating its contract with the Haas team and a separate statement from another Rich Energy entity called that a "rogue action," Storey said: "There has been an attempted coup of my position by a handful of shareholders who have a cosy relationship with Red Bull and Whyte Bikes."
  - o Do you know which shareholders he was referring to?
  - o Do you know what relationships he's referring to?
  - o Regardless, did Red Bull have a relationship with any Rich Energy shareholders?
  - o Can you tell us more?
- William Storey tweeted in July 2020: "Red Bull hated me in F1 & put Haas under huge pressure to try & oust me." Presumably, he meant the company, not the Red Bull Formula One team. Did this happen? What might have prompted this tweet?

Red Bull spokesperson Carly Loder declined to comment on any of the questions in an email to the authors, adding: "Good luck with the book! We wish you the best."[115] The authors sent a similar list to the Red Bull Racing Formula One team, with the addition of:

- In May 2020, William Storey said of his time in F1: "One of the problems was, we really pissed off Red Bull. The reason for that is that they spent 4 billion pounds in Formula One and they were thinking, 'Who on Earth is this hairy bloke walking around the paddock taking the piss out of us?' and they just really didn't like it. But, you know, that's a bit of fun, isn't it? As far as I'm concerned, we had a better product, a better brand, and why not?"
  - o How does Red Bull Racing feel about this depiction of what happened?
  - o Was Storey actively "taking the piss out of" Red Bull Racing?
  - o Was the rivalry even, in Red Bull Racing's eyes?

Aside from one spokesperson copying their colleagues on the email chain because they'd be out of the office for the deadline, Red Bull Racing didn't acknowledge the questions.

8

A VOLT OF HOPE

Midway through 2019, Rich Energy seemed to be on a better (or at least different) path. But with Rich Energy, outward appearances often didn't tell the whole story.

Companies House filings from July 16, just two days after the 2019 British Grand Prix, outlined Storey's termination as a director from Rich Energy and the company's name switch to "Lightning Volt Limited" in the registry. Other filings from the same day showed Zoran Terzic, who was listed as a "keep fit instructor" in the original Rich Energy documents, terminated as a director as well. English resident Matthew Bruce Kell was appointed in their place.[1] With the Haas partnership still intact and apparent new leadership at the company, it appeared a rebrand—and a new chapter—might be ahead.

It wasn't. William Storey's break from the helm of the company lasted just over a month. On August 29, 2019, new Companies House filings showed Storey and Terzic returning as directors. This time, Terzic's occupation was listed as simply "director."[2]

That day, Matthew Bruce Kell—the person appointed the day of the "Lightning Volt" name change and the original terminations of Storey and Terzic—was terminated as a director. The office address reverted back to its former location, and Storey regained all of the shares that had been transferred to Kell during the July 16 ousting: 6,400 of the 10,000 total.[3] Rich Energy was, it seemed, back to normal, with a new name on file at Companies House but the same name on the cans. At the time, neither Storey nor a contact line for Rich Energy responded to a request for comment about his reappointment—if the two weren't, in fact, one and the same.

But the reorganizations weren't the only unexplained events from that particular company shakeup. Three days after the original registry for Rich Energy became "Lightning Volt" on July 16, a separate filing for a new "Rich Energy Limited" appeared on Companies House with different leadership.[4]

The incorporation filing for the new "Rich Energy Limited," dated

July 19, listed a person named Steven Weston as its sole director.[5] Steven Weston isn't to be confused with Neville Weston, the minority shareholder in Rich Energy from 2018—the same one who received the apparent letter from Haas that said the team understood him to be "seeking to take control of the company away from Mr. Storey, the current CEO."[6] It was unclear if Neville Weston and Steven Weston were related.

Neville Weston retained shares in the original Rich Energy, still listed as "Lightning Volt," as did investment company Brandsellers Holdings Limited, soccer player Robert Lee, Charlie Simpson, Lloyd Tunicliffe, and Storey. All were listed as shareholders just a few months earlier when Rich Energy's investors reportedly wanted to "clear up the PR mess" created by the contract-termination tweet.[7] (Lee didn't respond to the authors' interview requests. Simpson, Tunicliffe, Terzic, and Kell couldn't be reached.)

The existence of two entities appearing to act as the same thing became the next big question about the company: Who, exactly, was Rich Energy? Had Lightning Volt become the brand, acting as "Rich Energy" in public but "Lightning Volt" in government filings? Or had this new Rich Energy filing adopted the entire identity of the old Rich Energy?

On May 12, 2021, Steven Weston's Rich Energy listing with Companies House posted an "Accounts for a dormant company" document. Companies House defined dormant companies as having "no 'significant' transactions in the financial year," and that was certainly true for Steven Weston's Rich Energy: At the time, its "cash at bank and in hand" was listed as 10 pounds.[8] When contacted by the authors for comment a few months later in August 2021, Steven Weston said: "I found your/*Jalopnik*'s reporting of William Storey's events from the outside back in 2019 quite fascinating and am sure your book will be also. Please forward what you, Elizabeth, and your coauthors have so far. Subject to the current legal proceedings in place against William, I may at least be able to confirm and correct any ambiguities."[9] The authors told Steven Weston via email that journalists can't provide drafts of stories to sources before they publish and asked for a detailed interview instead. Steven Weston did not respond to that email or any follow-ups; thus it was unclear what the original message meant by the "legal proceedings in place against William."

Meanwhile, back in 2019, the Rich Energy branding remained on the Haas cars after the new Rich Energy entity was formed, albeit without the infringing logo. The authors asked Storey, Rich Energy, and Haas at the time which entity—Rich Energy Limited or the company's original listing, which had become "Lightning Volt Limited"—remained partnered with the Formula One team. No one answered the question.

On August 29, 2019, the day of Storey's return as a director of the original Rich Energy, Haas team principal Guenther Steiner discussed the team's potential for a future with the brand, despite the legal letter from a month earlier stating Haas would accept Rich Energy's contract breach. In an audio clip provided to the authors by Haas spokesperson Stuart Morrison, Steiner told reporters the situation with Rich Energy had "calmed down," and it was time to "see where we go from here"—"we" meaning the team and its unruly sponsor.[10]

"First, we need to be calm and make a rational decision, and then it will be decided," Steiner said. "At the moment, [the Rich Energy branding is] on here—obviously, as you can see—so they need to decide where they want to go, not us. It is their decision, and then our one will follow—what we need to do. That should happen in the next week or so, and this time it will happen properly."[11]

When asked whether the decision would be made in regard to the full contract, which was originally meant to expire after the 2022 season, or just the remainder of 2019, Steiner wouldn't go into the details.

"I don't want to go into the contract," Steiner said. "It's more like for them to decide where they are with their company, you know, if it makes sense or not for them to continue. I'm not involved, therefore I cannot comment. I wouldn't be qualified to comment, because I've got enough on my plate. I don't need anybody else's problems, so we agreed that once they are ready to decide where they want to go, that they tell us what they want to do with us."[12]

When asked when Haas expected to know Rich Energy's decision—whichever faction of Rich Energy remained with the Haas team—Steiner said it would likely be after the 2019 Italian Grand Prix on September 8. That was only a few days away.

"I think it will be after Monza, because Monza is just next week," Steiner said. "It's very little time to do things properly. Hopefully, we can do things properly and respectfully."[13]

Aside from the audio clip, Morrison didn't weigh in on behalf of the team. "Take from that [audio file] what you wish," Morrison wrote via email. "No comment on anything else at this time."

Just as Steiner foretold, the fate of the Rich Energy–Haas partnership came to be the day after the Italian Grand Prix. The Haas F1 Team tweeted on September 9, 2019, that it was over.

"Haas F1 Team and Rich Energy have amicably agreed to end their partnership together in the FIA Formula One World Championship with immediate effect," the team said in a statement. It continued:

> While enjoying substantial brand recognition and significant exposure through its title partnership of the Haas F1 Team in 2019, a corporate restructuring process at Rich Energy will see the need for a revised global strategy. Subsequently, Haas F1 Team and Rich Energy concluded a termination of the

existing partnership was the best way forward for both parties. Haas F1 Team would like to express its thanks and best wishes to the stakeholders at Rich Energy.[14]

The same day, the Rich Energy account weighed in on its favorite medium, Twitter:

CEO William Storey "I would like to thank @HaasF1Team for great efforts in our partnership. It is regrettable they got caught in crossfire of a shareholder dispute which led to this wholly avoidable fiasco. I wish the team the very best & our passion for motorsport unabated" #F1[15]

The tweet included an image featuring Storey, Grosjean, Magnussen, and Steiner at the team's Rich Energy livery unveiling in London from February of that year. The photo was a cropped version of one taken by Getty Images' Bryn Lennon, posted without credit to the organization or photographer.

Not long after, Haas changed its name from the "Rich Energy Haas F1 Team" to "Haas F1 Team."[16] It was done.

On September 16, just one week after the split, the Haas team published photos of its new car livery ahead of that weekend's Singapore Grand Prix.[17] It was the same as before but without the "Rich Energy" wording, which was the only thing left after the team had to remove the infringing Rich Energy logo—a slow, symbolic disappearance of a company that had long refused to actually disappear.

Haas wouldn't shed the black-and-gold theme until the much delayed 2020 season that began in July instead of March due to the COVID-19 pandemic,[18] which Storey would frequently refer to as a "scamdemic" and "coronabollocks" on his personal Twitter account—despite the fact that it killed millions of people globally.[19] That year, Haas returned to the red, black, and lacquer gray Haas Automation CNC colors it wore before Rich Energy entered its universe.

But Rich Energy wasn't about to let the Haas F1 Team run the 2019 Singapore Grand Prix with all of the spotlight on it. The day of the race, September 22, the company account posted a cryptic tweet, tagging itself and adding an array of fun hashtags as usual: "Huge new motorsport announcements pending for the UK's premium energy drink @rich_energy #motorsport #F1 #speed #SingaporeGP #nobull #givesyouhorns."[20] "Gives you horns," of course, was the phrase Red Bull filed to sue Rich Energy over just two months earlier.

Things would only get weirder. Right around the start of the 2019 Russian Grand Prix on September 29, the Rich Energy account tweeted that, in fact, the Haas partnership was still on. "After review of dispute with investors who created havoc via UK distribution company Rich Energy CEO

& all stakeholders have asked @HaasF1Team to explain how they did a deal with unauthorized non officers of @rich_energy," the Rich Energy account wrote, again tagging itself in its own tweet. "As such title partnership is still on #RussianGP #F1 #NoDeal."[21] It was unclear what that tweet meant.

The Haas F1 team didn't run the Rich Energy branding in Russia. In fact, a "HaasCNC.com" label in what appeared to be a basic white Arial font was in Rich Energy's former place on the side of the car.

But Haas wasn't hurting for money. Less than a month after the official split on September 9, the team confirmed what everyone knew: that as it had done previously in both NASCAR and Formula One, Haas CNC would step in to sign the checks.[22]

On October 7, 2019, *Motorsport Network* publication *Autosport* quoted Steiner as saying Haas' commercial operations would have two monetary voids to fill that year: the one caused by Rich Energy and the one caused by the team's performance slump and drop in prize money. While Haas finished fifth of 10 in the 2018 constructor standings, it was sitting ninth of 10 at the time of the interview. It would finish there as well.[23]

"We haven't lost money, but luckily we've got Haas Automation as a good partner, and they'll support us for what the deal didn't bring to the final bit," Steiner said, referring to the Rich Energy deal that left Haas with a deficit of about 35 million pounds—more than $40 million at the time—through 2021.[24] Where Rich Energy got the money for the first payment, no one ever said.

Steiner told *Autosport* he was relieved the "Rich Energy" thing was over, even if it meant Haas Automation had to step in.[25] He continued:

The investors, they are good people. I don't know where they're going, but I'm relieved not to have to deal with it anymore because it gets old after a while.

When you don't make progress, you have to deal with the problem where there is no progress made. That is not satisfying in my life, and I'm not going out to fight with somebody just for the sake of it. If you cannot make progress, why waste energy?

So, it is disappointing that it ended how it ended, but again, with the investors in Rich Energy, we terminated on good standing, so you never know what happens in the future.[26]

* * *

For the former Haas F1 employees who spoke with the authors, the end of the Rich Energy era wasn't surprising. They saw the signs—many of the same signs bystanders saw. One sign came courtesy of comparing their workplace to other teams with drink sponsors, where there was always more than enough product for employees in the building. "At Red Bull at one point, I can't remember the official number, but it was something like they allocated six cans of Red Bull per day per employee," one former Haas employee said.[27] Another told the authors: "It's: 'How much can you physically consume without having a heart attack?' You can just keep on grabbing it. That seems to be the norm."[28]

"When a new drinks sponsor comes onto a race team, especially in F1, it's the norm for the product to be everywhere in the factory very quickly," another employee said. "I'd seen this in other, much larger teams. But that wasn't the case here. It was the opposite, in fact."[29]

The employees described seeing barely any Rich Energy at the team's facilities, if they saw it at all. Two said they saw about 48 cans arrive at their facilities within the first few months of the 2019 season. One said they didn't see any arrive at all. Another described essentially rationing the product supply that traveled from race to race to have enough for guests.

"They were treated like gold," a former employee said. "You'd expect the staff to be wandering around drinking it, or for it to be in reception, or to be in the cafeteria or wherever, but it was just nowhere."[30]

"I remember being told, 'Do not drink much,'" another said about the Rich Energy allotment at the track. "It was obvious there wasn't much of it. I know people at Red Bull. They have unlimited Red Bull available. You go into their hospitality and it's Red Bull everywhere, just free to take, while Rich Energy always came in very limited quantities."[31]

"The joke with us was like, 'When is the drink coming?'" one former employee said. "'Where's the money? When's the money coming?'"[32]

"We started to call it unicorn piss," another said. "It was a rare thing, like unicorn piss."[33]

More than one employee mentioned going on their own search for Rich Energy, to varying degrees of luck. "We just wanted to know: What is it? Does it taste like Red Bull?" one said. "Which, it does."[34]

"But the product itself was good," another said. "It looked good. I liked the taste, for sure."[35]

For former employees who spoke with the authors, another sign that the partnership probably wouldn't last was the constant news cycle—which, as one former employee described it: "We read a lot of it second-hand on, like, *Motorsport.com*."[36]

"At the height of when it was getting messy, some of the guys would be filling up their cars with gas in public, and random people would be like: 'What is going on at your place?'" another former employee said. "It became a comedy sketch."[37]

"A lot of the major details we found out in the news, and then I would go be like, 'Hey, what's going on? Do I need to be worried?'" another said. "That's the only information that we kind of got out of that, and I guess I'm glad because I probably would have left significantly earlier."[38]

When asked in separate interviews if Haas staff members were ever collectively reassured about the situation with Rich Energy—the questions from onlookers, the social media posts from the company, the public contract "termination," the legal actions—former employees who spoke with the authors said they generally weren't. "Guenther said: 'Don't worry about that, guys. It's bullshit,'" one former employee said. "That was true. It was bullshit. In the paddock, we speak a different language. We don't speak like when we're speaking to the media. When you speak to the media, you have to be nice."[39]

Another former employee described the atmosphere as: "Do your job. Keep the status quo. The less we talk about it, the more it will hopefully go away. If we keep going forward, it will get better. It can't get worse. Then it keeps getting worse. Then it gets worse after that."[40]

* * *

After its very public falling out from Formula One, many expected Rich Energy to take a step back for a while—at least from motorsport. It seemed like a sensible move: let the drama of the situation cool down before trying to secure another sponsorship.

That wasn't Rich Energy's style. On February 14, 2020, just five months after Rich Energy left Formula One, Storey and the owner of British Superbike Championship team OMG Racing, Alan Gardner, revealed a one-off livery at the Carole Nash MCN motorcycle show in London as a teaser of things to come[41]: Rich Energy signing on as OMG's title sponsor. Gardner was optimistic about the partnership with his three-year-old team, saying in a press release:

> We are delighted to announce Rich Energy as our title sponsor for the upcoming racing season and beyond, and to officially launch our 2020 Rich Energy OMG Racing BMW S1000RR.
> We are well aware of the previous controversy linked to Rich Energy.
> However, William Storey and the team at Rich Energy have been very transparent in their business dealings, to give us full confidence in our partnership to move ahead.
> We have always put our fans at the forefront of our plans, and this link gives us the opportunity to increase the amount we invest into new opportunities for our supporters to enhance their racing experience and build new audiences. The partnership also includes long-term commitments to develop both the OMG and Rich Energy brands as key supporters of British motorsport talent.[42]

Storey said in the same release: "The partnership with OMG is perfect. They have ripped up the rulebook in motorsport and come from nowhere to be one of the leading teams in the world. Their technical expertise, commitment to innovation, and support of riders is a perfect fit for

Rich Energy, and this wide-ranging partnership will also see the team become a major platform for the brand and driver of new distribution."[43]

So became Rich Energy OMG Racing, a team name many people found to be quite apt. The team announced the deal with a tweet saying it was "time to silence the critics."[44]

The Rich OMG website included a bizarre Q&A section on the deal, ensuring onlookers that, among other things, OMG Racing was fully funded and cans of Rich Energy actually existed. It read, typos included:

WHY ON EARTH HAVE OMG RACING SIGNED A DEAL WITH RICH ENERGY? HAVE THEY NOT LOOKED AT THE INTERNET?
Rich Energy have been a little 'eccentric' in the past on social media. But at the same time, we've made a seriously loud noise since appearing on the scene—like OMG. They are loud and aren't afraid to look a bit daft at times by doing things differently, like us. Together we are all about pushing sport to the next level.

BUT YOU CAN'T EVEN BUY A BL**DY CAN!?
You can now, we're distributing it right here—Here's the link to pre-order and as soon as we're ready to get moving, you'll be the first to know:

CAN BUY RICH ENERGY FROM OMG RACING?
Yes, you can. In fact they're so convinced that it's a good product, we'll have some free samples for you this year. So you'll be able to try some for yourself!

WHAT ABOUT THE RUMOURS THAT RICH ENERGY HAVEN'T PAID TEAMS/ATHLETES IN THE PAST, WHAT'S NEW HERE?
Not only are OMG Racing fully funded for the 2020 season and beyond, we are also ensuring that Rich Energy's existing sponsorship agreements are fully paid.

DIDN'T YOU FALL OUT WITH HAAS F1!
Haas' statement seems pretty amicable to us.

IS HE STILL INVOLVED? WHAT'S THE DEAL?
Yes HE is, given that William Storey is the CEO of Rich Energy. The enigmatic figurehead definitely gives us plenty of content. He's a big bike fan, and with a beard like that, we can't exactly disguise him. So yes, he'll be around. We were thinking a milk float for a paddock scooter....

SO WHERE WILL I BE ABLE TO SEE RICH ENERGY OMG RACING IN 2020?
Rich Energy will be the title sponsor across all racing activities, so that's British Superbikes, Northwest 200 and the legendary Isle of Man TT. It's going to be a busy year.

WAIT! I HAVE ANOTHER COMPLAINT!
We think we covered the main ones, but if you think we missed something in our due diligence then let us know at: hello@richenergy.com[45]

The milk float mention, of course, was a throwback to Rich Energy's infamous tweet about the Haas Formula One cars being as slow as milk floats at the British Grand Prix.

"OMG Racing LTD" became "Rich OMG LTD" on February 25, 2020, according to Companies House records, before switching to "Rich Energy OMG Racing" a month later. The company's most recent filing as of December 31, 2018, showed it having 24,262 pounds in the bank.[46]

OMG Racing had been part of the British Superbikes Paddock since 2018, two years before its Rich Energy partnership. The "about" section on its website described its mission as such:

> OMG Racing was born out of the passion of motorcycle racing fans, a desire to create a new type of racing team, putting its fans at the core of everything it does.
>
> Since joining the British Superbike paddock in 2018, OMG Racing has grown into one of the largest independent motorcycle racing outfits in the world, competing in the British Superbike Championship, National Superstock 1000 Championship, North West 200 and the iconic Isle of Man TT.
>
> The team also supports teams and riders in the National Superstock 600 and Junior Supersport Championships, as well as the inspiring True Heroes Racing Team.[47]

For Rich Energy's first season with OMG, 2020, team members included British Superbike riders Luke Mossey, Héctor Barberá, and Billy McConnell, alongside road and rally racers James Hillier and Davo Johnson.[48]

The 2020 British Superbikes season, although delayed by the COVID-19 pandemic, was a reasonable one for the team: Luke Mossey finished 11th of 25 riders in the championship standings while Barberá finished 17th. The best race finish for either driver was sixth place, which Mossey achieved twice. Barberá, though, did set the fastest lap of one race—a small consolation.[49]

The OMG Racing-Rich Energy partnership never seemed fraught with as many problems as the Haas one. The Rich Energy Twitter account made a handful of brief encouraging tweets, such as: "Rich Energy OMG Racing on fire! #RichEnergy #Motorsport"[50] and "British star @LukeMossey12 ahead of the pack in @OfficialBSB as he flies into the top 10 for Rich Energy OMG Racing #RichEnergy #BSBisOMG #SilverstoneBSB."[51]

Tweets from William Storey, OMG Racing, and Rich Energy's multiple accounts were a similar story: encouraging and straightforward, if a little boring. Even after difficult performances, no one at Rich Energy attempted to disavow OMG Racing, the riders, or British Superbikes as a whole.

Storey, though, wasn't one to be quiet. He and Rich Energy continued to tweet about Formula One, including photos of Haas cars from the previous year with praise for drivers Kevin Magnussen[52] and Romain Grosjean,[53] comments about track surface,[54] and performance analysis.[55] Storey also posted tweets from his personal account saying he was once again in talks to return to the Formula One grid in 2021.

Some of his tweets in 2020 included:

The Rich Energy Haas F1 car heading down to the harbour during the #Monaco Grand Prix in 2019. Next time we are in #F1 we aim to have a car capable of winning races. #F1 #GrandPrix #RichEnergy #British #energy #drink #EuropeDay
—**William Storey (@richenergyceo) May 9, 2020**[56]

Money was never an issue. Haas were seriously underperforming on track which was disappointing but worse was they decided to support a group of corporate investors & our competitors in trying to remove me. They backed the wrong horse but I found it extremely disappointing behaviour
—**William Storey (@richenergyceo) June 7, 2020**[57]

@F1 drivers must be dying of embarrassment wearing those ridiculous masks. Is nobody in #F1 aware of the #science, the efficacy of masks or infinitesimal risk of #COVID19? Supporting the #propaganda is pathetic. #coronabollocks #NoMasks #AustrianGP #Formula1 #Masks #lemmings @FT
—**William Storey (@richenergyceo) July 3, 2020**[58]

Another poor performance from @HaasF1Team in #Qualifying. Hopefully a better race awaits. A superb effort from @Carlossainz55 & for my money the top 3 today in the #wet are the best drivers in the sport. #F12020 #AustriaGP #LewisHamilton #RichEnergy #Formula1 #PolePosition
—**William Storey (@richenergyceo) July 11, 2020**[59]

Red Bull hated me in F1 & put Haas under huge pressure to try & oust me. Commercially that is a compliment but how could I continue with a team who reached an agreement with my competitors? I'm lucky to have some fantastic backers. I'm passionate about a Sunderland renaissance.
—**William Storey (@richenergyceo) July 26, 2020**[60]

I'm engaging on social to demonstrate that I'm a passionate football fan and that the F1 reporting a farce. Red Bull spent £4 billion in Formula One & hated my involvement. They put huge pressure on Haas to oust me. I can't work with a team who go behind my back.
—**William Storey (@richenergyceo) July 26, 2020**[61]

Haas made a catastrophic mistake in siding with my competitors in trying (and failing) to oust me from Rich Energy. Loyalty & integrity are extremely important #RichEnergy #HaasF1 #F1
—**William Storey (@richenergyceo) Dec. 17, 2020**[62]

As of July 2021, nearly two years removed from his stint in Formula One, Storey had about 7,700 Twitter followers. Rich Energy had 22,000. Red Bull had 2 million.

In his May 2020 interview with the *Chasin' the Racin'* podcast, Storey said "a lot" happened during his time in Formula One. "A lot of people in Formula One caused a lot of problems for us, and there were a lot of people who definitely wanted us not to succeed," he said. "I think the irony is, as you say, we projected our brand to a large number of people, and when—and it will be when—I buy a Formula One team, it will be very enjoyable to come back and start winning races. Because obviously the Haas team, unfortunately, they went backwards performance-wise."[63]

It wasn't just the Haas team Storey had issues with, though. It was much of the Formula One paddock. "Like a lot of things in life, because the barriers of entry are very high, what you tend to find is that most of the people in Formula One are very privileged rich kids," Storey added. "So if you can actually get in, you'll find that the gene pool is very shallow. I've said this for years and years and years, and I'm 100 percent right: There's 1,000 guys driving white vans in this country who wouldn't just beat, they would annihilate—piss all over—Lewis Hamilton. There's just no question about that, because so few people get the opportunity."[64]

That year, 2020, Hamilton won a seventh Formula One championship. It tied him with Michael Schumacher for most driver titles ever and made him statistically the most successful Formula One driver in history.

But, Storey said: "I'm always one for looking forward, not back."[65] Forecasting is always easier than critically reflecting, after all.

* * *

From its sports sponsorships to its overall vibe, Rich Energy's branding changed rapidly during and after its time in Formula One. At one point, Rich Energy redesigned its website—which was formerly a harsh black-and-gold theme—to a much lighter style including a photo of its can superimposed over a mountain background. The website would soon pivot to half black and half white with a stark divide down the middle. On the black side was the original version of Rich Energy's drink in its usual black can, and on the white side was its new, white-and-gold "zero sugar" line.

"Two drinks, one taste," it read, "...that simple."

At the time of the mountain theme, scrolling down revealed a 24-case of Rich Energy for sale, along with something called an "energy pack subscription" and described as:

> Join our fanbase with an energy pack subscription. You will receive 24 Rich Energy cans a month plus Rich Energy goodies throughout the year. You'll also be entered into exclusive draws and receive early access to Rich Energy events and parties. If you're a regular energy drink user then the Energy Pack is the way to go. It will save you money and guarantees you an ongoing supply of quality energy drink.[66]

Further down the homepage, the words "The Hunt: Not as hard to find as you think" were emblazoned over a photo of a car driving down a dark mountain road—an apparent reference to what little shelf presence the drink had.[67] There was, however, no website portal to explore the stores or countries that carried Rich Energy products.

Still, 2020 seemed to be a promising year for Rich Energy. On July 24, Storey announced on Twitter that he had made a "formal legal offer to buy the Sunderland AFC English football club."[68] (Sunderland finished eighth of 23 teams in the 2019–2020 championship standings for League One, the third tier of English football.[69]) Storey cited a non-disclosure agreement as the reason he was unable to say more about the situation at the time, but added that he had "significant funding from blue-chip backers." His tweet was accompanied by a photo of a Sunderland uniform with Rich Energy's name emblazoned proudly across the chest.

Storey's claims about the Sunderland bid were confusing. In a four-part interview with James Hunter of the *Chronicle Live* in December 2020, Storey dodged questions about money and conflicted with prior reports regarding bids for the team. At the time of the questioning, Hunter asked: "The [Sunderland] owners are currently in a period of exclusivity with another buyer, which means they can't talk to you, doesn't it?"

"No," Storey responded. "Because we were in talks with the club and have been in ongoing talks with the club since around about June, and those talks have continued. So if they are not allowed to continue with those talks, nobody has told us."

"So they are not in a period of exclusivity?" Hunter asked.

"You can conclude that, but the reality is that we have been in ongoing talks with them," Storey said. "The other thing that is relevant is that there were several other groups very interested in March or April, including an American consortium, and it was interesting that some of those people approached us in June to get involved with our bid. The reality is that, as it stands today, there are effectively two choices for the club in terms of proper fully funded, officially made opportunities. One is an investment-slash-loan … the other is a 100 percent takeover bid from my party."[70]

When asked specifics about where the money to buy Sunderland would come from, Storey took a similar approach to his Formula One days. "You're asking me a question about my personal resources," Storey said. "I'll phrase it elegantly: The total amount is fully costed and fully proved and fully backed. The exact source of all funds has been made available to the club, but clearly that is not for public information, because that would be reflected in the accounts of the company if and when we are successful in the purchase. But clearly the exact makeup of exactly where every pound is coming from is between me, the lawyers, the club, and my backers."

"The problem is that all fans have to go on is that you have stepped forward, said, 'I've made a bid of 45 million pounds, I have four blue-chip backers, but I can't tell you who they are,' and you are asking people to trust in you and believe in you on that," Hunter said later. "I could say that I have made a 100-million-pound bid funded by backers that I can't name."

"The difference is that the people who are selling the asset know who they are, and they have seen proof of funds," Storey said. "Therefore, the people that we are hoping to buy the club off have no doubts. Certain people at the *BBC* have seen the information, and when we meet, you will see the information. When you consider the quality of the people who have very generously backed me, I don't really take too kindly to it being questioned."[71]

If the reluctance to name backers sounds familiar, it's because Storey had repeated similar refrains throughout his career.

The *Guardian* reported that Sunderland's asking price was 37.6 million pounds, or U.S. $48.6 million.[72] The local *Sunderland Echo* newspaper also noted in July 2020 that Storey "claim[ed] to have previously been on the books of [fellow English football club Queens Park Rangers FC], only to be released before making a senior appearance."[73] That appeared to mean Storey claimed to have nearly been a professional football player, likely in part to establish himself as a viable candidate for the purchase.

Through a spokesperson, a Queens Park Rangers club historian told the authors in August 2021 that they searched the team's historical match records from the early 1990s onward and came back empty. "There is no record of a William Storey playing any matches from us in this period," they said. "I must admit it's not a name that is familiar to me at all."[74]

A lack of information was typical for Storey. As evidenced by his LinkedIn page, he was prone to making announcements without factual backup. While some of his sponsorship opportunities did come to fruition, others faded away as quickly as they appeared.

The Sunderland deal was a case of the latter, with French billionaire-heir Kyril Louis-Dreyfus—not Rich Energy—acquiring a controlling stake in the club from then-owner Stewart Donald. The *Guardian* reported at the time that at 23 years old, Louis-Dreyfus had become the youngest chair in English football.[75]

Storey lamented the news in a December 2020 tweet: "Very disappointing as we offered so much more. Sadly no shock as deal ensures Donald & Methven continue to suck on the teat of #Sunderland & take money OUT the club. I wish Dreyfus the best of luck & I hope he delivers what the fans deserve. A wonderful club #SAFC #Football."[76]

When asked about Sunderland's relationship with Storey—whether Storey put in an offer, how much it was for, why another offer was selected, and the overall experience with Rich Energy and Storey—a representative for the club told the authors in August 2021: "At this point in time, this isn't something that we are going to comment on, either on or off the record. Best of luck with the publication."[77]

Meanwhile, British Touring Car Championship driver Michael Crees signed on as a Rich Energy ambassador—once again announced by the company on Twitter in July 2020.[78] In response to the announcement, one Twitter user had nothing to offer but the usual complaint: "I've been trying to buy your cans for over 18 months. Can't check out on your website and out of stock on Amazon! William was actually going to send me some, none turned up! Please advise."[79]

Crees, who had about 2,700 Twitter followers as of 2021, had been successful in the touring-car world before the deal, winning several lower-level championships before moving up to British Touring Cars to pilot the BTC Racing team's Honda Civic Type R.[80] In a press release, Crees sounded optimistic and seemed to echo the reasoning OMG Racing gave for partnering with the brand:

> I am so excited to be working with such a big brand like Rich Energy and bringing them to the BTCC is going to be massive for all of us. I really feel that Rich Energy is a good fit for me, they're a bit cheeky and want to make an impact on the global market. The team are big supporters of motorsport and we've had good discussions about the future. I'm hoping that all my fans will support me in this journey and I'm delighted to have Rich Energy onboard for what's going to be an exciting 2020![81]

Criticism followed the driver's announcement, with Crees retweeting one Twitter user's defense of Rich Energy that read:

> You lot just can't let anything go FFS! Just give the brand a break??? Why are you not so critical of the Petrobras sponsor pulling on McLaren in the first season?? @OMGRacingUK seem quite confident with them. Best of luck to both team and sponsor!![82]

But 2020 wouldn't end on a high note for Rich Energy. On November 14 of that year, a new entry appeared in the Companies House registry for Lightning Volt Limited, widely known as Storey's Rich Energy UK registration: **ORDER OF COURT TO WIND UP.**[83] More than a year earlier in September 2019, according to the UK's *Gazette*, a petition to wind up had come from shareholder and Haas letter recipient Neville Weston, "claiming to be a creditor of the company."[84]

Rich Energy's UK arm appeared to be entering liquidation, yet Storey maintained he was actively seeking to return to the Formula One grid.

(When contacted by the authors for an interview, Neville Weston said: "Thank you for reaching out to me and giving me the heads up on the forth-coming publication. I would like to talk with you about your plans for the book. What is the best number to reach you on and what is a convenient time over the next few days?"[85] The authors sent multiple follow-up messages providing the information requested, but we never heard back again.)

A few days into 2021, Rich Energy's Formula One return would mate-rialize—or so Storey wanted everyone to think. On January 5, he tweeted:

> #F1 incoming.
> The best energy drink in the world mounting the biggest comeback since Lazarus
> Premium British performance. #RichEnergy #Motorsport #FormulaOne #British #Business #Entrepreneur[86]

"When is the announcement?" one Twitter user asked.[87]

"Official announcement from team first week of Feb.," Storey responded.[88]

Just over a week later on January 13, another new entry appeared in Companies House for Lightning Volt Limited: **APPOINTMENT OF A LIQUIDATOR**.[89] The liquidation process for Rich Energy's UK business appeared to be well underway, yet that same day, Storey tweeted:

> Having had a sneak preview of new cars, I can't wait to see #RichEnergy back in #F1 as we return to challenge our competitors on & off the track. Premium British performance
> #British #EnergyDrink #Business #FormulaOne #Entrepreneur #Competi-tion #Motorsport[90]

The next day, Formula One journalist Thomas Maher sent the authors record of a few private Twitter messages he'd exchanged with Storey.

"We are delighted to return," Storey wrote to Maher. "Rich Energy was valuable enough in 2019 for corporate investors to try and steal the brand (they failed) and [for] our major competitors to repeatedly take legal action. I said from day one we would beat the competition and our return to F1 is the next step of me being vindicated. Many journalists seem to favour the status quo but many fans actually support us, and we aim to add colour to a dreary corporate paddock."

"I presume this is viable despite the liquidation proceedings?" Maher responded.

"Rich Energy is an international group trading in multiple countries," Storey said, appearing to call the UK division irrelevant to the big pic-ture. "Mr. Weston tried and failed to steal the brand and blew up the UK distribution company in the process. Commercially idiotic and hubris-tic. He acted as a shadow director and unfortunately Haas believed the nonsense of his group, which they now regret. Despite that attack, I have led a renaissance of the brand worldwide and our return to F1 [is] merely the next step of our growth."[91]

After the exchange, Maher told the authors: "When you talk to him, if you weren't wise to him, you'd be fooled by him."[92]

*   *   *

A liquidation committee wouldn't officially be assigned to Lightning Volt Limited until March 26, 2021, but Storey kept busy in the meantime. Coincidentally, so did the Haas team.

Haas split with its longtime drivers, Romain Grosjean and Kevin Magnussen, after the 2020 season to bring in two rookies: Mick Schumacher, the son of seven-time Formula One champion Michael Schumacher, and Nikita Mazepin, the son of Russian billionaire Dmitry Mazepin.[93] Nikita Mazepin's arrival coincided with that of Haas' new sponsor: Uralkali, the Russian fertilizer company run by his father.[94] Signing Nikita Mazepin as a driver meant signing up for a large cash influx and a new Uralkali sponsorship, and Haas took the deal.

In December 2020, about a week after he was announced as a new Haas driver, the internet erupted with a video from 21-year-old Nikita Mazepin's Instagram story—a function on the photo- and video-sharing app where users could post videos, images, and other messages that would disappear after 24 hours. The video story was filmed from the front passenger seat of a Porsche, panning across the person driving before turning toward the back seat, where a woman sat. The woman, identified as model Andrea D'lVal, appeared intoxicated and was leaning forward in the seat when her dress strap and bra cup slipped down. As she reached down to catch them, the filmer—assumed to be Nikita Mazepin—reached back, groping her chest. She appeared to push back with her free hand before using it to give the camera the middle finger, all while the filmer's hand remained on her chest.[95] On December 9, 2020, the Haas team tweeted a statement about the incident.

"Haas F1 Team does not condone the behavior of Nikita Mazepin in the video recently posted on his social media," the statement read. "Additionally, the very fact that the video was posted on social media is also abhorrent to Haas F1 Team. The matter is being dealt with internally and no further comment shall be made at this time."[96]

Nikita Mazepin also tweeted a statement, which read: "I am sorry for the offense I have rightly caused and to the embarrassment I have brought to Haas F1 Team. I have to hold myself to a higher standard as a Formula One driver and I acknowledge I have let myself and many people down. I promise I will learn from this."[97]

Formula One and its governing body, the FIA, declined to step in. "We strongly support the Haas F1 Team in its response to the recent inappropriate actions of its driver, Nikita Mazepin," they said in a joint statement. "Mazepin has issued a public apology for his poor conduct and this matter will continue to be dealt with internally by the Haas F1 Team. The ethical principles and diverse and inclusive culture of our sport are of the utmost importance to the FIA and Formula One."[98]

The FIA took a far different approach when multi-time champion Lewis Hamilton wore a T-shirt calling for racial justice at the 2020 Tuscan Grand Prix, both before the race and during a podium celebration after winning it. Hamilton removed the top half of his racing suit to display the shirt, which was black and read "Arrest the cops who killed Breonna Taylor" in all caps, amid the stratospheric rise of the Black Lives Matter movement after the May 2020 police killing of George Floyd.[99] In March 2020, just two months before Floyd's death, American police in Louisville, Kentucky, shot and killed Taylor—a 26-year-old Black woman who worked as an emergency medical technician—in her home during a botched early-morning raid for narcotics. The suspect police were looking for wasn't there.

Despite Formula One promoting "End racism" and "We race as one" mottos during the racial-justice movement of 2020, the FIA quickly banned Hamilton's gesture. Before the next race, the *Motorsport Network* reported that the FIA added a new section to its rules requiring drivers to keep their race suits fully on—all the way to the neck, "not opened to the waist" as Hamilton's was—during the podium ceremony and post-race interviews. The FIA also changed pre-race procedures, the *Motorsport Network* reported, which had previously said drivers should wear its official anti-racism shirt or do "anything else a driver may feel comfortable" doing. The "anything else" line was deleted.[100]

The FIA often reminded onlookers of its priorities, and its decision to step in about Hamilton's T-shirt—not Nikita Mazepin groping a woman—was just another example. Mazepin's apology tweet would later be deleted while the Haas one stayed up, and no punishments, if there were any, became public.[101] Nikita Mazepin kept his seat for the 2021 season with his father's sponsorship on the Haas cars.

D'lVal initially defended the driver, posting her own statement in an Instagram story. "Hi guys, I just want to let you know Nikita and I have been good friends for a long time and nothing from that video was serious at all!" she said, according to *Sky Sports*. "We trust each other so much and this was a silly way of joking between us. I posted this video on his story as an internal joke. I am truly sorry. I can give you my word he's really a good person and he would never do anything to hurt or humiliate me."[102]

D'lVal's tone would soon change. Just over a week later, Spanish sports news site *Marca* shared screenshots of her Instagram story, where she posted a question prompt that read: "Advice to your younger self?"

"Mine would be: Don't let anyone touch you or disrespect you again," she answered. She posted the same advice prompt in another story, writing: "Don't drink with assholes."[103]

Around the same time, she posted a photo of a bathroom stall with a heart and "Protect drunk girls!" written on it in black marker.[104] (When the authors reached out to D'lVal to see if she'd like to share her experience, we did not hear back.)

About a month after the groping incident became public, Storey logged on yet again. He posted a picture of himself and team owner Gene Haas on Twitter, adding:

> Gene Haas made a mistake going against me after being misled by some corporate investors, however he has made a great move signing @nikita_mazepin & @SchumacherMick who are both world class talents. #Mazepin a future world champion in my view.
> #HaasF1 #FormulaOne #Business #F1[105]

In his rookie season with Haas, Nikita Mazepin would be the exact opposite. After one of Mazepin's multiple single-car spinouts at the season-opening 2021 Bahrain Grand Prix—this one during qualifying—the commentators said: "And that's not the first time we've seen the man from Moscow go for a spin on this track so far this weekend."[106] It wouldn't be the last, either. Three corners into the first lap of the Bahrain race, Mazepin spun out by himself yet again. He finished last, recording zero laps in his Formula One debut.[107]

Mazepin finished 17th at the next race in Italy, two laps down, ahead of only the three drivers who didn't finish the race at all. The same would be the case in the next two races in Portugal and Spain: In both, the Haas driver finished two laps down in 19th out of 20, ahead of only the drivers who did not finish the race at all.[108]

It wasn't until five races into his rookie season in Monaco that Mazepin didn't cross the line last on track. He finished ahead of one driver: his Haas teammate Mick Schumacher, who, like him, was three laps down from the leaders.[109]

Mazepin immediately earned the nickname "Mazespin," becoming such a meme that someone set up a website called "When Did Mazepin Spin?" with a collection of video embeds to his on-track woes. The website featured a cutout of Mazepin's head spinning in circles on a solid white background; under it, there was a clock counting up from his most recent spin and one counting down to his next drive on track. The longer the page stayed open, the faster Mazepin's head cutout spun.[110]

During the seventh of 23 scheduled race weekends in Mazepin's rookie 2021 season, the French Grand Prix, he spun during a practice session before the race. The administrator of the "When Did Mazepin Spin?" website recorded the time and date of the spin as usual, but captioned it to say it would be their final entry. "Mazepin spun on the last corner during practice," the caption read. "This is also the last update on this site. He spins way too much."[111]

At the time of the final entry, the website's unofficial tally was 12 spins in less than seven full race weekends. Another website dedicated to the same cause, Mazesp.in, had the same count at that point in the season.[112]

The controversy around Mazepin didn't end there. In 2022, Formula One's preseason testing took place in late February at Circuit de Barcelona-Catalunya in Spain.[113] On February 24, midway through testing, the world watched as Russia invaded Ukraine, sparking Europe's first major war in decades.[114] The attacks came at the command of Russian President Vladimir Putin, and many onlookers—including those in Formula One—voiced their support of Ukraine and its citizens.

As the invasion continued, many governments and organizations placed sanctions on Russia's economy and sports participation.[115-117] Formula One terminated its contract with the Russian Grand Prix promoter.[118] The FIA ruled that national symbols, anthems, colors, flags, or references to Russia or Belarus were essentially banned from use, and that Russian and Belarusian competitors would have to race under a neutral flag.[119]

With a Russian driver and sponsor, Haas F1 was immediately in the spotlight. The team, whose Uralkali car liveries mirrored the red, white, and blue hues of the Russian flag, stripped both the colors and branding from its cars for the final day of preseason testing on February 25.[120-121] Haas ran a plain white car instead.

Uralkali head Dmitry Mazepin, the father of Nikita Mazepin, was reported by ESPN on February 25 to be one of the business leaders who met with Putin to discuss sanctions in response to the invasion.[122] Meanwhile, Haas said it would decide on the future of its partnership with Uralkali—which funded Nikita Mazepin's spot on the team—once Barcelona testing ended.[123]

"Haas showed disloyalty to me going behind my back and working with my opponents," Storey tweeted on March 4, 2022, before Haas announced a decision.[124] "I hope they don't also do the dirty on Mazepin, who has worked hard for the team and done nothing wrong. Loyalty is a tremendously important characteristic for people of quality."

Less than a day later, Haas announced its termination of the partnership with Uralkali and Nikita Mazepin with immediate effect.

"As with the rest of the Formula One community, the team is shocked and saddened by the invasion of Ukraine and wishes a swift and peaceful end to the conflict," the announcement said.[125]

"An innocent young driver sacked because of nationality," Storey tweeted soon after the Haas announcement.[126] "Partisan, political, feeble, and wrong. Sets a terrible precedent and impugns the integrity of the sport. Spectacularly hypocritical and not thought through. Will the same apply to drivers from Saudi or the Congo? A farce."

Kevin Magnussen soon returned to Haas to take Mazepin's place, finishing fifth at the 2022 season opener in Bahrain.[127–128] That finish alone was worth 10 points—more than the entire Haas team scored in 2020 and 2021 combined.

If Mazepin were destined to be a Formula One champion as Storey predicted, it certainly wouldn't be anytime soon.

* * *

But Storey wasn't just a commenter on the Haas team's news cycle. He was a news cycle himself—or at least he wanted to be. On January 10, 2021, the Rich Energy account announced an announcement for the next day.[129]

The announcement came in a video posted to Storey's Twitter account, filmed in portrait orientation and without any fancy lighting or scenery. He sat on a dark leathery couch against a wall of wooden wainscoting, a hand on each leg. He wore all black, his beard and hair drooping to their signature mid-chest length, and he was positioned at the very bottom of the frame—similar to a casual photo taken by someone unfamiliar with a smartphone. A slight shake, in addition to the rest of the framing, indicated no tripod was used to film it.

"I'd like to thank the thousands of motorsport fans who have contacted us who are as excited as we are about the black and gold of Rich Energy returning to Formula One," Storey said. "As you know, in 2018, I signed a deal for Rich Energy to be the title sponsor of Haas, and in 2019, Rich Energy Haas Formula One competed with Ferrari engines in Formula One. We had some challenges in the summer of 2019 with some corporate stakeholders and our main competitors, costing us a lot of issues.

"We've overcome that and as the cofounder of the business, I've led a renaissance of Rich Energy around the world, and now we have, for example, one of the best motorbike teams in the world: Rich Energy OMG Racing. We have partnerships with some of the biggest motorsport manufacturers, and we now have some of the fastest men in the world as our ambassadors in addition to our ambassadors in many other sports. That includes, for example, Álvaro Bautista, the Spanish World Superbike superstar. We have James Hillier, the [Isle of Man] TT [motorcycle] legend, racing for Rich Energy in the Dakar Rally, and we have, among others, Davo Johnson, the Australian TT winner, representing Rich Energy in road racing.

"We're very, very excited about coming back to Formula One, and we look forward to really being very competitive in the pinnacle of motorsport. I thank all the supporters for their interest in what we are doing."[130]

All of Storey's claims about individual partnerships in the video were accurate—even if he double-dipped on Davo Johnson and James Hillier, who were both racing for the Rich Energy OMG team. But he only mentioned four specific partnerships: Rich Energy OMG, which everyone knew about; Bautista; Hillier; and Johnson. The rest of his claims were vague, much like the ones in his old LinkedIn blogs.

It also wasn't exactly the announcement advertised. The video, transcribed in full above, didn't reveal anything new about Rich Energy's road back to Formula One. Other than the partnership mentions and a recap of his season with Haas, Storey simply said Rich Energy was "very, very excited about coming back to Formula One"—not when, how, or with whom the company would return. Twitter users noticed immediately.

"So what happened to your announcement?" one account asked.[131]

"Does this utter tit womble think that nobody looks at Companies House!" another user said.[132] At the time, Companies House only showed that the Rich Energy listing had been ordered to wind up in the UK. The "appointment of a liquidator" documents would be published two days later.

Other responses included:

please no god no not again what team could be dumb enough to fall for this shit[133]

Absolute joke[134]

Hopefully whatever team agrees to this publicity stunt is smart enough to get paid in advance....[135]

Are you actually going to pay the team this time?[136]

why does he look like he's recruiting for a karate dojo?[137]

The roughly 200 replies to Storey's video announcement were overwhelmingly negative. But just a few days earlier on January 5, 2021, Storey had said an official announcement from the unnamed F1 team would come the first week of February—more than a month before the start of the 2021 season.[138] Perhaps all everyone needed was a little patience.

In the meantime, Rich Energy kept teasing its comeback. On February 7, 2021, the brand tweeted a photo of Storey with business titan Bernie Ecclestone, Formula One's longtime chief with an even longer history of controversy. The post read:

A huge thank you to the king of #F1 for being such a great supporter of our founder #WilliamStorey & for backing us. Our return to #FormulaOne due in no small part to the business genius of #BernieEcclestone. #RichEnergy #British #EnergyDrink #Entrepreneur #Motorsport[139]

The authors attempted to contact the closely guarded press representatives for Ecclestone, who was 90 years old at the time and whose honorific title of Formula One's chairman emeritus had expired more than a year before Rich Energy's tweet, to ask whether he was really involved. The attempt was unsuccessful.

On February 14, 2021, the Rich Energy Twitter account posted another video announcement. Storey, in what appeared to be the same outfit and same room as the January recording, opened by taking a drink from a Rich Energy can and loudly setting it on the table next to him.[140] The video quality, framing, and slight shake were all too reminiscent of the first.

"Magnificent," he said after taking a drink. "I'm delighted to announce that Rich Energy, the UK's premium energy drink, is coming back to Formula One. Ever since July 26, 2018, when I agreed to a deal with Vijay Mallya and [Indian conglomerate] Sahara to purchase the Force India Formula One team, we have been determined that Rich Energy will compete with Red Bull at the pinnacle of motorsport, Formula One. Unfortunately, our deal [to buy the] Force India Formula One team was derailed by [driver] Sergio Perez going for administration, and even though ourselves and a very well-funded Russian bid bidded more than Lawrence Stroll, Lawrence Stroll became the owner of Force India, which is now, of course, Aston Martin Racing."[141]

As previously noted, *Eurosport* reported in July 2018 that Rich Energy's offer to the Force India team totaled 30 million pounds.[142] Lawrence Stroll's consortium paid 90 million pounds, according to *Reuters*—three times the Rich Energy bid.[143]

"Subsequently, we then entered into detailed negotiations with McLaren and Williams before I decided that we could actually do a much better deal with Haas F1," Storey continued. "We then created the Rich Energy Haas F1 team, which was registered with the FIA, and actually, in my opinion, was the best looking car on the grid in 2019. Unfortunately, due to poor performance both on and off the track, regrettably I had to sack Haas."[144]

(As previously noted, Rich Energy's July 10, 2019, tweet "sacking" Haas prompted a statement from team principal Guenther Steiner: "Rich Energy is currently the title partner of Haas F1 Team. I cannot comment further on the contractual relationship between our two parties due to commercial confidentiality."[145] The Rich Energy Haas F1 partnership continued until September 9 of that year, when Haas announced it was over. After initially accepting the split, the Rich Energy account tweeted later in September: "After review of dispute with investors who created havoc via UK distribution company Rich Energy CEO & all stakeholders have asked @HaasF1Team to explain how they did a deal with unauthorized non officers of @rich_energy. As such title partnership is still on #RussianGP #F1 #NoDeal."[146])

Storey's video announcement went on: "I then entered into a series of legal problems with my main competitors, Red Bull, which have now all been dealt with, and in the last year, we've worked incredibly hard to lead a renaissance of Rich Energy worldwide, where millions of consumers are trying our drink, which we believe, and are very confident, is the best energy drink in the world.

"Rich Energy now have a raft of world-champion ambassadors. We have one of the best motorbike teams in the world, Rich Energy OMG Racing. We also have a partnership with the BMW factory World Superbike team and some of the fastest men in the TT, Macau Grand Prix, and World Superbikes—for example, Álvaro Bautista—as ambassadors.

"Since leaving Formula One, I've worked very diligently to engineer a return. And I've noticed, actually, there is a new financial reality in Formula One with terrestrial TV no longer really being prevalent and a paywall of viewers. Instead of 10 or 12 million people watching Formula One on *BBC*, it is actually a few hundred thousand on Sky.

"Subsequent damage that has been done to sponsorship has meant that there are a number of different teams [in financial trouble]. For example, McLaren have done the sale and lease back of their Woking technology center, and Williams were in financial problems until they were bailed out by our friends at Dorilton Capital. And obviously, even Haas have now had to go for pay drivers because of their weak financial position, so I've been looking for a way in which Rich Energy could return optimally both for us and to help the team that we are going to work with.

"A strategic ally of Rich Energy has agreed to purchase a majority stake in an existing team. We did explore with the new regulations actually entering our own team for 2022, which would be Rich Energy Formula One Team, but a friend of ours has agreed on a deal for a majority stake in a Formula One team, and we will become a partner of that team for 2021. Once that acquisition is announced, we will become the title sponsor for 2022.

"I'm really looking forward to competing with our competitors on track. I'll be at the first race, March 28 in Bahrain."

Despite Storey telling the world a month earlier that an "official announcement from [the] team" would come the first week of February, his February 14 video announcement came neither during the first week of the month nor from a team. It wasn't official, either—it was simply Storey further delaying his road to the "biggest comeback since Lazarus."

Rich Energy did not return to the Formula One grid in 2021, despite Storey's promises. Lazarus, it seemed, was dead as a doornail.

9

THE RICHEST PART

When the Haas Formula One team officially entered the paddock in 2016, America was in a strange place. The country was in the throes of a contentious election cycle, which would lead to business magnate and former reality television star Donald Trump assuming office over the career politicians who ran against him. Trump's presidency centered on shock value, with constant tweets and statements designed to keep his name at the forefront of the press.

The United States had become a global political spectacle, and Haas was representing it by default. "It was always going to be a divisive team," a former Haas F1 employee told the authors. "Being American, and especially in the period America was going through."[1]

Any American Formula One team would have struggled with the uphill battle of attaining international legitimacy in that climate. But Haas' problems were only exacerbated by having a title sponsor whose CEO took to Twitter to share his brash beliefs, yet struggled to legitimize his own brand's finances and product availability.

Team owner Gene Haas didn't have the rosiest business history himself. In 2006, Haas was arrested on charges of subscribing to false tax returns, witness intimidation, and conspiracy. The U.S. Department of Justice said Haas "allegedly orchestrat[ed] a scheme in which approximately $50 million of bogus expenses were put on the company's books in an attempt to avoid the payment of more than $20 million in federal income taxes," and he was sentenced to two years in prison.[2] He ultimately served 16 months.[3]

"Yes, Gene's got a bit of a sketchy past," the former employee continued. "We all know that. But it was 20-odd years ago. Not saying it's right, but he's a very quiet guy, he doesn't rub it down your throat. If you Google him, yes it comes up, but he's still got a billion-dollar company. So you don't forgive him, but you kind of park it. This other guy is blatant with it."[4]

* * *

When the authors started this book, we imagined this final chapter circling back around to the beginning: William Storey's beginning, since most people didn't know much about him outside of his tumultuous tenure in Formula One.

That's because as a public figure, Storey was a mystery. He arrived in the Formula One paddock one day with a long beard, black-and-gold swag, and his own branded team, only to disappear just as quickly. Everything we knew about Storey was in relation to his company or his time in motorsport—nothing before or adjacent to that. We imagined using this space to talk about his early life, his hobbies and interests, his schooling, and the details of how he came to be an entrepreneur in the first place. We then imagined getting to the harder questions: where the money was, why some of his claims didn't line up with the data (or often with his other claims), and what really happened with his investors and the Haas F1 Team.

But we never got to learn those things. Storey, who was usually keen to control the narrative around himself and his company, didn't respond to our interview requests or questions despite our messages being marked as "seen." Of the 112 questions we sent Storey, some of the most pressing were:

- What documentation or proof did you show Haas (and Williams, which you were close to a deal with) that your young brand could meet the financial requirements of sponsoring their F1 teams?
- In the Whyte Bikes judgment, judge Melissa Clarke described you as having an "apparently natural tendency to exaggerate," and as providing "different and inconsistent accounts" of the development of the Rich Energy logo, "which also conflicted to a large extent with the evidence of Mr. [Sean] Kelly." What do you have to say about this?
- When we asked in March 2019 about your Companies House financial statements—581 pounds in the bank in 2017 and 103 pounds in 2016—you wouldn't give financial information over but told us it would "very quickly become apparent that [Rich Energy was] very significantly bigger than one set of accounts from 2017 shows." Rich Energy's UK listing never uploaded more financial documents. What are your current finances like?
- Red Bull's claim cited IRI Worldwide data, which said between March 2017 and February 2019, approximately 1,025 cans of Rich Energy were sold with a value of £836. This conflates with your claims—first, that you'd sold in excess of 100 million cans during Rich Energy's lifetime, then that you'd sold circa 3 million in 2018. What is the real number of cans sold over the lifetime of the brand?

- You regularly teased announcements about your return to F1, but the announcements would end up being a recap of your current partnerships, with no new information aside from: "We're excited to return." When will Rich Energy return? What date? With whom?
- Do you care to share more about your views of the COVID-19 pandemic?

The Haas Formula One Team declined to participate in this book during the writing process—including a request to make team principal Guenther Steiner and owner Gene Haas available for interviews—through spokesperson Stuart Morrison. The authors first asked Haas about participating in the book months before it was finished, and the team declined to discuss the topic once again after receiving a final list of questions. Some of the most crucial questions we sent the Haas team were as follows:

- What research did you do into Rich Energy before signing the deal? What's your protocol for signing regular sponsors and title sponsors? How do you define "due diligence"?
- Did you know about Storey's history of failed businesses, whose records and financials are publicly accessible on Companies House?
- Haas wanted 35 million pounds in damages from the contract termination. Was this money ever received?
- William Storey tweeted in July 2020: "Red Bull hated me in F1 and put Haas under huge pressure to try and oust me." Did this happen?
- People on the internet very quickly and easily found Rich Energy's Companies House records, which said the company had 581 pounds in the bank in 2017 and 103 in 2016. Did Haas see this before going through with the partnership? If so, was there proof that Rich Energy had enough money for its sponsorship deal? What did Haas see that was different from what the public saw?

The full list of questions sent to both Storey and the Haas team can be found in Appendix A of this book.

The authors also didn't receive responses from public relations representatives for driver Kevin Magnussen in 2021, which made sense once he was called upon to return to the team in 2022. His former teammate Romain Grosjean seemed to take it pretty lightly those days, at least: At the 2021 U.S. Grand Prix, a few spectators spotted the authors and showed us a photo of Grosjean autographing one of their Rich Energy cans earlier that year.

During an interview in early 2022, Grosjean told the authors the Rich

Energy situation didn't impact him as a driver. He said the year wasn't really different from his other seasons in motorsport, at Haas or elsewhere.

"I didn't really care," Grosjean told the authors.[5] "For us, it didn't change anything. I know there was talk about it behind the scenes, but I think it was a lot made out of not much, if I may."

Despite onlookers researching Rich Energy's viability, Grosjean said he never did.

"I don't know the details behind it, but I guess they paid some money, so that was good for the team," Grosjean said. "I know it was not easy to find the Rich Energy cans. People were like, 'Where can we buy it?' I still have some in my fridge, so I kept them."

Aside from Rich Energy, the authors asked Grosjean what it was like looking back at Haas' performance three years later.

"I think we did a terrible job in 2019 and 2020," Grosjean said. "The car was just not fast, and there were issues. I fought really hard to get back to the Spec 1 car—the Melbourne one—during the season, because the update didn't work. But they wouldn't believe me. It was just a poorly designed car, sadly, and we were trying everything we could. The car was just not good enough."

"The team did admit toward the end of the 2019 season that they should have listened to you and Kevin more," the authors responded.[6]

"Yep," Grosjean said.[7] "But at the end of the season is a bit late, right?"

*   *   *

The silence from Storey and the Haas F1 Team left us with one final question: How does one end a story that hasn't quite ended?

As the authors brought this book to a close in December 2021, Storey remained adamant that Rich Energy would make a return to Formula One. Lightning Volt was still in liquidation, and the liquidators on its file—Chris Farrington and Ben Woodthorpe—did not provide comment to the authors.[8] Storey's Twitter bio proclaimed that he founded Wolf Data Systems and was the managing director of a company called WolfJerky. On November 30, 2021, he shared his feelings about what was then the latest variant of the virus that caused COVID-19, saying: "Omicron is an anagram of moronic. Aptly describes those who believe the Covid narrative."[9] Six days earlier, he tweeted a photo of a Rich Energy hospitality tent at sunset and said: "The Rich Club is raising the bar in motorsport hospitality. We have commissioned a new one for next year that will be making its debut in F1."[10]

But questions of Storey's life outside of Formula One weren't the only things we couldn't answer. With journalism, some of the most interesting details are the ones you can't quite publish—whether it be because not enough sources corroborate the claim, the sources lack documentation of what happened, or anything else.

For us, this happened on a few occasions. In total, we contacted or attempted to contact more than 150 people. We found the people said to be involved in the early stages of the Haas F1–Rich Energy introduction, but we couldn't get them to talk about how the deal went down. We heard about a rumored deal that would've made Rich Energy the title sponsor of a Formula One track, but non-disclosure agreements stifled our efforts to get more information. We learned of an apparently bizarre compensation agreement between Rich Energy and one of the racing teams it sponsored, but we couldn't get further documentation or sources to speak with us on the record. We reached out to Storey's partners and investors to ask what went down, but we didn't get very far with any of them. We tried to speak with countless numbers of other people involved with Storey in some way—athletes he sponsored, boxers he claimed to manage, employees who worked for him, friends, and family members—and rarely heard back.

Thus, questions lingered and anecdotes went unconfirmed. Perhaps that meant the story didn't end there. Perhaps it was only just beginning. Or, perhaps the Rich Energy tale peaked long before the end of 2021. As of this writing, the authors couldn't know.

Because of that, we handed the reins of this chapter to the people we spoke to while writing the book. The legacy of William Storey and Rich Energy, after all, was built on the vocalization of one person's impressions and opinions. It only seemed fitting that others should have their say.

*   *   *

People around William Storey described him as everything from a marketing mogul to a huge headache. When the authors had a chance to speak with extreme scooter rider Dakota Schuetz, the water had settled after his turbulent partnership with Rich Energy. Looking back, Schuetz said Storey was "just the best salesman ever."[11]

"If you ask him to sell you anything, and he believes in it, he can do it," Schuetz said. "The issue is it could be 50 percent B.S. I kind of knew [that] maybe halfway through, but it was a fun project if it worked, and we got to do a lot of cool things. I was already in these environments anyway, so it was easy to be with Rich Energy."[12]

"What made you start suspecting this wasn't what it seemed?" the authors asked.[13]

"It's just much smaller than they sell it to be," Schuetz said. "It was an energy-drink company. They had employees. I knew everybody. It wasn't like they didn't have anything. It was just much, much, much smaller. The term is just 'smoke and mirrors.' Like in any marketing company, you try to sell your company way, way bigger than it actually is. But when it comes down to it and you need to get paid, or need to go here and do this, then you find out what's the real deal."[14]

As for Storey, Schuetz didn't believe he was ever malicious in intent. He was just "the best and worst thing for Rich Energy. It's like he was the double-edged sword."[15]

Another person who worked with Storey faced a different set of extremes: deciding whether to quit their job or keep it due to the environment Rich Energy and its vocal CEO fostered. The person, whose identity was verified by the authors but who asked to remain anonymous to protect their career, worked with Storey during one of Rich Energy's many stints sponsoring motorsport athletes and teams. They eventually left their position, but they believed they might have stuck around had Rich Energy not been involved.

"[Rich Energy] added a massive headache for things," they said. "For all the ways forward [working with the brand] gave me, it also wrecked my own mental health and work ethic."[16]

It also changed their perception of their coworkers, including the people in positions of power who could have encouraged Storey to rein in some of his behavior but failed to speak up. "I was aware that they could see that William was doing things, and I always advocated for a harder response," they said. "It was just never taken."[17]

The person described Storey as a "rogue individual" and "one of these people that speaks in such hyperbole the whole time"—often loudly. "His opinion is bigger than your opinion, regardless of where you sit on things," they said. "You always need people that are very forceful of their opinions, but he'll say whatever he wants and won't back any of it up."[18]

Big opinions often attract big responses, and sim racer Azzy Iredale's experience was no different.

"I did receive a lot of backlash by some disgruntled F1 fans who obviously didn't like Rich Energy but didn't realize I was doing it for literally a joke," Iredale, whose brief Rich Energy sponsorship came after the company's falling-out with Haas, said. "I had everything get leaked. 'Oh, this person's email address is this.' I was like, 'Woah, woah, there's no need for that now.' I got a lot of abusive messages, comments on my personal Instagram and Twitter, and threats occasionally. It was crazy." (Iredale told the authors they deleted the comments and messages, thus they weren't able to provide screenshots or further evidence of them.[19])

After parting ways with Rich Energy, Iredale joined a furry-led community of gamers in an organization called Furtastic. It proved to be a more promising move for the racer, who planned to run a trans rights livery on their car soon after their August 2021 interview with the authors. That kind of message felt out of place alongside the Rich Energy logo, Iredale said, which "stood for everything against what I'm going for."

"The stuff that [Storey] was spouting on Twitter was just such a health hazard for people," Iredale said. "I don't associate with any of that stuff, and I do wear my heart on my sleeve when I race."[20]

Iredale said Furtastic was much more welcoming, providing them with gaming equipment soon after signing. "And they're a wee sports team compared to, let's say, an energy drinks company," they said.[21]

Perhaps the people most impacted by the Rich Energy saga had the least amount of influence. The five Haas F1 Team employees who spoke with the authors painted a picture of a tumultuous, painful, and confusing workplace characterized by unanswered questions in a period of already low performance. The biggest question of all, though, was a simple one: Why?

"I genuinely don't know," one employee said. "That's part of the troubling thing behind it, is: How did it even get to the point where we rolled out at Barcelona with black-and-gold cars and black-and-gold team uniforms and black-and-gold trucks, and everything black and gold? I'm not being derogatory, but if the likes of you and I can do the research, why couldn't Guenther and whoever else? And who was advising Guenther at the time?"[22]

Employees wondered what caused Steiner—a dependable leader in their eyes—to move forward with the Rich Energy contract. Did Steiner make that decision himself? Or was he influenced to do so in some way?

"Haas F1 was essentially Guenther's idea, so why would you jeopardize it by partnering with this guy who is very shady, has a very difficult history, and has a very poor financial record, you know?" an employee asked. "That side of it is the most intriguing and concerning at the same time. How did we get to that point where somebody's signature was on the line, and everything got to where it did? Because it just made them look like a laughing stock.

"It felt embarrassing as an employee to be part of it, and there was an element of concern and not understanding how senior management—whether it was Guenther or Gene or the guys in America, who were all a senior-management team—how they even got to that point of working with this guy. Which, hopefully, is what you're going to uncover."[23]

Answers failed to become apparent, both for Haas employees in 2019 and for the authors as we tried to track down the exact events that led up to the partnership. Employees couldn't compare their experience with Rich Energy to anything else in their professional lives; the CEO's conduct was as much of an enigma as the company itself. They felt that perhaps Gene

Haas truly knew Storey's credentials for entering the F1 scene, but neither he nor the Haas team provided hints as to what those credentials were.

Other employees quickly grew too tired to ask questions. The desire to leave their jobs—to find somewhere less tumultuous to work—was strong, largely due to the unrelenting nature of the Rich Energy news cycle. If there wasn't something going wrong with the Haas car on track, Storey was surely tweeting a news story into existence.

"Let's be honest," one former Haas employee said. "Most legal battles in Formula One—no matter whether they're sponsorship, or technical, or personal—are behind closed doors. They're very rarely played out on social media."[24]

"I'm sure the way William treated it was the only reason why it went big," another added. "That was the most interesting thing to us: He was tweeting stupid things."[25]

The former employees who spoke with the authors were irritated by Storey's social media habits—especially, in some cases, as it related to global politics. "I was thinking at the time, 'I don't like the way [Haas] is going, and also, it's allied itself with a very politically outspoken guy,'" one former employee said. "We had the whole Brexit thing going on, and regardless of my beliefs, Brexit caused huge problems with global travel and shipping in Formula One. To be allied and partnered with a company whose CEO was very pro–Brexit was very small-minded in my view. And it all added up, and I'm going, 'I can't be involved in the direction this company is taking.'"[26]

Other F1 team owners and title sponsors often had little to say about politics, the employee said, to the point where it could be challenging to posit exactly what that person or company believed. But with Storey, it was obvious, and they felt it reflected poorly on the team as a whole.

The employee became so uncomfortable with Storey's political alignment—and Haas' passive endorsement of those views, whether the team shared them or not, through its sponsorship agreement—that it had "quite a big bearing" in their ultimate departure from the team. They were concerned that future employers would see "Rich Energy" on their resume and pass them over.[27]

All roads, though, eventually led back to money. While Rich Energy might have taken over the identity of the Haas Formula One team, the numbers told a different story: Rich Energy only promised $20 million per year, compared to the team's $100 million annual budget. One former employee described the brand takeover as "disproportionate to the amount of money [Storey] was putting in."

"If he was on a level with [Dmitry] Mazepin or Gene [Haas] with the amount of money he was putting in, then you go, 'Maybe, OK, he's pushing his investment along,'" they said. "Then it's got some substance behind it."[28]

But there was never that feeling. The former employees who spoke to the authors were never assured that the money ever existed, or that, if it did, it had come from legitimate sources.

"I just had this feeling there was something sinister behind it all, and there often is—certainly in Formula One and in football, and all that kind of stuff," one former employee said. "There's often sinister, dirty money floating around. Look at Mazepin. Look at Vijay Mallya. It's been going on for years, but it just felt a bit sinister and a bit odd."[29]

Both Dmitry Mazepin and Mallya had money—that was never a question, even if there were moral or ethical concerns to be had with how they acquired it. Dmitry Mazepin, for example, was a majority shareholder in Uralkali, the company that went on to become Haas' title sponsor in 2021.[30] Uralkali mines created more than one large sinkhole in Russia that swallowed nearby homes.[31] Mallya was accused of money laundering in order to accumulate the fortune that allowed him to purchase and operate the Force India F1 team.[32]

But Storey, remember, praised Mallya for his "kamikaze" approach to running things and said he likely wasn't guilty of anything but "believing his lawyers and trusting those closest to him."[33]

Formula One was a perfect fit for Storey, an entrepreneur convinced his energy drink could take on Red Bull's Goliath. Storey, however, wasn't a perfect fit for Formula One. "It was the volume of what he was doing, and the volume he was doing it at," one former employee said. "It didn't add up. I think if you would have gone on Companies House or you did more of a search of him and it said 'multimillionaire William Storey,' or he's got a trail of very successful businesses behind him, you'll go, 'Well, OK, he's a loud-mouth billionaire or a loud-mouth millionaire, like Mallya was until he got caught up with.' Mallya was very brash, very loud, and OK he was dirty, but he could substantiate it with the money. You could look at him and go, 'He has got a fleet of 747s, he has got a lot of companies. Yes, he's very, very dodgy, but he can substantiate it because he's got 50 million quid in the bank.' But when [Storey's] got 200 quid in the bank and nobody really knows where his money's coming from, then he's just mouthing off. You'd think he would have gotten bored by now."[34]

*   *   *

Throughout Rich Energy's fraught time in Formula One, the same question kept coming up: Was this elusive drink—this unicorn piss, as some called it—actually better than Red Bull? Was it *anything* like Red Bull? Was it *too much* like Red Bull?

Matt Farah, automotive YouTube star and host of *The Smoking Tire* podcast, believed the latter: that Rich Energy tasted like "white-labeled

Red Bull."[35] Farah was so confident in that belief, he offered a blindfolded taste test with the help of *The Smoking Tire*'s producer, Zack Klapman.

Reclining in a chair on a video call with the authors, Farah said he wasn't a big fan of either Formula One or Red Bull. Someone gave him cans of Rich Energy "as a joke gift," he said, and the three unopened ones he had left expired in September 2020—a year after Rich Energy's time in Formula One ended and a year before this taste test occurred.

"Zack is around the corner," Farah said, pulling a royal blue sweatband over his eyes. "We have two cans of Red Bull and two cans of Rich Energy; one is room temperature, and one is cold. We've also got unmarked glasses to pour them in so I can't see a thing. I'm going to use my pilates headband as a blindfold, and I have some plain crackers here [as a palate cleanser]. They're appropriately stale."[36]

As Klapman prepared to round the corner with two champagne flutes of yellow liquids for the cold round, Farah asked the authors: "Is the whole thing a scam?"[37] It was a complicated question with no clear answer.

Unbeknownst to Farah, the first cold glass was Rich Energy. He brought it to his nose like a wine tasting.

"This smell," he said. "I know this smell so much. It's that cough-medicine-y smell."

"Now what does that one taste like?" the authors asked.

"Red Bull," he said. The sentiment was firm. "It tastes like Red Bull."

"Describe that," the authors said.

"It's very lightly carbonated, but it just generally has this medicinal taste," Farah responded. "It tastes like what the color orange would taste like. The taste is just a liquified version of the smell—just that medicine smell. I think that's definitely Red Bull. It's instantly familiar to me, and obviously in my life, I've had quite a bit of Red Bull. I probably haven't had a Red Bull in like two to three years, but it came right back as Red Bull."[38]

Farah wasn't told his first drink was, in fact, Rich Energy. As he picked up a stale cracker in between drinks, he added: "The funny thing about energy drinks is, they're so obviously not from Earth. It tastes like it was made in a lab."[39] Then he grabbed the chilled glass of Red Bull. "Now, this one smells like if you left the other one out in the sun for a few days and like 10 percent of the water content went out of it," Farah said. "Real similar to the first one, but denser, not as refined, and more like Triaminic cough syrup."[40]

He took a drink. "But the taste doesn't line up with the smell," he said. "It tastes much milder than it smells. It smells like dense syrup, and it tastes like—it's got the same kind of carbonation. It's definitely not as refined of a taste. I think the first one was Red Bull and the second one was Rich Energy."

As Klapman took notes of Farah's observations, not telling him he had the two backward, the authors asked: "Does the second one also taste like liquid orange, or a different flavor?"

"It's like brown," he said. "It tastes brown. It tastes like they were going for the same thing, but there were not nearly as many resources put into refining flavor. To try them just back to back, the first one is a much more drinkable flavor. It's still chemical-y and like medicine, but I could probably chug a whole can of it if I had to without, like, gagging. The second one is kind of—it's the denser medicine. I wouldn't want to take a big gulp of it."[41]

Klapman brought out another set of unmarked glasses, this time room temperature. The first one was Red Bull, but Farah didn't know that. "Smells definitely stronger," Farah said, sniffing the two room-temperature glasses interchangeably. Then he took a sip and clicked his lips. "Hmph. The smell matches the taste. This one tastes better at room temperature, actually."[42]

He would guess right this time around: that his first drink was Red Bull. Then came the Rich Energy. "That doesn't taste very good at all," Farah said, guessing its identity correctly as well. "This doesn't have much smell, but the taste is really, really, really medicine-y."[43]

Perhaps the taste of the Rich Energy at room temperature had to do with the expiration date, perhaps not. Farah hadn't yet learned which was which, but he had changed his mind from before: Rich Energy and Red Bull weren't the exact same thing. "I don't think they taste exactly the same," he said. "They taste like one is trying to copy the other but didn't have the resources to do it right. Did I guess right, Zack?"

"Only on half of them," Klapman said. "The cold ones, you got backwards. The first one you tried that was cold was Rich Energy, and you thought it was Red Bull."

"Oh shit!" Farah responded.

"This may just be the order because they taste so familiar, but your notes are interesting," Klapman said. "It almost makes it seem like the Rich Energy was watered-down Red Bull. The warm ones, you were correct."

"Am I the only person who actually owns a can of Rich Energy to drink?" Farah asked. "It's not the worst. I've drank some that are really, really horrible—like, the regular Monsters and the regular Rockstars are really gross. The flavored Red Bulls are terrible."[44]

Meanwhile, Klapman tried the drinks. "They do taste different," he said.

"They taste a little more different than I thought they would," Farah responded. "Being refrigerated really tamps down the flavor. I guess I actually thought the Rich Energy tasted better, didn't I?"[45] He did indeed—expired can and all.

＊　＊　＊

Rich Energy was never a fake company. It produced a real, tangible product—one that, to some, might have even tasted better than Red Bull. But with William Storey at the helm, that good product never got to shine on the world stage of motorsport, or even local supermarket shelves, like it could have. Rich Energy's wings were clipped long before it could take flight.

Many people said Storey could sell you the world, and he could. His pitches worked on everyone from small-time athletes to one of the world's most recognizable Formula One teams. Crucially, though, he was never able to create a narrative for his brand that answered the many questions his grandiose persona raised.

Onlookers struggled to follow the money despite Storey's consistent reassurances that he had "blue-chip backers"[46] and "sterling billionaires" at his disposal.[47] Few people could find the drink on shelves despite its positioning as an international brand. Meanwhile, Storey continued to shout his own praises. Two and two never quite equaled four.

Had Storey remained quiet, perhaps Rich Energy as a drink could have spoken for itself with its flavor and stylish black-and-gold branding. Perhaps the initial questions about the company's legitimacy would have simmered down. Perhaps Rich Energy as a company could have used its Formula One sponsorship to launch a successful rags-to-riches marketing campaign. But William Storey was Rich Energy's CEO, and he couldn't allow its narrative to exist without him at the center—to his own detriment, in many cases.

Yet to some degree, Storey was successful. He made it onto the world stage of motorsport and captivated its viewers, even if it wasn't always for the best reasons. He earned countless headlines, be they about his product or his antics. He made waves so big that a book—this book—was necessary to dissect them all. Even if Rich Energy never had a chance to fully thrive, one former Haas employee described it best: Storey had "some good marketing ideas."[48]

"Listen, I'll tell you something," they said. "If the whole story had been about making an energy drink popular and famous and well known, it would have worked. Everyone knows what Rich Energy is. It's famous."

"That bloke deserves some kudos. He did a good job."

APPENDIX A
Questions for William Storey

- Let's start at the very beginning: Tell us a little about your childhood, your family and schooling.
- You've seemed very entrepreneurial for years—when did you first realize that you wanted to start your own business?
- You've mentioned in previous interviews that you received your initial funding for Rich Energy from a tobacco farm. Tell us how you got involved with tobacco farming. Were you involved in any of your other businesses while you were overseas? How were you able to purchase that tobacco farm in the first place?
- Rich Energy wasn't your first attempt at starting a business; tell us about your previous explorations with tech companies and fashion brands.
- Many of your previous companies featured a very similar group of people that often took on roles within each company. Why was that? Tell us about them.
- What inspired you to opt for an energy drink brand? And why do you feel Rich Energy had a more public profile than other companies you've started?
- Did your promotion of Rich Energy in the sports sphere have anything to do with your decision to opt for an energy drink as opposed to a different product? Why or why not?
- What market research did you perform when it came to promoting products like energy drinks in the sports world? Do you have any of that research available for review?
- We've found similarities between Rich Energy and a Croatian energy drink company named Rich. What are the ties between your brands? Did you acquire the Croatian Rich company? What did you do with the brand after?

- An old version of the Rich Energy website says that you worked with experts to develop the Rich Energy recipe. What experts were those and what was their contribution?
- The cans list Rich Energy's manufacturing plant as being located in Austria. Where, exactly, in Austria is it? Do you have photos of the facility?
- In many of your LinkedIn posts, there seems to be a blend between athletes managed by William Storey Management and athletes sponsored by Rich Energy. Tell us about your management company and how the two became so intertwined?
- You've often promoted Rich Energy as a luxury brand with images of models or hotels that weren't what they seemed. How do you respond to that?
- It's appeared that entering F1 as a sponsor has been your goal for a long time. When did you first attempt to get involved in the sport? Is that where Force India came into play? What were your goals with Force India?
- A few publications reported that you were set to have meetings with Claire Williams during the 2018 U.S. Grand Prix, but that you didn't appear at the dinner. How long had your talks with Williams been going on? Why did that deal fall through?
- Was the deal that Haas was offering more attractive?
- Around this time, you also frequently mentioned you'd had cash infusions from four sterling billionaires. Who were those billionaires? Where did your involvement with them begin?
- What were your first impressions of the Haas team and its managers?
- You seemed to have a very small Rich Energy team when you entered F1, and it seemed like you managed your own PR. Was that by choice?
- Walk us through some of your other sponsorships. What fashion shows did you sponsor? What music festivals? What happened with your Isle of Man TT team? How did you get involved with Amber Lounge and Ultima Cars?
- Rich Energy has frequently mentioned its attempts to break into the American market, and there's even a U.S.–specific version of the Rich Energy website. What were your plans there?
- Rich Energy sponsored Jordan King for the Indy 500, but it was a one-off, and the brand never quite dug into the American motorsport market. Why?
- Two years ago, *Evo* magazine featured a full-page spread about Rich Energy that appeared to be an article but was titled as an advertisement. Did you commission that piece?

- When it came to your sponsorship of Haas, how did your relationship with the team begin to devolve?
- Did you believe there was a performance clause in your contract with Haas?
- Who were the investors who ousted you after Rich Energy tweeted about leaving F1?
- Can you tell us about the apparent Rich Energy talks with [*redacted*] to become the racetrack's headlining sponsor?
- Rich Energy once posted a photo of its "HQ," but it was actually a photo of the Bingham Riverhouse hotel in Richmond. Do you have an explanation for that? Was Bingham your HQ?
- The Rich Energy account also posted many pixelated stock photos from the internet without credit, over and over again—often claiming or insinuating that they had something to do with the company when they didn't. Examples include photos of airport hangars and hotels, taken from websites instead of by the social admin's phone. Why did this happen?
- What was the extent of Rich Energy's partnership with the 2017 West Ham player awards? Where did the brand appear? (Rich Energy didn't appear on the stand and repeat wall at the 2017 West Ham player awards or in the recap video from the event.)
- Who is Bernie Puz?
- Dakota Schuetz?
- The Whyte Bikes judgment said Melissa Clarke found the Rich Energy camp to be "poor witnesses" whose evidence she treated with a "high degree of caution." She also said she found some of your evidence to be "incorrect or misleading," and that she deemed you were "involved in the manufacture of documents during the course of litigation to provide additional support of the Defendants' case." Overall, how would you describe your court presence versus this description from the judgment?
- Adding to Clarke's suspicion about whether the logo was directly copied was your "unreasonable unwillingness to even countenance the possibility that [you] might have seen, but forgotten" during research. What is your response to that?
- Clarke described you as having an "apparently natural tendency to exaggerate," and as providing "different and inconsistent accounts" of the development of the Rich Energy logo, "which also conflicted to a large extent with the evidence of Mr. Kelly." What do you have to say about this?
- Clarke cited examples of your sales during court. You said in February 2019, the month before the trial, that Rich Energy had

produced 90 million cans. When questioned in court on March 12 and 13, 2019, you clarified that Rich Energy "had produced 90 million cans, but had not yet filled and sold them." But the next day on March 14, 2019, you told Alanis King on the phone that Rich Energy had sold "in excess of 100 million cans." These numbers don't add up. Can you explain the discrepancies?

- Clarke said you wouldn't admit that the Rich Energy and Whyte Bikes logos were closely similar. Why not?
- You've said before, and said in the court proceedings, that Rich Energy was named for Richmond. But then you've gone back on that and said it was serendipitous that the brand you bought had a similar name. Why didn't you say that the first time?
- Clarke wrote: "I am satisfied on the balance of probabilities that both Mr. Kelly and Mr. Storey have lied about not being familiar with [Whyte Bikes' logo]. I find it more likely than not that they were familiar with it, and that they directly and knowingly copied [it] in designing [the Rich Energy logo]." Do you stand by what you said in court: that you hadn't seen the Whyte Bikes logo?
- In 2019, Rich Energy tweeted a photo of a black helicopter with a gold Rich Energy logo, saying: "Fly high with @rich_energy and @castleairltd." The photo was the exact same one the account had used in at least one other tweet, dated nearly two years earlier on November 22, 2017. Why repeat the photos?
- In a November 2020 tweet with a "MAGA" hashtag, you wore a "Make America Great Again" hat. Before Trump's November 2016 election victory over Hillary Clinton, you bet on him winning in a LinkedIn blog but claimed not to be cheering him on. When did that change?
- Have you paid Whyte Bikes its 35,416 pounds?
- In another case, Red Bull settled with Rich Energy, and damages totaled 25,000 pounds from the company. The first 5,000 pounds was due on October 21, 2019, another 10,000 pounds was due on January 2, 2020, and the final 10,000 pounds was due on February 1, 2020. Was this paid?
- Azzy Iredale said they received a 24 pack of Rich Energy but no other support, despite saying you said you'd send it. Did you send anything else?
- How many Rich Energy cans did you provide the Haas team total? How many were provided to the U.S., the UK, the traveling race team, and Italy, if applicable?
- Do you have proof of an offer for Sunderland? How much was it for?

- For a long time, Rich Energy's Wikipedia page said it was "a British beverage company that claims to manufacture the Rich Energy energy drink." The "claims" part was edited out sometime around 2021. Do you know who edited it out? Why do you think it was that way before?
- In early 2019 and throughout your 2019 season, it was mostly you handling press inquiries to the Rich Energy press email. Did you intend for it to be you handling press? Was it out of necessity—monetary or otherwise—or was that just the best move for your company, since many companies have other people handle public relations?
- Who is Zoran Terzic, one of the original Rich Energy directors? How is he involved?
- Who is Richard Fletcher, one of the original Rich Energy directors? How was he involved before his termination as a director in June 2017?
- When we asked in March 2019 about your Companies House financial statements—581 pounds in the bank in 2017 and 103 pounds in 2016—you wouldn't give financial information over but told us it would "very quickly become apparent that [Rich Energy was] very significantly bigger than one set of accounts from 2017 shows." Rich Energy's UK listing never uploaded more financial documents. What are your current finances like?
- You told *Motorsport.com* in 2018 that you were backed by four sterling billionaires, reported to include David Sullivan and David Gold. Who were the other two?
- On LinkedIn in March 2018, you wrote: "Rich Energy chosen as trailblazing brand in city awards as company raises £220m. Delighted to be recognised by multiple financial institutions as a company at the forefront of innovation with a compelling proposition and business model as we take our international expansion to the next level. We now have the financial firepower to take on the established corporates. And win. Rich Energy is on the acquisition trail and moves further on trajectory of establishing a world class British performance brand." What city were these awards for? What financial institutions? Where did the 220 million pounds come from?
- Did you run Rich Energy's Twitter account? Were you responsible for the tweets with Chris Harris, Whyte Bikes, about Red Bull, and all of the early ones with photos of women and tigers and such?
- One of Rich Energy's most famous tweets showed a photo of a pool with the Rich Energy logo Photoshopped onto the bottom, and

it was captioned: "A swim on New Year's day with Rich Energy."
Why Photoshop this?

- The Rich Energy account used to post a stock photo of a couple in black-tie attire, and the woman had a tattoo of the original Rich Energy logo and name on her shoulder. The photo was commonly used on romance and erotic-fiction books, and someone Photoshopped the Rich Energy logo in. Why Photoshop this?
- There was also an image taken from a Paco Rabanne perfume ad with the Rich Energy logo Photoshopped in. This is someone else's work and promotional materials—did Rich Energy ask for permission before using it?
- The same goes for an image from an Estee Lauder ad. Did Rich Energy ask for permission before using it?
- The same goes for an image from the 2012 *Sports Illustrated* swimsuit edition. Did Rich Energy ask for permission before using it?
- The same goes for an image from a 2009 *Harper's Bazaar* issue. Did Rich Energy ask for permission before using it?
- In April 2017, the Rich Energy account tweeted: "A great view enjoying a cool Vodka Rich cocktail." It was a photo of the St. Regis Bangkok hotel, taken from the Marriott website. Why take a photo from Marriott and claim it's Rich Energy's own view that night?
- In February 2017, the Rich Energy account posted a photo of a plane in a hangar with the caption: "A night trip with Rich Energy." The photo was actually from a 2010 post on a U.S. government website. It featured a plane at the Yokota Air Base in Japan. Why was this taken from that website and claimed to be a night trip with Rich Energy?
- In April 2017, Rich Energy tweeted: "Early flight to Europe for @ rich_energy management team this morning. Expansion in new markets." The photo with it showed a private jet and Bentley at dawn, and the same photo often appeared on Pinterest and had been posted online as early as 2012—five years before Rich Energy's tweet. Why claim that this is where the Rich Energy account is?
- On December 26, 2016, the Rich Energy account tweeted "Thank you Santa" with a photo of a Ferrari Enzo. The photo frequently appeared on websites to download computer wallpapers, some as early as May 2016—seven months before Rich Energy's tweet. Why make it seem like this belongs to Rich Energy when it's a photo from the internet?
- Were you behind the Rich Energy Twitter account during and before its time in Formula One?

- Rich Energy USA listed three members of its "executive team" as of September 2020: Jesse Gordon, creative director; Lance Henderson, vice president of branding and marketing; and Blake Farhoumand, CEO. What can you tell us about them?
- The Rich Energy USA website, as of September 2020, still used the original company logo—the one Rich Energy itself had to stop using more than a year earlier in July 2019 thanks to its trip to copyright court. Why?
- Red Bull said before its copyright claim in June 2019, it contacted the defendants (you and Rich Energy) on March 21, 2019. What did Red Bull say, and did you respond?
- If you responded, what did you say?
- Red Bull's copyright claim said Rich Energy admitted a couple of things in discussions with Red Bull long before the official court action: that the Red Bull trademarks the brand was using had a reputation, and that anyone reading the #BetterThanRedBull hashtag would read it as "Better than Red Bull." Thus, why did the Rich Energy account use the Better Than Red Bull hashtag when tweeting a photo of the claim document?
- In the July 2019 tweet about the Red Bull claim, the Rich Energy account posted: "Now @redbull are taking William Storey to court. A cynic might see a pattern emerging! #richenergy #betterthanredbull #williamstorey #BusinessIntelligence." But Red Bull reached out months earlier—why not mention anything then?
- Red Bull's claim cited IRI Worldwide data, which said between March 2017 and February 2019, approximately 1,025 cans of Rich Energy were sold with a value of £836. This conflicts with your claims—first, that you'd sold in excess of 100 million cans during Rich Energy's lifetime, then that you'd sold circa 3 million in 2018. What is your response to this claim? What is the real number of cans sold over the lifetime of the brand?
- Red Bull's claim said Rich Energy took unfair advantage of its marketing by trying to "create a link" between their brand and Red Bull "in the mind of the average consumer seeing the phrases complained of." How do you feel about this? Do you think this is what Rich Energy was trying to do?
- On July 16, 2019, an order from the court in the *Red Bull v. Rich Energy* copyright case granted Brandsmiths' application to no longer represent Rich Energy. Civil Procedure Rule 42.3(2)(a), as mentioned in the order, falls under "Order that a solicitor has ceased to act." Lexology calls terminating a retainer "an

exceptional course of action" and gives examples as to when it would happen: a "breakdown in confidence," an inability "to obtain proper instructions," a construction of facts that the solicitor does "not consider to be properly arguable," and a "failure by a client … to pay a reasonable sum." Did any of this happen with Rich Energy? Why did Brandsmiths terminate its agreement?

- It appeared that after Brandsmiths left, you represented yourself in the legal proceedings with Red Bull. Did this happen? Why?
- How much did you pay esports racer Azzy Iredale? How long did that partnership last?
- Do you care to share more about your views of the COVID-19 pandemic?
- During the 2020 Austrian races, the Rich Energy account tweeted a photo of a Super Formula car with the caption: "Now this is a beautiful car. We can't wait to beat the competition in #F1." Why use a Super Formula car for an F1 tweet?
- *ESPN* reported that during the USGP weekend in October 2018, Claire Williams and several senior team members were left waiting for you at an Austin restaurant on the evening of the race to finalize the terms of the deal, but you never showed up, and a few days later, the Haas partnership was announced. Did this happen?
- *ESPN* also said it wasn't clear how much Haas knew about the Williams situation. Did Haas know?
- What documentation or proof did you show Haas (and Williams, which you were close to a deal with) that your young brand could meet the financial requirements of sponsoring their F1 teams?
- You admitted that you'd produced 90 million cans but not yet filled and sold them. (Then, we assume, that was also the case when you said "in excess of 100 million" to us.) Where did those cans go after Whyte Bikes won its copyright case?
- How many cans have you actually sold now?
- Speaking to the *Sun*, you said: "Red Bull have spent £250 billion in F1 and last year across Toro Rosso and Red Bull, there or there abouts, £400 million." The 400 million figure was near the actual number, but where did you get 250 billion? Did you mean over their lifetime?
- In June 2019, the Rich Energy account tweeted an image of a Rich Energy can lined up next to a Red Bull can and a Monster can, captioning it: "Delighted with feedback from the beverage industry. A quiet revolution happening with @rich_energy." An account called *MsportXtra*, which asked Rich Energy many times where to buy its products but never got an answer aside

from "hundreds of supermarkets" despite Rich Energy saying it would provide a list, pointed out the strange timing in a June 18 tweet: "Feedback from beverage industry ??? It was done by Dutch 'Livingproof' who are a mum and dad with a few kids that try out stuff." (For what it's worth, the team behind the "livingproof" account described themselves as simply "BFFs for eternity.") Was this what that tweet was referring to?

- Did Rich Energy provide those cans for Livingproof's test?
- After the Haas F1 contract-termination tweet and a separate statement from another Rich Energy entity calling it a "rogue action," you said: "There has been an attempted coup of my position by a handful of shareholders who have a cosy relationship with Red Bull and Whyte Bikes." Which shareholders did you mean?
- How did you know they had a cozy relationship with Whyte Bikes and Red Bull? Do you have proof?
- You also said you had support from all key stakeholders. Who?
- Who didn't support you? Why?
- You said in your termination email to Guenther Steiner that Rich Energy had paid for 10 races and Silverstone was the 10th. How much was paid for 10 races?
- The weekend of the Canadian Grand Prix, Rich Energy said it was the company's idea to remove its logos from the Haas cars after the Whyte Bikes loss. In the termination email to Guenther Steiner, you implied it was Haas' decision. Which is the truth?
- Haas wanted 35 million pounds in damages from the contract termination. Was this money ever paid to Haas?
- On July 16, 2019, Matthew Bruce Kell took over as a director of Rich Energy, which became Lightning Volt Limited, while you were terminated. What happened?
- After the change, Rich Energy tweeted: "William Storey founder of @rich_energy has sold his majority stake in the legal entity of Rich Energy Ltd to a third party. This was in disgust at conduct of duplicitous minority stakeholders. In the words of @Schwarzenegger he'll be back!#richenergy #F1 #nobull #williamstorey." Can you tell us more about this?
- The Matthew Kell changeover lasted about a month. What happened over this period of time? Why were you and Zoran Terzic restored as directors and Matthew Kell removed?
- The existence of two entities made everyone wonder: Who, exactly, was Rich Energy? Had Lightning Volt become the brand, acting as "Rich Energy" in public but "Lightning Volt" in government

filings? Or had this new Rich Energy adopted the entire identity of the old Rich Energy? Tell us.

- Haas and Rich Energy announced the contract termination to be official in early September. Later that month, the Rich Energy account tweeted: "After review of dispute with investors who created havoc via UK distribution company Rich Energy CEO & all stakeholders have asked @HaasF1Team to explain how they did a deal with unauthorized non officers of @rich_energy. As such title partnership is still on #RussianGP #F1 #NoDeal." What was this about? What made you think this? Why?
- How did you get involved with OMG Racing? Where did you meet and whose idea was the deal?
- OMG said in an announcement that despite the Rich Energy controversy, "William Storey and the team at Rich Energy have been very transparent in their business dealings, to give us full confidence in our partnership to move ahead." What transparency did you provide? Documents? Financial information?
- Monetarily, what was the nature of the Rich Energy OMG sponsorship deal?
- You tweeted in July 2020: "Red Bull hated me in F1 & put Haas under huge pressure to try & oust me." Did this happen? What proof do you have that Red Bull put Haas under huge pressure to try and oust you?
- You said in 2020 that you'd made a formal legal offer to buy Sunderland. How much did you offer?
- The local *Sunderland Echo* newspaper also noted in July 2020 that you "claim[ed] to have previously been on the books of [fellow English football club Queens Park Rangers FC], only to be released before making a senior appearance." Does this mean you were very nearly a professional player?
- You have claimed that Neville Weston blew up the UK distribution company listed by Companies House, which is in liquidation. Where is Rich Energy's main company listing? How do we find it?
- How much money does the main company have?
- You regularly teased announcements about your return to F1, but the announcements would end up being a recap of your current partnerships, with no new information aside from "we're excited to return." When will Rich Energy return? What date? With whom?
- You said in January 2021 that an official announcement from the F1 team would come in early February. An announcement never came. What was this announcement supposed to be? With whom? What happened to it?

- You said in February 2021: "A huge thank you to the king of #F1 for being such a great supporter of our founder #WilliamStorey & for backing us. Our return to #FormulaOne due in no small part to the business genius of #BernieEcclestone. #RichEnergy #British #EnergyDrink #Entrepreneur #Motorsport." Does this mean Bernie Ecclestone was working with you? Was he financially involved with Rich Energy?
- In February 2021, you said: "Unfortunately, our deal [to buy the] Force India Formula One team was derailed by [driver] Sergio Perez going for administration, and even though ourselves and a very well-funded Russian bid bidded more than Lawrence Stroll, Lawrence Stroll became the owner of Force India, which is now, of course, Aston Martin Racing." What was your offer? What was Lawrence Stroll's?
- Your offer was reported to be 30 million pounds and Stroll's was 90 million. Why did you say yours was more?
- You said in February 2021: "A strategic ally of Rich Energy has agreed to purchase a majority stake in an existing team. We did explore with the new regulations actually entering our own team for 2022, which would be Rich Energy Formula One Team, but a friend of ours has agreed a deal for a majority stake in a Formula One team, and we will become a partner of that team for 2021. Once that acquisition is announced, we will become the title sponsor for 2022." This has yet to happen. What is the team? Why hasn't this happened?

Appendix B
Questions for Haas F1 Team

- In *Drive to Survive*'s second season, Gene Haas said: "The Rich Energy deal was supposed to be worth $60 million. Other than the initial payment, that was the only money we ever received." Has this changed since the filming?
- What research did you do into Rich Energy before signing the deal? What's your protocol for signing regular sponsors and title sponsors? How do you define "due diligence"?
- After Haas' 15th- and 16th-place qualifying efforts at the 2020 season opener, Storey tweeted on his personal account: "The #FridayFeeling when you know you made the right decision." After the race, he tweeted: "Another million dollars saved. Serendipity for #RichEnergy." During the pandemic, he tweeted a photo of Guenther Steiner that said, verbatim: "Fucking hell Gene, vis ze gimp masks ve look like a bunch of vankers." Do you have any response to his and Rich Energy's tweets of this nature?
- Did you know about Storey's history of failed businesses, whose records and financials are publicly accessible on Companies House?
- *ESPN* reported that during the 2018 USGP weekend in October: *Claire Williams and several senior team members were left waiting for Storey at an Austin restaurant on the evening of the race to finalize the terms of their deal. He never showed up, and a few days later the Haas partnership was announced. It has never been clear how much of this Haas was aware of at the time.* Did the Haas team know Rich Energy was talking to Williams? Was the team aware of this apparent meeting and that Storey was reported to have not shown up?
- On July 11, after Rich Energy's contract-termination tweet, a

statement from a seemingly new Rich Energy entity came out, attributing the "rogue" actions to a person Rich Energy was "in the process of legally removing … from all executive responsibilities." Storey told us at the time that this move was led by Charlie Simpson and Neville Weston, the latter of whom Haas had apparently contacted to say: *We understand that you are seeking to take control of the company away from Mr Storey, the current CEO. If that comes to pass, then our client will be happy to engage in without prejudice conversations with you but they will need to see clear and unambiguous evidence that Mr Storey has been removed as a director of the company and that a new CEO has been validly appointed in his place.* What was going on between Haas and Neville Weston at the time?

- Had Weston shown Haas that his version of Rich Energy could financially support the partnership? Why did Haas stay in it?
- Is the version of Rich Energy Haas was talking to at this point related to the new Companies House listing for Rich Energy Limited, incorporated in July 2019 under Steven Weston?
- Storey said in his apparent termination email to Guenther Steiner that Rich Energy had paid for 10 races and Silverstone was the 10th. Had Rich Energy paid for 10 races?
- The weekend of the Canadian Grand Prix, Rich Energy said it was the company's idea to remove its logos from the Haas cars after the Whyte Bikes loss. In the apparent termination email to Guenther Steiner, Storey implied it was Haas' decision. Which is the truth?
- If the assertion that it was Rich Energy's idea was wrong, why didn't Haas correct the record during the race weekend?
- Haas wanted 35 million pounds in damages from the contract termination. Was this money ever received?
- In July 2019, Rich Energy became Lightning Volt Limited with Companies House and a new Rich Energy was established. Did the new Rich Energy entity become the partner with the Haas team? Or did Haas' partner remain Lightning Volt?
- After Haas accepted Rich Energy's contract breach, Guenther Steiner said on August 29, 2019: "First, we need to be calm and make a rational decision, and then it will be decided. At the moment, [the Rich Energy logos] are on here—obviously, as you can see—so they need to decide where they want to go, not us. It is their decision, and then our one will follow—what we need to do. That should happen in the next week or so, and this time it will happen properly." Was there any idea that the partnership would go on, under a new entity perhaps? Or was this just a way of

avoiding the question until Haas made its official announcement about the end of the partnership in September?
- William Storey tweeted in July 2020: "Red Bull hated me in F1 and put Haas under huge pressure to try and oust me." Did this happen?
- Storey said the Haas team "believed the nonsense of [Neville Weston's] group, which they now regret." What does Haas say to this?
- On March 14, 2019, you answered our questions for a Rich Energy story on *Jalopnik* as such (answers in italics). Have any of those answers changed? Would the team like to elaborate on any?
    - o The most recent Companies House balance sheets for Rich Energy (from September of 2017) show 581 pounds in the bank, and that number (along with limited product availability, past failed companies run by CEO William Storey, etc.) has gotten a lot of attention online. Guenther Steiner has said Haas vetted the company, so can the team comment on the vetting process it used to confirm Rich Energy's legitimacy? *Our due diligence of potential partners is a confidential matter.*
    - o How did the findings of Haas' vetting differ from what people have found online? *Our due diligence of potential partners is a confidential matter.*
    - o What is the level of partnership Rich Energy has with Haas, considering that Haas is able to support itself and has in other seasons? How much of a stake does the company have in the team? *Rich Energy is Title Partner to Haas F1 Team (as announced 25th October 2018). Rich Energy has no stake in Haas F1 Team.*
- People on the internet very quickly and easily found Rich Energy's Companies House records, which said the company had 581 pounds in the bank in 2017 and 103 in 2016. Did Haas see this before going through with the partnership? If so, was there proof that Rich Energy had enough money for its sponsorship deal? What did Haas see that was different from what the public saw?
- We were told when it came to the tweets and claims from Rich Energy during the 2019 season, Guenther Steiner reassured employees by saying: "Don't worry about that. It's bullshit." Does Haas have any comment on whether this was the messaging from Guenther?

CHAPTER NOTES

Chapter 1

1. Courtenay-Stamp, Jeremy. Letter to William Storey, July 11, 2019.

2. "Filing History for Lightning Volt Limited (09791667)." Gov. uk. 2017. https://find-and-update.-company-information.service.gov.uk/company/09791667/filing-history.

3. "Ten Fascinating Facts About the Very First F1 Race." 2016. F1. https://www.formula1.com/en/latest/features/2016/5/-f1-first-race-1950-silverstone.html.

4. Duxbury, Anna. 2020. "How Much Does an F1 Car Cost, and Other F1 Questions Answered." *Autosport*. https://www.autosport.com/f1/news/how-much-does-an-f1-car-cost-and-other-f1-questions-answered-4983337/4983337/.

5. "Organisation | Federation Internationale De L'Automobile." n.d. FIA. https://www.fia.com/organisation.

6. "Fastest Speed Outright in a Formula One Grand Prix." 2005. Guinness World Records. https://www.guinnessworldrecords.com/world-records/fastest-speed-outright-in-a-formula-one-grand-prix.

7. "Can an F1 Car REALLY Drive Upside Down? Aerodynamics EXPLAINED." YouTube, 2020. https://www.youtube.com/watch?time_continue=4&v=iUu7d8AnZ_Y&feature=emb_logo&ab_channel=Mercedes-AMGPetronasFormulaOneTeam.

8. FIA. 2017. "Halo Protection System to Be Introduced for 2018." F1. https://www.formula1.com/en/latest/headlines/2017/7/halo-protection-system-to-be-introduced-for-2018.html.

9. Barretto, Lawrence. 2019. "Fight Night: How brutal Singapore GP pushes drivers to the limit." F1. https://www.formula1.com/en/latest/article.fight-night-why-brutal-singapore-gp-pushes-drivers-to-the-limit.6CWlvmuJZnPFm9KbBE0Zzk.html

10. Warren, Katie. 2019. "15 Wild Facts About Monaco, Where 32% of Residents Are Millionaires." *Business Insider*. https://www.businessinsider.com/mind-blowing-facts-about-monaco-wealth-2019-5.

11. Ruhling, Nancy A. 2019. "Buyers in Monte Carlo Have Access to a Billionaires' Playground." Mansion Global. https://www.mansionglobal.com/articles/-buyers-in-monte-carlo-have-access-to-a-billionaires-playground-202155.

12. F1. May 21, 2020, 1:31 PM. Twitter Post. https://twitter.com/f1/status/1263537794481348608?lang=en

13. "Monaco 2006 Epic Kimi Räikkönen—Going Straight to His Yacht After Heat Shield Blow Up!" YouTube, 2018. https://www.youtube.com/watch?v=ZMzeluIxblY&ab_channel=Kimiisland.

14. Reuters. 2020. "Mercedes F1 Spent $442 Million in 2019 but Still Made Money." *ESPN*. https://www.espn.com/f1/story/_/id/29823419/mercedes-f1-spent-442-million-2019-made-money.

15. "Rich Energy Haas F1 Team 2019 Livery Unveiled." 2019. Haas F1 Team. https://media.haasf1team.com/files/pdf/FINAL%20070219%20VF-19%20Livery%20Unveil%20Release-475.pdf.

16. "Haas 2019 F1 Livery Launch." YouTube, 2019. https://www.youtube.com/watch?v=PGrBWoMqpVI&ab_channel=Autosport.

17. *Ibid.*

18. Mitchell, Scott. 2019. "Haas Title

Sponsor Likens Doubters to Moon Landing Truthers." *Motorsport.com.* https://us.motorsport.com/f1/news/haas-rich-energy-doubters-moon-landing/4333923/.

19. *Ibid.*

20. *Ibid.*

21. "Red Bull." n.d. Forbes. https://www.forbes.com/companies/red-bull/#36ccfb2861ce.

22. *Ibid.*

23. Mitchell, Scott. 2019. "Haas Title Sponsor Likens Doubters to Moon Landing Truthers." *Motorsport.com.* https://us.motorsport.com/f1/news/haas-rich-energy-doubters-moon-landing/4333923/.

24. King, Alanis. William Storey. Personal, March 14, 2019.

25. Red Bull GmbH vs. Rich Energy Limited (Business and Property Court of England and Wales June 11, 2019).

26. Tran, Mark. 2004. "Red Bull Buys Jaguar F1 Team | Business." *The Guardian.* https://www.theguardian.com/business/2004/nov/15/formulaone.money.

27. Reuters. 2019. "Toro Rosso F1 Team Pushing for Name Change." *ESPN.* https://www.espn.com/f1/story/_/id/27742970/-toro-rosso-f1-team-pushing-name-change.

28. King, Alanis. William Storey. Personal, March 14, 2019.

29. *Ibid.*

30. ATB Sales Limited v Rich Energy Limited and Ors (Business and Property Courts of England and Wales May 14, 2019).

31. Red Bull GmbH vs. Rich Energy Limited: Tomlin Order (Business and Property Court of England and Wales September 30, 2019).

32. "Twitter Advanced Search: 'Rich Energy 581.'" Twitter. https://twitter.com/search?f=tweets&q=rich+energy+581&src=typd.

33. "What Is 'Rich Energy'?—Racing Comments—The Autosport Forums." 2018. *Autosport* Forums. https://forums.autosport.com/topic/211627-what-is-rich-energy/.

34. *Ibid.*

35. *Ibid.*

36. *Ibid.*

37. "Is Rich Energy, a Scam? r/formula1." 2018. Reddit. https://www.reddit.com/r/formula1/comments/94h0p1/is_rich_energy_a_scam/.

38. *Ibid.*

39. *Ibid.*

40. "What Is Rich Energy?: r/formula1." 2018. Reddit. https://www.reddit.com/r/formula1/comments/a4ih0y/what_is_rich_energy/.

41. *Ibid.*

42. *Ibid.*

43. "HaasF1 and Rich Energy—the Inside Story (1/2)." YouTube, 2018. https://www.youtube.com/watch?v=Cr8icp8vEIY&ab_channel=peterwindsor.

44. "Registrirajte SE." RICH d.o.o.—prihod, dobit, zaposleni, analiza, kontakt podaci. http://www.poslovna.hr/(X(1)S(mhcwoppto5azmaaelcmxipju))/lite/rich/1267894/subjekti.aspx?AspxAutoDetectCookieSupport=1.

45. "TULUMARENJE: Počinje Party League Croatia Uz Energetski Napitak Rich | Zagreb...." 2011. MojZagreb.info. https://mojzagreb.info/zagreb/tulumarenje-pocinje-party-league-croatia-uz-energetski-napitak-rich.

46. "Rich Energy Drink (Archived)," n.d. https://web.archive.org/web/20130616032122/http://richenergydrink.com/.

47. Gerrard, Bradley, Ben Woods, Matt Oliver, Rachel Millard, Simon Foy, and Oliver Gill. 2018. "Rich Energy Chief: 'I Fell Into the Drinks Business After Meeting a Mad Scientist.'" *Telegraph.* https://www.telegraph.co.uk/business/2018/03/30/-rich-energy-chief-fell-drinks-business-meeting-mad-scientist/.

48. King, Alanis. William Storey. Personal, March 14, 2019.

49. "Rich Energy Drink (Archived)," n.d. https://web.archive.org/web/20130616032122/http://richenergydrink.com/.

50. Mitchell, Scott. 2019. "Haas Title Sponsor Likens Doubters to Moon Landing Truthers." *Motorsport.com.* https://us.motorsport.com/f1/news/haas-rich-energy-doubters-moon-landing/4333923/.

51. Sylt, Christian. 2019. "Revealed: The $285 Million Cost of Winning the F1 Championship." *Forbes.* April 26. https://www.forbes.com/sites/csylt/2019/04/26/revealed-the-285-million-cost-of-winning-the-f1-championship/?sh=6c97dda223d8.

52. *Ibid.*

53. *Ibid.*

54. Cooper, Adam. 2020. "Mercedes Spent Over £333m to Win the 2019 F1 Title." *Motorsport.com.* https://www.motorsport.com/f1/news/mercedes-2019-budget-revealed/4868650/.

55. Sylt, Christian. 2020. "Revealed: The 1,000% Increase in F1 Team Spending." Forbes. February 9. https://www.forbes.com/sites/csylt/2020/02/09/-revealed-the-1000-increase-in-f1-team-spending/?sh=77b22713d93e.

56. "Williams Could Sell F1 Team as Board Announces £13m Loss in 2019 and Split from Title Sponsor." 2020. F1. https://www.formula1.com/en/latest/article.williams-could-sell-f1-team-as-board-announces-gbp13m-loss-in-2019-and-split.455wGjds3WOQf7gdSuqJRf.html.

57. Baldwin, Alan. 2018. "Motor Racing: Williams Losing Title Sponsor Martini at End of Year." *Reuters.* https://www.reuters.com/article/us-motor-f1-williams-martini/motor-racing-williams-losing-title-sponsor-martini-at-end-of-year-idUSKCN1GB1IO.

58. Dixon, Ed. 2020. "Report: Williams F1 Lose Another Major Sponsor with Rexona Exit." *SportsPro Media.* https://www.sportspromedia.com/news/williams-f1-rexona-sponsor-exit-tata-omnitude-symantec/.

59. Barretto, Lawrence. 2020. "ANALYSIS: What Lies Ahead for Williams After Shock Financial News?" F1. https://www.formula1.com/en/latest/article.analysis-what-lies-ahead-for-williams-after-shock-financial-news.3jtmzE7GixI3a1DGwiwv3I.html.

60. Konotey, Olivia. 2020. "F1 GP, Formula One News: Loan from Nicholas Latifi's Dad." *Bloomberg.com.* https://www.bloomberg.com/news/articles/2020-04-11/canadian-food-tycoon-rescues-struggling-formula-1-team.

61. "Williams Announce Sale of F1 Team to U.S. Investment Company." 2020. F1. https://www.formula1.com/en/latest/article.breaking-williams-announce-sale-of-f1-team-to-us-investment-company.5hjIdxTo9MOBOlHkmfGjo.html.

62. Cooper, Adam. 2020. "Why the Once Mighty Williams F1 Team Is Up for Sale." *Motorsport.com.* https://www.motorsport.com/f1/news/williams-teams-sale-analysis/4798512/.

63. Jacobs, Caleb. 2020. "Now Rich Energy Wants to Sponsor the Ailing Williams F1 Team." *The Drive.* https://www.thedrive.com/accelerator/33780/now-rich-energy-wants-to-sponsor-the-ailing-williams-f1-team.

64. Anderson, Ben. 2018. "Perez 'Heartbroken' Over Force India Legal Action to 'Save Team.'" *Autosport.* https://www.autosport.com/f1/news/perez-heart broken-over-force-india-legal-action-to-save-team-5293468/5293468/.

65. Storey, William. 2018. "Rich Energy Launch Official £100m Takeover of Force India." LinkedIn. https://www.linkedin.com/pulse/rich-energy-launch-official-100m-takeover-force-india-william-storey/.

66. Mitchell, Scott. 2018. "British Firm Not Ready to 'Relinquish' Force India Bid." *Motorsport.com.* https://us.motorsport.com/f1/news/rich-energy-force-india-buyout/3152345/.

67. "Breaking News: William Storey on Force India's Future." YouTube, 2018. https://www.youtube.com/watch?v=0uhAWuMwyyo&ab_channel=peter windsor.

68. Gilboy, James. 2018. "Haas F1 Signs Soft Drink Startup Rich Energy as 2019 Title Sponsor." *The Drive.* https://www.thedrive.com/accelerator/24506/haas-f1-signs-soft-drink-startup-rich-energy-as-2019-title-sponsor.

69. Saunders, Nate. 2020. "The Bizarre Haas-Rich Energy Saga Explained." *ESPN.* https://www.espn.com/f1/story/_/id/27221746/the-bizarre-haas-rich-energy-saga-explained.

70. "News: Rich Energy Announced as Haas F1 Team Title Partner." 2018. Haas F1 Team. https://www.haasf1team.com/news/news-rich-energy-announced-haas-f1-team-title-partner.

71. King, Alanis. Haas Employee 5. Personal Interview, August 2021.

72. "What's the Storey?" 2020. *Chasin' the Racin'.* https://www.youtube.com/watch?v=xBEyFflfz4w.

73. Vertuno, Jim. "Haas F1 Tussling in Middle of Pack in 2nd Season." 2017. *AP News,* October 21. https://apnews.com/article/f45db47719e844ef8bc6e88dbb891908.

74. "Gene Haas—The Official Stewart-Haas Racing Website." n.d. Stewart-Haas Racing. https://www.stewarthaasracing.com/gene-haas/.

75. Noble, Jonathan. 2015. "Haas Formula 1 Squad Buys Marussia Factory but Not the Team." *Autosport*. https://www.autosport.com/f1/news/haas-formula-1-squad-buys-marussia-factory-but-not-the-team-5019509/5019509/.

76. "The Italian Job." 2016. Haas F1 Team. https://www.haasf1team.com/news/italian-job.

77. Sylt, Christian. 2016. "What Really Fuelled Gene Haas' $1 Billion F1 Bet." *Forbes*, March 25. https://www.forbes.com/sites/csylt/2016/03/25/what-really-fuelled-gene-haas-1-billion-f1-bet/?sh=647bb62b14c6.

78. "Guenther Steiner." n.d. Haas F1 Team. https://www.haasf1team.com/season/team/guenther-steiner.

79. "2016 Constructor Standings." n.d. F1. https://www.formula1.com/en/results.html/2016/team.html.

80. "2018 Constructor Standings." n.d. F1. https://www.formula1.com/en/results.html/2018/team.html.

81. "Rich Energy Haas F1 Team 2019 Livery Unveiled." 2019. Haas F1 Team. https://media.haasf1team.com/files/pdf/FINAL%20070219%20VF-19%20Livery%20Unveil%20Release-475.pdf.

82. "2019 Race Results." n.d. F1. https://www.formula1.com/en/results.html/2019/races.html.

83. "Boiling Point." 2020. Episode. *Formula 1: Drive to Survive* 2, no. 2. Netflix. https://www.netflix.com/title/80204890.

84. *Ibid.*

85. "2019 Race Results." n.d. F1. https://www.formula1.com/en/results.html/2019/races.html.

86. ATB Sales Limited v Rich Energy Limited and Ors (Business and Property Courts of England and Wales May 14, 2019).

87. Patterson, Ross, July 12, 2019.

88. King, Alanis. 2019. "Haas F1 Sponsor Rich Energy Claims to Have Terminated Contract, Citing 'PC Attitude' [Update: Haas Says They're Still Partners]." *Jalopnik*. https://jalopnik.com/haas-f1-sponsor-rich-energy-claims-to-have-terminated-c-1836250021.

89. King, Alanis. 2019. "Power Struggle Continues at F1 Sponsor Rich Energy." *Jalopnik*. https://jalopnik.com/power-struggle-at-rich-energy-continues-as-its-accused-1836316162.

90. Saunders, Nate. 2020. "The Bizarre Haas-Rich Energy Saga Explained." *ESPN*. https://www.espn.com/f1/story/_/id/27221746/the-bizarre-haas-rich-energy-saga-explained.

91. "Boiling Point." 2020. Episode. *Formula 1: Drive to Survive* 2, no. 2. Netflix. https://www.netflix.com/title/80204890.

92. Marchetti, Silvia. 2014. "The South Tyrol Identity Crisis: To Live in Italy, but Feel Austrian." *The Guardian*. https://www.theguardian.com/education/2014/may/30/south-tyrol-live-in-italy-feel-austrian.

93. "Boiling Point." 2020. Episode. *Formula 1: Drive to Survive* 2, no. 2. Netflix. https://www.netflix.com/title/80204890.

94. *Ibid.*

95. "Bernie Ecclestone Says Hitler Was a Man Who Got Things Done." 2009. *The Guardian*. https://www.theguardian.com/sport/2009/jul/04/bernie-ecclestone-interview-hitler-saddam.

96. "Bernie Ecclestone: Women Drivers in F1 Would Not Be Taken Seriously." 2016. *BBC*. https://www.bbc.com/sport/formula1/36086363.

97. "Jeffrey Epstein's Little Black Book." Scribd. https://www.scribd.com/document/416489768/Jeffrey-Epstein-s-Little-Black-Book.

98. Reuters. 2019. "Bahrain: Formula 1 Ignores Rights Commitments." Human Rights Watch. https://www.hrw.org/news/2019/03/22/bahrain-formula-1-ignores-rights-commitments.

99. McVeigh, Tracy. 2016. "As F1 Roars Into Baku, Activists Tell Drivers: Help Our Fight for Human Rights." *The Guardian*. https://www.theguardian.com/world/2016/jun/18/baku-formula-one-grand-prix-azerbaijan-human-rights.

100. *Ibid.*

101. Boucey, Bertrand. 2009. "Jean Todt Replaces Mosley as FIA President." *Reuters*. https://www.reuters.com/article/idINIndia-43388920091023.

102. "Case of Mosley V. the United Kingdom." n.d. Global Freedom of Expression. https://globalfreedomofexpression.columbia.edu/cases/case-mosley-v-united-kingdom/.

103. *Ibid.*
104. *Ibid.*
105. Dowell, Ben. 2008. "Max Mosley V News of the World Timeline." *The Guardian.* https://www.theguardian.com/media/2008/jul/24/privacy.newsoftheworld.
106. Salisbury, Matt. 2007. "Stepney Leaves Ferrari." *Crash.Net.* https://www.crash.net/f1/news/59106/1/ferrari-dismisses-stepney.
107. Spence, Steve. 2007. "Big Scandal, Big Comedy at the Formula 1 Show." *Car and Driver.* https://www.caranddriver.com/features/a15146433/big-scandal-big-comedy-at-the-formula-1-show/.
108. Spurring, Quentin. 2007. "McLaren F1 Team Fined $100 Million: Disqualified from 2007 Season." *Autoweek.* https://www.autoweek.com/news/a2058376/mclaren-f1-team-fined-100-million-disqualified-2007-season/.
109. "Stepney—Not My Fault." 2008. *Sky Sports.* https://www.skysports.com/f1/news/12433/3067476/stepney-not-my-fault.
110. Williamson, Martin. n.d. "Crashgate Explained." *ESPN.* http://en.espn.co.uk/f1/motorsport/story/14272.html.
111. Noble, Jonathan. 2009. "Renault Given Two-year Suspended Ban." *Autosport.* https://www.autosport.com/f1/news/renault-given-two-year-suspended-ban-4433045/4433045/.

Chapter 2

1. Blackstock, Elizabeth. Luke Smith. Personal, August 2021.
2. Blackstock, Elizabeth. Stuart Taylor (Chain Bear). Personal, August 2021.
3. *Ibid.*
4. "Rich Energy (Archived)." Wikipedia, n.d. https://web.archive.org/web/20210213122656/https://en.wikipedia.org/wiki/Rich_Energy.
5. "Rich Energy." n.d. Wikipedia. https://en.wikipedia.org/wiki/Rich_Energy.
6. "Registrirajte SE." RICH D.o.o.—prihod, dobit, zaposleni, analiza, kontakt podaci. http://www.poslovna.hr/(X(1)S(mhcwoppto5azmaaelcmxipju))/lite/rich/1267894/subjekti.aspx?AspxAutoDetectCookieSupport=1.
7. "Tulumarenje: Počinje Party League Croatia Uz Energetski Napitak Rich." 2011. MojZagreb.info. https://mojzagreb.info/zagreb/tulumarenje-pocinje-party-league-croatia-uz-energetski-napitak-rich.
8. "Registrirajte SE." RICH D.o.o.—prihod, dobit, zaposleni, analiza, kontakt podaci. http://www.poslovna.hr/(X(1)S(mhcwoppto5azmaaelcmxipju))/lite/rich/1267894/subjekti.aspx?AspxAutoDetectCookieSupport=1.
9. "I-Nova Medicinska Istrazivanja D.o.o. Company Profile." Dun & Bradstreet. https://www.dnb.com/-business-directory/company-profiles.-i-nova_medicinska_istrazivanja_doo.8227661231ff7ac8040cbc035b3cffc0.html?aka_re=2%3Faka_re.
10. Blackstock, Elizabeth, and Alanis King. 2019. "What You Find When You Look Into Rich Energy, the Mystery Sponsor of America's F1 Team." *Jalopnik.* https://jalopnik.com/what-you-find-when-you-look-into-rich-energy-the-myste-1833303620.
11. "Osječka Robna Burza." OSRB. https://osrb.hr/.
12. Majstrović, Dražen, August 26, 2021.
13. *Ibid.*
14. "Filing History for Lightning Volt Limited (09791667)." 2017. Gov.uk. https://find-and-update.-company-information.service.gov.uk/company/09791667/filing-history.
15. King, Alanis. William Storey. Personal, March 14, 2019.
16. Gerrard, Bradley. 2018. "Rich Energy Chief: 'I Fell Into the Drinks Business After Meeting a Mad Scientist.'" *The Telegraph.* https://www.telegraph.co.uk/business/2018/03/30/rich-energy-chief-fell-drinks-business-meeting-mad-scientist/.
17. "Filing History for Lightning Volt Limited (09791667)." Gov.uk. 2017. https://find-and-update.company-information.service.gov.uk/company/09791667/filing-history.
18. Sylt, Christian. 2018. "Haas: The Formula for Reducing F1's Costs." Forbes, August 20. https://www.forbes.com/sites/csylt/2018/08/20/haas-the-formula-for-reducing-f1s-costs/?sh=77eff4552c31.
19. "Rich Energy (Archived)." Rich

Energy, n.d. https://web.archive.org/web/20190123072246/https://richenergy.com/.

20. Blackstock, Elizabeth, and Alanis King. 2019. "What You Find When You Look Into Rich Energy, the Mystery Sponsor of America's F1 Team." *Jalopnik.* https://jalopnik.com/what-you-find-when-you-look-into-rich-energy-the-myste-1833303620.

21. "Rich Energy Drink—Better Business Bureau® Profile." n.d. BBB. https://www.bbb.org/us/ne/lincoln/profile/-food-manufacturer/rich-energy-drink-0714-300172708.

22. King, TJ. 2013. "Rich Bar & Lounge Opens in Once-controversial Location." *Lincoln Journal Star.* https://journalstar.com/entertainment/misc/rich-bar-lounge-opens-in-once-controversial-location/article_7c979246-946f-562a-bc30-7e4279f17e94.html.

23. "Rich Energy Drink (Archived)," n.d. https://web.archive.org/web/20130620163255/http://richenergydrink.com.ia18.4w.com/?page_id=21.

24. Bowling, Chris. 2014. "Rich Lounge Provides Relaxed Atmosphere for Bar Goers." *Daily Nebraskan.* http://www.dailynebraskan.com/culture/rich-lounge-provides-relaxed-atmosphere-for-bar-goers/article_ef793f60-4472-11e4-a1f6-001a4bcf6878.html.

25. *Ibid.*

26. Blackstock, Elizabeth. Lawrence Chatters. Personal, December 2021.

27. *Ibid.*

28. *Ibid.*

29. *Ibid.*

30. Blackstock, Elizabeth. Dakota Schuetz. Personal, August 2021.

31. *Ibid.*

32. *Ibid.*

33. *Ibid.*

34. *Ibid.*

35. *Ibid.*

36. "Filing History for Lightning Volt Limited (09791667)." Gov.uk. 2017. https://find-and-update.company-information.service.gov.uk/company/09791667/filing-history.

37. ATB Sales Limited v Rich Energy Limited and Ors (Business and Property Courts of England and Wales May 14, 2019).

38. Gerrard, Bradley. 2018. "Rich Energy Chief: 'I Fell Into the Drinks Business After Meeting a Mad Scientist.'" *The Telegraph.* https://www.telegraph.co.uk/business/2018/03/30/rich-energy-chief-fell-drinks-business-meeting-mad-scientist/.

39. ATB Sales Limited v Rich Energy Limited and Ors (Business and Property Courts of England and Wales May 14, 2019).

40. King, Alanis. William Storey. Personal, March 14, 2019.

41. *Ibid.*

42. "Rich Energy (Archived)." Rich Energy, n.d. https://web.archive.org/web/20190123072246/https://richenergy.com/.

43. King, Alanis. William Storey. Personal, March 14, 2019.

44. Gerrard, Bradley. 2018. "Rich Energy Chief: 'I Fell Into the Drinks Business After Meeting a Mad Scientist.'" *The Telegraph.* https://www.telegraph.co.uk/business/2018/03/30/rich-energy-chief-fell-drinks-business-meeting-mad-scientist/.

45. "David Sullivan—Living a Dream in Theydon Bois, Essex." 2010. *Great British Life.* https://www.essexlifemag.co.uk/people/celebrity-interviews/david-sullivan-living-a-dream-in-theydon-bois-essex-1-1639861.

46. "The Big Interview: David Sullivan—The Freedom Fighter." 2012. *Evening Standard.* https://www.standard.co.uk/sport/football/the-big-interview-david-sullivan-the-freedom-fighter-6802989.html.

47. Mitchell, Scott. 2018. "British Firm Not Ready to 'Relinquish' Force India Bid." *Motorsport.com.* https://us.motorsport.com/f1/news/rich-energy-force-india-buyout/3152345/.

48. Storey, William. 2018. "British Billionaire David Sullivan Acquires Stake in Rich Energy." LinkedIn. October 12. https://www.linkedin.com/pulse/british-billionaire-david-sullivan-acquires-stake-rich-william-storey/?trk=aff_src.aff-lilpar_c.partners_pkw.10078_net.mediapartner_plc.Skimbit+Ltd._pcrid.449670_learning&veh=aff_src.aff-lilpar_c.partners_pkw.10078_net.mediapartner_plc.Skimbit+Ltd._pcrid.449670_learning&irgwc=1.

49. King, Alanis. Haas Employee 1. Personal Interview, August 2021.

50. "Rich Energy." n.d. West Ham United. https://www.whufc.com/teams/women/partners/rich-energy.

51. Campbell, Ben. 2021. *Questions Re: West Ham's Involvement with Rich Energy*, August 23.

52. *Ibid.*

53. Sowery, Toby. 2016. Instagram Post. June 11. https://www.instagram.com/p/BGgX2bkAabx/.

54. Storey, William. 2018. "Rich Energy Sponsor British Superbikes." LinkedIn. March 8. https://www.linkedin.com/pulse/rich-energy-sponsor-british-superbikes-william-storey/.

55. Fort Wayne Music Festival. Facebook Page. https://www.facebook.com/richenergy.us/photos/a.967691673435348/1045526448985203/?type=1&theater.

56. Storey, William. 2018. "GGG at West Ham." LinkedIn. March 8. https://www.linkedin.com/pulse/ggg-west-ham-william-storey/?lipi=urn%3Ali%3Apage%3Ad_flagship3_profile_view_base_post_details%3BLMaLl98eR8a5u%2F0I2j2lqA%3D%3D.

57. Storey, William. 2018. "Kidd Dynamite Signs with William Storey Management." LinkedIn. March 8. https://www.linkedin.com/pulse/kidd-dynamite-signs-william-storey-management-william-storey/?lipi=urn%3Ali%3Apage%3Ad_flagship3_profile_view_base_post_details%3BLMaLl98eR8a5u%2F0I2j2lqA%3D%3D.

58. Storey, William. 2018. "William Storey Management in Extreme Sports." LinkedIn. March 8. https://www.linkedin.com/pulse/william-storey-management-extreme-sports-william-storey/?lipi=urn%3Ali%3Apage%3Ad_flagship3_profile_view_base_post_details%3BLMaLl98eR8a5u%2F0I2j2lqA%3D%3D.

59. Storey, William. 2018. "William Storey Luxury Brands." LinkedIn. July 27. https://www.linkedin.com/pulse/william-storey-luxury-brands-william-storey/.

60. Storey, William. 2018. "Rich Energy Sign Exclusive Deal with Multiple Festivals for Summer 2017." LinkedIn. March 8. https://www.linkedin.com/pulse/rich-energy-sign-exclusive-deal-multiple-festivals-summer-storey/.

61. Fort Wayne Music Festival. Facebook Page. https://www.facebook.com/richenergy.us/photos/a.967691673435348/1045526448985203/?type=1&theater.

62. Storey, William. 2018. "William Storey Management in F1." LinkedIn. July 30. https://www.linkedin.com/pulse/william-storey-management-f1-william-storey/.

63. *Ibid.*

64. Storey, William. 2018. "Rich Energy Commence International Media Campaign Across Motor Racing, Boxing, Football and Extreme Sports." LinkedIn. March 8. https://www.linkedin.com/pulse/rich-energy-commence-international-media-campaign-across-storey/.

65. Storey, William. 2018. "Rich Energy Beat Red Bull to Corporate Accounts." LinkedIn. March 9. https://www.linkedin.com/pulse/rich-energy-beat-red-bull-corporate-accounts-william-storey/.

66. Storey, William. 2016. "William Storey TT Races." LinkedIn. August 30. https://www.linkedin.com/pulse/william-storey-tt-races-william-storey/.

67. Storey, William. 2018. "Rich Energy Fuel the Party at Monaco GP." LinkedIn. March 9. https://www.linkedin.com/pulse/rich-energy-fuel-party-monaco-gp-william-storey/.

68. Watson, Calvin. 2021. "A Few Quick Questions About the Amber Lounge's Partnership with Rich Energy," August 21.

69. Storey, William. 2018. "Rich Energy Sponsor British Superbikes." LinkedIn. March 8. https://www.linkedin.com/pulse/rich-energy-sponsor-british-superbikes-william-storey/.

70. Storey, William. 2018. "Ex Sas V Navy Seals Charity Boxing." LinkedIn. March 8. https://www.linkedin.com/pulse/ex-sas-v-navy-seals-charity-boxing-william-storey/.

71. Storey, William. 2018. "Rich Energy Supporting Lamborghini Race Series as Part of Motorsport Investment." LinkedIn. March 9. https://www.linkedin.com/pulse/rich-energy-supporting-lamborghini-race-series-part-william-storey/.

72. *Ibid.*

73. Storey, William. 2018. "Rich Energy Support Paris Dakar Competitors for 2018." LinkedIn. March 9. https://www.linkedin.com/pulse/rich-energy-support-

paris-dakar-competitors-2018-william-storey/.

74. Storey, William. 2018. "Rich Energy Have Large Scale Activations at Monaco Grand Prix and TT Races on Successive Weekends." LinkedIn. May 23. https://www.linkedin.com/pulse/rich-energy-have-large-scale-activations-monaco-grand-william-storey/.

75. Storey, William. 2018. "Rich Energy Confirm IOM TT Motorbike Races." LinkedIn. March 21. https://www.linkedin.com/pulse/rich-energy-confirm-iom-tt-motorbike-races-william-storey/.

76. Rich Energy. 2016. Twitter Post. November 20. https://twitter.com/rich_energy/status/800404910709899264.

77. Storey, William. 2018. "Rich Energy and Noble Automotive." LinkedIn. March 12. https://www.linkedin.com/pulse/rich-energy-noble-automotive-william-storey/.

78. Storey, William. 2018. "Rich Energy Partner UK's Premier Helicopter Service." LinkedIn. March 8. https://www.linkedin.com/pulse/rich-energy-partner-uks-premier-helicopter-service-william-storey/.

79. Storey, William. 2018. "William Storey Signs Deal with Alex Thomson Racing and Hugo Boss." LinkedIn. March 8. https://www.linkedin.com/pulse/william-storey-signs-deal-alex-thomson-racing-hugo-boss-storey/.

80. Storey, William. 2018. "Rich Energy Sponsor West Ham Player Awards 2017." LinkedIn. March 10. https://www.linkedin.com/pulse/rich-energy-sponsor-west-ham-player-awards-2017-william-storey/.

81. Storey, William. 2018. "Rich Energy Aviation." LinkedIn. March 8. https://www.linkedin.com/pulse/rich-energy-aviation-william-storey/.

82. Storey, William. 2018. "Rich Energy Sponsor Surfing Worldwide." LinkedIn. March 9. https://www.linkedin.com/pulse/rich-energy-sponsor-surfing-worldwide-william-storey/.

83. Storey, William. 2018. "Rich Energy Target World Titles in Powerboat Racing." LinkedIn. May 30. https://www.linkedin.com/pulse/rich-energy-target-world-titles-powerboat-racing-william-storey/.

84. Storey, William. 2018. "Rich Energy Sign Football Deals." LinkedIn. March 8. https://www.linkedin.com/pulse/rich-energy-sign-football-deals-william-storey/.

85. Storey, William. 2018. "Heavyweight Boxing Star Lucas 'Big Daddy' Browne Signed by Rich Energy." LinkedIn. March 19. https://www.linkedin.com/pulse/heavyweight-boxing-star-lucas-big-daddybrowne-signed-rich-storey/.

86. Storey, William. 2018. "Rich Energy Sign Vegas Casinos." LinkedIn. March 9. https://www.linkedin.com/pulse/rich-energy-sign-vegas-casinos-william-storey/.

87. Storey, William. 2018. "Rich Energy Win Hilton and Marriot Hotels." LinkedIn. March 7. https://www.linkedin.com/pulse/rich-energy-win-hilton-marriot-hotels-william-storey/.

88. *Ibid.*

89. "MP 644: The Week in IndyCar, Sept 4, with Jack Harvey and Toby Sowery," 2019. https://youtu.be/pmDSrahPvok?t=4722.

90. "Toby Sowery." n.d. IndyCar.com. https://www.indycar.com/Series/Indy-Lights/Toby-Sowery.

91. Browne, Lucas. 2019. Twitter Post. July 24. https://twitter.com/lucasBrowne/status/1154034678896050176.

92. Browne, Lucas. 2019. Twitter Post. July 27. https://twitter.com/lucasBrowne/status/1155114005029097472.

93. Parfitt Jr., Rick. 2019. Twitter Post. July 19. https://twitter.com/RickParfittJnr/status/1152263609524850688.

94. "Carroll and Fernandes Scoop Player Awards." 2017. West Ham United. https://www.whufc.com/news/articles/2017/may/09-may/carroll-and-fernandes-scoop-player-awards.

95. "Player Awards 2016/17." 2017. YouTube. https://www.youtube.com/watch?v=KvVealqyymo&ab_channel=WestHamUnitedFC.

96. Storey, William. 2018. "Rich Energy Launch Official £100m Takeover of Force India." LinkedIn. https://www.linkedin.com/pulse/rich-energy-launch-official-100m-takeover-force-india-william-storey/.

97. Storey, William. 2019. "Rich Energy Chosen as Trailblazing Brand in City Awards as Company Raises £220m." LinkedIn. January 23. https://www.linkedin.com/pulse/rich-energy-chosen-trailblazing-brand-city-awards-company-storey/.

98. Storey, William. 2018. "Why Now Is the Time to Bet on Trump." LinkedIn. March 9. https://www.linkedin.com/pulse/why-now-time-bet-trump-william-storey/.

99. Storey, William. 2018. "Congratulations President Trump." LinkedIn. March 8. https://www.linkedin.com/pulse/congratulations-president-trump-william-storey/?articleId=825929294 2518347985.

100. Storey, William. 2018. "Rich Energy Enjoys International Export Boom Post Brexit Vote." LinkedIn. March 9. https://www.linkedin.com/pulse/rich-energy-enjoys-international-export-boom-post-brexit-storey/?lipi=urn%3Ali%3Apage%3Ad_flagship3_profile_view_base_post_details%3BLMaLl98eR8a5u%2F0I2j2lqA%3D%3D.

101. Wood, Rachel, and Matthew Knight. 2017. "Bernie Ecclestone 'Made Some Enemies … but He Did a Lot of Good.'" *CNN*. https://www.cnn.com/2017/03/21/motorsport/f1-bernie-ecclestone-maurice-hamilton/index.html.

102. "Bernie Ecclestone Says Hitler Was a Man Who Got Things Done." 2009. *The Guardian*. https://www.theguardian.com/sport/2009/jul/04/bernie-ecclestone-interview-hitler-saddam.

103. "Ecclestone Challenges $1.5 Billion Tax Demand." 2015. *CNBC*. https://www.cnbc.com/2015/05/22/ecclestone-challenges-15-billion-tax-demand.html.

104. Sylt, Christian. 2014. "The Real Reason Bernie Ecclestone Settled His Bribery Trial." Forbes. https://www.forbes.com/sites/csylt/2014/08/20/the-real-reason-bernie-ecclestone-settled-his-bribery-trial/#b4a7bba34204.

105. "Bernie Ecclestone: Women Drivers in F1 Would Not Be Taken Seriously." 2016. BBC. https://www.bbc.com/sport/formula1/36086363.

106. "Ecclestone: Hamilton Racism Row 'Nonsense.'" 2008. *The Guardian*. https://www.theguardian.com/sport/2008/nov/06/lewishamilton-formulaone.

107. Davies, Amanda, and George Ramsay. 2020. "Often 'Black People Are More Racist Than White People,' Says Ex-F1 Supremo Bernie Ecclestone." *CNN*. https://edition.cnn.com/2020/06/26/motorsport/bernie-ecclestone-formula-one-motorsport-lewis-hamilton-spt-intl/index.html.

108. Robinson, Joshua. 2017. "Liberty Media Names Chase Carey as Formula One CEO, Replacing Bernie Ecclestone." *Wall Street Journal*. https://www.wsj.com/articles/chase-carey-replaces-formula-ones-bernie-ecclestone-as-ceo-1485210949.

109. Storey, William. 2018. "Lie with Snakes and Drink Poison." LinkedIn. March 9. https://www.linkedin.com/pulse/-lie-snakes-drink-poison-william-storey/.

110. Williamson, Martin. n.d. "Monaco Grand Prix 1958—Trintignant Wins on Home Soil." *ESPN*. http://en.espn.co.uk/f1/motorsport/story/16050.html.

111. King, Alanis. 2019. "Looks Like Haas F1 Is Going After Rich Energy." *Jalopnik*. https://jalopnik.com/looks-like-haas-f1-is-going-after-rich-energy-1836358665.

112. Larson, Selena. 2017. "Welcome to a World with 280-character Tweets." *CNN Business*. https://money.cnn.com/2017/11/07/technology/twitter-280-character-limit/index.html.

113. Rich Energy. 2019. Twitter Post. January 1. https://twitter.com/okeefe_92/status/1130861975058173957/.

114. Rich Energy. 2017. Twitter Post. January 12. https://twitter.com/rich_energy/status/819601310760767488.

115. Rich Energy. 2015. Twitter Post. November 30. https://twitter.com/rich_energy/status/671290053675585536.

116. Rich Energy. 2016. Twitter Post. April 11. https://twitter.com/rich_energy/status/719424340685676544.

117. Rich Energy. 2016. Twitter Post. April 22. https://twitter.com/rich_energy/status/72340674781830348.

118. Rich Energy. 2016. Twitter Post. April 22. https://twitter.com/rich_energy/status/723414862810882049.

119. "Constance Jablonski for Estée Lauder Idealist Campaign." *Fashion Gone Rogue*, October 27. https://www.fashiongonerogue.com/constance-jablonski-estee-lauder-campaign/.

120. "Soprano Ice Hair Removal." n.d. Nation Light. http://nationlight.ca/soprano-ice-platinum/.

121. Rich Energy. 2016. Twitter Post. September 24. https://twitter.com/rich_energy/status/779727522808401921.

122. Rich Energy. 2016. Twitter post. December 20. https://twitter.com/rich_energy/status/811339338898440193.

123. Rutherford, Chrissy. 2021. "Happy Birthday, Naomi Campbell! See Her Top 10 Moments in Bazaar." *Harper's Bazaar.* March 3. https://www.harpersbazaar.com/fashion/photography/g2048/naomi-campbell-in-bazaar/?slide=1.

124. Rich Energy. 2017. Twitter Post. February 21. https://twitter.com/rich_energy/status/834256010646867969.

125. Rich Energy. 2017. Twitter Post. April 27. https://twitter.com/rich_energy/status/857808866532352004.

126. "The St. Regis Bangkok." Marriott International. https://www.marriott.com/hotels/hotel-photos/bkkxr-the-st-regis-bangkok/.

127. Rich Energy. 2017. Twitter Post. February 5. https://twitter.com/rich_energy/status/828386103258406912.

128. "NOAA's Gulfstream IV in the Hangar at Yokota Airforce Base in Japan." NOAA's Gulfstream IV in the hangar at Yokota Airforce Base in Japan | Office of Marine and Aviation Operations, January 10, 2022. https://www.omao.noaa.gov/find/media/images/noaas-gulfstream-iv-hangar-yokota-airforce-base-japan.

129. Rich Energy. 2017. Twitter Post. April 7. https://twitter.com/rich_energy/status/850241400255926274.

130. Rich Energy. 2016. Twitter Post. December 28. https://twitter.com/rich_energy/status/814103229080436736.

131. "Used Ferrari for Sale (with Photos)." n.d. CarGurus. https://www.cargurus.com/Cars/l-Used-Ferrari-Enzo-d442.

132. Rich Energy. 2016. Twitter Post. April 10. https://twitter.com/rich_energy/status/719246172741902336.

133. Rich Energy. 2016. Twitter Post. May 23. https://twitter.com/rich_energy/status/734791458490843136.

134. Rich Energy. 2016. Twitter Post. May 21. https://twitter.com/rich_energy/status/734039561697959941.

135. Rich Energy. 2016. Twitter Post. June 21. https://twitter.com/rich_energy/status/745292899714207744.

136. Rich Energy. 2016. Twitter Post. June 16. https://twitter.com/rich_energy/status/743480927993626624.

137. Kerr, Luke. 2015. "Watch as a Terrifying Shark Swims Into Someone's Backyard." *USA Today's FTW.* https://ftw.usatoday.com/2015/04/terrifying-shark-swims-backyard-video.

138. Rich Energy USA (Archived), n.d. https://web.archive.org/web/20190527144841/https://www.richenergy.us/.

139. *Ibid.*

140. *Ibid.*

141. Rich Energy U.S. 2019. Instagram Post. June 18. https://www.instagram.com/p/By3mnTyA6Hg/.

142. ATB Sales Limited v Rich Energy Limited and Ors (Business and Property Courts of England and Wales May 14, 2019).

143. King, Alanis. Anonymous. Personal Interview, August 2021.

144. Farhoumand, Blake, September 1, 2021.

145. Henderson, Lance, August 25, 2021.

146. Puz, Bernard, November 26, 2021.

147. Puz, Bernard, August 16, 2021.

148. Storey, William. 2018. "Rich Energy Appoint City Veteran to Management Team." LinkedIn. December 11. https://www.linkedin.com/pulse/rich-energy-appoint-city-veteran-manage ment-team-william-storey/.

149. Hope, Craig. 2018. "British Energy Drinks Company in Talks to Buy Force India." *Daily Mail.* https://www.dailymail.co.uk/sport/formulaone/article-5414721/British-energy-drinks-company-talks-buy-Force-India.html.

150. "What's the Storey?" *Chasin' the Racin',* 2020. https://www.youtube.com/watch?v=xBEyFflfz4w.

151. *Ibid.*

152. "William Storey—Founder—Rich Energy." LinkedIn. https://uk.linkedin.com/in/william-storey-58598356.

153. "Rich Energy." LinkedIn. https://www.linkedin.com/company/rich-energy-beverages.

154. "John Morris—Company Director—ML-Leisure Ltd." LinkedIn. https://uk.linkedin.com/in/john-morris-7637a7127.

155. *Ibid.*

156. "Company Overview for Danieli UK Holding Limited (02997333)." Gov.uk. https://find-and-update.company-information.service.gov.uk/company/02997333.

157. "Wales | History, Geography, Facts, & Points of Interest." 2021. Britannica. https://www.britannica.com/place/Wales.
158. "Company Overview for Tryfan Technologies Limited (07405925)." Gov.uk. https://find-and-update.company-information.service.gov.uk/company/07405925.
159. *Ibid.*
160. "Staxoweb," n.d. https://staxoweb.com/.
161. *Ibid.*
162. ATB Sales Limited v Rich Energy Limited and Ors (Business and Property Courts of England and Wales May 14, 2019).
163. "William Storey Management," n.d. williamstorey.com
164. Kalinauckas, Alex. 2019. "Rich Energy "Bringing Back" JPS Lotus Look with Haas Livery." *Motorsport.com*. https://us.motorsport.com/f1/news/haas-rich-energy-jps-lotus-look/4334026/.
165. "Company Overview for Tryfan Technologies Limited (07405925)." Gov.uk. https://find-and-update.company-information.service.gov.uk/company/07405925.
166. *Ibid.*
167. "What Does Business Recovery Actually Mean? Can My Company Be Rescued?" 2021. Real Business Rescue. https://www.realbusinessrescue.co.uk/articles/business-insolvency/what-does-business-recovery-actually-mean-can-my-company-be-rescued.
168. "Company Overview for Tryfan Technologies Limited (07405925)." Gov.uk. https://find-and-update.company-information.service.gov.uk/company/07405925.
169. "Wind Up a Company That Owes You Money." n.d. Gov.uk. https://www.gov.uk/wind-up-a-company-that-owes-you-money.
170. "Company Overview for Tryfan Technologies Limited (07405925)." Gov.uk. https://find-and-update.company-information.service.gov.uk/company/07405925.
171. *Ibid.*
172. *Ibid.*
173. "Company Overview for Wise Guy Boxing (08260818)." Gov.uk. https://find-and-update.company-information.service.gov.uk/company/08260818.
174. *Ibid.*
175. Buglioni, Frank, March 2019.
176. "Company Overview for Danieli UK Holding Limited (02997333)." Gov.uk. https://find-and-update.company-information.service.gov.uk/company/02997333.
177. Danieli Style. Twitter Account. https://twitter.com/Danieli_Style.
178. "Danieli Style," n.d. https://web.archive.org/web/20140517050512/http://danielistyle.com/.
179. *Ibid.*
180. *Ibid.*
181. "Company Overview for Danieli UK Holding Limited (02997333)." Gov.uk. https://find-and-update.company-information.service.gov.uk/company/02997333.
182. "Company Overview for Wise Guy Boxing (08260818)." Gov.uk. https://find-and-update.company-information.service.gov.uk/company/08260818.
183. "Company Overview for Danieli UK Holding Limited (02997333)." Gov.uk. https://find-and-update.company-information.service.gov.uk/company/02997333.
184. "Company Overview for Tryfan LED Limited (09580846)." Gov.uk. https://find-and-update.company-information.service.gov.uk/company/09580846.
185. *Ibid.*
186. King, Alanis. William Storey. Personal, March 14, 2019.
187. *Ibid.*
188. *Ibid.*
189. Storey, William, March 14, 2019.
190. Morrison, Stuart, March 14, 2019.
191. King, Alanis. Haas Employee 5. Personal Interview, August 2021.
192. Cooper, Adam. 2018. "Haas: Due Diligence Completed on New 2019 Title Sponsor Rich Energy." *Autosport*. https://www.autosport.com/f1/news/139664/haas-due-diligence-done-on-new-title-sponsor.

Chapter 3

1. Blackstock, Elizabeth. Luke Smith. Personal, August 2021.
2. *Ibid.*
3. Doodson, Mike, and Simon Arron. n.d. "Elio De Angelis: Money Greased the Wheels, but Talent Turned Them."

Motor Sport Magazine. https://www. motorsportmagazine.com/archive/article/- june-2011/68/money-greased-wheels- talent-turned-them.

4. Galarza, Daniela. 2015. "Why You Should Know the Name Roger Vergé." *Eater*. https://www.eater.com/2015/6/8/8745361/ chef-roger-verge-died.

5. "Police Arrested American Oil Financier David Thieme on Allega- tions..." 1981. UPI. https://www.upi.com/ Archives/1981/04/14/Police-arrested- American-oil-financier-David-Thieme- on-allegations/2698356072400/.

6. Bruce, Chris. 2016. "Banned Lotus 88 F1 Car Explained by Colin Chapman's Son." *Autoblog*. https://www.autoblog. com/2016/04/04/lotus-88-carbon-fiber- f1-aerodynamics-video/.

7. "F1 Launches on the Grand Scale." *ESPN*, January 2014. http://en.espnf1.com/ blogs/motorsport/story/142963.html.

8. Ferrier, Laurent, François Sérv- anin, and François Trisconi. n.d. "70 Years of Porsche Sports Cars—70 Years of Porsche Sports Cars." https://presskit. porsche.de/anniversaries/en/70-years- porsche-sports-cars/topic/category/ motorsporterfolge/items/en-le-mans- 1979-the-year-of-the-935-721.html.

9. Watkins, Gary. 2014. "Stand-in Delivers January 2008." *Motor Sport Magazine*. https://www.motorsport magazine.com/archive/article/january- 2008/96/stand-in-delivers.

10. "Police Arrested American Oil Financier David Thieme on Allega- tions..." 1981. UPI. https://www.upi.com/ Archives/1981/04/14/Police-arrested- American-oil-financier-David-Thieme- on-allegations/2698356072400/.

11. AP. 1981. "Lotus Car Is Banned." 1981. *The Ithaca Journal*, April 24, 13. https://www.newspapers.com/image /255057644/?terms=Associated%20 Press%20150000%20bail%20david%20 thieme&match=1.

12. Somerfield, Matt. 2020. "Banned: Why Lotus' Twin-chassis Concept Was Outlawed." *Motorsport.com*. https:// us.motorsport.com/f1/news/banned-tech- twin-chassis-lotus/4780031/.

13. "Lotus Type 88—The BANNED F1 Car. YouTube." YouTube, 2016. https://www.youtube.com/watch?v=DMtk RcqvGaU&feature=emb_title.

14. *Ibid.*

15. Walsworth, Jack. 2015. "Lotus Founder Colin Chapman Dies at Age 54." *Automotive News*. https://www. autonews.com/article/20151215/ CCHISTORY/151219934/lotus-founder- colin-chapman-dies-at-age-54.

16. Spurgeon, Brad. 2012. "What's in a Formula One Name?" *The New York Times*. https://www.nytimes.com/2012/03/17/ sports/autoracing/17iht-srf1prix17.html.

17. Miles, Ben. 2020. "The Nine Most Successful F1 Teams of All Time (List)." Goodwood. https://www.goodwood.com/ grr/race/historic/2020/4/the-nine-most- successful-f1-teams-of-all-time/.

18. Casert, Raf. 1990. "Down and Out in Belgium." *Associated Press*. https:// apnews.com/article/988c08a37242dd72c8 1ec4e0c1fe5952.

19. "Jean-Pierre Van Rossem Obit- uary." 2019. *The Times*. https://www. thetimes.co.uk/article/jean-pierre-van- rossem-obituary-0z5khsxm8.

20. "Obituary: Jean-Pierre Van Ros- sem." 2018. *Independent.ie*. https:// www.independent.ie/world-news/ europe/obituary-jean-pierre-van- rossem-37652550.html.

21. *Ibid.*

22. Casert, Raf. 1990. "Down and Out in Belgium." *Associated Press*. https:// apnews.com/article/988c08a37242dd72c8 1ec4e0c1fe5952.

23. "Jean-Pierre Van Rossem Obituary | Register." 2019. *The Times*. https://www. thetimes.co.uk/article/jean-pierre-van- rossem-obituary-0z5khsxm8.

24. "1989 Race Results." n.d. F1. https:// www.formula1.com/en/results.html/1989/ races.html.

25. *Ibid.*

26. Casert, Raf. 1990. "Down and Out in Belgium." *Associated Press*. https:// apnews.com/article/988c08a37242dd72c8 1ec4e0c1fe5952.

27. *Ibid.*

28. "Jean-Pierre Van Rossem Obit- uary." 2019. *The Times*. https://www. thetimes.co.uk/article/jean-pierre-van- rossem-obituary-0z5khsxm8.

29. Watkins, Gary. 2018. "Jean-Pierre Van Rossem, Onyx Formula 1 Team Backer, Dies." *Autosport*. https://www. autosport.com/f1/news/140665/backer- behind-onyx-f1-team-dies.

30. Partridge, Matthew. 2020. "Great Frauds in History: Jean-Pierre Van Rossem's Money-making Machine." *Money Week*. https://moneyweek.com/invest ments/investment-strategy/601415/-great-frauds-in-history-jean-pierre-van-rossems-money-making.

31. Straw, Edd. 2020. "The Lost F1 Team That Launched Newey." *Motorsport.com*. https://us.motorsport.com/f1/news/adrian-newey-leyton-house-march/4809840/?nrt=54.

32. "1987 Kremer Porsche 962C." n.d. Gooding & Company. https://www.goodingco.com/vehicle/1987-kremer-porsche-962c/.

33. Chira, Susan. 1988. "Japan's Big Spenders." *The New York Times*. https://www.nytimes.com/1988/04/10/magazine/japan-s-big-spenders.html.

34. *Ibid.*

35. Straw, Edd. 2020. "The Lost F1 Team That Launched Newey." *Motorsport.com*. https://us.motorsport.com/f1/news/adrian-newey-leyton-house-march/4809840/?nrt=54.

36. *Ibid.*

37. McRae, Donald. 2011. "Why Adrian Newey Just Cannot Bear to Watch the New Senna Movie." *The Guardian*. https://www.theguardian.com/sport/2011/may/17/-adrian-newey-red-bull-ayrton-senna.

38. Hong, K.P. 1990. "World Bank Suspends Nomura, Nikko Securities; Gangster Ties Reported Reason." *Associated Press*. https://apnews.com/article/ee901cf4fc731ebdbf9ea023856b8f27.

39. Simmons, Marcus. 2014. "The Short, Dazzling Story of Leyton House in F1: Marching to Civil War." *Motor Sport Magazine*. https://www.motorsportmagazine.com/archive/article/june-2005/82/marching-to-civil-war.

40. "Monaco 1989: Brabham's Final Fling." *Yahoo Sports AU*, n.d. https://au.sports.yahoo.com/monaco-1989-brabham-final-fling-145520384.html.

41. Lovell, Terry. *Bernie Ecclestone: King of Sport*. Readhowyouwant.com Ltd., 2014.

42. *Ibid.*

43. *Ibid.*

44. *Ibid.*

45. *Ibid.*

46. *Ibid.*

47. Thomsen, Ian. 1993. "Ligier's De Rouvre: Man of Many Parts." *The New York Times*. https://www.nytimes.com/1993/05/21/sports/IHT-ligiers-de-rouvre-man-of-many-parts.html.

48. Henry, Alan. 1993. "Brundle Could Give Ligier an All-British Line-up." *The Guardian*, January 13, 1993, 17. https://www.newspapers.com/image/260295409/?terms=Cyril%20Rouvre%20ligier&match=1.

49. "Cyril De Rouvre Sort De La Route." 2021. *L'Humanité*, March 28. https://www.humanite.fr/node/72016.

50. MacDonald, Ian. 1993. "Englishmen Become Driving Force for French Team Ligier." *The Gazette*, June 11, 51. https://www.newspapers.com/image/424316949/?terms=cyril%20rouvre&match=1.

51. "Les Millions De Cyril." 1994. L'Express.fr, January 6. https://www.lexpress.fr/informations/les-millions-de-cyril_596731.html.

52. "Cyril De Rouvre." *Libération*. https://www.liberation.fr/futurs/1994/12/24/cyril-de-rouvre_116185.

53. "Arab Cleared of £300,000 'Con Tricks.'" 1999. *The Guardian*. https://www.theguardian.com/uk/1999/nov/09/3.

54. "'Fake Sheikh' Gave Cher Sports Car." 1999. *BBC News*. http://news.bbc.co.uk/2/hi/uk_news/479506.stm.

55. "Fake Sheikh Lavished 'Gift' on Singer Cher." 1999. *Oxford Mail*. https://www.oxfordmail.co.uk/news/6635042.-fake-sheikh-lavished-gift-singer-cher/.

56. *Ibid.*

57. "'Fake Sheikh' Gave Cher Sports Car." 1999. *BBC News*. http://news.bbc.co.uk/2/hi/uk_news/479506.stm.

58. *Ibid.*

59. Spurgeon, Brad. 1998. "Pollock Engineers the Deals at the Tyrrell Formula One Team: A Young Owner on the Fast Track (Published 1998)." *The New York Times*. https://www.nytimes.com/1998/08/15/sports/IHT-pollock-engineers-the-deals-at-the-tyrrell-formula-one-team-a.html.

60. Mitchell, Scott. 2019. "McLaren Signs Deal with British American Tobacco." *Motorsport.com*. https://us.motorsport.com/f1/news/british-american-tobacco-mclaren-deal/4335601/.

61. "Japanese GP Tyrrell Friday Notes." 1999. Motorsport. https://au.motorsport.

com/f1/news/japanese-gp-tyrrell-friday-notes/1731108/.

62. "Africa | Nigerian Businessman Gets Into Formula One." 1999. *BBC News.* http://news.bbc.co.uk/2/hi/africa/254363.stm.

63. "Prince Out After Boardroom Tussle." *Autosport,* n.d. https://www.autosport.com/f1/news/6509/prince-out-after-boardroom-tussle.

64. Weeks, Jim. 2017. "The Mysterious Nigerian Prince Who Scammed His Way Into Owning an F1 Team." *VICE.* https://www.vice.com/en/article/gvawv7/the-mysterious-nigerian-prince-who-scammed-his-way-into-owning-an-f1-team.

65. *Ibid.*

66. "1999 Constructor Standings." n.d. F1. https://www.formula1.com/en/results.html/1999/team.html.

67. Valentine, Ian. 2002. "Future Bleak for Arrows F1 Team as Orange Mulls Sponsorship Deal." *Campaign.* https://www.campaignlive.co.uk/article/future-bleak-arrows-f1-team-orange-mulls-sponsorship-deal/150688.

68. "BBC Sport—Gloucester Owner and Former F1 Boss Tom Walkinshaw Dies." 2010. *BBC News.* http://news.bbc.co.uk/sport2/hi/front_page/9280301.stm.

69. Davison, Drew. 2016. "From Hay Farmer to Daytona 500: The Improbable Story of Robert Richardson, Jr." *Fort Worth Star-Telegram.* https://www.star-telegram.com/sports/nascar-auto-racing/article61378457.html.

70. Gallagher, Danny. 2008. "Jury Acquits Ibrahim of Theft, Deception Charges | News | Starlocalmedia.com." *Star Local Media.* https://starlocalmedia.com/mckinneycouriergazette/news/jury-acquits-ibrahim-of-theft-deception-charges/article_385dc42a-8fce-5805-8fbf-5f66ed9af3f2.html.

71. Ujah, Emma. 2017. "We'll Deliver Electric Cars to Nigerian Market in 2018, Says Prince Ado Ibrahim." *Vanguard News.* https://www.vanguardngr.com/2017/08/-well-deliver-electric-cars-nigerian-market-2018-says-prince-ado-ibrahim/.

72. Associated Press. 1992. "Andrea Moda to Start Two GP Cars." *Courier-Post,* January 23, 32. https://www.newspapers.com/image/182844498/?terms=andrea%20moda%20formula&match=1.

73. Henry, Alan. 1992. "Italy's Fast Lady Chases the Right Formula." *Guardian,* February 28, 17. https://www.newspapers.com/image/259960752/?terms=andrea%20moda%20formula&match=1.

74. *El Nuevo Herald.* 1992. "Mañana Se Larga GP De Sudáfrica." February 29, 27. https://www.newspapers.com/image/636767918/?terms=andrea%20moda&match=1.

75. *Guardian.* 1992. "Motor Racing." March 31, 19. https://www.newspapers.com/image/260289624/?terms=andrea%20moda&match=1.

76. Henry, Alan. 1992. "McLaren Teething Troubles Leave Senna Down in Mouth." *Guardian,* April 4, 14. https://www.newspapers.com/image/260291252/?terms=andrea%20moda&match=1.

77. Henry, Alan. 1992. "Mansell Firmly in the Driving Seat." *Guardian,* May 2, 19. https://www.newspapers.com/image/260291252/?terms=andrea%20moda&match=1.

78. Associated Press. 1992. "Auto Racing." *Kansas City Star,* September 9, 1992, 34. https://www.newspapers.com/image/682342914/?terms=andrea%20moda%20monaco%2011%20laps&match=1.

79. "Belgian Grand Prix—QUALIFYING 1." 1992. F1. https://www.formula1.com/en/results.html/1992/races/585/belgium/qualifying-1.html.

80. Associated Press. 1992. "Auto Racing." *Kansas City Star,* September 9, 34. https://www.newspapers.com/image/682342914/?terms=andrea%20moda%20monaco%2011%20laps&match=1.

81. Associated Press. 1992. "Andrea Moda Team Ruled Out of Formula 1 Season." *Courier-Journal,* September 9, 40. https://www.newspapers.com/image/110705185/.

82. Miller, Robin. 1993. "Rookie Driver Makes Impressive Debut." *Indianapolis Star,* June 14, 33. https://www.newspapers.com/image/107339687/?terms=andrea%20Montermini%20detroit&match=1.

83. "Parmalat: 40-year History at Stake—Dec. 23, 2003." 2003. *CNN.* https://www.cnn.com/2003/BUSINESS/12/22/italy.parmalat.sidebar/.

84. "Parmalat." 2016. Financial Scandals, Scoundrels & Crises. https://www.econcrises.org/2016/11/29/parmalat/.
85. "Lauda Seeks New Sponsor for Famous Red Cap." 2010. *Motorsport.com*. https://us.motorsport.com/f1/news/-lauda-seeks-new-sponsor-for-famous-red-cap/2452740/.
86. "Parmalat Funds Siphoned by Tanzi." 2003. *BBC News*. http://news.bbc.co.uk/2/hi/business/3355605.stm.
87. Noble, Jonathan. 2007. "Super Aguri to Sue SS United." *Autosport*. https://www.autosport.com/f1/news/61700/super-aguri-to-sue-ss-united.
88. "Super Aguri Acquisition." n.d. Magma Group. http://magmagroup.co/insight/case-studies/super-aguri-acquisition/.
89. "Super Aguri Withdraw from F1 Championship." 2008. *Reuters*. https://www.reuters.com/article/idINIndia-33426520080506.
90. "Quantum Still Plotting Lotus Buy-in." 2014. *Yahoo News Singapore*. https://sg.news.yahoo.com/quantum-still-plotting-lotus-buy-072933109.html.
91. "Mansoor Ijaz: Fixer in Pakistan's 'Memogate' Row." 2012. *BBC*. https://www.bbc.com/news/world-asia-16649034.
92. Winderman, Ira, and Anthony Lednovich. 1986. "Auto Racing Faces Problem Of Drug Money Financing." *Sun Sentinel*. https://www.sun-sentinel.com/news/fl-xpm-1986-03-23-8601180194-story.html.
93. Skalocky, Stephen. n.d. "Randy Lanier: IndyCar Driver and Drug Smuggler | Longform—SI.com." *Sports Illustrated*. https://www.si.com/longform/true-crime/randy-lanier-indycar-drug-smuggler/index.html.
94. Schrader, Stef. 2017. "The Drug-Running Team Who Got Into Racing with a Bag Full of Cash at Le Mans." *Jalopnik*. https://jalopnik.com/the-drug-running-team-who-got-into-racing-with-a-bag-fu-1821122960.
95. "History | Results | Statistics." n.d. 24 Hours of Le Mans. https://assets.lemans.org/explorer/pdf/courses/2018/-24-heures-du-mans/press-kit/uk/-statistiques-historiques-en.pdf.
96. "Cannot Race Indy 500." 1986. UPI. https://www.upi.com/Archives/1986/05/08/Cannot-race-Indy-500/4197515908800/.
97. "Photo of the Day—John Paul, Sr.'s Porsche at the 1978 24 Hours of Le Mans." 2016. 24 Heures du Mans. https://www.24h-lemans.com/en/news/photo-of-the-day-john-paul-sr-s-porsche-at-the-1978-24-hours-of-le-mans-43873.
98. Pagliery, Jose. 2016. "Race Car Driver Arrested in Alleged $2 Billion Payday Lending Empire." *CNN Business*. https://money.cnn.com/2016/02/10/news/payday-lending-scott-tucker-arrest/.
99. Pruett, Marshall. 2020. "Figueiredo Linked to Investigation Into Embezzlement, Money Laundering." *RACER*. https://racer.com/2020/06/26/figueiredo-embezzlement-money-laundering/.
100. *Ibid*.
101. Cairone, Andrea. 2013. "Venezuelan Scandal Freezes Motorsport Assets—Racing News." *Road & Track*. https://www.roadandtrack.com/motorsports/news/a5774/venezuelan-financial-scandal-cuts-motorsport-sponsorship/.
102. Wallis, Daniel. 2013. "Venezuela Investigates Sports Stars in Big Currency Scam." *Reuters*. https://www.reuters.com/article/amp/idUKBRE99H03920131018?-edition-redirect=uk.
103. Perez, Jerry. 2018. "Show Me the Money: The Finances Behind IndyCar, NASCAR, and Formula 1." *The Drive*. https://www.thedrive.com/accelerator/22168/behind-the-shadowy-billion-dollar-payouts-of-f1-nascar-and-indycar.
104. Richards, Giles. 2020. "F1 Teams Agree to Introduce Budget Cap from 2021 Onwards." *Guardian*. https://www.theguardian.com/sport/2020/may/23/f1-teams-agree-to-introduce-budget-cap-from-2021-onwards.
105. "2021 NTT IndyCar Series Car Specifications." n.d. IndyCar.com. https://www.indycar.com/Fan-Info/INDYCAR-101/The-Car-Dallara/IndyCar-Series-Chassis-Specifications.
106. Perez, Jerry. 2018. "Show Me the Money: The Finances Behind IndyCar, NASCAR, and Formula 1." *The Drive*. https://www.thedrive.com/accelerator/22168/behind-the-shadowy-billion-dollar-payouts-of-f1-nascar-and-indycar.
107. Haislop, Tadd. 2020. "Indy 500 Purse, Payout Breakdown: How Much Prize Money Does the Winner Get in

2020?" *Sporting News.* https://www.
sportingnews.com/us/motorsports/news/
indy-500-payouts-purse-2020-prize-
money/16x9jbef8xozf102akgurl2cjm.

108. Smith, Steven C. 2009. "Racing Rip
Job: Pro Drivers Allegedly Burned by Con
Man." *Autoweek.* https://www.autoweek.
com/racing/more-racing/a2027001/
racing-rip-job-pro-drivers-allegedly-
burned-con-man/.

109. Pruett, Marshall. 2017. "The
Ponzi-Scheming Scumbags of Sports
Car Racing That Were on Par with Bernie Madoff." *Road & Track.* https://
www.roadandtrack.com/motorsports/
a32941/sports-car-ponzi-schemes/.

110. Dagys, John. 2014. "Zogaib, Loles
Sentenced to Prison Terms." *Sportscar365.*
https://sportscar365.com/imsa/zogaib-
loles-sentenced-to-prison-terms/.

111. UPI. 1982. "$40,000 Swindle
Charged to 'Mystery Driver.'" *The Town
Talk,* June 26, 11. https://www.newspapers.
com/image/?clipping_id=29781516&fcf
Token=eyJhbGciOiJIUzI1NiIsInR5cCI6
IkpXVCJ9.eyJmcmVlLXZpZXctaWQiO
jIxNTk3NzAyMywiaWF0IjoxNjQxNTg
3OTk2LCJleHAiOjE2NDE2NzQzOTZ9.
wb4O8yq3d9-EiBE929hgDK6-PJpee_
l9jPzJp6JiMSM.

112. "EarthWater Exclusively Sold
on Amazon Joins BK Racing Team
as the Official Bottled Water for the
2018 NASCAR Season." 2018. *Yahoo
Finance.* https://www.yahoo.com/news/-
earthwater-exclusively-sold-amazon-
joins-180000112.html.

113. *Ibid.*

114. *Ibid.*

115. "Black Water? EarthWater
Fulhum (Amazon Review)." YouTube,
2017. https://www.youtube.com/watch?
v=vA2TSNC4lrM.

116. *Ibid.*

117. *Ibid.*

118. *Ibid.*

119. Ellis, Ryan. 2020. Twitter Post. July
18. https://twitter.com/ryanellisracing/
status/1284671648814305280.

120. Ellis, Ryan. 2020. Twitter Post. July
18. https://twitter.com/ryanellisracing/
status/1284673196487331840.

121. Barr, Daylon. 2020. Twitter Post.
July 18. https://twitter.com/BarrVisuals/
status/1284670972642156544.

122. Comu, CJ. 2018. Twitter Post.

April 27. https://twitter.com/cjcomu1/
status/989858521893294081/.

123. Comu, CJ. 2018. Twitter Post.
May 31. https://twitter.com/cjcomu1/
status/1002209774413500417.

124. Accesswire. 2019. "EarthWater
Founder & CEO Enters Local Politics."
Associated Press. https://apnews.com/-
press-release/pr-accesswire/defe8bdc21fb
5dbf022870348d4f7cfe.

125. "May 4 Unofficial Election Results
for Addison City Council Race." 2019.
Visit Addison. https://visitaddison.com/
marketing/may-4-unofficial-election-
results-addison-city-council-race.

126. "Six Men Charged for Role in
Five-Year High-Yield Investment Fraud
Scheme." 2019. Department of Justice.
https://www.justice.gov/opa/pr/six-men-
charged-role-five-year-high-yield-
investment-fraud-scheme.

127. "Pending Criminal Division
Cases." 2021. Department of Justice.
https://www.justice.gov/archives/
criminal-vns/case/EarthWater/update.

128. "Two Former EarthWa-
ter Executives Plead Guilty for Investment Fraud Scheme Targeting Elderly
Victims." 2020. Department of Justice. https://www.justice.gov/opa/
pr/two-former-earthwater-executives-
plead-guilty-investment-fraud-scheme-
targeting-elderly.

129. *Ibid.*

130. *Ibid.*

131. Krause, Kevin. 2020. "Top Execs
of Dallas-area 'Miracle' Mineral Water
Company Admit to Massive Fraud." *Dallas Morning News.* https://www.dallas
news.com/business/local-companies/
2020/06/12/top-execs-of-dallas-miracle-
mineral-water-company-admit-to-
massive-fraud/.

132. *Ibid.*

133. Long, Dustin. 2018. "Bankruptcy Judge Appoints Trustee to Manage BK Racing." *NASCAR on NBC Sports.*
https://nascar.nbcsports.com/2018/03/28/
bankruptcy-judge-appoints-trustee-to-
manage-bk-racing/.

134. "r/NASCAR—Earthwater CEO
Admits Via Linkedin That They Aren't
Paying for Sponsorship on the No. 23,
Only Providing the Team with Free Water.
This Would Mean BK Racing Has No Pay-
ing Sponsors Through the First 4 Races of

2018." reddit. https://www.reddit.com/r/NASCAR/comments/82yfuw/earthwater_ceo_admits_via_linkedin_that_they/.

135. *Ibid.*

136. Edwards, Jim. 2013. "Here's What It Costs to Sponsor a NASCAR." *Business Insider.* https://www.businessinsider.com/heres-what-it-costs-to-sponsor-a-nascar-2013-1.

137. "r/NASCAR—Earthwater CEO Admits Via Linkedin That They Aren't Paying for Sponsorship on the No. 23, Only Providing the Team with Free Water. This Would Mean BK Racing Has No Paying Sponsors Through the First 4 Races of 2018." reddit. https://www.reddit.com/r/NASCAR/comments/82yfuw/earthwater_ceo_admits_via_linkedin_that_they/.

138. "Boston Departs from KBM, Bell in for Kentucky." *Popular Speed,* n.d. https://popularspeed.com/boston-departs-from-kbm-bell-in-for-kentucky/.

139. "Federal Indictment Charges Founders of Defunct Hickory E-Waste Company with Defrauding Victims of at Least $25 Million." 2017. Department of Justice. https://www.justice.gov/usao-wdnc/pr/federal-indictment-charges-founders-defunct-hickory-e-waste-company-defrauding-victims.

140. *Ibid.*

141. *Ibid.*

142. *Ibid.*

143. King, Alanis. 2017. "Driver Tied to Alleged $25 Million Scheme to Fund His Career Owes Former Team a Lot of Money." *Jalopnik.* https://jalopnik.com/driver-tied-to-alleged-25-million-scheme-to-fund-his-c-1819621478.

144. "Founder and CEO of Charlotte Area Start-Up Company Sentenced to 10 Years for Defrauding Victims of More Than $25 Million." 2018. Department of Justice. https://www.justice.gov/usao-wdnc/pr/founder-and-ceo-charlotte-area-start-company-sentenced-10-years-defrauding-victims-more.

145. *Ibid.*

146. *Ibid.*

147. *Ibid.*

148. "DC Solar Expands Partnership with Kyle Larson, CGR." 2018. NASCAR.com. https://www.nascar.com/news-media/2018/01/16/kyle-larson-jamie-mcmurray-sponsor-dc-solar/.

149. "DC Solar to Expand Partnership with CGR to Include a Full-Time NXS Entry in 2019 with Ross Chastain." 2018. Chip Ganassi Racing. http://www.chipganassiracing.com/News/2018/11/-DC-Solar-to-Expand-Partnership-with-CGR-to-Include-a-Full-Time-NXS-Entry-in-2019-with-Ross-Chastain.aspx.

150. *Ibid.*

151. Hurd, Rick. 2018. "Martinez: FBI Raids Home of Martinez Clippers Owners." *Mercury News.* https://www.mercurynews.com/2018/12/20/fbi-raids-home-of-martinez-clippers-owners/.

152. *Ibid.*

153. McFadin, Daniel. 2018. "FBI Conducts Raid of DC Solar's Headquarters, CEO's Home—NASCAR Talk." *NASCAR on NBC Sports.* https://nascar.nbcsports.com/2018/12/21/report-fbi-conducts-raid-of-dc-solars-headquarters-ceos-home/.

154. *Ibid.*

155. *Ibid.*

156. Chip Ganassi Racing. 2019. Twitter Post. January 4. https://twitter.com/CGRTeams/status/1081253816224436224.

157. *Ibid.*

158. Whitman, Elizabeth. n.d. "DC Solar Powers Electric Cars in Arizona Parking Lots, NASCAR Races." *Phoenix New Times.* https://www.phoenixnewtimes.com/news/dc-solar-offers-free-power-in-phoenix-parking-lots-and-nascar-races-11071663.

159. *Ibid.*

160. Weaver, Matt. 2019. "NASCAR Team and Track Sponsor DC Solar Files for Chapter 11 Bankruptcy." *Autoweek.* https://www.autoweek.com/racing/nascar/a1716071/nascar-team-and-track-sponsor-files-chapter-11-bankruptcy/.

161. "Top Executives Plead Guilty to Participating in a Billion Dollar Ponzi Scheme—the Biggest Criminal Fraud Scheme in the History of the Eastern District of California." 2020. Department of Justice. https://www.justice.gov/usao-edca/pr/top-executives-plead-guilty-participating-billion-dollar-ponzi-scheme-biggest-criminal.

162. *Ibid.*

163. *Ibid.*

164. *Ibid.*

165. *Ibid.*

166. *Ibid.*

167. "Court Orders Final Forfeiture of Over $54 Million in Connection

with Billion Dollar Ponzi Scheme." 2020. Department of Justice. https://www.justice.gov/usao-edca/pr/court-orders-final-forfeiture-over-54-million-connection-billion-dollar-ponzi-scheme.

168. "U.S. Marshals Auctioning Collection of 149 Classic, Luxury Vehicles." 2019. Department of Justice. https://www.justice.gov/usao-edca/pr/us-marshals-auctioning-collection-149-classic-luxury-vehicles.

169. McFadin, Daniel. 2019. "DC Solar Bankruptcy Auction Includes Kyle Larson's Daytona-Winning Car." *NASCAR on NBC Sports.* https://nascar.nbcsports.com/2019/09/25/dc-solar-bankruptcy-auction-includes-kyle-larsons-daytona-winning-car/.

170. "Court Orders Final Forfeiture of Over $54 Million in Connection with Billion Dollar Ponzi Scheme." 2020. Department of Justice. https://www.justice.gov/usao-edca/pr/court-orders-final-forfeiture-over-54-million-connection-billion-dollar-ponzi-scheme.

171. Stemple, Jonathan. 2020. "Owners of Solar Company That Caused Loss for Buffett Plead Guilty Over Ponzi Scheme." *Reuters.* https://www.reuters.com/article/usa-crime-dc-solar-fraud-idAFL1N29T1JN.

172. "DC Solar Owner Sentenced to 30 Years in Prison for Billion Dollar Ponzi Scheme." 2021. Department of Justice. https://www.justice.gov/usao-edca/pr/dc-solar-owner-sentenced-30-years-prison-billion-dollar-ponzi-scheme.

173. "Sean Ragan Named Special Agent in Charge of the Sacramento Field Office." 2017. FBI. https://www.fbi.gov/news/pressrel/press-releases/sean-ragan-named-special-agent-in-charge-of-the-sacramento-field-office.

174. *Ibid.*

175. Ballaban, Michael. 2019. "What Is Scuderia Ferrari's Mission Winnow Sponsor?" *Jalopnik.* https://jalopnik.com/what-the-fuck-is-mission-winnow-explained-1832730465.

176. Medland, Chris. 2019. "Ferrari to Run Special Livery in Australia." *RACER.* https://racer.com/2019/03/13/ferrari-to-run-special-livery-in-australia/.

177. "Williams Could Sell F1 Team as Board Announces £13m Loss in 2019 and Split from Title Sponsor." 2020. F1.

https://www.formula1.com/en/latest/article.williams-could-sell-f1-team-as-board-announces-gbp13m-loss-in-2019-and-split.455wGjds3WOQf7gdSuqJRf.html

178. Williams, Andrew. 2019. "The Rokit IO Pro 3D Is a Strange, Pointless Zombie of a Phone." *Wired UK.* https://www.wired.co.uk/article/rokit-io-pro-3d-review.

179. Barretto, Lawrence. 2020. "ANALYSIS: What Lies Ahead for Williams After Shock Financial News?." F1. https://www.formula1.com/en/latest/article.analysis-what-lies-ahead-for-williams-after-shock-financial-news.3jtmzE7GixI3a1DGwiwv3I.html

180. *Ibid.*

181. *Ibid.*

182. Associated Press. 2020. "Frank Williams Leaving F1 Team Will Daughter Claire After 40 Years in Series." *NBC Sports' MotorSportsTalk.* https://motorsports.nbcsports.com/2020/09/03/frank-williams-claire-f1-team/.

183. Barretto, Lawrence. 2020. "'It Feels Like Grieving'—Claire Williams Opens Up on Her Family Leaving F1 for Good." F1. https://www.formula1.com/en/latest/article.it-feels-like-grieving-claire-williams-opens-up-on-her-family-leaving-f1-for.4AGYGdRBwxUDsOtQjmSkYJ.html.

184. Storey, William. Twitter Post. September 3, 2020. https://twitter.com/richenergyceo/status/1301499475521929232?lang=en.

185. Scicluna, Tony. n.d. "FIA Stands for Ferrari International Assistance." *Bleacher Report.* https://bleacherreport.com/articles/57410-fia-stands-for-ferrari-international-assistance.

186. Noble, Jonathan. 2019. "Ferrari Will Retain F1 Veto as Part of New 2021 Concorde Agreement." *Autosport.* https://www.autosport.com/f1/news/147422/-ferrari-will-retain-veto-in-new-concorde-agreement.

187. Sylt, Christian. 2017. "Exclusive: Ferrari's $100 Million F1 Bonus at Risk." Forbes. https://www.forbes.com/sites/csylt/2017/01/21/exclusive-ferraris-100-million-f1-bonus-at-risk/.

188. "Bernie Ecclestone Defends Ferrari's $100 Million Bonus." 2017. *Eurosport.* https://www.eurosport.

com/formula-1/bernie-ecclestone-defends-ferrari-s-100-million-bonus_sto6098061/story.shtml.

189. Collantine, Keith. 2020. "Seven F1 Teams Demand Explanation Over Secret FIA-Ferrari Settlement." *RaceFans.* https://www.racefans.net/2020/03/04/-seven-non-ferrari-f1-teams-say-they-are-shocked-by-fias-power-unit-settlement/.

190. Benson, Andrew. 2020. "Formula 1: Teams Formally Object to Ferrari Engine Settlement." *BBC.* https://www.bbc.com/sport/formula1/51736247.

191. Edmondson, Laurence. 2020. "FIA Offers Clarification Over Ferrari Engine Settlement Following Backlash from Rival Teams." *ESPN.* https://www.espn.com/f1/story/_/id/28842333/fia-offers-clarification-ferrari-engine-settlement.

192. Hall, Sam. 2017. "Bernie Ecclestone: FIA Conspired to Help Ferrari Gain an Advantage in F1." *Autoweek.* https://www.autoweek.com/racing/formula-1/a1833766/-bernie-ecclestone-fia-conspired-help-ferrari-gain-advantage-f1/.

193. "Monaco Announce Cancellation of 2020 F1 Race Due to Coronavirus." 2020. F1. https://www.formula1.com/en/latest/article.monaco-announce-cancellation-2020-f1-race.4tpwalvxWpDL0uwRMnV9TI.html.

Chapter 4

1. "Haas F1 Team Secures 2017 Driver Lineup by Signing Kevin Magnussen to Join Romain Grosjean." 2016. Haas F1 Team. https://www.haasf1team.com/news/haas-f1-team-secures-2017-driver-lineup-signing-kevin-magnussen-join-romain-grosjean.

2. King, Alanis. Peter Habicht. Personal Interview, August 2021.

3. "Haas F1 Team Earns Points in Debut Race." 2016. Haas F1 Team. https://www.haasf1team.com/news/haas-f1-team-earns-points-debut-race.

4. King, Alanis. Peter Habicht. Personal Interview, August 2021.

5. *Ibid.*

6. *Ibid.*

7. *Ibid.*

8. "F1–2016 Australian Grand Prix—Friday Press Conference | Federation Internationale De L'Automobile." 2016.

FIA. https://www.fia.com/news/f1-2016-australian-grand-prix-friday-press-conference.

9. Barnes, Joey. 2020. "Red Bull Racing Exec Touts Young American Driver Jak Crawford." *Autoweek.* https://www.autoweek.com/racing/formula-1/a31649109/red-bull-racing-exec-touts-american-development-driver-jak-crawford/.

10. "Toro Rosso | Formula One." n.d. *Guardian.* https://www.theguardian.com/sport/2007/mar/12/formulaone.motorsports32.

11. Vaughn, Mark. 2019. "Alexander Rossi Not Holding His Breath Waiting for F1 Call from Ferrari, Mercedes." *Autoweek.* https://www.autoweek.com/racing/indycar/a1719416/alexander-rossi-being-american-f1/.

12. "U.S. Driver Scott Speed Dropped by Toro Rosso." 2007. *ESPN.* https://www.espn.com/racing/news/story?id=2955466&seriesId=6.

13. *Ibid.*

14. Hynes, Justin. 2017. "Sebastian Vettel Crowned 2013 F1 Champion." Red Bull. https://www.redbull.com/us-en/-sebastian-vettel-f1-champion-2013.

15. "Sebastian Vettel." n.d. F1. https://www.formula1.com/en/drivers/hall-of-fame/Sebastian_Vettel.html.

16. "How F1 Technology Has Supercharged the World." 2019. F1. https://www.formula1.com/en/latest/article.how-f1-technology-has-supercharged-the-world.6Gtk3hBxGyUGbNH0q8vDQK.html.

17. Richards, Giles. 2014. "Sebastian Vettel Goes to Ferrari for More Than Cash and a Quick Car." *The Guardian.* https://www.theguardian.com/sport/blog/2014/oct/04/sebastian-vettel-ferrari-red-bull-cash.

18. "Marussia Hand Rossi Race Debut in Singapore." 2015. F1. https://www.formula1.com/en/latest/headlines/2015/9/-marussia-hand-rossi-race-debut-in-singapore.html.

19. "Spurned from F1, Rossi Joins Andretti IndyCar Team." 2016. *Reuters.* https://www.reuters.com/article/us-motor-indycar-rossi/spurned-from-f1-rossi-joins-andretti-indycar-team-idUSKCN0VW2JL.

20. "Haas F1 Team Earns Points in Debut Race." 2016. Haas F1 Team. https://

www.haasf1team.com/news/haas-f1-team-earns-points-debut-race.

21. "News." n.d. Haas F1 Team. https://www.haasf1team.com/news/haas-f1-team-names-guti%C3%A9rrez-2016-race-seat.

22. "Haas F1 Team Secures 2017 Driver Lineup by Signing Kevin Magnussen to Join Romain Grosjean." 2016. Haas F1 Team. https://www.haasf1team.com/news/haas-f1-team-secures-2017-driver-lineup-signing-kevin-magnussen-join-romain-grosjean.

23. Blackstock, Elizabeth. Bex Foot. Personal, August 2021.

24. "Haas VF-19: All the Angles of the 2019 F1 Car." 2019. F1. https://www.formula1.com/en/latest/article.first-look-all-the-angles-of-haas-new-2019-livery.l4qlJmDtedmTkv0zan1bH.html.

25. "Club History." n.d. Royal Automobile Club. https://www.royalautomobileclub.co.uk/about-the-club/history/.

26. "Haas Unveil New Black-and-gold F1 Livery for 2019." 2019. F1. https://www.formula1.com/en/latest/article.haas-unveil-new-black-and-gold-f1-livery-for-2019.3fIfnfT5NoMoLcuitzNJrt.html.

27. King, Alanis. Haas Employee 1. Personal Interview, August 2021.

28. "Boiling Point." Episode. *Formula 1: Drive to Survive* 2, no. 2. Netflix, 2020. https://www.netflix.com/title/80204890.

29. *Ibid.*

30. King, Alanis. Haas Employee 5. Personal Interview, August 2021.

31. *Ibid.*

32. "Rich Energy Haas F1 Team 2019 Livery Unveiled." 2019. Haas F1 Team. https://media.haasf1team.com/files/pdf/FINAL%20070219%20VF-19%20Livery%20Unveil%20Release-475.pdf.

33. *Ibid.*

34. *Ibid.*

35. Galloway, James, and Matt Morlidge. 2019. "Haas Reveal Striking New Black and Gold Livery for F1 2019 Car." *Sky Sports.* https://www.skysports.com/f1/news/12433/11601806/haas-reveal-striking-new-black-and-gold-livery-for-f1-2019-car.

36. King, Alanis. Haas Employee 5. Personal Interview, August 2021.

37. Blackstock, Elizabeth. Bex Foot. Personal, August 2021.

38. Noble, Jonathan. 2019. "Ferrari's New Matte Paint a Performance Benefit." *Motorsport.com.* https://us.motorsport.com/f1/news/ferrari-matte-paint-performance-benefit/4338383/.

39. Hughes, Mark, and Giorgio Piola. 2018. "Analysing the Aerodynamic Changes Coming to F1 in 2019." F1. https://www.formula1.com/en/latest/article.tech-tuesday-looking-ahead-to-the-aerodynamic-changes-coming-to-f1-in-2019.3G8r94lzEAEiG8WS0oCm8y.html.

40. King, Alanis. Haas Employee 5. Personal Interview, August 2021.

41. *Ibid.*

42. *Ibid.*

43. Rencken, Dieter. 2018. "2018 Formula 1 Team Budgets Revealed: Part Two." *RaceFans.* https://www.racefans.net/2018/12/26/the-cost-of-f1-revealed-how-much-teams-spent-in-2018-part-two/.

44. King, Alanis. Haas Employee 5. Personal Interview, August 2021.

45. "F1 Pre-Season Testing 2019 Day 2: Ferrari Fastest for Second Straight Day with Charles Leclerc." 2019. F1. https://www.formula1.com/en/latest/article.f1-pre-season-testing-leclerc-puts-ferrari-fastest-for-second-straight-day.7J8rU3ThUz1uDErC0VBB3x.html.

46. Blackstock, Elizabeth. Luke Smith. Personal, August 2021.

47. Rich Energy. 2019. Twitter Post. February 18. Deleted.

48. "Steiner: 'Annoying' Electronic Issues Hampering Haas." 2019. F1. https://www.formula1.com/en/latest/article.steiner-%27annoying%27-electronic-issues-hampering-haas.3VT5p1fClGzQwDGemrLgH8.html.

49. *Ibid.*

50. *Ibid.*

51. *Ibid.*

52. "2019 Race Results." n.d. F1. https://www.formula1.com/en/results.html/2019/races.html.

53. "Guenther Steiner 'More Amazed Than Upset' at Haas Pace Loss at Bahrain Grand Prix 2019." 2019. F1. https://www.formula1.com/en/latest/article.steiner-more-amazed-than-upset-at-haas-pace-loss-in-bahrain.3XCL1obSlJgcnnySobdaVR.html.

54. *Ibid.*

55. "Grosjean: Haas Had the Pace to Split Red Bulls in China Qualifying." 2019. F1. https://www.formula1.com/en/latest/ article.grosjean-haas-had-the-pace-to-split-red-bulls.6vwD0pC8iE0N595mh1tJio. html.

56. "Tyre Issues to Blame Again for Haas's 2019 Chinese Grand Prix Woe." 2019. F1. https://www.formula1.com/ en/latest/article.tyre-issues-to-blame-again-for-haas-china-woe.3J9MJC 6O0akPEkh5AxAQKj.html.

57. *Ibid.*

58. "2019 Race Results." n.d. F1. https:// www.formula1.com/en/results.html/2019/ races.html.

59. "Tyre Issues to Blame Again for Haas's 2019 Chinese Grand Prix Woe." 2019. F1. https://www.formula1.com/en/ latest/article.tyre-issues-to-blame-again-for-haas-china-woe.3J9MJC6O0ak PEkh5AxAQKj.html.

60. *Ibid.*

61. "Haas 'Cautiously Optimistic' Ahead of 'Significant' Upgrade for Spain." 2019. F1. https://www.formula1.com/en/ latest/article.haas-cautiously-optimistic-ahead-of-significant-upgrade-for-spain.4l0q0sXlTBzxRwaYyKpwPr.html.

62. "2019 Race Results." n.d. F1. https:// www.formula1.com/en/results.html/2019/ races.html.

63. "Haas' Problems Cannot Get Any Worse—Steiner." 2019. F1. https:// www.formula1.com/en/latest/article.-haas-form-cannot-get-any-worse-steiner.1dX5xlgx5t0GlzeUT9t903.html.

64. "French Grand Prix: Race Recap." 2019. Haas F1 Team. https:// www.haasf1team.com/news/french-grand-prix-race-recap-0.

65. "Haas Declare France Their 'Worst Weekend' Ever in F1." 2019. F1. https:// www.formula1.com/en/latest/article.haas-france-was-our-worst-weekend-in-f1-ever.4ZbcoyIt8HEQh50KZaSSOW.html.

66. *Ibid.*

67. "Boiling Point." 2020. Episode. *Formula 1: Drive to Survive* 2, no. 2. Netflix. https://www.netflix.com/title/80204890.

68. *Ibid.*

69. *Ibid.*

70. *Ibid.*

71. "Magnussen Gets Haas Aero Upgrades for Germany as Grosjean Keeps Australia Spec." 2019. F1. https://www. formula1.com/en/latest/article. magnussen-gets-haas-upgrades-for-germany-grosjean-keeps-australia-spec.6f9k2Xx9XK2whjtB9yswsg.html.

72. Cooper, Adam. 2019. "Grosjean Reverts to Melbourne-spec Haas for Silverstone." *Autosport.* https://www.auto sport.com/f1/news/grosjean-reverts-to-melbourne-spec-haas-for-silverst one-4991394/4991394/.

73. "Magnussen Gets Haas Aero Upgrades for Germany as Grosjean Keeps Australia Spec." 2019. F1. https:// www.formula1.com/en/latest/article. magnussen-gets-haas-upgrades-for-germany-grosjean-keeps-australia-spec.6f9k2Xx9XK2whjtB9yswsg.html.

74. "British Grand Prix: Race Recap." 2019. Haas F1 Team. https:// www.haasf1team.com/news/british-grand-prix-race-recap-0.

75. *Ibid.*

76. "Boiling Point." 2020. Episode. *Formula 1: Drive to Survive* 2, no. 2. Netflix. https://www.netflix.com/title/80204890.

77. *Ibid.*

78. "Magnussen: Haas Upgrade Performance Deficit 'Confusing'." 2019. F1. https://www.formula1.com/en/latest/ article.magnussen-haas-upgrade-performance-deficit-confusing.19ZjXDoD E8fvOuaEnRzZQ0.html.

79. *Ibid.*

80. *Ibid.*

81. "2019 Race Results." n.d. F1. https://www.formula1.com/en/results. html/2019/races.html.

82. "Haas Still Perplexed by 'Weird' Pace After Hungarian Grand Prix." 2019. F1. https://www.formula1.com/en/latest/ article.haas-still-perplexed-by-weird-pace-fluctuations.1BINaE4frvYMCplEGd 5I4D.html.

83. *Ibid.*

84. "2019 RACE RESULTS." n.d. F1. https://www.formula1.com/en/results. html/2019/races.html.

85. "Haas Won't Take Chance on Rookie After 2019 Struggles—Guenther Steiner." 2019. F1. https://www.formula1. com/en/latest/article.haas-unlikely-to-chance-a-rookie-after-2019-struggles-says-steiner.6yp1Cu4mFvIgTBXIspDnLQ. html.

86. "Belgian Grand Prix 2019: Both Grosjean and Magnussen to Run Latest

Haas Aero Spec at Spa." F1. https://www.formula1.com/en/latest/article.both-grosjean-and-magnussen-to-run-latest-haas-aero-spec-at-spa.GTo9zn7bXkfmlf8ddZyCH.html.

87. "Grosjean Baffled After Haas Lack Pace in Italy." 2019. F1. https://www.formula1.com/en/latest/article.grosjean-baffled-after-haas-lack-pace-in-italy.5taGJIz5JC8KuHE4mekbrw.html.

88. "Steiner Saw 'Nothing Encouraging' from Haas in Belgium." 2019. F1. https://www.formula1.com/en/latest/article.steiner-saw-nothing-encouraging-from-haas-in-belgium.3IoVoRnuYDALq3jKSKBhIl.html.

89. "Steiner Fined for Critical Russian GP Radio Message." 2019. F1. https://www.formula1.com/en/latest/article.steiner-fined-for-critical-russian-gp-radio-message.5CuAO9DJR6ejq3or42zznz.html.

90. "Steiner—Low Expectations Numbed Haas's Mexico Disappointment." 2019. F1. https://www.formula1.com/en/latest/article.steiner-low-expectations-numbed-haass-mexico-disappointment.7jIaxhAQgQZUED5ihJ49C8.html.

91. Blackstock, Elizabeth. Luke Smith. Personal, August 2021.

92. "'We Have Nothing'—Steiner Admits Haas Can't Wait for 2020 After Difficult USGP." 2019. F1. https://www.formula1.com/en/latest/article.we-have-nothing-steiner-admits-haas-cant-wait-for-2020-after-difficult-home.7jMGGn7a093sJlqfsAkiYP.html.

93. Ibid.

94. King, Alanis. Haas Employee 3. Personal Interview, August 2021.

95. "Formula 1 Etihad Airways Abu Dhabi Grand Prix 2019—Qualifying." 2021. F1. https://www.formula1.com/en/results.html/2019/races/1020/abu-dhabi/qualifying.html.

96. "Abu Dhabi Grand Prix 2019: 'Bloody Undriveable' Haas 'Won't Go in the Museum', Says Grosjean After Q1 Exit." 2019. F1. https://www.formula1.com/en/latest/article.bloody-undriveable-haas-wont-go-in-a-museum-says-grosjean-after-q1-exit.41weK9iMt9BHTaPEH1UDcT.html.

97. "Haas Ready to Forget 2019 After Final 'Hard Fight' in Abu Dhabi." 2019. F1. https://www.formula1.com/en/latest/article.haas-ready-to-forget-2019-after-final-hard-fight-in-abu-dhabi.3I2p3AfoKMJ4NSHzLBLexV.html.

98. "2020 Constructor Standings." n.d. F1. https://www.formula1.com/en/results.html/2020/team.html.

99. Blackstock, Elizabeth. Stuart Taylor (Chain Bear). Personal, August 2021.

100. Mitchell, Scott. 2019. "Gunther Steiner Needs 'Thinking Hat' Amid Haas F1 Income Drop." Autosport. https://www.autosport.com/f1/news/gunther-steiner-needs-thinking-hat-amid-haas-f1-income-drop-4987752/4987752/.

101. "Haas Ready to Forget 2019 After Final 'Hard Fight' in Abu Dhabi." 2019. F1. https://www.formula1.com/en/latest/article.haas-ready-to-forget-2019-after-final-hard-fight-in-abu-dhabi.3I2p3AfoKMJ4NSHzLBLexV.html.

102. "What the Teams Said—Race Day in Abu Dhabi." 2019. F1. https://www.formula1.com/en/latest/article.what-the-teams-said-race-day-in-abu-dhabi-2019.1qnfNvoo4bGGsDu8ehcUFQ.html.

103. Ibid.

104. "Boiling Point." Episode. Formula 1: Drive to Survive 2, no. 2. Netflix, 2020. https://www.netflix.com/title/80204890.

105. Ibid.

106. Noble, Jonathan. 2021. "Gunther Steiner: Haas F1 Concept Inspired by Domenicali." Motorsport.com. https://us.motorsport.com/f1/news/steiner-haas-f1-business-model-inspired-by-domenicali/5325509/.

107. "Boiling Point." Episode. Formula 1: Drive to Survive 2, no. 2. Netflix, 2020. https://www.netflix.com/title/80204890.

108. King, Alanis. Haas Employee 1. Personal Interview, August 2021.

109. King, Alanis. Haas Employee 5. Personal Interview, August 2021.

110. Blackstock, Elizabeth. Stuart Taylor (Chain Bear). Personal, August 2021.

111. King, Alanis. Haas Employee 5. Personal Interview, August 2021.

112. Ibid.

113. King, Alanis. Haas Employee 1. Personal Interview, August 2021.

114. Ibid.

115. King, Alanis. Haas Employee 3. Personal Interview, August 2021.

116. Ibid.

117. King, Alanis. Haas Employee 5. Personal Interview, August 2021.

118. Sylt, Christian. 2018. "Haas: The

Formula for Reducing F1's Costs." *Forbes*, August 20. https://www.forbes.com/sites/csylt/2018/08/20/haas-the-formula-for-reducing-f1s-costs/?sh=77eff4552c31.

119. King, Alanis. Haas Employee 5. Personal Interview, August 2021.

120. *Ibid.*

121. King, Alanis. Haas Employee 1. Personal Interview, August 2021.

122. King, Alanis. Haas Employee 3. Personal Interview, August 2021.

123. King, Alanis. Haas Employee 5. Personal Interview, August 2021.

124. King, Alanis. Haas Employee 3. Personal Interview, August 2021.

125. *Ibid.*

126. *Ibid.*

127. King, Alanis. Haas Employee 5. Personal Interview, August 2021.

128. King, Alanis. Haas Employee 3. Personal Interview, August 2021.

129. King, Alanis. Haas Employee 5. Personal Interview, August 2021.

130. King, Alanis. Haas Employee 3. Personal Interview, August 2021.

131. King, Alanis. Haas Employee 1. Personal Interview, August 2021.

132. King, Alanis. 2018. "Force India F1 Forfeits Its Title Points and Changes Its Name Right Before the Belgian Grand Prix." *Jalopnik*. https://jalopnik.com/-force-india-f1-forfeits-its-title-points-and-changes-it-1828558256.

133. Mitchell, Scott. 2018. "Why Perez Led Action Against Force India Formula 1 Team." *Autosport*. https://www.autosport.com/f1/news/why-perez-led-action-against-force-india-formula-1-team-5293431/5293431/.

134. Storey, William. 2018. "Rich Energy Launch Official £100m Takeover of Force India." LinkedIn. https://www.linkedin.com/pulse/rich-energy-launch-official-100m-takeover-force-india-william-storey/.

135. *Ibid.*

136. Mitchell, Scott. 2018. "British Firm Not Ready to "relinquish" Force India Bid." *Motorsport.com.* https://us.motorsport.com/f1/news/rich-energy-force-india-buyout/3152345/.

137. *Breaking News: William Storey on Force India's Future.* YouTube, 2018. https://www.youtube.com/watch?v=0uhAWuMwyyo&ab_channel=peterwindsor.

138. *Ibid.*

139. *Ibid.*

140. *Ibid.*

141. "peterwindsor." n.d. YouTube. https://www.youtube.com/channel/UCPwy2q7BNjdLYu1kM_OEJVw.

142. Windsor, Peter. *Interview Request | Rich Energy, the Book*, September 1, 2021.

143. Mitchell, Scott. 2018. "Why Perez Led Action Against Force India Formula 1 Team." *Autosport*. https://www.autosport.com/f1/news/why-perez-led-action-against-force-india-formula-1-team-5293431/5293431/.

144. *Breaking News: William Storey on Force India's Future.* YouTube, 2018. https://www.youtube.com/watch?v=0uhAWuMwyyo&ab_channel=peterwindsor.

145. Mitchell, Scott. 2018. "Why Perez Led Action Against Force India Formula 1 Team." *Autosport*. https://www.autosport.com/f1/news/why-perez-led-action-against-force-india-formula-1-team-5293431/5293431/.

146. Mitchell, Scott. 2018. "British Firm Not Ready to "relinquish" Force India Bid." *Motorsport.com.* https://us.motorsport.com/f1/news/rich-energy-force-india-buyout/3152345/.

147. *Breaking News: William Storey on Force India's Future.* YouTube, 2018. https://www.youtube.com/watch?v=0uhAWuMwyyo&ab_channel=peterwindsor.

148. *Ibid.*

149. Gilboy, James. 2018. "Former Force India F1 Team Owner Vijay Mallya to Be Extradited to India, UK Court Approves." *The Drive*. https://www.thedrive.com/accelerator/25406/former-force-india-f1-team-owner-vijay-mallya-to-be-extradited-to-india-uk-court-approves.

150. Neate, Rupert. 2020. "Fugitive Indian Tycoon Vijay Mallya Applies for UK Asylum." *The Guardian*. https://www.theguardian.com/law/2020/jun/10/-fugitive-indian-tycoon-vijay-mallya-applies-for-uk-asylum.

151. "Breaking News: William Storey on Force India's Future." 2018. YouTube. https://www.youtube.com/watch?v=0uhAWuMwyyo&ab_channel=peterwindsor.

152. *Ibid.*

153. *Ibid.*

154. King, Alanis. 2018. "Lance Stroll

Joins F1 Team His Father Bought a Few Months Ago." *Jalopnik*. https://jalopnik.com/nepotism-wins-1830766974.

155. Baldwin, Alan. 2018. "Canadian Group Led by Stroll Paid $117 Million for Force India." *Reuters*. https://www.reuters.com/article/uk-motor-f1-forceindia/canadian-group-led-by-stroll-paid-117-million-for-force-india-idUKKCN1ME1LV.

156. GMM. 2016. "Report: Lance Stroll's Father Spent $80 Million to Get Son Williams F1 Seat." *Autoweek*. https://www.autoweek.com/racing/formula-1/a1857276/report-lance-strolls-father-spent-80-million-get-son-f1-seat/.

157. Saunders, Nate. 2020. "The Bizarre Haas-Rich Energy Saga Explained." *ESPN*. https://www.espn.com/f1/story/_/id/27221746/the-bizarre-haas-rich-energy-saga-explained.

158. Gilboy, James. 2018. "Haas F1 Signs Soft Drink Startup Rich Energy as 2019 Title Sponsor." *The Drive*. https://www.thedrive.com/accelerator/24506/-haas-f1-signs-soft-drink-startup-rich-energy-as-2019-title-sponsor.

159. Rencken, Dieter, and Keith Collantine. 2018. "Haas-Rich Energy 2019 F1 Deal Came About Quickly—Steiner." *RaceFans*. https://www.racefans.net/2018/10/26/haas-rich-energy-deal-came-about-quickly-steiner/.

160. Gilboy, James. 2018. "Haas F1 Signs Soft Drink Startup Rich Energy as 2019 Title Sponsor." *The Drive*. https://www.thedrive.com/accelerator/24506/-haas-f1-signs-soft-drink-startup-rich-energy-as-2019-title-sponsor.

161. Cooper, Adam. 2018. "Haas: Due Diligence Completed on New 2019 Title Sponsor Rich Energy." *Autosport*. https://www.autosport.com/f1/news/139664/-haas-due-diligence-done-on-new-title-sponsor.

162. Blackstock, Elizabeth. Bex Foot. Personal, August 2021.

163. Cooper, Adam. 2018. "Haas: Due Diligence Completed on New 2019 Title Sponsor Rich Energy." *Autosport*. https://www.autosport.com/f1/news/139664/-haas-due-diligence-done-on-new-title-sponsor.

164. "Breaking News: William Storey on Force India's Future." YouTube, 2018. https://www.youtube.com/watch?v=0uhAWuMwyyo&ab_channel=peterwindsor.

165. Cooper, Adam. 2018. "Haas: Due Diligence Completed on New 2019 Title Sponsor Rich Energy." *Autosport*. https://www.autosport.com/f1/news/139664/-haas-due-diligence-done-on-new-title-sponsor.

166. *Ibid.*

167. Blackstock, Elizabeth. 2019. "You Can Finally Buy Rich Energy in the U.S. Through Walmart." *Jalopnik*. https://jalopnik.com/you-can-finally-buy-rich-energy-in-the-u-s-through-wal-1835479976.

168. King, Alanis. William Storey. Personal, March 14, 2019.

169. *Ibid.*

170. ATB Sales Limited v Rich Energy Limited and Ors (Business and Property Courts of England and Wales May 14, 2019).

171. King, Alanis. William Storey. Personal, March 14, 2019.

172. *Ibid.*

173. *Ibid.*

174. *Ibid.*

175. *Ibid.*

176. *Ibid.*

177. "Red Bull." n.d. Forbes. https://www.forbes.com/companies/red-bull/#36ccfb2861ce.

178. King, Alanis. William Storey. Personal, March 14, 2019.

179. *Ibid.*

180. *Ibid.*

181. *Ibid.*

182. Errington, Tom. 2019. "Haas Sets Date for Expected Rich Energy-style 2019 F1 Livery Unveil." *Autosport*. https://www.autosport.com/f1/news/haas-sets-date-for-expected-rich-energy-style-2019-f1-livery-unveil-5283412/5283412/.

183. "Haas F1 Reveal as Rich Energy Counters Criticism—Formula 1 Videos." 2019. *Motorsport.com*. https://www.motorsport.com/f1/video/haas-f1-reveal-as-rich-energy-counters-criticism/382091/.

184. Kalinauckas, Alex. 2019. "Rich Energy 'Bringing Back' JPS Lotus Look with Haas Livery." *Motorsport.com*. https://www.motorsport.com/f1/news/-haas-rich-energy-jps-lotus-look/4334023/.

185. Noble, Jonathan. 2019. "The Key Battle Facing Rich Energy." *Motorsport*.

com. https://www.motorsport.com/f1/news/the-key-battle-facing-rich-energy/4373126/.

186. Mitchell, Scott. 2018. "British Firm Not Ready to 'Relinquish' Force India Bid." *Motorsport.com.* https://us.motorsport.com/f1/news/rich-energy-force-india-buyout/3152345/.

187. Noble, Jonathan. 2019. "Haas Defends Rich Energy's Aim of Beating Red Bull in Formula 1." *Autosport.* https://www.autosport.com/f1/news/141372/haas-beating-red-bull-is-the-right-ambition.

188. Hardigree, Matt. 2014. "Bernie Ecclestone Doesn't Care About Social Media, Because Greed." *Jalopnik.* https://jalopnik.com/bernie-ecclestone-doesnt-care-about-social-media-becau-1586477212#!.

189. Schrader, Stef. 2014. "Bernie Ecclestone Doesn't Like Bloggers Very Much." *Jalopnik.* https://jalopnik.com/-bernie-ecclestone-doesnt-like-us-very-much-1660017542.

190. King, Alanis. 2016. "Lewis Hamilton Gets Banned from Using Snapchat in F1 Paddock, Does It Anyway." *Jalopnik.* https://jalopnik.com/snapchat-helped-f1-during-the-australian-gp-snapchat-1768691589.

191. Schrader, Stef. 2017. "Formula One Starts Acting Like a Modern Racing Series or Something." *Jalopnik.* https://jalopnik.com/formula-one-starts-acting-like-a-modern-racing-series-o-1792784970.

192. Schrader, Stef. 2017. "F1 Is Finally Posting Its Most Incredible Moments on YouTube and That Rules." *Jalopnik.* https://jalopnik.com/f1-is-finally-posting-its-most-incredible-moments-on-yo-1794132326.

193. King, Alanis. 2017. "Bernie Ecclestone Hates These Damn Kids and Their Social Media." *Jalopnik.* https://jalopnik.com/bernie-ecclestone-hates-these-damn-kids-and-their-socia-1795651283.

194. "Rich Energy: Haas Vastly Superior to Rivals | PlanetF1." 2019. Planet F1. https://www.planetf1.com/news/rich-energy-haas-vastly-superior-to-rivals/.

195. Hunt, Ben. 2019. "Haas F1 Team Will BEAT Red Bull This Season, According to Sponsors Rich Energy." *The Sun.* https://www.thesun.co.uk/sport/motorsport/8372522/f1-haas-beat-red-bull-2019/.

196. Rencken, Dieter. 2018. "2018 Formula 1 Team Budgets Revealed: Part Two." *RaceFans.* https://www.racefans.net/2018/12/26/the-cost-of-f1-revealed-how-much-teams-spent-in-2018-part-two/.

197. Barretto, Lawrence. 2019. "The Winners and Losers of F1's First Pre-season Test of 2019." F1. https://www.formula1.com/en/latest/article.the-winners-and-losers-of-f1s-first-pre-season-test.12114NyKbJEWOy8PjJfDjj.html.

198. Rich Energy. 2019. Twitter Post. February 18. Deleted.

199. van Wingerden, Joas. 2019. "F1 Pre-season Test Results: Fastest Laps, Full Lap Count." *GPFans.* https://www.gpfans.com/en/articles/4275/f1-pre-season-test-results-fastest-laps-full-lap-count/.

200. Cobb, Haydn. 2019. "F1 Barcelona F1 Test 1 Times—Monday 1PM | F1 | Crash—2019 Barcelona Pre-Season Test 1 Barcelona F1 Test 1 Times—Monday 1PM | F1." *Crash.Net.* https://www.crash.net/f1/results/913037/1/barcelona-f1-test-1-times-monday-1pm.

201. Rich Energy. 2019. Twitter Post. April 28. https://twitter.com/okeefe_92/status/1130861906858840072.

202. Rich Energy. 2019. Twitter Post. May 14. https://twitter.com/rich_energy/status/1128309045050388481?ref_src=twsrc%5Etfw.

203. Whyte Bikes. 2019. Twitter Post. May 18. https://twitter.com/WhyteBikes/status/1129772100204601344.

204. Windsor, Peter. 2018. Twitter Post. May 17. https://twitter.com/PeterDWindsor/status/1129455626080403457.

205. Rich Energy. 2019. Twitter Post. May 18. https://twitter.com/okeefe_92/status/1130862173276835840/photo/1.

206. Rich Energy. 2019. Twitter Post. May 18. https://twitter.com/okeefe_92/status/1130862173276835840/photo/1.

207. Rich Energy. 2018. Twitter Post. May 19. https://twitter.com/okeefe_92/status/1130862186006482945/photo/1.

208. Rich Energy. 2019. Twitter Post. June 8. https://twitter.com/natesaunders F1/status/1137449926546415616?s=20.

209. Rich Energy. 2019. Twitter Post. June 8. https://twitter.com/rich_energy/status/1137442693087453185?ref_src=twsrc%5Etfw.

210. Blackstock, Elizabeth. Bex Foot. Personal, August 2021.

211. Benson, Andrew. 2012. "Belgian Grand Prix Crash: Romain Grosjean Banned for One Race." *BBC*. https://www.bbc.com/sport/formula1/19458954.

212. Blackstock, Elizabeth. Bex Foot. Personal, August 2021.

213. MsportXtra and William Storey exchange. Twitter Post. June 12, 2019. https://twitter.com/MsportXtra/status/1138827226458275841.

214. *Ibid.*

215. *Ibid.*

216. *Ibid.*

217. *Ibid.*

218. *Ibid.*

219. *Ibid.*

220. *Ibid.*

221. Rich Energy. 2019. Twitter Post. June 18. https://twitter.com/okeefe_92/status/1141040086194282496

222. livingproef. 2019. Instagram Post. June 18. https://www.instagram.com/p/By2RCv0oECb/.

223. MsportXtra. 2019. Twitter Post. June 18. https://twitter.com/MsportXtra/status/1141065513960972288.

224. "Our Story | LIVINGPROEF." https://www.livingproef.nl/our-story.

225. King, Alanis. William Storey. Personal, March 14, 2019.

Chapter 5

1. "Rich Energy Haas F1 Team Title Sponsor Loses Court Case for Copying Whyte Bikes' Stag Logo," May 14, 2019. Whyte Bikes. https://web.archive.org/web/20190516005143/https://whyte.bike/pages/stag.

2. *Ibid.*

3. *Ibid.*

4. ATB Sales Limited v Rich Energy Limited and Ors (Business and Property Courts of England and Wales May 14, 2019).

5. *Ibid.*

6. "History—Whyte Bikes USA." n.d. Whyte Bikes USA. https://www.whyteusa.bike/pages/history.

7. ATB Sales Limited v Rich Energy Limited and Ors (Business and Property Courts of England and Wales May 14, 2019).

8. *Ibid.*

9. *Ibid.*

10. *Ibid.*

11. *Ibid.*

12. *Ibid.*

13. *Ibid.*

14. *Ibid.*

15. *Ibid.*

16. *Ibid.*

17. *Ibid.*

18. *Ibid.*

19. Mitchell, Scott. 2019. "Haas Title Sponsor Likens Doubters to Moon Landing Truthers." *Motorsport.com*. https://us.motorsport.com/f1/news/-haas-rich-energy-doubters-moon-landing/4333923/.

20. ATB Sales Limited v Rich Energy Limited and Ors (Business and Property Courts of England and Wales May 14, 2019).

21. *Ibid.*

22. King, Alanis. William Storey. Personal, March 14, 2019.

23. ATB Sales Limited v Rich Energy Limited and Ors (Business and Property Courts of England and Wales May 14, 2019).

24. *Ibid.*

25. *Ibid.*

26. *Ibid.*

27. *Ibid.*

28. *Ibid.*

29. *Ibid.*

30. *Ibid.*

31. *Ibid.*

32. Blackstock, Elizabeth, and Alanis King. 2019. "What You Find When You Look Into Rich Energy, the Mystery Sponsor of America's F1 Team." *Jalopnik*. https://jalopnik.com/what-you-find-when-you-look-into-rich-energy-the-myste-1833303620.

33. ATB Sales Limited v Rich Energy Limited and Ors (Business and Property Courts of England and Wales May 14, 2019).

34. *Ibid.*

35. *Ibid.*

36. *Ibid.*

37. *Ibid.*

38. *Ibid.*

39. *Ibid.*

40. *Ibid.*

41. *Ibid.*

42. *Ibid.*

43. *Ibid.*

44. *Ibid.*

45. *Ibid.*

46. *Ibid.*

47. *Ibid.*

48. Storey, William, May 14, 2019.

49. Edmondson, Laurence. "Haas Title Sponsor Rich Energy Loses Court Case Over Logo." *ESPN. ESPN Internet Ventures*, May 14, 2019. https://www.espn.com/f1/story/_/id/26744828/haas-title-sponsor-rich-energy-loses-court-case-logo.

50. Rich Energy. 2019. Twitter Post. May 16. https://twitter.com/okeefe_92/status/1130861946671124480.

51. Rich Energy. 2019. Twitter Post. May 17. https://twitter.com/okeefe_92/status/1130861946671124480.

52. Rich Energy. 2019. Twitter Post. May 19. Deleted.

53. Storey, William. 2020. Twitter Post. April 28. https://twitter.com/richenergyceo/status/1255192575956353024.

54. Storey, William. 2020. Twitter Post. May 24. https://twitter.com/richenergyceo/status/1264706284366020608.

55. Storey, William. 2020. Twitter Post. May 25. https://twitter.com/richenergyceo/status/1265009434595639300.

56. Storey, William. 2020. Twitter Post. July 6. https://twitter.com/richenergyceo/status/1280220838638358536.

57. Storey, William. 2021. Twitter Post. August 26. https://twitter.com/richenergyceo/status/1430899924804145152.

58. Storey, William. 2021. Twitter Post. August 31. https://twitter.com/richenergyceo/status/1432658498148515841.

59. Colson, Thomas. 2019. "Full Text: Read Theresa May's Resignation Speech in Full." *Business Insider.* https://www.businessinsider.com/full-text-theresa-may-resignation-speech-2019-5.

60. Rich Energy. 2020. Twitter Post. May 24. Deleted.

61. Rich Energy. 2020. Twitter Post. May 28. Deleted.

62. Rich Energy. 2020. Twitter Post. June 1. Deleted.

63. King, Alanis. 2019. "Rich Energy Pulls Logo from Haas F1 Cars After Loss in Copyright Case." *Jalopnik.* https://jalopnik.com/rich-energy-pulls-logo-from-haas-f1-cars-after-loss-in-1835322740.

64. Noble, Jonathan. 2019. "Rich Energy Asks Haas to Remove Contested Logo for Canada." *Motorsport.com.* https://www.motorsport.com/f1/news/haas-rich-energy-logo-canada/4454083/.

65. *Ibid.*

66. King, Alanis. Haas Employee 1. Personal Interview, August 2021.

67. *Ibid.*

68. King, Alanis. 2019. "Final Wheel Movement Decided Controversial Penalty That Undid Ferrari's F1 Win: Report." *Jalopnik.* https://jalopnik.com/final-wheel-movement-decided-controversial-penalty-that-1835372654.

69. Mattzel89. 2019. Twitter Post. June 9. https://twitter.com/Mattzel89/status/1137810230929219587.

70. Mitchell, Scott. 2019. "Vettel Explains Why He Returned to Canadian GP Podium." *Motorsport.com.* https://us.motorsport.com/f1/news/vettel-explains-return-podium-canada/4461873/.

71. King, Alanis. 2019. "Sebastian Vettel's F1 Canadian Grand Prix 'Win' Immortalized by Very Unusual Diecast." *Jalopnik.* https://jalopnik.com/sebastian-vettel-s-f1-canadian-grand-prix-win-immorta-1835908480

72. Rich Energy. 2019. Twitter Post. June 9. https://web.archive.org/web/20190710183929/twitter.com/rich_energy.

73. King, Alanis. 2019. "In Memoriam: Rich Energy's Tweets." *Jalopnik.* https://jalopnik.com/in-memoriam-rich-energys-tweets-1839096792.

74. King, Alanis. 2019. "Power Struggle Continues at F1 Sponsor Rich Energy." *Jalopnik.* https://jalopnik.com/power-struggle-at-rich-energy-continues-as-its-accused-1836316162.

75. King, Alanis. 2019. "In Memoriam: Rich Energy's Tweets." *Jalopnik.* https://jalopnik.com/in-memoriam-rich-energys-tweets-1839096792.

76. Harris, Chris. 2019. Twitter Post. June 10. https://twitter.com/harrismonkey/status/1138121473447604226.

77. Storey, William. 2020. Twitter Post. April 12. https://twitter.com/richenergyceo/status/1249359303380787207.

78. Storey, William. 2020. Twitter Post. August 27. https://twitter.com/richenergyceo/status/1299114017957478402.

79. Storey, William. 2021. Twitter Post. January 18. https://twitter.com/richenergyceo/status/1351291593832148995.

80. Storey, William. 2020. Twitter Post. November 29. https://twitter.com/richenergyceo/status/1333028320771010562.

81. Storey, William. 2021. Twitter Post. January 2. https://twitter.com/richenergyceo/status/134533254889807 0530.

82. Storey, William. 2020. Twitter Post. November 29. https://twitter.com/richenergyceo/status/1333028320771010562.

83. Storey, William. 2018. "Why Now Is the Time to Bet on Trump." LinkedIn. March 9. https://www.linkedin.com/pulse/why-now-time-bet-trump-william-storey/.

84. Rich Energy. 2019. Twitter Post. June 10. Deleted.

85. *Ibid.*

86. *Ibid.*

87. *Ibid.*

88. *Ibid.*

89. *Ibid.*

90. *Ibid.*

91. *Ibid.*

92. *Ibid.*

93. *Ibid.*

94. King, Alanis. 2019. "In Memoriam: Rich Energy's Tweets." *Jalopnik.* https://jalopnik.com/in-memoriam-rich-energys-tweets-1839096792.

95. King, Alanis. 2019. "Haas F1 Sponsor Rich Energy Denied Appeal After Losing Logo Case." *Jalopnik.* https://jalopnik.com/haas-f1-sponsor-rich-energy-denied-appeal-after-losing-1835947104.

96. *Ibid.*

97. *Ibid.*

98. "Filing History for Lightning Volt Limited (09791667)." Gov.uk. 2017. https://find-and-update.company-information.service.gov.uk/company/09791667/filing-history.

99. Maher, Thomas. 2021. "Formula 1—Storey: Rich Energy's Return to F1 Will Be 'vindication.'" *Formula Spy.* https://formulaspy.com/f1/storey-rich-energys-return-to-f1-will-be-vindication-73267.

Chapter 6

1. *Breaking News: William Storey on Force India's Future.* YouTube, 2018. https://www.youtube.com/watch?v=0uhAWuMwyyo&ab_channel=peter windsor.

2. Blackstock, Elizabeth. Luke Smith. Personal, August 2021.

3. King, Alanis. 2019. "Haas F1 Sponsor Rich Energy Claims to Have Terminated Contract, Citing 'PC Attitude' [Update: Haas Says They're Still Partners]." *Jalopnik.* https://jalopnik.com/haas-f1-sponsor-rich-energy-claims-to-have-terminated-c-1836250021.

4. Haas F1 Team. 2019. Twitter Post. July 11. https://twitter.com/HaasF1Team/status/1149234399982100481?s=20.

5. Morrison, Stuart, July 12, 2019.

6. Maher, Thomas. 2019. "Formula 1—Rich Energy Confirm Contentious Tweet Was 'rogue.'" *Formula Spy.* https://formulaspy.com/f1/rich-energy-confirm-contentious-tweet-was-rogue-62549.

7. King, Alanis. 2019. "Power Struggle Continues at F1 Sponsor Rich Energy." *Jalopnik.* https://jalopnik.com/power-struggle-at-rich-energy-continues-as-its-accused-1836316162.

8. *Ibid.*

9. Cooper, Adam. 2019. "Rich Energy Investors Trying to Save Haas F1 Deal." *Motorsport.com.* https://www.motorsport.com/f1/news/rich-energy-investors-save-haas-deal/4492346/.

10. *Ibid.*

11. *Ibid.*

12. Mitchell, Scott. 2019. "Haas Will Run Rich Branding at British GP, Says Steiner." *Motorsport.com.* https://www.motorsport.com/f1/news/haas-rich-energy-british-gp/4492480/.

13. Collantine, Keith. 2019. "F1: 'Surprised' Haas Will Run Rich Energy Logos at Silverstone." *RaceFans.* https://www.racefans.net/2019/07/11/surprised-haas-will-run-rich-energy-logos-at-silverstone/.

14. *Ibid.*

15. Blackstock, Elizabeth. Luke Smith. Personal, August 2021.

16. Medland, Chris. 2019. "INSIGHT: Behind the Rich Energy Mess at Haas." *RACER.* https://racer.com/2019/07/15/insight-behind-the-rich-energy-mess-at-haas/.

17. *Ibid.*

18. *Ibid.*

19. *Ibid.*

20. George, Patrick. 2019. "F1 Sponsor

Rich Energy Now Blames Rogue Employee for Yesterday's Bizarre 'PC Attitude' Tweet [UPDATE]." *Jalopnik*. https://jalopnik.com/f1-sponsor-rich-energy-now-blames-rogue-employee-for-ye-1836281581.

21. Rich Energy. 2019. Twitter Post. July 11. Deleted.

22. King, Alanis. 2019. "Power Struggle Continues at F1 Sponsor Rich Energy." *Jalopnik*. https://jalopnik.com/power-struggle-at-rich-energy-continues-as-its-accused-1836316162.

23. *Ibid.*

24. *Ibid.*

25. Morrison, Stuart, July 12, 2019.

26. Patterson, Ross, July 12, 2019.

27. "FP1: Grosjean Loses Front Wing in Bizarre Pit-exit Spin." 2019. F1. https://www.formula1.com/en/video/2019/7/FP1__Grosjean_loses_front_wing_in_bizarre_pit-exit_spin.html.

28. King, Alanis. 2019. "In Memoriam: Rich Energy's Tweets." *Jalopnik*. https://jalopnik.com/in-memoriam-rich-energys-tweets-1839096792.

29. *Ibid.*

30. *Ibid.*

31. Storey, William. July 14, 2019.

32. Storey, William. Email to Guenther Steiner, July 10, 2019.

33. King, Alanis. Haas Employee 1. Personal Interview, August 2021.

34. Storey, William. July 14, 2019.

35. "Filing History for Lightning Volt Limited (09791667)." Gov.uk. 2017. https://find-and-update.company-information.service.gov.uk/company/09791667/filing-history.

36. King, Alanis. William Storey. Personal, March 14, 2019.

37. Sylt, Christian. 2013. "What's It Cost to Compete in Formula One? An Indy-Car Comparison." *NBC Sports' Motor-SportsTalk*. https://motorsports.nbcsports.com/2013/05/22/whats-it-cost-to-compete-in-formula-one-an-indycar-comparison/.

38. King, Alanis. 2019. "In Memoriam: Rich Energy's Tweets." *Jalopnik*. https://jalopnik.com/in-memoriam-rich-energys-tweets-1839096792.

39. Sylt, Christian. 2019. "Revealed: Sponsors Fuel Formula One with $30 Billion." Forbes. https://www.forbes.com/sites/csylt/2019/05/19/revealed-sponsors-fuel-formula-one-with-30-billion/#4ba8baec2416.

40. Storey, William. Email to Guenther Steiner, July 10, 2019.

41. King, Alanis. 2019. "In Memoriam: Rich Energy's Tweets." *Jalopnik*. https://jalopnik.com/in-memoriam-rich-energys-tweets-1839096792.

42. Rich Energy. 2019. Twitter Post. June 6. Deleted.

43. King, Alanis. 2019. "In Memoriam: Rich Energy's Tweets." *Jalopnik*. https://jalopnik.com/in-memoriam-rich-energys-tweets-1839096792.

44. "British Grand Prix: Race Recap." 2019. Haas F1 Team. https://www.haasf1team.com/news/british-grand-prix-race-recap-0.

45. *Ibid.*

46. "Boiling Point." 2020. Episode. *Formula 1: Drive to Survive* 2, no. 2. Netflix. https://www.netflix.com/title/80204890.

47. Rich Energy. 2019. Twitter Post. July 14. Deleted.

48. Hunt, Ben. 2019. "Rich Energy Drink Chief Labels F1 Team Haas 'milk Float at Back of Grid' After Pulling Plug on Sponsorship." *The Sun*. https://www.thesun.co.uk/sport/motorsport/9483957/rich-energy-f1-haas-team-sponsorship/.

49. *Ibid.*

50. *Ibid.*

51. "Grosjean and Magnussen's Driving 'Not Acceptable' Says Furious Steiner." 2019. F1. https://www.formula1.com/en/latest/article.grosjean-and-magnussens-driving-not-acceptable-says-furious-steiner.3l9S6OTuC5opdznf2ZTGms.html.

52. Morrison, Stuart, July 15, 2019.

53. Cooper, Adam. 2019. "Haas Denies Reputation Harmed by Rich Energy Saga." *Motorsport.com*. https://www.motorsport.com/f1/news/haas-reputation-rich-energy-saga/4494414/.

54. *Ibid.*

55. *Ibid.*

56. *Ibid.*

57. *Ibid.*

58. Collantine, Keith. 2019. "RaceFans Round-up: Steiner 'Doesn't Care' About Rich Energy Tweets." *RaceFans*. https://www.racefans.net/2019/07/16/racefans-round-up-16-07-2/.

59. "Filing History for Lightning Volt Limited (09791667)." Gov.uk. 2017. https://find-and-update.company-information.service.gov.uk/company/09791667/filing-history.

60. *Ibid.*
61. Rich Energy. 2019. Twitter Post. July 16. Deleted.
62. King, Alanis. Haas Employee 1. Personal Interview, August 2021.
63. King, Alanis. Haas Employee 5. Personal Interview, August 2021.
64. King, Alanis. Haas Employee 3. Personal Interview, August 2021.
65. Blackstock, Elizabeth. Stuart Taylor (Chain Bear). Personal, August 2021.
66. Blackstock, Elizabeth. Luke Smith. Personal, August 2021.
67. "2020 Constructor Standings." n.d. F1. https://www.formula1.com/en/results.html/2020/team.html.
68. "2021 Constructor Standings." n.d. F1. https://www.formula1.com/en/results.html/2021/team.html.
69. Pryson, Mike. 2021. "Uralkali Haas F1 Team to Reveal VF-21 at Bahrain Test." *Autoweek.* https://www.autoweek.com/racing/formula-1/a35769654/uralkali-haas-f1-team-reveal-vf21-bahrain/.
70. Blackstock, Elizabeth. Stuart Taylor (Chain Bear). Personal, August 2021.
71. Blackstock, Elizabeth. Luke Smith. Personal, August 2021.

Chapter 7

1. "Red Bull Energy Drink—Official Website :: Energy Drink." n.d. Red Bull. https://www.redbull.com/us-en/energydrink/company-profile.
2. Pangarkar, Nitin, and Mohit Agarwal. 2013. "The Wind Behind Red Bull's Wings." Forbes. https://www.forbes.com/sites/forbesasia/2013/06/24/the-wind-behind-red-bulls-wings/.
3. "Red Bull Energy Drink." n.d. Red Bull CA (EN). https://www.redbull.com/ca-en/energydrink/contact-sponsorship.
4. "Multi-platform Media Company." n.d. Red Bull Media House. https://www.redbullmediahouse.com/en/about-us.
5. Rich Energy. 2019. Twitter Post. July 18. Deleted.
6. *Ibid.*
7. "Red Bull." n.d. Forbes. https://www.forbes.com/companies/red-bull/#36ccfb2861ce.
8. *Ibid.*
9. King, Alanis. 2019. "Now Red Bull Might Be Suing Rich Energy." *Jalopnik.* https://jalopnik.com/now-red-bull-might-be-suing-rich-energy-1836490303.
10. Red Bull GmbH vs. Rich Energy Limited (Business and Property Court of England and Wales June 11, 2019).
11. *Ibid.*
12. *Ibid.*
13. *Ibid.*
14. *Ibid.*
15. *Ibid.*
16. *Ibid.*
17. *Ibid.*
18. *Ibid.*
19. *Ibid.*
20. *Ibid.*
21. *Ibid.*
22. *Ibid.*
23. *Ibid.*
24. *Ibid.*
25. *Ibid.*
26. *Ibid.*
27. *Ibid.*
28. Red Bull GmbH vs. Rich Energy Limited (Business and Property Court of England and Wales July 16, 2019).
29. "About." n.d. Brandsmiths. https://brandsmiths.co.uk/about/.
30. ATB Sales Limited v Rich Energy Limited and Ors (Business and Property Courts of England and Wales May 14, 2019).
31. Red Bull GmbH vs. Rich Energy Limited (Business and Property Court of England and Wales July 16, 2019).
32. "Part 42—Change of Solicitor—Civil Procedure Rules." n.d. Justice.gov.uk. https://www.justice.gov.uk/courts/procedure-rules/civil/rules/part42.
33. Hardman, Kim. 2010. "How Can a Solicitor Cease to Act for a Client?" Lexology. https://www.lexology.com/library/detail.aspx?g=e8a0b5fb-41a7-495d-b6f2-62d276c71f7d.
34. *Ibid.*
35. *Ibid.*
36. *Ibid.*
37. Red Bull GmbH vs. Rich Energy Limited: Tomlin Order (Business and Property Court of England and Wales September 30, 2019).
38. *Ibid.*
39. "Represent Yourself in Court." n.d. Gov.uk. https://www.gov.uk/represent-yourself-in-court.
40. Red Bull GmbH vs. Rich Energy Limited: Tomlin Order (Business and

Property Court of England and Wales September 30, 2019).

41. *Ibid.*

42. *Ibid.*

43. "Red Bull." n.d. Forbes. https://www.forbes.com/companies/red-bull/#36ccfb2861ce.

44. King, Alanis. 2019. "In Memoriam: Rich Energy's Tweets." *Jalopnik.* https://jalopnik.com/in-memoriam-rich-energys-tweets-1839096792.

45. Rich Energy. 2019. Twitter Post. October 16. Deleted.

46. Rich Energy. 2019. Twitter Post. September 29. Deleted.

47. Storey, William. 2020. Twitter Post. September 13. https://twitter.com/richenergyceo/status/1305114602334806016.

48. Rich Energy. 2016. Twitter Post 1. October 21. Deleted.

49. Rich Energy. 2016. Twitter Post 2. October 21. Deleted.

50. Rich Energy. 2016. Twitter Post. December 4. Deleted.

51. "Fire Breathing While BASE Jumping, What Could Go Wrong? | EpicTV Choice Cuts." YouTube, 2015. https://www.youtube.com/watch?v=dAeUYRfMV38.

52. de Kam, JP. August 20, 2021.

53. Stern, Adam. 2020. Twitter Post. June 17. https://mobile.twitter.com/A_S12/status/1273432840278102028.

54. *Ibid.*

55. Rich Energy HQ. 2020. Twitter Post. June 26. https://twitter.com/rich_energy/status/1276569770188582912.

56. Iredale, Azzy. 2020. Twitter Post. May 25. https://twitter.com/AzzyIredale37/status/1264987551347195907.

57. Iredale, Azzy. 2020. Twitter Post. May 25. https://twitter.com/AzzyIredale37/status/1264995588237602816.

58. Iredale, Azzy. 2020. Twitter Post. May 25. https://twitter.com/AzzyIredale37/status/1264995941825814528.

59. Storey, William. 2020. Twitter Post. May 28. https://mobile.twitter.com/richenergyceo/status/1265942658142306304.

60. Dolan, Simon. 2020. Twitter Post. May 28. Deleted.

61. Iredale, Azzy. 2020. Twitter Post. June 9. https://mobile.twitter.com/AzzyIredale37/status/1270394601979904001.

62. *Ibid.*

63. Blackstock, Elizabeth. Azzy Iredale. Personal, August 2021.

64. *Ibid.*

65. *Ibid.*

66. *Ibid.*

67. *Ibid.*

68. *Ibid.*

69. Blackstock, Elizabeth. Anonymous Motorsport Employee. Personal, August 2021.

70. *Ibid.*

71. Iredale, Azzy. 2020. Twitter Post. December 26. https://twitter.com/AzzyIredale37/status/1343011883633291267.

72. Blackstock, Elizabeth. Azzy Iredale. Personal, August 2021.

73. *Ibid.*

74. "What's the Storey?" 2020. *Chasin' the Racin'.* https://www.youtube.com/watch?v=xBEyFflfz4w.

75. *Ibid.*

76. "Brazilian Grand Prix 2019: Hamilton Admits Albon Crash 'Completely My Fault.'" 2019. F1. https://www.formula1.com/en/latest/article.hamilton-says-albon-crash-completely-my-fault.245RL043CRlvS8fBy1rDnh.html.

77. "2019 Constructor Standings." n.d. F1. https://www.formula1.com/en/results.html/2019/team.html.

78. Tran, Mark. 2004. "Red Bull Buys Jaguar F1 Team." *The Guardian.* https://www.theguardian.com/business/2004/nov/15/formulaone.money.

79. Davies, Alex. 2014. "One of F1's Most Dangerous Tracks Is Back." *WIRED.* https://www.wired.com/2014/06/f1-austria-grand-prix-track/.

80. King, Alanis. 2020. Twitter Post. July 5. https://twitter.com/alanisnking/status/1279809985703301120.

81. "Formula 1 Rolex Grosser Preis Von Österreich 2020—Qualifying." 2020. F1. https://www.formula1.com/en/results.html/2020/races/1045/austria/qualifying.html.

82. Storey, William. 2020. Twitter Post. July 3. https://twitter.com/richenergyceo/status/1279121089029906433.

83. Gomez, Dessi. 2020. "Watch First 'Hamilton' Film Trailer Ahead of Disney+ Release." *Los Angeles Times.* https://www.latimes.com/entertainment-arts/movies/story/2020-06-22/first-hamilton-film-trailer-disney.

84. Maxouris, Christina. 2020. "Judge

Sets Derek Chauvin's Bail at $1.25 Million in George Floyd's Death." *CNN.* https://www.cnn.com/2020/06/08/us/derek-chauvin-court-monday-george-floyd-latest/index.html.

85. "Formula 1 Rolex Grosser Preis Von Österreich 2020—Race Result." 2020. F1. https://www.formula1.com/en/results.html/2020/races/1045/austria/race-result.html.

86. "'We Didn't Expect It to Be This Big of an Issue'—Steiner Explains Haas Double DNF in Austria." 2020. F1. https://www.formula1.com/en/latest/article.we-didnt-expect-it-to-be-this-big-of-an-issue-steiner-explains-haas-double.6DF2ZPyJu8dW89q2BLJzqh.html.

87. Storey, William. 2020. Twitter Post. July 5. https://mobile.twitter.com/richenergyceo/status/1279847197425709060?lang=ar.

88. Cooper, Adam. 2020. "Radio Controlled Podium Robots "weird", Says Hamilton." *Motorsport.com.* https://us.motorsport.com/f1/news/podium-robots-weird-ott-hamilton/4833912/.

89. Storey, William. 2020. Twitter Post. July 5. https://twitter.com/richenergyceo/status/1279824307540103168.

90. Storey, William. 2020. Twitter Post. July 4. https://twitter.com/richenergyceo/status/1279520330806165506.

91. Storey, William. 2020. Twitter Post. July 4. https://twitter.com/richenergyceo/status/1279534838769422340.

92. Dolan, Simon. 2020. Twitter Post. July 6. https://twitter.com/simondolan/status/1280149505413976066.

93. Storey, William. 2020. Twitter Post. July 6. https://twitter.com/richenergyceo/status/1280198064310018048.

94. "Listings of WHO's Response to COVID-19." 2020. World Health Organization. https://www.who.int/news-room/detail/29-06-2020-covidtimeline.

95. Dolan, Simon. 2020. Twitter Post. July 1. https://twitter.com/simondolan/status/1278347032072241152.

96. Storey, William. 2020. Twitter Post. December 26. https://twitter.com/richenergyceo/status/1342882235922456583.

97. Storey, William. 2021. Twitter Post. March 27. https://twitter.com/richenergyceo/status/1375820740939878400.

98. "F1 Calendar 2020—Enjoy a Record-breaking 22 Races in the 2020 Season." 2019. F1. https://www.formula1.com/en/latest/article.record-breaking-22-race-f1-calendar-set-for-2020.7vdbREiAYJKP5Ey8whglC2.html.

99. "Formula 1 Pirelli Grosser Preis Der Steiermark 2020—Race Result." 2020. F1. https://www.formula1.com/en/results.html/2020/races/1046/austria/race-result.html.

100. Storey, William. 2020. Twitter Post. July 11. https://twitter.com/richenergyceo/status/1282037409610379265.

101. Rich Energy HQ. 2020. Twitter Post. July 12. https://twitter.com/rich_energy/status/1282300664882880514.

102. Boulter, Scott. 2020. Twitter Post. July 12. https://twitter.com/scott_boulter/status/1282364981812617218.

103. Harry, Rob. 2020. Twitter Post. July 12. https://twitter.com/robharry/status/1282320331152273409.

104. Ericsson, Simon. 2020. Twitter Post. July 12. https://twitter.com/simonerkss/status/1282342588033441793.

105. Jake. 2020. Twitter Post. July 12. https://twitter.com/jakevdW/status/1282314314540515329.

106. broodjie. 2020. Twitter Post. July 12. https://twitter.com/BroodjeF1/status/1282333076664864768.

107. Rich Energy HQ. 2020. Twitter Post. July 12. https://twitter.com/rich_energy/status/1282333333310132224.

108. Rich Energy HQ. 2020. Twitter Post. July 18. https://twitter.com/rich_energy/status/1284577608286470146.

109. King, Alanis. Haas Employee 5. Personal Interview, August 2021.

110. King, Alanis. Haas Employee 1. Personal Interview, August 2021.

111. King, Alanis. Haas Employee 5. Personal Interview, August 2021.

112. King, Alanis. Haas Employee 1. Personal Interview, August 2021.

113. King, Alanis. Haas Employee 5. Personal Interview, August 2021.

114. King, Alanis. Haas Employee 1. Personal Interview, August 2021.

115. Loder, Carly. "Request for Comment | Rich Energy, the Book," September 8, 2021.

Chapter 8

1. "Filing History for Lightning Volt Limited (09791667)." 2017.

Gov.uk. https://find-and-update. company-information.service.gov.uk/ company/09791667/filing-history.

2. *Ibid.*

3. *Ibid.*

4. "RichEnergyLimitedOverview—Find and Update Company Information—Gov. uk." n.d. Companies House. https://find-and-update.company-information.service. gov.uk/company/12112427.

5. *Ibid.*

6. *Ibid.*

7. "Filing History for Lightning Volt Limited (09791667)." 2017. Gov. uk. https://find-and-update.company-information.service.gov.uk/company/ 09791667/filing-history.

8. "Rich Energy Limited Overview— Find and Update Company Information—Gov.uk." n.d. Companies House. https://find-and-update.company-information.service.gov.uk/company/ 12112427.

9. Weston, Steve, August 31, 2021.

10. Smith, Luke. 2019. "Rich Energy Future to Be Decided by Singapore." *Crash.Net*. https://www.crash.net/f1/ news/928439/1/rich-energy-future-be-decided-singapore.

11. *Ibid.*

12. *Ibid.*

13. *Ibid.*

14. Haas F1 Team. 2019. Twitter Post. September 9. https://twitter.com/ HaasF1Team/status/117104561809939251 3?s=20.

15. Rich Energy. 2019. Twitter Post. September 9. Deleted.

16. Collantine, Keith. 2019. "F1: Rich Energy Officially Dropped from Haas Team Name." *RaceFans*. https://www. racefans.net/2019/09/12/rich-energy-officially-dropped-from-haas-team-name/.

17. Cobb, Haydn. 2019. "Haas Reveals Tweaked Livery After Rich Energy Split." *Crash.Net*. https://www.crash.net/f1/ news/929316/1/haas-reveals-tweaked-livery-after-rich-energy-split.

18. "2020 Constructor Standings." n.d. F1. https://www.formula1.com/en/results. html/2020/team.html.

19. Storey, William. 2020. Twitter Post. October 23. https://twitter.com/ richenergyceo/status/131965297566 5623043.

20. King, Alanis. 2019. "Rich Energy: Not Dead Yet!" *Jalopnik*. https:// jalopnik.com/rich-energy-not-dead-yet-1838359045.

21. Rich Energy. 2019. Twitter Post. September 29. Deleted.

22. Haas F1 Team. 2019. Twitter Post. September 9. https://twitter.com/ HaasF1Team/status/117104561809939251 3?s=20.

23. Mitchell, Scott. 2019. "Gunther Steiner Needs 'Thinking Hat' Amid Haas F1 Income Drop." *Autosport*. https:// www.autosport.com/f1/news/gunther-steiner-needs-thinking-hat-amid-haas-f1-income-drop-4987752/4987752/.

24. *Ibid.*

25. *Ibid.*

26. *Ibid.*

27. King, Alanis. Haas Employee 5. Personal Interview, August 2021.

28. King, Alanis. Haas Employee 3. Personal Interview, August 2021.

29. King, Alanis. Haas Employee 5. Personal Interview, August 2021.

30. King, Alanis. Haas Employee 5. Personal Interview, August 2021.

31. King, Alanis. Haas Employee 1. Personal Interview, August 2021.

32. King, Alanis. Haas Employee 5. Personal Interview, August 2021.

33. King, Alanis. Haas Employee 1. Personal Interview, August 2021.

34. King, Alanis. Haas Employee 3. Personal Interview, August 2021.

35. King, Alanis. Haas Employee 1. Personal Interview, August 2021.

36. King, Alanis. Haas Employee 3. Personal Interview, August 2021.

37. King, Alanis. Haas Employee 5. Personal Interview, August 2021.

38. King, Alanis. Haas Employee 3. Personal Interview, August 2021.

39. King, Alanis. Haas Employee 1. Personal Interview, August 2021.

40. King, Alanis. Haas Employee 3. Personal Interview, August 2021.

41. Duncan, Lewis. 2020. "Rich Energy to Sponsor Road Racing Team OMG." *Motorsport.com*. https://us.motorsport. com/bike/news/rich-energy-omg-racing-sponsorship/4685676/.

42. "OMG Racing Announces New Title Sponsorship with Rich Energy," February 14, 2020. https://www. britishsuperbike.com/news/omg-racing-

announces-new-title-sponsorship-partnership-with-rich-energy/.

43. *Ibid.*

44. RICH Energy OMG Racing. 2020. Twitter Post. February 14. https://twitter.com/omgracinguk/status/1228300679061680128?lang=en

45. "Q&A—." n.d. Rich OMG. https://www.richomg.com/qanda.

46. "OMG Racing Limited Overview—Find and Update Company Information—Gov.uk." n.d. Companies House. https://beta.companieshouse.gov.uk/company/11074788.

47. "OMG Racing—About," n.d. https://www.omgracing.co.uk/about.

48. Rich Energy OMG Racing. Twitter Post. October 26. https://mobile.twitter.com/OMGRacingUK/status/1320711903165952000.

49. "2020 British Superbikes Points," n.d. https://www.britishsuperbike.com/media/727576/superbike-points.pdf.

50. Rich Energy HQ. 2020. Twitter Post. September 10. https://twitter.com/rich_energy/status/1303992498143080448.

51. Rich Energy HQ. 2020. Twitter Post. September 6. https://twitter.com/rich_energy/status/1302640301878771714.

52. Storey, William. 2020. Twitter Post. October 22. https://twitter.com/richenergyceo/status/1319291891263795200.

53. Storey, William. 2020. Twitter Post. December 6. https://twitter.com/richenergyceo/status/1335625360147419150.

54. Rich Energy HQ. 2020. Twitter Post. July 19. https://twitter.com/rich_energy/status/1284803950592643072.

55. Storey, William. 2020. Twitter Post. July 11. https://twitter.com/richenergyceo/status/1282037409610379265.

56. Storey, William. 2020. Twitter Post. May 9. https://twitter.com/richenergyceo/status/1259252610890190848.

57. Storey, William. 2020. Twitter Post. June 7. https://twitter.com/richenergyceo/status/1269736639250792449.

58. Storey, William. 2020. Twitter Post. July 3. https://twitter.com/richenergyceo/status/1278990388980862976.

59. Storey, William. 2020. Twitter Post. July 11. https://twitter.com/richenergyceo/status/1282037409610379265.

60. Storey, William. 2020. Twitter Post. July 26. https://twitter.com/richenergyceo/status/1287496139181359114

61. Storey, William. 2020. Twitter Post. July 26. https://twitter.com/richenergyceo/status/1287498187624910849

62. Storey, William. 2020. Twitter Post. December 17. https://twitter.com/richenergyceo/status/1339541516096856065

63. "What's the Storey?" *Chasin' the Racin'.* 2020. https://www.youtube.com/watch?v=xBEyFflfz4w.

64. *Ibid.*

65. *Ibid.*

66. "Energy Pack Subscription." Rich Energy, n.d. https://web.archive.org/web/20200413145532/https://www.richenergy.life/.

67. *Ibid.*

68. Storey, William. 2020. Twitter Post. July 24. https://twitter.com/richenergyceo/status/1286608356388540416

69. "League One Table & Standings." 2020. League One Table & Standings—Sky Sports Football. https://www.skysports.com/league-1-table/2019.

70. Hunter, James. 2020. "William Storey on Why He Cannot Name His 'blue Chip' Backers, in Part Two of Our Q&A." *Evening Chronicle.* https://www.chroniclelive.co.uk/sport/football/football-news/william-storey-cannot-name-blue-19486649.

71. *Ibid.*

72. Taylor, Louise. 2020. "Founder of Soft Drinks Firm Rich Energy Bids to Buy Sunderland." *The Guardian.* https://www.theguardian.com/football/2020/jul/24/founder-of-soft-drinks-firm-rich-energy-bids-to-buy-sunderland.

73. Donnelly, Mark. 2020. "Who Is William Storey? The Rich Energy CEO Claiming to Have Launched a Take-over Bid for Sunderland AFC." *Sunderland Echo.* https://www.sunderlandecho.com/sport/football/sunderland-afc/who-william-storey-rich-energy-ceo-claiming-have-launched-takeover-bid-sunderland-afc-2923233.

74. Morrissey, Paul. "A Quick Question About a Former QPR Player," August 22, 2021.

75. Neate, Rupert. 2021. "Meet Kyril Louis-Dreyfus, 23—English Football's Youngest Chairman." *The Guardian.* https://www.theguardian.com/football/

2021/feb/20/meet-kyril-louis-dreyfus-23-english-football-youngest-chairman.

76. Storey, William. 2020. Twitter Post. December 24. https://twitter.com/richenergyceo/status/1342173566608015368?lang=en.

77. Chamberlain, Oscar. "A Few Quick Questions About Sunderland AFC-Rich Energy," August 23, 2021.

78. We Are Rich Energy. 2020. Twitter Post. July 27. https://twitter.com/weareRichEnergy/status/1288036499133538308.

79. BroadleyF1, Roland. 2020. Twitter Post. July 28. https://twitter.com/RolandBroadley/status/1288134547255832577.

80. "About." n.d. Michael Crees. https://michaelcreesracing.com/about/.

81. "Fan-Favourite British Touring Car Star Michael Crees Links Up with Rich Energy." 2020. Michael Crees. https://michaelcreesracing.com/fan-favourite-british-touring-car-star-michael-crees-links-up-with-rich-energy/.

82. Busso, Ashton. 2020. Twitter Post. July 28. https://twitter.com/TheAshtonBusso/status/1288067934078763009.

83. "Filing History for Lightning Volt Limited (09791667)." 2017. Gov.uk. https://find-and-update.company-information.service.gov.uk/company/09791667/filing-history.

84. "Lightning Volt Limited: Petitions to Wind Up ." *The Gazette*. https://www.thegazette.co.uk/notice/3406114/.

85. Weston, Neville. "Interview Request | Rich Energy, the Book," August 16, 2021.

86. Storey, William. 2021. Twitter Post. January 5. https://twitter.com/richenergyceo/status/1346580504963911692.

87. The Pob. 2021. Twitter Post. January 5. https://twitter.com/Quemerford/status/1346581179085053953.

88. Storey, William. 2021. Twitter Post. January 5. https://twitter.com/richenergyceo/status/134658189067807539 2.

89. "Filing History for Lightning Volt Limited (09791667)." Gov.uk. 2017. https://find-and-update.company-information.service.gov.uk/company/09791667/filing-history.

90. Storey, William. 2021. Twitter Post.

January 13. https://twitter.com/richenergyceo/status/1349417385858633734.

91. Storey, William. 2021. Letter to Thomas Maher, January.

92. Maher, Thomas, January 14, 2021.

93. "Grosjean and Magnussen Announce They Are to Leave Haas at the End of 2020." 2020. F1. https://www.formula1.com/en/latest/article.breaking-grosjean-and-magnussen-announce-they-are-to-leave-haas-at-the-end.5pXS3lUq9uQIbBZvXo41cV.html.

94. "Board of Directors URAL-CHEM, JSC." n.d. Uralchem. https://www.uralchem.com/corporate_management/corporate-governance/board-of-directors-uralchem-jsc/.

95. "Haas 'Dealing With' Nikita Mazepin, F1 Team Taking Actions 'Seriously.'" 2020. *Sky Sports*. https://www.skysports.com/f1/news/32133/12158139/haas-dealing-with-nikita-mazepin-f1-team-taking-actions-seriously.

96. Haas F1 Team. 2020. Twitter Post. December 9. https://twitter.com/HaasF1Team/status/133661769319417856 0.

97. Church, Ben. 2020. "Nikita Mazepin: F1 Driver Apologizes for 'inappropriate Behavior.'" *CNN*. https://www.cnn.com/2020/12/10/motorsport/nikita-mazepin-haas-apology-video-spt-intl/index.html.

98. Morlidge, Matt. 2021. "Haas F1 Condemn 'abhorrent' Nikita Mazepin Actions, Social Media Video." *Sky Sports*. https://www.skysports.com/f1/news/12433/12155959/haas-f1-condemn-abhorrent-nikita-mazepin-actions-social-media-video.

99. Galloway, James. 2020. "Lewis Hamilton Expects New Guidelines After Wearing Breonna Taylor T-shirt." *Sky Sports*. https://www.skysports.com/f1/news/24181/12080537/lewis-hamilton-expects-new-guidelines-after-wearing-breonna-taylor-t-shirt.

100. Cooper, Adam. 2020. "FIA Tightens Podium Rules After Hamilton's Breonna Taylor Protest." *Motorsport.com*. https://us.motorsport.com/f1/news/fia-bans-t-shirts-f1-podium-ceremonies/4882622/.

101. Morlidge, Matt. 2021. "Haas F1 Condemn 'Abhorrent' Nikita Mazepin Actions, Social Media Video." *Sky*

Sports. https://www.skysports.com/f1/news/12433/12155959/haas-f1-condemn-abhorrent-nikita-mazepin-actions-social-media-video.

102. *Ibid*.

103. "Instagrammer Who Was Groped by Mazepin Speaks Out Against 2021 Haas Driver." 2020. *MARCA*. https://www.marca.com/en/lifestyle/2020/12/18/5fdcb7c2ca47416d1c8b4571.html.

104. *Ibid*.

105. Storey, William. 2021. Twitter Post. January 23. https://twitter.com/richenergyceo/status/1353008987432767492.

106. "2021 Bahrain GP Qualifying: Mazepin Spins at Turn 13." 2021. F1. https://www.formula1.com/en/latest/video.2021-bahrain-gp-qualifying-mazepin-spins-at-turn-13.1696505121639107291.html.

107. "Formula 1 Gulf Air Bahrain Grand Prix 2021—Race Result." 2021. F1. https://www.formula1.com/en/results.html/2021/races/1064/bahrain/race-result.html.

108. "2021 Driver Standings: Nikita Mazepin." n.d. F1. https://www.formula1.com/en/results.html/2021/drivers/NIKMAZ01/nikita-mazepin.html.

109. *Ibid*.

110. "When Did Mazepin Spin?" n.d. When did Mazepin spin? https://whendidmazepinspin.com/.

111. *Ibid*.

112. "Mazesp.in." n.d. Nikita Mazespin. http://mazesp.in.

113. "2022 F1 Pre-Season Track Session—Barcelona." Formula 1®—The Official F1® Website. https://www.formula1.com/en/racing/2022/Pre-Season-Track-Session.html.

114. Kirby, Jen, and Jonathan Guyer. 2022. "Russia's War in Ukraine, Explained." Vox. February 24. https://www.vox.com/2022/2/23/22948534/russia-ukraine-war-putin-explosions-invasion-explained.

115. "Fact Sheet: United States, G7 and EU Impose Severe and Immediate Costs on Russia." 2022. The White House. April 6. https://www.whitehouse.gov/briefing-room/statements-releases/2022/04/06/fact-sheet-united-states-g7-and-eu-impose-severe-and-immediate-costs-on-russia/.

116. Sweet, Ken, and Fatima Hussein. 2022. "Sanctions Hit Russian Economy, Although Putin Says Otherwise." AP News. April 23. https://apnews.com/article/russia-ukraine-business-europe-economy-dd7bcb1c09b4020a3f75048c4045fa90.

117. Sung, Patrick, and Wayne Sterling. 2022. "These Are the Sports That Russia Has Been Suspended From." CNN. March 7. https://www.cnn.com/2022/03/01/sport/sports-russia-banned-from-football-rugby-spt-intl/.

118. F1. 2019. "Haas: We Should Have Listened to the Drivers More amid Struggles: Formula 1." F1. October 17. https://www.formula1.com/en/latest/article.haas-we-should-have-listened-to-the-drivers-more-amid-struggles.1AeEknt0XzyECdaCRSu0kh.html.

119. "FIA Announces World Motor Sport Council Decisions in Relation to the Situation in Ukraine." Federation Internationale de l'Automobile, March 2, 2022. https://www.fia.com/news/fia-announces-world-motor-sport-council-decisions-relation-situation-ukraine.

120. "Haas to Use All-White Livery on Final Day of Barcelona Pre-Season Running: Formula 1." F1. https://www.formula1.com/en/latest/article.haas-to-use-all-white-livery-on-final-day-of-barcelona-pre-season-running.4yJ2e7yoN2hWYrTWFXBzk6.html.

121. Alonso, Eric. 2022. Formula 1 Testing in Barcelona—Day 2. Photograph. Barcelona, Spain, February 24. Getty.

122. Saunders, Nate. 2022. "Haas Formula One to Decide on Nikita Mazepin; Drops Uralkali Branding from Car after Russian Invasion of Ukraine." ESPN. February 25. https://www.espn.com/f1/story/_/id/33368180/haas-decide-nikita-mazepin-uralkali-next-week.

123. Storey, William. 2022. Twitter Post. March 4. https://twitter.com/richenergyceo/status/1499722983656542211.

124. Haas F1 Team. 2022. Twitter Post. March 5. https://twitter.com/HaasF1Team/status/1500031737581158412?ref_src=twsrc%5Egoogle%7Ctwcamp%5Eserp%7Ctwgr%5Etweet.

125. Storey, William. 2022. Twitter Post. March 5. https://twitter.com/richenergyceo/status/1500055378041741314.

126. Haas F1 Team. 2022. Twitter Post. March 9. https://twitter.com/Haas F1Team/status/1501632476619452427?s=2 0&t=xC_Tl9Q1mjfjsDnDdNNsVw.

127. "Formula 1 Gulf Air Bahrain Grand Prix 2022—Race Result." 2022. F1. https://www.formula1.com/en/results.html/2022/races/1124/bahrain/race-result.html.

128. Storey, William. 2021. Twitter Post. January 10. https://twitter.com/rich_energy/status/1348304019253579777.

129. Storey, William. 2021. Twitter Post. January 11. https://twitter.com/richenergyceo/status/1348388318120173568.

130. Gilles Rosso. 2021. Twitter Post. January 12. https://twitter.com/GillesRosso27/status/13489215758825579969.

131. Bown, Paul. 2021. Twitter Post. January 11. https://twitter.com/bownerp/status/1348682863760306183.

132. omerta. 2021. Twitter Post. January 11. https://twitter.com/ineedmclrnsenna/status/1348611412004892673.

133. Davies, Garth. 2021. Twitter Post. January 11. https://twitter.com/ggaazzz/status/1348697457019019269.

134. Oki Dingo. 2021. Twitter Post. January 12. https://twitter.com/Oki_Dingo/status/1348947014000627714.

135. Bracken. 2021. Twitter Post. January 12. https://twitter.com/brackendawson/status/1349197530014343176.

136. Avila, Jason. 2021. Twitter Post. January 11. https://twitter.com/thatbrokenkouki/status/1348586748394102784.

137. Storey, William. 2021. Twitter Post. January 5. https://twitter.com/richenergyceo/status/1346581890678075392.

138. Rich Energy. 2021. Twitter Post. February 7. https://twitter.com/rich_energy/status/135841735116792217 8?s=20.

139. Rich Energy. 2021. Twitter Post. February 14. https://twitter.com/rich_energy/status/1360972079722618888.

140. *Ibid.*

141. "Why Sergio Perez Took Action Against Force India." 2018. *Eurosport.* https://www.eurosport.com/formula-1/why-sergio-perez-took-action-against-force-india_sto6865773/story.shtml.

142. Baldwin, Alan. 2018. "Canadian Group Led by Stroll Paid $117 Million for Force India." *Reuters.* https://www.reuters.com/article/uk-motor-f1-forceindia/canadian-group-led-by-stroll-paid-117-million-for-force-india-idUKKCN1ME1LV.

143. Rich Energy. 2021. Twitter Post. February 14. https://twitter.com/rich_energy/status/1360972079722618888.

144. Haas F1 Team. 2019. Twitter Post. July 11. https://twitter.com/HaasF1Team/status/1149234399982100481?s=20.

145. Rich Energy. 2021. Twitter Post. September 29. Deleted.

146. Rich Energy. 2021. Twitter Post. February 14. https://twitter.com/rich_energy/status/1360972079722618888.

Chapter 9

1. King, Alanis. Haas Employee 5. Personal, August 2021.

2. "USAO/CDCA Press Release." 2006. Department of Justice. https://www.justice.gov/archive/tax/usaopress/2006/txdv06_077.html.

3. Hoops, Stephanie. 2009. "Haas About to Leave Prison." Home. https://archive.vcstar.com/business/haas-about-to-leave-prison-ep-371964445-350884221.html.

4. King, Alanis. Haas Employee 5. Personal, August 2021.

5. King, Alanis. Romain Grosjean. Personal, March 2022.

6. F1. "Haas: We Should Have Listened to the Drivers More amid Struggles: Formula 1." October 17, 2019. https://www.formula1.com/en/latest/article.haas-we-should-have-listened-to-the-drivers-more-amid-struggles.1AeEkn t0XzyECdaCRSu0kh.html.

7. King, Alanis. Romain Grosjean. Personal, March 2022.

8. "Filing History for Lightning Volt Limited (09791667)." 2017. Gov.uk. https://find-and-update.company-information.service.gov.uk/company/09791667/filing-history.

9. Storey, William. 2021. Twitter Post. November 30. https://twitter.com/richenergyceo/status/1465758826796400645.

10. Storey, William. 2021. Twitter Post. November 24. https://twitter.com/richenergyceo/status/1463638814577106949.

11. Blackstock, Elizabeth. Azzy Iredale. Personal, August 2021.

12. *Ibid.*

13. *Ibid.*

14. *Ibid.*

15. *Ibid.*

16. Blackstock, Elizabeth. Anonymous Motorsport Employee. Personal, August 2021.

17. *Ibid.*

18. *Ibid.*

19. Blackstock, Elizabeth. Azzy Iredale. Personal, August 2021.

20. *Ibid.*

21. *Ibid.*

22. King, Alanis. Haas Employee 5. Personal, August 2021.

23. *Ibid.*

24. *Ibid.*

25. King, Alanis. Haas Employee 1. Personal, August 2021.

26. King, Alanis. Haas Employee 5. Personal, August 2021.

27. *Ibid.*

28. *Ibid.*

29. *Ibid.*

30. "Uralkali Announces Partnership with Haas F1 Team." 2021. Press Releases PJSC Uralkali. https://www.uralkali.com/press_center/press_releases/item43939/.

31. Service, Robert. 2015. "The Crater That Keeps Swallowing Up Houses." *Siberian Times*. https://siberiantimes.com/other/others/news/n0388-the-crater-that-keeps-swallowing-up-houses/.

32. Ghosh, Suvashree. 2021. "Banks Recover Nearly $1 Billion from India's 'King of Good Times' Mallya." *Bloomberg.com*. https://www.bloomberg.com/news/articles/2021-06-23/banks-recover-about-1-billion-from-indian-ex-billionaire-mallya.

33. "Breaking News: William Storey on Force India's Future." YouTube, 2018. https://www.youtube.com/watch?v=0uhAWuMwyyo&ab_channel=peterwindsor

34. King, Alanis. Haas Employee 5. Personal, August 2021.

35. Farah, Matt. 2021. Twitter Post. August 20, 2021. https://twitter.com/TheSmokingTire/status/1428831761530642433

36. King, Alanis. Matt Farah taste test. Personal, 2021.

37. *Ibid.*

38. *Ibid.*

39. *Ibid.*

40. *Ibid.*

41. *Ibid.*

42. *Ibid.*

43. *Ibid.*

44. *Ibid.*

45. *Ibid.*

46. Hunter, James. 2020. "William Storey on Why He Cannot Name His 'Blue Chip' Backers, in Part Two of Our Q&A." *Evening Chronicle*. https://www.chroniclelive.co.uk/sport/football/football-news/william-storey-cannot-name-blue-19486649.

47. Blackstock, Elizabeth, and Alanis King. 2019. "What You Find When You Look Into Rich Energy, the Mystery Sponsor of America's F1 Team." *Jalopnik*. https://jalopnik.com/what-you-find-when-you-look-into-rich-energy-the-myste-1833303620.

48. King, Alanis. Haas Employee 1. Personal, August 2021. .

BIBLIOGRAPHY

Books

Lovell, Terry. *Bernie Ecclestone: King of Sport*. Readhowyouwant Com Ltd, 2014.

Films and Video

"Black Water? EarthWater Fulhum (Amazon Review)." 2017. YouTube. https://www.youtube.com/watch?v=vA2TSNC4lrM.

"Boiling Point." 2020. Episode. *Formula 1: Drive to Survive* 2, no. 2. Netflix. https://www.netflix.com/title/80204890.

"Breaking News: William Storey on Force India's Future." 2018. YouTube. https://www.youtube.com/watch?v=0uhAWuMwyyo&ab_channel=peterwindsor.

"Can an F1 Car REALLY Drive Upside Down? Aerodynamics EXPLAINED." 2020. YouTube. https://www.youtube.com/watch?time_continue=4&v=iUu7d8AnZ_Y&feature=emb_logo&ab_channel=Mercedes-AMGPetronasFormulaOneTeam.

"Fire Breathing While BASE Jumping, What Could Go Wrong? EpicTV Choice Cuts." 2015. YouTube. https://www.youtube.com/watch?v=dAeUYRfMV38.

"Haas 2019 F1 Livery Launch." 2019. YouTube. https://www.youtube.com/watch?v=PGrBWoMqpVI&ab_channel=Autosport.

"HaasF1 and Rich Energy—the Inside Story (1/2)." 2018. YouTube. https://www.youtube.com/watch?v=Cr8icp8vEIY&ab_channel=peterwindsor.

"Lotus Type 88—the BANNED F1 Car."

2016. YouTube. https://www.youtube.com/watch?v=DMtkRcqvGaU&feature=emb_title.

"Monaco 2006 Epic Kimi Räikkönen—Going Straight to His Yacht After Heat Shield Blow Up!" 2018. YouTube. https://www.youtube.com/watch?v=ZMzeluIxblY&ab_channel=Kimiisland.

"MP 644: The Week in IndyCar, Sept 4, with Jack Harvey and Toby Sowery." 2019. YouTube. https://youtu.be/pmDSrahPvok?t=4722.

"Player Awards 2016/17." 2017. YouTube. https://www.youtube.com/watch?v=KvVealqyymo&ab_channel=WestHamUnitedFC.

"What's the Storey?" 2020. *Chasin' the Racin'*. https://www.youtube.com/watch?v=xBEyFflfz4w.

Government and Court Documents

ATB Sales Limited v Rich Energy Limited and Ors (Business and Property Courts of England and Wales May 14, 2019).

"Company Overview for Danieli UK Holding Limited (02997333)." Gov.uk. https://find-and-update.company-information.service.gov.uk/company/02997333.

"Company Overview for Tryfan LED Limited (09580846)." Gov.uk. https://find-and-update.company-information.service.gov.uk/company/09580846.

"Company Overview for Tryfan Technologies Limited (07405925)." Gov.uk. https://find-and-update.company-information.service.gov.uk/company/07405925.

"Company Overview for Wise Guy Boxing (08260818)." Gov.uk. https://find-and-update.company-information.service.gov.uk/company/08260818.

"Court-Orders Final Forfeiture of Over $54 Million in Connection with Billion-Dollar Ponzi Scheme." 2020. Department of Justice. https://www.justice.gov/usao-edca/pr/court-orders-final-forfeiture-over-54-million-connection-billion-dollar-ponzi-scheme.

"DC Solar Owner Sentenced to 30 Years in Prison for Billion-Dollar Ponzi Scheme." 2021. Department of Justice. https://www.justice.gov/usao-edca/pr/-dc-solar-owner-sentenced-30-years-prison-billion-dollar-ponzi-scheme.

"Federal Indictment Charges Founders of Defunct Hickory E-Waste Company with Defrauding Victims of at Least $25 Million." 2017. Department of Justice. https://www.justice.gov/usao-wdnc/pr/-federal-indictment-charges-founders-defunct-hickory-e-waste-company-defrauding-victims.

"Filing History for Lightning Volt Limited (09791667)." 2017. Gov.uk. https://find-and-update.company-information.service.gov.uk/company/09791667/filing-history.

"Founder and CEO of Charlotte Area Start-Up Company Sentenced to 10 Years for Defrauding Victims of More Than $25 Million." 2018. Department of Justice. https://www.justice.gov/usao-wdnc/pr/founder-and-ceo-charlotte-area-start-company-sentenced-10-years-defrauding-victims-more.

"Lightning Volt Limited: Petitions to Wind Up." *The Gazette.* https://www.thegazette.co.uk/notice/3406114/.

"OMG Racing Limited Overview—Find and Update Company Information—Gov.uk." n.d. Companies House. https://beta.companieshouse.gov.uk/company/11074788.

"Pending Criminal Division Cases." 2021. Department of Justice. https://www.justice.gov/archives/criminal-vns/case/EarthWater/update.

Red Bull GmbH vs. Rich Energy Limited (Business and Property Court of England and Wales July 16, 2019).

Red Bull GmbH vs. Rich Energy Limited (Business and Property Court of England and Wales June 11, 2019).

Red Bull GmbH vs. Rich Energy Limited: Tomlin Order (Business and Property Court of England and Wales September 30, 2019).

"Rich Energy Limited Overview—Find and Update Company Information—Gov.uk." n.d. Companies House. https://find-and-update.company-information.service.gov.uk/company/12112427.

"Sean Ragan Named Special Agent in Charge of the Sacramento Field Office—FBI." 2017. FBI. https://www.fbi.gov/news/pressrel/press-releases/sean-ragan-named-special-agent-in-charge-of-the-sacramento-field-office.

"Six Men Charged for Role in Five-Year High-Yield Investment Fraud Scheme." 2019. Department of Justice. https://www.justice.gov/opa/pr/six-men-charged-role-five-year-high-yield-investment-fraud-scheme.

"Top Executives Plead Guilty to Participating in a Billion Dollar Ponzi Scheme—the Biggest Criminal Fraud Scheme in the History of the Eastern District of California." 2020. Department of Justice. https://www.justice.gov/usao-edca/pr/top-executives-plead-guilty-participating-billion-dollar-ponzi-scheme-biggest-criminal.

"Two Former EarthWater Executives Plead Guilty for Investment Fraud Scheme Targeting Elderly Victims." 2020. Department of Justice. https://www.justice.gov/opa/pr/two-former-earthwater-executives-plead-guilty-investment-fraud-scheme-targeting-elderly.

"U.S. Marshals Auctioning Collection of 149 Classic, Luxury Vehicles." 2019. Department of Justice. https://www.justice.gov/usao-edca/pr/us-marshals-auctioning-collection-149-classic-luxury-vehicles.

"USAO/CDCA Press Release." 2006. Department of Justice. https://www.justice.gov/archive/tax/usaopress/2006/txdv06_077.html.

Social Media

Avila, Jason. January 11, 2021. Twitter Post. https://twitter.com/thatbrokenkouki/status/1348586748394102784.

Barr, Daylon. July 18, 2020. Twitter Post.

https://twitter.com/BarrVisuals/status/1284670972642156544.

Boulter, Scott. July 12, 2020. Twitter Post. https://twitter.com/scott_boulter/status/1282364981812617218.

Bown, Paul. January 11, 2021. Twitter Post. https://twitter.com/bownerp/status/1348682863760306183.

Bracken. January 12, 2021. Twitter Post. https://twitter.com/brackendawson/status/1349197530014343176.

BroadleyF1, Roland. July 28, 2020. Twitter Post. https://twitter.com/RolandBroadley/status/1288134547255832577.

broodjie. July 12, 2020. Twitter Post. https://twitter.com/BroodjeF1/status/1282333076664864768.

Browne, Lucas. July 24, 2019. Twitter Post. https://twitter.com/lucasBrowne/status/1154034678896050176.

Browne, Lucas. July 27, 2019. Twitter Post. https://twitter.com/lucasBrowne/status/1155114005029097472.

Busso, Ashton. July 28, 2020. Twitter Post. https://twitter.com/TheAshtonBusso/status/1288067934078763009.

Chip Ganassi Racing. January 4, 2019. Twitter Post. https://twitter.com/CGRTeams/status/1081253816224436224.

Comu, CJ. April 27, 2018. Twitter Post. https://twitter.com/cjcomul/status/989858521893294081/.

Comu, CJ. May 31, 2018. Twitter Post. https://twitter.com/cjcomul/status/1002209774413500417.

Danieli Style. Twitter Account. https://twitter.com/Danieli_Style.

Davies, Garth. January 11, 2021. Twitter Post. https://twitter.com/ggaazzz/status/1348697457019019269.

Dolan, Simon. July 1, 2020. Twitter Post. https://twitter.com/simondolan/status/1278347032072241152.

Dolan, Simon. July 6, 2020. Twitter Post. https://twitter.com/simondolan/status/1280149505413976066.

Dolan, Simon. May 28, 2020. Twitter Post. Deleted.

Ellis, Ryan. July 18, 2020. Twitter Post. https://twitter.com/ryanellisracing/status/1284671648814305280.

Ellis, Ryan. July 18, 2020. Twitter Post. https://twitter.com/ryanellisracing/status/1284673196487331840.

Ericsson, Simon. July 12, 2020. Twitter Post. https://twitter.com/simonerkss/status/1282342588033441793.

F1. May 21, 2020, 1:31 PM. Twitter Post. https://twitter.com/f1/status/1263537794481348608?lang=en.

Farah, Matt. August 20, 2021. Twitter Post. https://twitter.com/TheSmokingTire/status/1428831761530642433.

Fort Wayne Music Festival. Facebook Page. https://www.facebook.com/richenergy.us/photos/a.967691673435348/1045526448985203/?type=1&theater.

Gilles Rosso. January 12, 2021. Twitter Post. https://twitter.com/GillesRosso27/status/1348921575882579969.

Haas F1 Team. December 9, 2020. Twitter Post. https://twitter.com/HaasF1Team/status/1336617693194178560.

Haas F1 Team. July 11, 2019. Twitter Post. https://twitter.com/HaasF1Team/status/1149234399982100481?s=20.

Haas F1 Team. Twitter Post. March 5, 2022. https://twitter.com/HaasF1Team/status/1500031737581158412?ref_src=twsrc%5Egoogle%7Ctwcamp%5Eserp%7Ctwgr%5Etweet.

Haas F1 Team. Twitter Post. March 9, 2022. https://twitter.com/HaasF1Team/status/1501632476619452427?s=20&t=xC_Tl9Q1mjfjsDnDdNNsVw.

Haas F1 Team. September 9, 2019. Twitter Post. https://twitter.com/HaasF1Team/status/1171045618099392513?s=20

Harris, Chris. June 10, 2019. Twitter Post. https://twitter.com/harrismonkey/status/1138121473447604226.

Harry, Rob. July 12, 2020. Twitter Post. https://twitter.com/robharry/status/1282320331152273409.

Iredale, Azzy. December 26, 2020. Twitter Post. https://twitter.com/AzzyIredale37/status/1343011883663291267.

Iredale, Azzy. June 9, 2020. Twitter Post. https://mobile.twitter.com/AzzyIredale37/status/1270394601979904001.

Iredale, Azzy. May 25, 2020. Twitter Post. https://twitter.com/AzzyIredale37/status/1264987551347195907.

Iredale, Azzy. May 25, 2020. Twitter Post. https://twitter.com/AzzyIredale37/status/1264995588237602816.

Iredale, Azzy. May 25, 2020. Twitter Post. https://twitter.com/AzzyIredale37/status/1264995941825814528.

"Is Rich Energy, a Scam?: r/formula1." 2018. Reddit. https://www.reddit.com/r/formula1/comments/94h0p1/is_rich_energy_a_scam/.

Jake. July 12, 2020. Twitter Post. https://twitter.com/jakevdW/status/1282314314540515329.

"John Morris—Company Director—ML-Leisure Ltd | Linkedin." https://uk.linkedin.com/in/john-morris-7637a7127.

King, Alanis. July 5, 2020. Twitter Post. https://twitter.com/alanisnking/status/1279809985703301120.

livingproef. June 18, 2019. Instagram Post. https://www.instagram.com/p/By2RCv0oECb/.

Mattzel89. June 9, 2019. Twitter Post. https://twitter.com/Mattzel89/status/1137810230929219587.

MsportXtra and William Storey exchange. June 12, 2019. Twitter Post. https://twitter.com/MsportXtra/status/1138827226458275841

MsportXtra. June 18, 2019. Twitter Post. https://twitter.com/MsportXtra/status/1141065513960972288.

Oki Dingo. January 12, 2021. Twitter Post. https://twitter.com/Oki_Dingo/status/1348947014000627714.

omerta. January 11, 2021. Twitter Post. https://twitter.com/ineedmclrnsenna/status/1348611412004892673.

Parfitt Jnr., Rick. July 19, 2019. Twitter Post. https://twitter.com/RickParfittJnr/status/1152263609524850688.

The Pob. January 5, 2021. Twitter Post. https://twitter.com/Quemerford/status/1346581179085053953.

"r/NASCAR—Earthwater CEO Admits Via LinkedIn That They Aren't Paying for Sponsorship on the No. 23, Only Providing the Team with Free Water. This Would Mean BK Racing Has No Paying Sponsors Through the First 4 Races of 2018." Reddit. https://www.reddit.com/r/NASCAR/comments/82yfuw/earthwater_ceo_admits_via_linkedin_that_they/.

Rich Energy. April 10, 2016. Twitter Post. https://twitter.com/rich_energy/status/719246172741902336.

Rich Energy. April 11, 2016. Twitter Post. https://twitter.com/rich_energy/status/719424340685676544.

Rich Energy. April 22, 2016. Twitter Post. https://twitter.com/rich_energy/status/723406747818303488.

Rich Energy. April 22, 2016. Twitter Post. https://twitter.com/rich_energy/status/723414862810882049.

Rich Energy. April 27, 2017. Twitter Post. https://twitter.com/rich_energy/status/857808866532352004.

Rich Energy. April 28, 2019. Twitter Post. https://twitter.com/okeefe_92/status/1130861906858840072.

Rich Energy. April 7, 2017. Twitter Post. https://twitter.com/rich_energy/status/850241400255926274.

Rich Energy. December 20, 2016. Twitter Post. https://twitter.com/rich_energy/status/811339338898440193.

Rich Energy. December 28, 2016. Twitter Post. https://twitter.com/rich_energy/status/814103229080436736.

Rich Energy. December 4, 2016. Twitter Post. Deleted.

Rich Energy. February 14, 2021. Twitter Post. https://twitter.com/rich_energy/status/1360972079722618888.

Rich Energy. February 18, 2019. Twitter Post. Deleted.

Rich Energy. February 21, 2017. Twitter Post. https://twitter.com/rich_energy/status/834256010646867969.

Rich Energy. February 5, 2017. Twitter Post. https://twitter.com/rich_energy/status/828386103258406912.

Rich Energy. February 7, 2021. Twitter Post. https://twitter.com/rich_energy/status/1358417351167922178?s=20.

Rich Energy. January 1, 2019. Twitter Post. https://twitter.com/okeefe_92/status/1130861975058173957/.

Rich Energy. January 12, 2017. Twitter Post. https://twitter.com/rich_energy/status/819601310760767488.

Rich Energy. July 11, 2019. Twitter Post. Deleted.

Rich Energy. July 14, 2019. Twitter Post. Deleted.

Rich Energy. July 16, 2019. Twitter Post. Deleted.

Rich Energy. July 18, 2019. Twitter Post. Deleted.

Rich Energy. June 1, 2020. Twitter Post. Deleted.

Rich Energy. June 10, 2019. Twitter Post. Deleted.

Rich Energy. June 16, 2016. Twitter Post.

https://twitter.com/rich_energy/
status/743480927993626624.

Rich Energy. June 18, 2019. Twitter
Post. https://twitter.com/okeefe_92/
status/1141040086194282496.

Rich Energy. June 21, 2016. Twitter Post.
https://twitter.com/rich_energy/
status/745292899714207744.

Rich Energy. June 6, 2019. Twitter Post.
Deleted.

Rich Energy. June 8, 2019. Twitter Post.
https://twitter.com/natesaundersF1/stat
us/1137449926546415616?s=20.

Rich Energy. June 8, 2019. Twitter Post.
https://twitter.com/rich_energy/
status/1137442693087453185?ref_
src=twsrc%5Etfw.

Rich Energy. June 9, 2019. Twitter Post. https://web.archive.org/
web/20190710183929/twitter.com/
rich_energy.

Rich Energy. May 14, 2019. Twitter Post.
https://twitter.com/rich_energy/
status/1128309045050388481?ref_
src=twsrc%5Etfw.

Rich Energy. May 16, 2019. Twitter
Post. https://twitter.com/okeefe_92/
status/1130861946671124480.

Rich Energy. May 17, 2019. Twitter Post.
Deleted.

Rich Energy. May 17, 2 Twitter Post.
019. https://twitter.com/okeefe_92/
status/1130861946671124480.

Rich Energy. May 18, 2019. Twitter
Post. https://twitter.com/okeefe_
92/status/1130862173276835840/
photo/1.

Rich Energy. May 19, 2018. Twitter Post.
https://twitter.com/okeefe_92/
status/1130862186006482945/photo/1.

Rich Energy. May 21, 2016. Twitter Post.
https://twitter.com/rich_energy/
status/734039561697959941.

Rich Energy. May 23, 2016. Twitter Post.
https://twitter.com/rich_energy/
status/734791458490843136.

Rich Energy. May 24, 2020. Twitter Post.
Deleted.

Rich Energy. May 28, 2020. Twitter Post.
Deleted.

Rich Energy. November 20, 2016. Twitter
Post. https://twitter.com/rich_energy/
status/800404910709899264.

Rich Energy. November 30, 2015. Twitter
Post. https://twitter.com/rich_energy/
status/671290053675585536.

Rich Energy. October 16, 2019. Twitter
Post. Deleted.

Rich Energy. September 24, 2016. Twitter
Post. https://twitter.com/rich_energy/
status/779727522808401921.

Rich Energy. September 29, 2019. Twitter
Post. Deleted.

Rich Energy. September 9, 2019. Twitter
Post. Deleted.

Rich Energy. October 21, 2016. Twitter Post
1. Deleted.

Rich Energy. October 21, 2016. Twitter Post
2. Deleted.

"Rich Energy | LinkedIn." https://
www.linkedin.com/company/rich-
energy-beverages.

Rich Energy HQ. July 12, 2020. Twitter
Post. https://twitter.com/rich_energy/
status/1282300664882880514.

Rich Energy HQ. July 12, 2020. Twitter
Post. https://twitter.com/rich_energy/
status/1282333333310132224.

Rich Energy HQ. July 18, 2020. Twitter
Post. https://twitter.com/rich_energy/
status/1284577608286470146.

Rich Energy HQ. July 19, 2020. Twitter
Post. https://twitter.com/rich_energy/
status/1284803950592643072.

Rich Energy HQ. June 26, 2020. Twitter
Post. https://twitter.com/rich_energy/
status/1276569770188582912.

Rich Energy HQ. September 10,
2020. Twitter Post. https://twitter.
com/rich_energy/status/1303992498
143080448.

Rich Energy HQ. September 6, 2020.
Twitter Post. https://twitter.com/rich_
energy/status/1302640301878771
714.

RICH Energy OMG Racing. February 14,
2020. Twitter Post. https://twitter.com/
omgracinguk/status/1228300679061680
128?lang=en.

RICH Energy OMG Racing. October 26, 2020. Twitter Post. https://
mobile.twitter.com/OMGRacingUK/
status/1320711903165952000.

Rich Energy US. June 18, 2019. Instagram
Post.https://www.instagram.com/p/
By3mnTyA6Hg/.

Sowery, Toby. June 11, 2016. Instagram
Post. https://www.instagram.com/p/
BGgX2bkAabx/.

Stern, Adam. June 17, 2020. Twitter Post.
https://mobile.twitter.com/A_S12/
status/1273432840278102028.

Storey, William. October 12, 2018. "British Billionaire David Sullivan Acquires Stake in Rich Energy." LinkedIn. https://www.linkedin.com/pulse/british-billionaire-david-sullivan-acquires-stake-rich-william-storey/?trk=aff_src.aff-lilpar_c.partners_pkw.10078_net.mediapartner_plc.Skimbit+Ltd._pcrid.449670_learning&veh=aff_src.aff-lilpar_c.partners_pkw.10078_net.mediapartner_plc.Skimbit+Ltd._pcrid.449670_learning&irgwc=1.

Storey, William. March 8, 2018. "Congratulations President Trump." LinkedIn. https://www.linkedin.com/pulse/congratulations-president-trump-william-storey/?articleId=8259292942518347985.

Storey, William. March 8, 2018. "Ex Sas V Navy Seals Charity Boxing." LinkedIn. https://www.linkedin.com/pulse/-ex-sas-v-navy-seals-charity-boxing-william-storey/.

Storey, William. March 8, 2018. "GGG at West Ham." LinkedIn. https://www.linkedin.com/pulse/ggg-west-ham-william-storey/?lipi=urn%3Ali%3Apage%3Ad_flagship3_profile_view_base_post_details%3BLMaLl98eR8a5u%2F0I2j2lqA%3D%3D.

Storey, William. March 19, 2018. "Heavyweight Boxing Star Lucas 'Big Daddy' Browne Signed by Rich Energy." LinkedIn. https://www.linkedin.com/pulse/heavyweight-boxing-star-lucas-big-daddybrowne-signed-rich-storey/.

Storey, William. March 8, 2018. "Kidd Dynamite Signs with William Storey Management." LinkedIn. https://www.linkedin.com/pulse/kidd-dynamite-signs-william-storey-management-william-storey/?lipi=urn%3Ali%3Apage%3Ad_flagship3_profile_view_base_post_details%3BLMaLl98eR8a5u%2F0I2j2lqA%3D%3D.

Storey, William. March 9, 2018. "Lie with Snakes and Drink Poison." LinkedIn. https://www.linkedin.com/pulse/lie-snakes-drink-poison-william-storey/.

Storey, William. March 12, 2018. "Rich Energy and Noble Automotive." LinkedIn. https://www.linkedin.com/pulse/rich-energy-noble-automotive-william-storey/.

Storey, William. December 11, 2018. "Rich Energy Appoint City Veteran to Management Team." LinkedIn. https://www.linkedin.com/pulse/rich-energy-appoint-city-veteran-management-team-william-storey/.

Storey, William. March 8, 2018. "Rich Energy Aviation." LinkedIn. https://www.linkedin.com/pulse/rich-energy-aviation-william-storey/.

Storey, William. March 9, 2018. "Rich Energy Beat Red Bull to Corporate Accounts." LinkedIn. https://www.linkedin.com/pulse/rich-energy-beat-red-bull-corporate-accounts-william-storey/.

Storey, William. January 23, 2019. "Rich Energy Chosen as Trailblazing Brand in City Awards as Company Raises £220m." LinkedIn. https://www.linkedin.com/pulse/rich-energy-chosen-trailblazing-brand-city-awards-company-storey/.

Storey, William. March 8, 2018. "Rich Energy Commence International Media Campaign Across Motor Racing, Boxing, Football and Extreme Sports." LinkedIn. https://www.linkedin.com/pulse/rich-energy-commence-international-media-campaign-across-storey/.

Storey, William. March 21, 2018. "Rich Energy Confirm IOM TT Motorbike Races." LinkedIn. https://www.linkedin.com/pulse/rich-energy-confirm-iom-tt-motorbike-races-william-storey/.

Storey, William. March 9, 2018. "Rich Energy Enjoys International Export Boom Post Brexit Vote." LinkedIn. https://www.linkedin.com/pulse/-rich-energy-enjoys-international-export-boom-post-brexit-storey/?lipi=urn%3Ali%3Apage%3Ad_flagship3_profile_view_base_post_details%3BLMaLl98eR8a5u%2F0I2j2lqA%3D%3D.

Storey, William. March 9, 2018. "Rich Energy Fuel the Party at Monaco GP." LinkedIn. https://www.linkedin.com/pulse/rich-energy-fuel-party-monaco-gp-william-storey/.

Storey, William. May 23, 2018. "Rich Energy Have Large Scale Activations at Monaco Grand Prix and TT Races on Successive Weekends." LinkedIn. https://www.linkedin.com/pulse/rich-energy-have-large-scale-activations-monaco-grand-william-storey/.

Storey, William. March 8, 2018. "Rich Energy Partner UK's Premier Helicopter Service." LinkedIn. https://www.linkedin.com/pulse/rich-energy-partner-uks-premier-helicopter-service-william-storey/.

Storey, William. March 8, 2018. "Rich Energy Sign Exclusive Deal with Multiple Festivals for Summer 2017." LinkedIn. https://www.linkedin.com/pulse/rich-energy-sign-exclusive-deal-multiple-festivals-summer-storey/.

Storey, William. March 8, 2018. "Rich Energy Sign Football Deals." LinkedIn. https://www.linkedin.com/pulse/rich-energy-sign-football-deals-william-storey/.

Storey, William. March 9, 2018. "Rich Energy Sign Vegas Casinos." LinkedIn. https://www.linkedin.com/pulse/rich-energy-sign-vegas-casinos-william-storey/.

Storey, William. March 8, 2018. "Rich Energy Sponsor British Superbikes." LinkedIn. https://www.linkedin.com/pulse/rich-energy-sponsor-british-superbikes-william-storey/.

Storey, William. March 9, 2018. "Rich Energy Sponsor Surfing Worldwide." LinkedIn. https://www.linkedin.com/pulse/rich-energy-sponsor-surfing-worldwide-william-storey/.

Storey, William. March 10, 2018. "Rich Energy Sponsor West Ham Player Awards 2017." LinkedIn. https://www.linkedin.com/pulse/rich-energy-sponsor-west-ham-player-awards-2017-william-storey/.

Storey, William. March 9, 2018. "Rich Energy Support Paris Dakar Competitors for 2018." LinkedIn. https://www.linkedin.com/pulse/rich-energy-support-paris-dakar-competitors-2018-william-storey/.

Storey, William. March 9, 2018. "Rich Energy Supporting Lamborghini Race Series as Part of Motorsport Investment." LinkedIn. https://www.linkedin.com/pulse/rich-energy-supporting-lamborghini-race-series-part-william-storey/.

Storey, William. May 30, 2018. "Rich Energy Target World Titles in Powerboat Racing." LinkedIn. https://www.linkedin.com/pulse/rich-energy-target-world-titles-powerboat-racing-william-storey/.

Storey, William. March 7, 2018. "Rich Energy Win Hilton and Marriot Hotels." LinkedIn. https://www.linkedin.com/pulse/rich-energy-win-hilton-marriot-hotels-william-storey/.

Storey, William. March 9, 2018. "Why Now Is the Time to Bet on Trump." LinkedIn. https://www.linkedin.com/pulse/why-now-time-bet-trump-william-storey/.

Storey, William. July 27, 2018. "William Storey Luxury Brands." LinkedIn. https://www.linkedin.com/pulse/william-storey-luxury-brands-william-storey/.

Storey, William. March 8, 2018. "William Storey Management in Extreme Sports." LinkedIn. https://www.linkedin.com/pulse/william-storey-management-extreme-sports-william-storey/?lipi=urn%3Ali%3Apage%3Ad_flagship3_profile_view_base_post_details%3BLMaLl98eR8a5u%2F0I2j2lqA%3D%3D.

Storey, William. July 30, 2018. "William Storey Management in F1." LinkedIn. https://www.linkedin.com/pulse/william-storey-management-f1-william-storey/.

Storey, William. March 8, 2018. "William Storey Signs Deal with Alex Thomson Racing and Hugo Boss." LinkedIn. https://www.linkedin.com/pulse/william-storey-signs-deal-alex-thomson-racing-hugo-boss-storey/.

Storey, William. August 30, 2016. "William Storey TT Races." LinkedIn. https://www.linkedin.com/pulse/william-storey-tt-races-william-storey/.

Storey, William. April 12, 2020. Twitter Post. https://twitter.com/richenergyceo/status/1249359303380787207.

Storey, William. April 28, 2020. Twitter Post. https://twitter.com/richenergyceo/status/1255192575956353024.

Storey, William. August 26, 2021. Twitter Post. https://twitter.com/richenergyceo/status/1430899924804145152.

Storey, William. August 27, 2020. Twitter Post. https://twitter.com/richenergyceo/status/1299114017957478402.

Storey, William. August 31, 2021. Twitter Post. https://twitter.com/richenergyceo/status/1432658498148515841.

Storey, William. December 17, 2020. Twitter Post. https://twitter.com/richenergyceo/status/1339541516096856065

Storey, William. December 24, 2020. Twitter Post. https://twitter.com/richenergyceo/status/1342173566608015368?lang=en.

Storey, William. December 26, 2020. Twitter Post. https://twitter.com/richenergyceo/status/1342882235922456583.

Storey, William. December 6, 2020. Twitter Post. https://twitter.com/richenergyceo/status/1335625360147419150.

Storey, William. January 10, 2021. Twitter Post. https://twitter.com/rich_energy/status/1348304019253579777.

Storey, William. January 10, 2021. Twitter Post. https://twitter.com/richenergyceo/status/1348388318120173568.

Storey, William. January 13, 2021. Twitter Post. https://twitter.com/richenergyceo/status/1349417385858633734.

Storey, William. January 18, 2021. Twitter Post. https://twitter.com/richenergyceo/status/1351291593832148995.

Storey, William. January 2, 2021. Twitter Post. https://twitter.com/richenergyceo/status/1345332548898070530.

Storey, William. January 23, 2021. Twitter Post. https://twitter.com/richenergyceo/status/1353008987432767492.

Storey, William. January 5, 2021. Twitter Post. https://twitter.com/richenergyceo/status/1346580504963911692.

Storey, William. January 5, 2021. Twitter Post. https://twitter.com/richenergyceo/status/1346581890678075392.

Storey, William. July 11, 2020. Twitter Post. https://twitter.com/richenergyceo/status/1282037409610379265.

Storey, William. July 24, 2020. Twitter Post. https://twitter.com/richenergyceo/status/1286608356388540416.

Storey, William. July 26, 2020. Twitter Post. https://twitter.com/richenergyceo/status/1287496139181359114.

Storey, William. July 26, 2020. Twitter Post. https://twitter.com/richenergyceo/status/1287498187624910849.

Storey, William. July 3, 2020. Twitter Post. https://twitter.com/richenergyceo/status/1278990388980862976.

Storey, William. July 3, 2020. Twitter Post. https://twitter.com/richenergyceo/status/1279121089029906433.

Storey, William. July 4, 2020. Twitter Post. https://twitter.com/richenergyceo/status/1279520330806165506.

Storey, William. July 4, 2020. Twitter Post. https://twitter.com/richenergyceo/status/1279534838769422340.

Storey, William. July 5, 2020. Twitter Post. https://mobile.twitter.com/richenergyceo/status/1279847197425709060?lang=ar.

Storey, William. July 5, 2020. Twitter Post. https://twitter.com/richenergyceo/status/1279824307540103168.

Storey, William. July 6, 2020. Twitter Post. https://twitter.com/richenergyceo/status/1280198064310018048.

Storey, William. July 6, 2020. Twitter Post. https://twitter.com/richenergyceo/status/1280220838638358536.

Storey, William. June 7, 2020. Twitter Post. https://twitter.com/richenergyceo/status/1269736639250792449.

Storey, William. March 27, 2021. Twitter Post. https://twitter.com/richenergyceo/status/1375820740939878400.

Storey, William. May 24, 2020. Twitter Post. https://twitter.com/richenergyceo/status/1264706284366020608.

Storey, William. May 25, 2020. Twitter Post. https://twitter.com/richenergyceo/status/1265009434595639300.

Storey, William. May 28, 2020. Twitter Post. https://mobile.twitter.com/richenergyceo/status/1265942658142306304.

Storey, William. May 9, 2020. Twitter Post. https://twitter.com/richenergyceo/status/1259252610890190848.

Storey, William. November 24, 2021. Twitter Post. https://twitter.com/richenergyceo/status/1463638814577106949,

Storey, William. November 29, 2020. Twitter Post. https://twitter.com/richenergyceo/status/1333028320771010562.

Storey, William. November 30, 2021. Twitter Post. https://twitter.com/richenergyceo/status/1465758826796400645.

Storey, William. October 22, 2020. Twitter Post. https://twitter.com/richenergyceo/status/1319291891263795200.

Storey, William. October 23, 2020. Twitter Post. https://twitter.com/richenergyceo/status/1319652975665623043.

Storey, William. September 13, 2020. Twitter Post. https://twitter.com/richenergyceo/status/1305114602334806016.

Storey, William. September 3, 2020. Twitter Post. https://twitter.com/

richenergyceo/status/1301499475521929
232?lang=en.

Storey, William. Twitter Post. March 4, 2022. https://twitter.com/richenergy ceo/status/1499722983656542211.

Storey, William. Twitter Post. March 5, 2022. https://twitter.com/rich energyceo/status/1500055378041741314.

Storey, William. 2018. "Rich Energy Launch Official £100m Takeover of Force India." LinkedIn. https://www. linkedin.com/pulse/rich-energy-launch-official-100m-takeover-force-india-william-storey/.

"Twitter Advanced Search: 'Rich Energy 581.'" Twitter. https://twitter.com/searc h?f=tweets&q=rich+energy+581&src=t ypd.

WE ARE RICH ENERGY. July 27, 2020. Twitter Post. https://twitter.com/ weareRichEnergy/status/1288036 499133538308.

"What Is 'Rich Energy'?—Racing Comments—The Autosport Forums." 2018. *Autosport* Forums. https://forums. autosport.com/topic/211627-what-is-rich-energy/.

"What Is Rich Energy? : R/formula1." 2018. Reddit. https://www.reddit.com/ r/formula1/comments/a4ih0y/what_is_ rich_energy/.

Whyte Bikes. May 18, 2019. Twitter Post. https://twitter.com/WhyteBikes/ status/1129772100204601344.

"William Storey—Founder—Rich Energy | LinkedIn." https://uk.linkedin.com/ in/william-storey-58598356.

Windsor, Peter. May 17, 2018. Twitter Post. https://twitter.com/PeterDWindsor/ status/1129455626080403457.

Interviews

Blackstock, Elizabeth. Anonymous Motorsport Employee. Personal, August 2021.

Blackstock, Elizabeth. Azzy Iredale. Personal, August 2021.

Blackstock, Elizabeth. Bex Foot. Personal, August 2021.

Blackstock, Elizabeth. Dakota Schuetz. Personal, August 2021.

Blackstock, Elizabeth. Lawrence Chatters. Personal, December 2021.

Blackstock, Elizabeth. Luke Smith. Personal, August 2021.

Blackstock, Elizabeth. Stuart Taylor (Chain Bear). Personal, August 2021.

Courtenay-Stamp, Jeremy. Letter to William Storey, July 11, 2019.

King, Alanis. Anonymous. Personal, August 2021.

King, Alanis. Haas Employee 1. Personal, August 2021.

King, Alanis. Haas Employee 2. Personal, August 2021.

King, Alanis. Haas Employee 3. Personal, August 2021.

King, Alanis. Haas Employee 4. Personal, August 2021.

King, Alanis. Haas Employee 5. Personal, August 2021.

King, Alanis. Matt Farah taste test. Personal, 2021.

King, Alanis. Peter Habicht. Personal, August 2021.

King, Alanis. Romain Grosjean. Personal, March 2022.

King, Alanis. William Storey. Personal, March 14, 2019.

Emails and messages

Buglioni, Frank, March 2019.

Campbell, Ben. *Questions Re: West Ham's Involvement with Rich Energy,* August 23, 2021.

Chamberlain, Oscar. *A Few Quick Questions About Sunderland AFC-Rich Energy,* August 23, 2021.

de Kam, JP, August 20, 2021.

Farhoumand, Blake, September 1, 2021.

Henderson, Lance, August 25, 2021.

Loder, Carly. *Request for Comment | Rich Energy, the Book,* September 8, 2021.

Maher, Thomas, January 14, 2021.

Majstrović, Dražen, August 26, 2021.

Morrison, Stuart, July 15, 2019.

Morrison, Stuart, July 12, 2019.

Morrison, Stuart, March 14, 2019.

Morrissey, Paul. *A Quick Question About a Former QPR Player,* August 22, 2021.

Patterson, Ross, July 12, 2019.

Puz, Bernard, August 16, 2021.

Puz, Bernard, November 26, 2021.

Storey, William. Email to Guenther Steiner, July 10, 2019.

Storey, William. Email to Thomas Maher, January 2021.

Storey, William. July 14, 2019.

Storey, William, March 14, 2019.

Storey, William, May 14, 2019.

Watson, Calvin. *A Few Quick Questions About the Amber Lounge's Partnership with Rich Energy,* August 21, 2021.

Weston, Neville. *Interview Request | Rich Energy, the Book,* August 16, 2021.

Weston, Steve, August 31, 2021.

Windsor, Peter. *Interview Request | Rich Energy, the Book,* September 1, 2021.

Webpages

"1987 Kremer Porsche 962C." n.d. Gooding & Company. https://www.goodingco.com/vehicle/1987-kremer-porsche-962c/.

"1989 Race Results." n.d. F1. https://www.formula1.com/en/results.html/1989/races.html.

"1999 Constructor Standings." n.d. F1. https://www.formula1.com/en/results.html/1999/team.html.

"2016 Constructor Standings." n.d. F1. https://www.formula1.com/en/results.html/2016/team.html.

"2018 Constructor Standings." n.d. F1. https://www.formula1.com/en/results.html/2018/team.html.

"2019 Constructor Standings." n.d. F1. https://www.formula1.com/en/results.html/2019/team.html.

"2019 Race Results." n.d. F1. https://www.formula1.com/en/results.html/2019/races.html.

"2020 British Superbikes Points," n.d. https://www.britishsuperbike.com/media/727576/superbike-points.pdf.

"2020 Constructor Standings." n.d. F1. https://www.formula1.com/en/results.html/2020/team.html.

"2021 Bahrain GP Qualifying: Mazepin Spins at Turn 13." 2021. F1. https://www.formula1.com/en/latest/video.2021-bahrain-gp-qualifying-mazepin-spins-at-turn-13.1696505121639107291.html.

"2021 Constructor Standings." n.d. F1. https://www.formula1.com/en/results.html/2021/team.html.

"2021 Driver Standings: Nikita Mazepin." n.d. F1. https://www.formula1.com/en/results.html/2021/drivers/NIKMAZ01/-nikita-mazepin.html.

"2021 NTT IndyCar Series Car Specifications." n.d. IndyCar.com. https://www.indycar.com/Fan-Info/INDYCAR-101/The-Car-Dallara/IndyCar-Series-Chassis-Specifications.

"2022 F1 Pre-Season Track Session—Barcelona." Formula 1®—The Official F1® Website. https://www.formula1.com/en/racing/2022/Pre-Season-Track-Session.html.

"About." n.d. Brandsmiths. https://brandsmiths.co.uk/about/.

"About." n.d. Michael Crees. https://michaelcreesracing.com/about/.

"Abu Dhabi Grand Prix 2019: 'Bloody Undriveable' Haas 'Won't Go in the Museum,' Says Grosjean After Q1 Exit." 2019. F1. https://www.formula1.com/en/latest/article.bloody-undriveable-haas-wont-go-in-a-museum-says-grosjean-after-q1-exit.41weK9iMt9BHTaPEH1UDcT.html

Accesswire. 2019. "EarthWater Founder & CEO Enters Local Politics." *Associated Press.* https://apnews.com/press-release/pr-accesswire/defe8bdc21fb5dbf022870348d4f7cfe.

"Africa | Nigerian Businessman Gets Into Formula One." 1999. *BBC News.* http://news.bbc.co.uk/2/hi/africa/254363.stm.

Alonso, Eric. 2022. *Formula 1 Testing in Barcelona—Day 2.* Photograph. Barcelona, Spain, February 24. Getty.

Anderson, Ben. 2018. "Perez 'Heartbroken' Over Force India Legal Action to 'Save Team.'" *Autosport.* https://www.autosport.com/f1/news/perez-heartbroken-over-force-india-legal-action-to-save-team-5293468/5293468/.

"Arab Cleared of £300,000 'Con Tricks.'" 1999. *The Guardian.* https://www.theguardian.com/uk/1999/nov/09/3.

Associated Press. 1981. "Lotus Car Is Banned." *The Ithaca Journal,* April 24, 1981, 13. https://www.newspapers.com/image/255057644/?terms=Associated%20Press%20150000%20bail%20david%20thieme&match=1.

Associated Press. 1992. "Andrea Moda Team Ruled Out of Formula 1 Season." *Courier-Journal,* September 9, 1992, 40. https://www.newspapers.com/image/110705185/.

Associated Press. 1992. "Andrea Moda to Start Two GP Cars." *Courier-Post,* January 23, 1992, 32. https://www.newspapers.com/image/182844

498/?terms=andrea%20moda%20 formula&match=1.

Associated Press. 1992. "Auto Racing." *Kansas City Star,* September 9, 1992, 34. https://www.newspapers.com/ image/682342914/?terms=andrea%20 moda%20monaco%2011%20laps& match=1.

Associated Press. 2020. "Frank Williams Will Leave Family's F1 Team After 43 Years." *NBC Sports' MotorSportsTalk.* https://motorsports.nbcsports. com/2020/09/03/frank-williams-claire-f1-team/.

Baldwin, Alan. 2018. "Canadian Group Led by Stroll Paid $117 Million for Force India." *Reuters.* https://www. reuters.com/article/uk-motor-f1-forceindia/canadian-group-led-by-stroll-paid-117-million-for-force-india-idUKKCN1ME1LV.

Baldwin, Alan. 2018. "Motor Racing: Williams Losing Title Sponsor Martini at End of Year." *Reuters.* https:// www.reuters.com/article/us-motor-f1-williams-martini/motor-racing-williams-losing-title-sponsor-martini-at-end-of-year-idUSKCN1GB1IO.

Ballaban, Michael. 2019. "What Is Scuderia Ferrari's Mission Winnow Sponsor?" *Jalopnik.* https://jalopnik. com/what-the-fuck-is-mission-winnow-explained-1832730465.

Barnes, Joey. 2020. "Red Bull Racing Exec Touts Young American Driver Jak Crawford." *Autoweek.* https:// www.autoweek.com/racing/formula-1/ a31649109/red-bull-racing-exec-touts-american-development-driver-jak-crawford/.

Barretto, Lawrence. 2019. "Fight Night: How Brutal Singapore GP Pushes Drivers to the Limit." F1. https:// www.formula1.com/en/latest/ article.fight-night-why-brutal-singapore-gp-pushes-drivers-to-the-limit.6CWlvmuJZnPFm9KbBE0Zzk. html

Barretto, Lawrence. 2019. "The Winners and Losers of F1's First Pre-season Test of 2019." F1. https://www.formula1. com/en/latest/article.the-winners-and-losers-of-f1s-first-pre-season-test.12114NyKbJEWOy8PjJfDjj.html.

Barretto, Lawrence. 2020. "ANALYSIS: What Lies Ahead for Williams

After Shock Financial News?" F1. https://www.formula1.com/en/latest/ article.analysis-what-lies-ahead-for-williams-after-shock-financial-news.3jtmzE7GixI3a1DGwiwv3I.html.

Barretto, Lawrence. 2020. "'It Feels Like Grieving'—Claire Williams Opens Up on Her Family Leaving F1 for Good." F1. https://www. formula1.com/en/latest/article.it-feels-like-grieving-claire-williams-opens-up-on-her-family-leaving-f1-for.4AGYGdRBwxUDsOtQjmSkYJ. html.

"BBC Sport—Gloucester Owner and Former F1 Boss Tom Walkinshaw Dies." 2010. *BBC News.* http://news.bbc.co.uk/ sport2/hi/front_page/9280301.stm.

"Belgian Grand Prix 2019: Both Grosjean and Magnussen to Run Latest Haas Aero Spec at Spa." 2019. F1. https://www.formula1.com/en/latest/ article.both-grosjean-and-magnussen-to-run-latest-haas-aero-spec-at-spa. GTo9zn7bXkfmlf8ddZyCH.html.

"Belgian Grand Prix—Qualifying 1." 1992. F1. https://www.formula1.com/en/ results.html/1992/races/585/belgium/-qualifying-1.html.

Benson, Andrew. 2012. "Belgian Grand Prix Crash: Romain Grosjean Banned for One Race." *BBC.* https://www.bbc. com/sport/formula1/19458954.

Benson, Andrew. 2020. "Formula 1: Teams Formally Object to Ferrari Engine Settlement." *BBC.* https://www.bbc.com/ sport/formula1/51736247.

"Bernie Ecclestone Defends Ferrari's $100 Million Bonus." 2017. *Eurosport.* https:// www.eurosport.com/formula-1/bernie-ecclestone-defends-ferrari-s-100-million-bonus_sto6098061/story.shtml.

"Bernie Ecclestone Says Hitler Was a Man Who Got Things Done | Bernie Ecclestone." 2009. *The Guardian.* https:// www.theguardian.com/sport/2009/ jul/04/bernie-ecclestone-interview-hitler-saddam.

"Bernie Ecclestone: Women Drivers in F1 Would Not Be Taken Seriously." 2016. *BBC.* https://www.bbc.com/sport/ formula1/36086363.

"The Big Interview: David Sullivan—The Freedom Fighter." 2012. *Evening Standard.* https://www.standard.co.uk/ sport/football/the-big-interview-david-sullivan-the-freedom-fighter-6802989. html.

Blackstock, Elizabeth. 2019. "You Can Finally Buy Rich Energy in the US Through Walmart." *Jalopnik*. https://jalopnik.com/you-can-finally-buy-rich-energy-in-the-u-s-through-wal-1835479976.

Blackstock, Elizabeth, and Alanis King. 2019. "What You Find When You Look Into Rich Energy, the Mystery Sponsor of America's F1 Team." *Jalopnik*. https://jalopnik.com/what-you-find-when-you-look-into-rich-energy-the-myste-1833303620.

"Board of Directors Uralchem, JSC." n.d. Uralchem. https://www.uralchem.com/corporate_management/corporate-governance/board-of-directors-uralchem-jsc/.

"Boston Departs from KBM, Bell in for Kentucky." *Popular Speed*, n.d. https://popularspeed.com/boston-departs-from-kbm-bell-in-for-kentucky/.

Boucey, Bertrand. 2009. "Jean Todt Replaces Mosley as FIA President." *Reuters*. https://www.reuters.com/article/idINIndia-43388920091023.

Bowling, Chris. 2014. "Rich Lounge Provides Relaxed Atmosphere for Bar Goers." *Daily Nebraskan*. http://www.dailynebraskan.com/culture/rich-lounge-provides-relaxed-atmosphere-for-bar-goers/article_ef793f60-4472-11e4-a1f6-001a4bcf6878.html.

"Brazilian Grand Prix 2019: Hamilton Admits Albon Crash 'Completely My Fault.'" 2019. F1. https://www.formula1.com/en/latest/article.hamilton-says-albon-crash-completely-my-fault.245RL043CRlvS8fBy1rDnh.html.

"British Grand Prix: Race Recap." 2019. Haas F1 Team. https://www.haasf1team.com/news/british-grand-prix-race-recap-0.

Bruce, Chris. 2016. "Banned Lotus 88 F1 Car Explained by Colin Chapman's Son." *Autoblog*. https://www.autoblog.com/2016/04/04/lotus-88-carbon-fiber-f1-aerodynamics-video/.

Cairone, Andrea. 2013. "Venezuelan Scandal Freezes Motorsport Assets." *Road & Track*. https://www.roadandtrack.com/motorsports/news/a5774/venezuelan-financial-scandal-cuts-motorsport-sponsorship/.

"Cannot Race Indy 500." 1986. UPI. https://www.upi.com/Archives/1986/05/08/-Cannot-race-Indy-500/4197515908800/.

"Carroll and Fernandes Scoop Player Awards." 2017. West Ham United. https://www.whufc.com/news/articles/2017/may/09-may/carroll-and-fernandes-scoop-player-awards.

Casert, Raf. 1990. "Down and Out in Belgium." *Associated Press*. https://apnews.com/article/988c08a37242dd72c8lec4e0c1fe5952.

Chira, Susan. 1988. "JAPAN'S BIG SPENDERS." *The New York Times*. https://www.nytimes.com/1988/04/10/magazine/japan-s-big-spenders.html.

Church, Ben. 2020. "Nikita Mazepin: F1 Driver Apologizes for 'Inappropriate Behavior.'" *CNN*. https://www.cnn.com/2020/12/10/motorsport/nikita-mazepin-haas-apology-video-spt-intl/index.html.

"Club History." n.d. Royal Automobile Club. https://www.royalautomobileclub.co.uk/about-the-club/history/.

Cobb, Haydn. 2019. "F1 Barcelona F1 Test 1 Times—Monday 1PM | F1 | Crash-2019 Barcelona Pre-Season Test 1." *Crash.Net*. https://www.crash.net/f1/results/913037/1/barcelona-f1-test-1-times-monday-1pm.

Cobb, Haydn. 2019. "Haas Reveals Tweaked Livery After Rich Energy Split." *Crash.Net*. https://www.crash.net/f1/news/929316/1/haas-reveals-tweaked-livery-after-rich-energy-split.

Collantine, Keith. 2019. "F1: 'Surprised' Haas Will Run Rich Energy Logos at Silverstone." *RaceFans*. https://www.racefans.net/2019/07/11/surprised-haas-will-run-rich-energy-logos-at-silverstone/.

Collantine, Keith. 2019. "F1: Rich Energy Officially Dropped from Haas Team Name." *RaceFans*. https://www.racefans.net/2019/09/12/rich-energy-officially-dropped-from-haas-team-name/.

Collantine, Keith. 2019. "RaceFans Round-up: Steiner 'Doesn't Care' About Rich Energy Tweets." *RaceFans*. https://www.racefans.net/2019/07/16/racefans-round-up-16-07-2/.

Collantine, Keith. 2020. "Seven F1 Teams Demand Explanation Over

Secret FIA-Ferrari Settlement." *RaceFans.* https://www.racefans. net/2020/03/04/seven-non-ferrari-f1-teams-say-they-are-shocked-by-fias-power-unit-settlement/.

Colson, Thomas. 2019. "Full Text: Read Theresa May's Resignation Speech in Full." *Business Insider.* https://www. businessinsider.com/full-text-theresa-may-resignation-speech-2019-5.

"Constance Jablonski for Estée Lauder Idealist Campaign." 2017. *Fashion Gone Rogue,* October 27. https://www. fashiongonerogue.com/constance-jablonski-estee-lauder-campaign/.

Cooper, Adam. 2020. "FIA Tightens Podium Rules After Hamilton's Breonna Taylor Protest." *Motorsport. com.* https://us.motorsport.com/f1/news/fia-bans-t-shirts-f1-podium-ceremonies/4882622/.

Cooper, Adam. 2019. "Grosjean Reverts to Melbourne-spec Haas for Silverstone." *Autosport.* https://www. autosport.com/f1/news/grosjean-reverts-to-melbourne-spec-haas-for-silverstone-4991394/4991394/.

Cooper, Adam. 2019. "Haas Denies Reputation Harmed by Rich Energy Saga." *Motorsport.com.* https://www. motorsport.com/f1/news/haas-reputation-rich-energy-saga/4494414/.

Cooper, Adam. 2018. "Haas: Due Diligence Completed on New 2019 Title Sponsor Rich Energy." *Autosport.* https:// www.autosport.com/f1/news/139664/-haas-due-diligence-done-on-new-title-sponsor.

Cooper, Adam. 2020. "Mercedes Spent Over £333m to Win the 2019 F1 Title." *Motorsport.com.* https://www. motorsport.com/f1/news/mercedes-2019-budget-revealed/4868650/.

Cooper, Adam. 2019. "Rich Energy Investors Trying to Save Haas F1 Deal." *Motorsport.com.* https://www. motorsport.com/f1/news/rich-energy-investors-save-haas-deal/4492346/.

Cooper, Adam. 2020. "Radio Controlled Podium Robots 'Weird,' Says Hamilton." *Motorsport.com.* https:// us.motorsport.com/f1/news/podium-robots-weird-ott-hamilton/4833912/.

Cooper, Adam. 2020. "Why the Once Mighty Williams F1 Team Is Up for Sale." *Motorsport.com.* https://www.

motorsport.com/f1/news/williams-teams-sale-analysis/4798512/.

"Cyril De Rouvre." Libération. https:// www.liberation.fr/futurs/1994/12/24/-cyril-de-rouvre_116185.

"Cyril De Rouvre Sort De La Route." 2021. *L'Humanité,* March 28. https://www. humanite.fr/node/72016.

Dagys, John. 2014. "Zogaib, Loles Sentenced to Prison Terms." *Sportscar365.* https://sportscar365.com/imsa/zogaib-loles-sentenced-to-prison-terms/.

"Danieli Style," n.d. https://web.archive. org/web/20140517050512/http:// danielistyle.com/.

"David Sullivan—living a Dream in Theydon Bois, Essex." 2010. *Great British Life.* https://www.essexlifemag.co.uk/ people/celebrity-interviews/david-sullivan-living-a-dream-in-theydon-bois-essex-1-1639861.

Davies, Alex. 2014. "One of F1's Most Dangerous Tracks Is Back." *WIRED.* https:// www.wired.com/2014/06/f1-austria-grand-prix-track/.

Davies, Amanda, and George Ramsay. 2020. "Often 'Black People Are More Racist Than White People,' Says Ex-F1 Supremo Bernie Ecclestone." *CNN.* https://edition.cnn.com/2020/06/26/ motorsport/bernie-ecclestone-formula-one-motorsport-lewis-hamilton-spt-intl/index.html.

Davison, Drew. 2016. "From Hay Farmer to Daytona 500: The Improbable Story of Robert Richardson, Jr." *Fort Worth Star-Telegram.* https://www.star-telegram.com/sports/nascar-auto-racing/article61378457.html.

"DC Solar Expands Partnership with Kyle Larson, CGR." 2018. NASCAR. com. https://www.nascar.com/news-media/2018/01/16/kyle-larson-jamie-mcmurray-sponsor-dc-solar/.

"DC Solar to Expand Partnership with CGR to Include a Full-Time NXS Entry in 2019 with Ross Chastain." 2018. Chip Ganassi Racing. http:// www.chipganassiracing.com/ News/2018/11/DC-Solar-to-Expand-Partnership-with-CGR-to-Include-a-Full-Time-NXS-Entry-in-2019-with-Ross-Chastain.aspx.

Dixon, Ed. 2020. "Report: Williams F1 Lose Another Major Sponsor with Rexona Exit." *SportsPro Media.* https://

www.sportspromedia.com/news/-williams-f1-rexona-sponsor-exit-tata-omnitude-symantec/

Donnelly, Mark. 2020. "Who Is William Storey? The Rich Energy CEO Claiming to Have Launched a Takeover Bid for Sunderland AFC." *Sunderland Echo.* https://www.sunderlandecho.com/sport/football/sunderland-afc/-who-william-storey-rich-energy-ceo-claiming-have-launched-takeover-bid-sunderland-afc-2923233.

Doodson, Mike, and Simon Arron. n.d. "Elio De Angelis: Money Greased the Wheels, but Talent Turned Them." *Motor Sport Magazine.* https://www.motorsportmagazine.com/archive/article/june-2011/68/money-greased-wheels-talent-turned-them.

Dowell, Ben. 2008. "Max Mosley V News of the World Timeline." *The Guardian.* https://www.theguardian.com/media/2008/jul/24/privacy.newsoftheworld.

Duncan, Lewis. 2020. "Rich Energy to Sponsor Road Racing Team OMG." *Motorsport.com.* https://us.motorsport.com/bike/news/rich-energy-omg-racing-sponsorship/4685676/.

Duxbury, Anna. 2020. "How Much Does an F1 Car Cost, and Other F1 Questions Answered." *Autosport.* https://www.autosport.com/f1/news/how-much-does-an-f1-car-cost-and-other-f1-questions-answered-4983337/4983337/.

"EarthWater Exclusively Sold on Amazon Joins BK Racing Team as the Official Bottled Water for the 2018 NASCAR Season." 2018. *Yahoo Finance.* https://www.yahoo.com/news/earth water-exclusively-sold-amazon-joins-180000112.html.

"Ecclestone Challenges $1.5 Billion Tax Demand." 2015. *CNBC.* https://www.cnbc.com/2015/05/22/ecclestone-challenges-15-billion-tax-demand.html.

"Ecclestone: Hamilton Racism Row 'Nonsense.'" 2008. *The Guardian.* https://www.theguardian.com/sport/2008/nov/06/lewishamilton-formulaone.

Edmondson, Laurence. 2020. "FIA Offers Clarification Over Ferrari Engine Settlement Following Backlash from Rival Teams." *ESPN.* https://www.espn.com/f1/story/_/id/28842 333/fia-offers-clarification-ferrari-engine-settlement.

Edmondson, Laurence. 2019. "Haas Title Sponsor Rich Energy Loses Court Case Over Logo." *ESPN.* ESPN Internet Ventures, May 14. https://www.espn.com/f1/story/_/id/26744828/haas-title-sponsor-rich-energy-loses-court-case-logo.

Edwards, Jim. 2013. "Here's What It Costs to Sponsor a NASCAR." *Business Insider.* https://www.businessinsider.com/heres-what-it-costs-to-sponsor-a-nascar-2013-1.

El Nuevo Herald. 1992. "Mañana Se Larga GP De Sudáfrica." February 29, 27. https://www.newspapers.com/image/636767918/?terms=andrea%20moda&match=1.

"Energy Pack Subscription." Rich Energy, n.d. https://web.archive.org/web/20200413145532/https://www.richenergy.life/.

Errington, Tom. 2019. "Haas Sets Date for Expected Rich Energy-style 2019 F1 Livery Unveil." *Autosport.* https://www.autosport.com/f1/news/haas-sets-date-for-expected-rich-energy-style-2019-f1-livery-unveil-5283412/5283412/.

"F1 Calendar 2020—Enjoy a Record-breaking 22 Races in the 2020 Season." 2019. F1. https://www.formula1.com/en/latest/article.record-breaking-22-race-f1-calendar-set-for-2020.7vdbREiAYJKP5Ey8whglC2.html

"FP1: Grosjean Loses Front Wing in Bizarre Pit-exit Spin." 2019. F1. Https://www.formula1.com/en/video/2019/7/FP1__Grosjean_loses_front_wing_in_bizarre_pit-exit_spin.html.

"F1 Launches on the Grand Scale." *ESPN,* January 2014. http://en.espnf1.com/blogs/motorsport/story/142963.html.

"F1 Pre-Season Testing 2019 Day 2: Ferrari Fastest for Second Straight Day with Charles Leclerc." 2019. F1. https://www.formula1.com/en/latest/article.-f1-pre-season-testing-leclerc-puts-ferrari-fastest-for-second-straight-day.7J8rU3ThUzIuDErC0VBB3x.html.

"F1-2016 Australian Grand Prix—Friday Press Conference | Federation Internationale De L'Automobile." 2016. FIA. https://www.fia.com/news/f1-2016-australian-grand-prix-friday-press-conference.

F1. 2019. "Haas: We Should Have Listened to the Drivers More amid Struggles: Formula 1." October 17. https://www.formula1.com/en/latest/article.haas-we-should-have-listened-to-the-drivers-more-amid-struggles.1AeEknt0XzyECdaCRSu0kh.html.

"Fact Sheet: United States, G7 and EU Impose Severe and Immediate Costs on Russia." 2022. The White House. April 6. https://www.whitehouse.gov/briefing-room/statements-releases/2022/04/06/fact-sheet-united-states-g7-and-eu-impose-severe-and-immediate-costs-on-russia/.

"'Fake Sheikh' Gave Cher Sports Car." 1999. *BBC News.* http://news.bbc.co.uk/2/hi/uk_news/479506.stm.

"Fake Sheikh Lavished 'Gift' on Singer Cher." 1999. *Oxford Mail.* https://www.oxfordmail.co.uk/news/6635042.fake-sheikh-lavished-gift-singer-cher/.

"Fan-Favourite British Touring Car Star Michael Crees Links Up with Rich Energy." 2020. Michael Crees. https://michaelcreesracing.com/fan-favourite-british-touring-car-star-michael-crees-links-up-with-rich-energy/.

"Fastest Speed Outright in a Formula One Grand Prix." 2005. Guinness World Records. https://www.guinnessworldrecords.com/world-records/fastest-speed-outright-in-a-formula-one-grand-prix.

Ferrier, Laurent, François Sérvanin, and François Trisconi. n.d. "70 Years of Porsche Sports Cars." https://presskit.porsche.de/anniversaries/en/70-years-porsche-sports-cars/topic/category/motorsporterfolge/items/en-le-mans-1979-the-year-of-the-935-721.html.

FIA. 2017. "Halo Protection System to Be Introduced for 2018." F1. https://www.formula1.com/en/latest/headlines/2017/7/halo-protection-system-to-be-introduced-for-2018.html.

"FIA Announces World Motor Sport Council Decisions in Relation to the Situation in Ukraine." Federation Internationale de l'Automobile, March 2, 2022. https://www.fia.com/news/fia-announces-world-motor-sport-council-decisions-relation-situation-ukraine.

"Formula 1 Etihad Airways Abu Dhabi Grand Prix 2019—Qualifying." 2021. F1. https://www.formula1.com/en/results.html/2019/races/1020/abu-dhabi/qualifying.html.

"Formula 1 Gulf Air Bahrain Grand Prix 2022—Race Result." 2022. F1. https://www.formula1.com/en/results.html/2022/races/1124/bahrain/race-result.html.

"Formula 1 Gulf Air Bahrain Grand Prix 2021—Race Result." 2021. F1. https://www.formula1.com/en/results.html/2021/races/1064/bahrain/race-result.html.

"Formula 1 Pirelli Grosser Preis Der Steiermark 2020—Race Result." 2020. F1. https://www.formula1.com/en/results.html/2020/races/1046/austria/race-result.html.

"Formula 1 Rolex Grosser Preis Von Österreich 2020—Qualifying." 2020. F1. https://www.formula1.com/en/results.html/2020/races/1045/austria/qualifying.html.

"Formula 1 Rolex Grosser Preis Von Österreich 2020—Race Result." 2020. F1. https://www.formula1.com/en/results.html/2020/races/1045/austria/race-result.html.

Freeman, Glenn. 2018. "Sebastien Bourdais Hits Back at Haas F1 Claims About American Drivers." *Autosport.* https://www.autosport.com/f1/news/sebastien-bourdais-hits-back-at-haas-f1-claims-about-american-drivers-4987138/4987138/.

"French Grand Prix: Race Recap." 2019. Haas F1 Team. https://www.haasf1team.com/news/french-grand-prix-race-recap-0.

Galarza, Daniela. 2015. "Why You Should Know the Name Roger Vergé." *Eater.* https://www.eater.com/2015/6/8/8745361/chef-roger-verge-died.

Gallagher, Danny. 2008. "Jury Acquits Ibrahim of Theft, Deception Charges | News | Starlocalmedia.com." *Star Local Media.* https://starlocalmedia.com/mckinneycouriergazette/news/jury-acquits-ibrahim-of-theft-deception-charges/article_385dc42a-8fce-5805-8fbf-5f66ed9af3f2.html.

Galloway, James. 2020. "Lewis Hamilton Expects New Guidelines After Wearing Breonna Taylor T-shirt." *Sky Sports.* https://www.skysports.com/f1/news/24181/12080537/lewis-hamilton-expects-new-guidelines-after-wearing-breonna-taylor-t-shirt.

Galloway, James, and Matt Morlidge. 2019. "Haas Reveal Striking New Black and Gold Livery for F1 2019 Car." *Sky Sports*. https://www.skysports.com/f1/news/12433/11601806/haas-reveal-striking-new-black-and-gold-livery-for-f1-2019-car

"Gene Haas—The Official Stewart-Haas Racing Website." n.d. Stewart-Haas Racing. https://www.stewarthaasracing.com/gene-haas/.

George, Patrick. 2019. "F1 Sponsor Rich Energy Now Blames Rogue Employee for Yesterday's Bizarre 'PC Attitude' Tweet [UPDATE]." *Jalopnik*. https://jalopnik.com/f1-sponsor-rich-energy-now-blames-rogue-employee-for-ye-1836281581.

Gerrard, Bradley. 2018. "Rich Energy Chief: 'I Fell Into the Drinks Business After Meeting a Mad Scientist.'" *The Telegraph*. https://www.telegraph.co.uk/business/2018/03/30/rich-energy-chief-fell-drinks-business-meeting-mad-scientist/.

Ghosh, Suvashree. 2021. "Banks Recover Nearly $1 Billion from India's 'King of Good Times' Mallya." *Bloomberg.com*. https://www.bloomberg.com/news/articles/2021-06-23/banks-recover-about-1-billion-from-indian-ex-billionaire-mallya.

Gilboy, James. 2018. "Former Force India F1 Team Owner Vijay Mallya to Be Extradited to India, UK Court Approves." *The Drive*. https://www.thedrive.com/accelerator/25406/former-force-india-f1-team-owner-vijay-mallya-to-be-extradited-to-india-uk-court-approves.

Gilboy, James. 2018. "Haas F1 Signs Soft Drink Startup Rich Energy as 2019 Title Sponsor." *The Drive*. https://www.thedrive.com/accelerator/24506/-haas-f1-signs-soft-drink-startup-rich-energy-as-2019-title-sponsor.

"Global Freedom of Expression | Case of Mosley V. the United Kingdom—Global Freedom of Expression." n.d. Global Freedom of Expression. https://globalfreedomofexpression.columbia.edu/cases/case-mosley-v-united-kingdom/.

GMM. 2016. "Report: Lance Stroll's Father Spent $80 Million to Get Son Williams F1 Seat." *Autoweek*. https://www.autoweek.com/racing/formula-1/a1857276/report-lance-strolls-father-spent-80-million-get-son-f1-seat/.

Gomez, Dessi. 2020. "Watch First 'Hamilton' Film Trailer Ahead of Disney+ Release." *Los Angeles Times*. https://www.latimes.com/entertainment-arts/movies/story/2020-06-22/first-hamilton-film-trailer-disney.

"Grosjean and Magnussen Announce They Are to Leave Haas at the End of 2020." 2020. F1. https://www.formula1.com/en/latest/article.breaking-grosjean-and-magnussen-announce-they-are-to-leave-haas-at-the-end.5pXS3lUq9uQIbBZvXo4lcV.html.

"Grosjean and Magnussen's Driving 'not Acceptable' Says Furious Steiner| Formula 1°." 2019. F1. https://www.formula1.com/en/latest/article.grosjean-and-magnussens-driving-not-acceptable-says-furious-steiner.3l9S6OTuC5opdznf2ZTGms.html.

"Grosjean Baffled After Haas Lack Pace in Italy." 2019. F1. https://www.formula1.com/en/latest/article.grosjean-baffled-after-haas-lack-pace-in-italy.5taGJIz5JC8KuHE4mekbrw.html.

"Grosjean: Haas Had the Pace to Split Red Bulls in China Qualifying." 2019. F1. https://www.formula1.com/en/latest/article.grosjean-haas-had-the-pace-to-split-red-bulls.6vwD0pC8iE0N595mhItJio.html.

Guardian. 1992. "Motor Racing." March 31, 19. https://www.newspapers.com/image/260289624/?terms=andrea%20moda&match=1.

"Guenther Steiner." n.d. Haas F1 Team. https://www.haasf1team.com/season/team/guenther-steiner.

"Guenther Steiner 'More Amazed Than Upset' at Haas Pace Loss at Bahrain Grand Prix 2019." 2019. F1. https://www.formula1.com/en/latest/article.steiner-more-amazed-than-upset-at-haas-pace-loss-in-bahrain.3XCL1obSlJgcnnySobdaVR.html.

"Haas 'Dealing With' Nikita Mazepin, F1 Team Taking Actions 'Seriously.'" 2020. *Sky Sports*. https://www.skysports.com/f1/news/32133/12158139/haas-dealing-with-nikita-mazepin-f1-team-taking-actions-seriously.

"Haas 'Cautiously Optimistic' Ahead of 'Significant' Upgrade for Spain." 2019. F1. https://www.formula1.com/en/latest/article.haas-cautiously-optimistic-ahead-of-significant-upgrade-for-spain.4l0q0sXlTBzxRwaYyKpwPr.html

"Haas Declare France Their 'Worst Weekend' Ever in F1." 2019. F1. https://www.formula1.com/en/latest/article.haas-france-was-our-worst-weekend-in-f1-ever.4ZbcoyIt8HEQh50KZaSSOW.html.

"Haas F1 Reveal as Rich Energy Counters Criticism—Formula 1 Videos." 2019. *Motorsport.com*. https://www.motorsport.com/f1/video/haas-f1-reveal-as-rich-energy-counters-criticism/382091/.

"Haas F1 Team Earns Points in Debut Race." 2016. Haas F1 Team. https://www.haasf1team.com/news/haas-f1-team-earns-points-debut-race.

"Haas F1 Team Secures 2017 Driver Lineup by Signing Kevin Magnussen to Join Romain Grosjean." 2016. Haas F1 Team. https://www.haasf1team.com/news/haas-f1-team-secures-2017-driver-lineup-signing-kevin-magnussen-join-romain-grosjean.

"Haas Ready to Forget 2019 After Final 'Hard Fight' in Abu Dhabi." 2019. F1. https://www.formula1.com/en/latest/article.haas-ready-to-forget-2019-after-final-hard-fight-in-abu-dhabi.3I2p3AfoKMJ4NSHzLBLexV.html.

"Haas Still Perplexed by 'Weird' Pace After Hungarian Grand Prix." 2019. F1. https://www.formula1.com/en/latest/article.haas-still-perplexed-by-weird-pace-fluctuations.1BINaE4frvYMCplEGd5I4D.html.

"Haas to Use All-White Livery on Final Day of Barcelona Pre-Season Running: Formula 1." F1. https://www.formula1.com/en/latest/article.haas-to-use-all-white-livery-on-final-day-of-barcelona-pre-season-running.4yJ2e7yoN2hWYrTWFXBzk6.html.

"Haas Unveil New Black-and-Gold F1 Livery for 2019." 2019. F1. https://www.formula1.com/en/latest/article.haas-unveil-new-black-and-gold-f1-livery-for-2019.3fIfnfT5NoMoLcuitzNJrt.html.

"Haas VF-19: All the Angles of the 2019 F1 Car." 2019. F1. https://www.formula1.com/en/latest/article.first-look-all-the-angles-of-haas-new-2019-livery.l4qlJmDtedmTkv0zan1bH.html.

"Haas Won't Take Chance on Rookie After 2019 Struggles—Guenther Steiner." 2019. F1. https://www.formula1.com/en/latest/article.haas-unlikely-to-chance-a-rookie-after-2019-struggles-says-steiner.6yp1Cu4mFvIgTBXIspDnLQ.html.

"Haas' Problems Cannot Get Any Worse—Steiner." 2019. F1. https://www.formula1.com/en/latest/article.haas-form-cannot-get-any-worse-steiner.1dX5xlgx5t0GlzeUT9t903.html.

Haislop, Tadd. 2020. "Indy 500 Purse, Payout Breakdown: How Much Prize Money Does the Winner Get in 2020?" *Sporting News*. https://www.sportingnews.com/us/motorsports/news/indy-500-payouts-purse-2020-prize-money/16x9jbef8xozfl02akgurl2cjm.

Hall, Sam. 2017. "Bernie Ecclestone: FIA Conspired to Help Ferrari Gain an Advantage in F1." *Autoweek*. https://www.autoweek.com/racing/formula-1/a1833766/bernie-ecclestone-fia-conspired-help-ferrari-gain-advantage-f1/.

Hardigree, Matt. 2014. "Bernie Ecclestone Doesn't Care About Social Media, Because Greed." *Jalopnik*. https://jalopnik.com/bernie-ecclestone-doesnt-care-about-social-media-becau-1586477212#!.

Henry, Alan. 1992. "Italy's Fast Lady Chases the Right Formula." *Guardian*, February 28, 1992, 17. https://www.newspapers.com/image/259960752/?terms=andrea%20moda%20formula&match=1.

Henry, Alan. 1992. "Mansell Firmly in the Driving Seat." *Guardian*, May 2, 1992, 19.

Henry, Alan. 1992. "McLaren Teething Troubles Leave Senna Down in Mouth." *Guardian*, April 4, 1992, 14. https://www.newspapers.com/image/260291252/?terms=andrea%20moda&match=1.

Henry, Alan. 1993. "Brundle Could Give Ligier an All-British Line-up." *The Guardian*, January 13, 1993, 17. https://www.newspapers.com/image/260295409/?terms=Cyril%20Rouvre%20ligier&match=1.

"History | Results | Statistics." n.d. 24 Hours of Le Mans. https://assets. lemans.org/explorer/pdf/courses/2018/-24-heures-du-mans/press-kit/uk/-statistiques-historiques-en.pdf.

"History—Whyte Bikes USA." n.d. Whyte Bikes USA. https://www.whyteusa.bike/pages/history.

Hong, K.P. 1990. "World Bank Suspends Nomura, Nikko Securities; Gangster Ties Reported Reason." *Associated Press.* https://apnews.com/article/ee901 cf4fc731ebdbf9ea023856b8f27.

Hoops, Stephanie. 2009. "Haas About to Leave Prison." Home. https://archive. vcstar.com/business/haas-about-to-leave-prison-ep-371964445-350884221. html.

Hope, Craig. 2018. "British Energy Drinks Company in Talks to Buy Force India." *Daily Mail.* https://www. dailymail.co.uk/sport/formulaone/-article-5414721/British-energy-drinks-company-talks-buy-Force-India.html.

"How F1 Technology Has Supercharged the World." 2019. F1. https://www. formula1.com/en/latest/article.how-f1-technology-has-supercharged-the-world.6Gtk3hBxGyUGbNH0q8vDQK. html.

Hughes, Mark, and Giorgio Piola. 2018. "Analysing the Aerodynamic Changes Coming to F1 in 2019." F1. https:// www.formula1.com/en/latest/article. tech-tuesday-looking-ahead-to-the-aerodynamic-changes-coming-to-f1-in-2019.3G8r94lzEAEiG8WS0oCm8y.html.

Hunt, Ben. 2019. "Haas F1 Team Will Beat Red Bull This Season, According to Sponsors Rich Energy." *The Sun.* https://www.thesun.co.uk/sport/motorsport/8372522/f1-haas-beat-red-bull-2019/.

Hunt, Ben. 2019. "Rich Energy Drink Chief Labels F1 Team Haas 'Milk Float at Back of Grid' After Pulling Plug on Sponsorship." *The Sun.* https://www.thesun. co.uk/sport/motorsport/9483957/rich-energy-f1-haas-team-sponsorship/.

Hunter, James. 2020. "William Storey on Why He Cannot Name His 'Blue Chip' Backers, in Part Two of Our Q&A." *Evening Chronicle.* https://www. chroniclelive.co.uk/sport/football/-football-news/william-storey-cannot-name-blue-19486649.

Hurd, Rick. 2018. "Martinez: FBI Raids Home of Martinez Clippers Owners." *The Mercury News.* https://www. mercurynews.com/2018/12/20/fbi-raids-home-of-martinez-clippers-owners/.

Hynes, Justin. 2017. "Sebastian Vettel Crowned 2013 F1 Champion." Red Bull. https://www.redbull.com/us-en/-sebastian-vettel-f1-champion-2013.

"I-Nova Medicinska Istrazivanja D.O.O. Company Profile." Dun & Bradstreet. https://www.dnb.com/business-directory/company-profiles. i-nova_medicinska_istrazivanja_doo .8227661231ff7ac8040cbc035b3cffc0. html?aka_re=2%3Faka_re.

"Instagrammer Who Was Groped by Mazepin Speaks Out Against 2021 Haas Driver." 2020. *MARCA.* https://www. marca.com/en/lifestyle/2020/12/18/5fdc b7c2ca47416d1c8b4571.html.

"The Italian Job." 2016. Haas F1 Team. https://www.haasf1team.com/news/italian-job.

Jacobs, Caleb. 2020. "Now Rich Energy Wants to Sponsor the Ailing Williams F1 Team." *The Drive.* https://www. thedrive.com/accelerator/33780/now-rich-energy-wants-to-sponsor-the-ailing-williams-f1-team.

"Japanese GP Tyrrell Friday Notes." 1999. *Motorsport.* https://au.motorsport.com/f1/news/japanese-gp-tyrrell-friday-notes/1731108/.

"Jean-Pierre Van Rossem Obituary | Register." 2019. *The Times.* https://www. thetimes.co.uk/article/jean-pierre-van-rossem-obituary-0z5khsxm8.

"Jeffrey Epstein's Little Black Book." Scribd. https://www.scribd.com/document/416489768/Jeffrey-Epstein-s-Little-Black-Book.

Kalinauckas, Alex. 2019. "Rich Energy 'Bringing Back" JPS Lotus Look with Haas Livery." *Motorsport.com.* https:// us.motorsport.com/f1/news/haas-rich-energy-jps-lotus-look/4334026/.

Kerr, Luke. 2015. "Watch as a Terrifying Shark Swims Into Someone's Backyard." *USA Today's FTW.* https://ftw.usatoday. com/2015/04/terrifying-shark-swims-backyard-video.

King, Alanis. 2016. "Lewis Hamilton Gets Banned from Using Snapchat in F1 Paddock, Does It Anyway." *Jalopnik.*

https://jalopnik.com/snapchat-helped-f1-during-the-australian-gp-snapchat-1768691589.

King, Alanis. 2017. "Bernie Ecclestone Hates These Damn Kids and Their Social Media." *Jalopnik.* https://jalopnik.com/bernie-ecclestone-hates-these-damn-kids-and-their-socia-1795651283.

King, Alanis. 2017. "Driver Tied to Alleged $25 Million Scheme to Fund His Career Owes Former Team a Lot of Money." *Jalopnik.* https://jalopnik.com/driver-tied-to-alleged-25-million-scheme-to-fund-his-c-1819621478.

King, Alanis. 2018. "Force India F1 Forfeits Its Title Points and Changes Its Name Right Before the Belgian Grand Prix." *Jalopnik.* https://jalopnik.com/force-india-f1-forfeits-its-title-points-and-changes-it-1828558256.

King, Alanis. 2018. "Lance Stroll Joins F1 Team His Father Bought a Few Months Ago." *Jalopnik.* https://jalopnik.com/nepotism-wins-1830766974.

King, Alanis. 2019. "Final Wheel Movement Decided Controversial Penalty That Undid Ferrari's F1 Win: Report." *Jalopnik.* https://jalopnik.com/final-wheel-movement-decided-controversial-penalty-that-1835372654.

King, Alanis. 2019. "Haas F1 Sponsor Rich Energy Claims to Have Terminated Contract, Citing 'PC Attitude' [Update: Haas Says They're Still Partners]." *Jalopnik.* https://jalopnik.com/haas-f1-sponsor-rich-energy-claims-to-have-terminated-c-1836250021.

King, Alanis. 2019. "Haas F1 Sponsor Rich Energy Denied Appeal After Losing Logo Case." *Jalopnik.* https://jalopnik.com/haas-f1-sponsor-rich-energy-denied-appeal-after-losing-1835947104.

King, Alanis. 2019. "In Memoriam: Rich Energy's Tweets." *Jalopnik.* https://jalopnik.com/in-memoriam-rich-energys-tweets-1839096792.

King, Alanis. 2019. "Looks Like Haas F1 Is Going After Rich Energy." *Jalopnik.* https://jalopnik.com/looks-like-haas-f1-is-going-after-rich-energy-1836358665.

King, Alanis. 2019. "Now Red Bull Might Be Suing Rich Energy." *Jalopnik.* https://jalopnik.com/now-red-bull-might-be-suing-rich-energy-1836490303.

King, Alanis. 2019. "Power Struggle Continues at F1 Sponsor Rich Energy." *Jalopnik.* https://jalopnik.com/power-struggle-at-rich-energy-continues-as-its-accused-1836316162.

King, Alanis. 2019. "Rich Energy Pulls Logo from Haas F1 Cars After Loss in Copyright Case." *Jalopnik.* https://jalopnik.com/rich-energy-pulls-logo-from-haas-f1-cars-after-loss-in-1835322740.

King, Alanis. 2019. "Rich Energy: Not Dead Yet!" *Jalopnik.* https://jalopnik.com/rich-energy-not-dead-yet-1838359045.

King, Alanis. 2019. "Sebastian Vettel's F1 Canadian Grand Prix 'Win' Immortalized by Very Unusual Diecast." *Jalopnik.* https://jalopnik.com/sebastian-vettels-f1-canadian-grand-prix-win-immorta-1835908480.

King, TJ. 2013. "Rich Bar & Lounge Opens in Once-Controversial Location." *Lincoln Journal Star.* https://journalstar.com/entertainment/misc/rich-bar-lounge-opens-in-once-controversial-location/article_7c979246-946f-562a-bc30-7e4279f17e94.html.

Kirby, Jen, and Jonathan Guyer. 2022. "Russia's War in Ukraine, Explained." *Vox.* February 24. https://www.vox.com/2022/2/23/22948534/russia-ukraine-war-putin-explosions-invasion-explained.

Konotey, Olivia. 2020. "F1 GP, Formula One News: Loan from Nicholas Latifi's Dad." *Bloomberg.com.* https://www.bloomberg.com/news/articles/2020-04-11/canadian-food-tycoon-rescues-struggling-formula-1-team.

Krause, Kevin. 2020. "Top Execs of Dallas-area 'Miracle' Mineral Water Company Admit to Massive Fraud." *Dallas Morning News.* https://www.dallasnews.com/business/local-companies/2020/06/12/top-execs-of-dallas-miracle-mineral-water-company-admit-to-massive-fraud/.

Larson, Selena. 2017. "Welcome to a World with 280-character Tweets." *CNN Business.* https://money.cnn.com/2017/11/07/technology/twitter-280-character-limit/index.html.

"Lauda Seeks New Sponsor for Famous Red Cap." 2010. *Motorsport.com.* https://us.motorsport.com/f1/

news/lauda-seeks-new-sponsor-for-famous-red-cap/2452740/.

"League One Table & Standings." 2020. Sky Sports Football. https://www.skysports.com/league-1-table/2019.

"Les Millions De Cyril." L'Express.fr, January 6, 1994. https://www.lexpress.fr/informations/les-millions-de-cyril_596731.html.

"Listings of WHO's Response to COVID-19." 2020. World Health Organization. https://www.who.int/news-room/detail/29-06-2020-covidtimeline

Long, Dustin. 2018. "Bankruptcy Judge Appoints Trustee to Manage BK Racing—NASCAR Talk." *NBC Sports*. https://nascar.nbcsports.com/2018/03/28/bankruptcy-judge-appoints-trustee-to-manage-bk-racing/.

MacDonald, Ian. 1993. "Englishmen Become Driving Force for French Team Ligier." *The Gazette*, June 11, 1993, 51. https://www.newspapers.com/image/424316949/?terms=cyril%20rouvre&match=1.

"Magnussen Gets Haas Aero Upgrades for Germany as Grosjean Keeps Australia Spec." 2019. F1. https://www.formula1.com/en/latest/article.-magnussen-gets-haas-upgrades-for-germany-grosjean-keeps-australia-spec.6f9k2Xx9XK2whjtB9yswsg.html.

"Magnussen: Haas Upgrade Performance Deficit 'Confusing'." 2019. F1. https://www.formula1.com/en/latest/article.-magnussen-haas-upgrade-performance-deficit-confusing.19ZjXDoDE8fvOuaEnRzZQ0.html.

Maher, Thomas. 2019. "Formula 1—Rich Energy Confirm Contentious Tweet Was 'Rogue.'" *Formula Spy*. https://formulaspy.com/f1/rich-energy-confirm-contentious-tweet-was-rogue-62549.

Maher, Thomas. 2021. "Formula 1—Storey: Rich Energy's Return to F1 Will Be 'Vindication.'" *Formula Spy*. https://formulaspy.com/f1/storey-rich-energys-return-to-f1-will-be-vindication-73267.

"Mansoor Ijaz: Fixer in Pakistan's 'Memogate' Row." 2012. BBC. https://www.bbc.com/news/world-asia-16649034.

Marchetti, Silvia. 2014. "The South Tyrol Identity Crisis: To Live in Italy, but Feel Austrian." *The Guardian*. https://www.theguardian.com/education/2014/may/30/south-tyrol-live-in-italy-feel-austrian.

"Marussia Hand Rossi Race Debut in Singapore." 2015. F1. https://www.formula1.com/en/latest/headlines/2015/9/-marussia-hand-rossi-race-debut-in-singapore.html.

Maxouris, Christina. 2020. "Judge Sets Derek Chauvin's Bail at $1.25 Million in George Floyd's Death." *CNN*. https://www.cnn.com/2020/06/08/us/derek-chauvin-court-monday-george-floyd-latest/index.html.

"May 4 Unofficial Election Results for Addison City Council Race." 2019. Visit Addison. https://visitaddison.com/marketing/may-4-unofficial-election-results-addison-city-council-race.

"Mazesp.in." n.d. Nikita Mazespin. http://mazesp.in.

McFadin, Daniel. 2018. "FBI Conducts Raid of DC Solar's Headquarters, CEO's Home." *NASCAR on NBC Sports*. https://nascar.nbcsports.com/2018/12/21/-report-fbi-conducts-raid-of-dc-solars-headquarters-ceos-home/.

McFadin, Daniel. 2019. "DC Solar Bankruptcy Auction Includes Kyle Larson's Daytona-winning Car." *NASCAR on NBC Sports*. https://nascar.nbcsports.com/2019/09/25/dc-solar-bankruptcy-auction-includes-kyle-larsons-daytona-winning-car/.

McRae, Donald. 2011. "Why Adrian Newey Just Cannot Bear to Watch the New Senna Movie." *The Guardian*. https://www.theguardian.com/sport/2011/may/17/adrian-newey-red-bull-ayrton-senna.

McVeigh, Tracy. 2016. "As F1 Roars Into Baku, Activists Tell Drivers: Help Our Fight for Human Rights." *The Guardian*. https://www.theguardian.com/world/2016/jun/18/baku-formula-one-grand-prix-azerbaijan-human-rights.

Medland, Chris. 2019. "Ferrari to Run Special Livery in Australia." *RACER*. https://racer.com/2019/03/13/ferrari-to-run-special-livery-in-australia/.

Medland, Chris. 2019. "INSIGHT: Behind the Rich Energy Mess at Haas." *RACER*. https://racer.com/2019/07/15/insight-behind-the-rich-energy-mess-at-haas/.

Miles, Ben. 2020. "The Nine Most Successful F1 Teams of All Time (List)." Goodwood. https://www.goodwood.com/grr/

race/historic/2020/4/the-nine-most-successful-f1-teams-of-all-time/.

Miller, Robin. 1993. "Rookie Driver Makes Impressive Debut." *Indianapolis Star,* June 14, 33. https://www.newspapers.com/image/107339687/?terms=andrea%20Montermini%20detroit&match=1.

Mitchell, Scott. 2018. "British Firm Not Ready to 'Relinquish' Force India Bid." *Motorsport.com.* https://us.motorsport.com/f1/news/rich-energy-force-india-buyout/3152345/.

Mitchell, Scott. 2019. "Gunther Steiner Needs 'Thinking Hat' Amid Haas F1 Income Drop." *Autosport.* https://www.autosport.com/f1/news/gunther-steiner-needs-thinking-hat-amid-haas-f1-income-drop-4987752/4987752/.

Mitchell, Scott. 2019. "Haas Title Sponsor Likens Doubters to Moon Landing Truthers." *Motorsport.com.* https://us.motorsport.com/f1/news/haas-rich-energy-doubters-moon-landing/4333923/.

Mitchell, Scott. 2019. "Haas Will Run Rich Branding at British GP, Says Steiner." *Motorsport.com.* https://www.motorsport.com/f1/news/haas-rich-energy-british-gp/4492480/.

Mitchell, Scott. 2019. "McLaren Signs Deal with British American Tobacco." *Motorsport.com.* https://us.motorsport.com/f1/news/british-american-tobacco-mclaren-deal/4335601/.

Mitchell, Scott. 2019. "Vettel Explains Why He Returned to Canadian GP Podium." *Motorsport.com.* https://us.motorsport.com/f1/news/vettel-explains-return-podium-canada/4461873/.

Mitchell, Scott. 2018. "Why Perez Led Action Against Force India Formula 1 Team." *Autosport.* https://www.autosport.com/f1/news/why-perez-led-action-against-force-india-formula-1-team-5293431/5293431/.

"Monaco 1989: Brabham's Final Fling." n.d. *Yahoo Sports AU.* https://au.sports.yahoo.com/monaco-1989-brabham-final-fling-145520384.html.

"Monaco Announce Cancellation of 2020 F1 Race Due to Coronavirus." 2020. F1. https://www.formula1.com/en/latest/article.monaco-announce-cancellation-2020-f1-race.4tpwalvxWpDL0uwRMnV9TI.html.

Morlidge, Matt. 2021. "Haas F1 Condemn 'Abhorrent' Nikita Mazepin Actions, Social Media Video." *Sky Sports.* https://www.skysports.com/f1/news/12433/12155959/haas-f1-condemn-abhorrent-nikita-mazepin-actions-social-media-video.

"Multi-platform Media Company." n.d. Red Bull Media House https://www.redbullmediahouse.com/en/about-us.

Neate, Rupert. 2020. "Fugitive Indian Tycoon Vijay Mallya Applies for UK Asylum." *The Guardian.* https://www.theguardian.com/law/2020/jun/10/-fugitive-indian-tycoon-vijay-mallya-applies-for-uk-asylum.

Neate, Rupert. 2021. "Meet Kyril Louis-Dreyfus, 23—English Football's Youngest Chairman." *The Guardian.* https://www.theguardian.com/football/2021/feb/20/meet-kyril-louis-dreyfus-23-english-football-youngest-chairman.

"News." n.d. Haas F1 Team. https://www.haasf1team.com/news/haas-f1-team-names-guti%C3%A9rrez-2016-race-seat.

"News: Rich Energy Announced as Haas F1 Team Title Partner." 2018. Haas F1 Team. https://www.haasf1team.com/news/-news-rich-energy-announced-haas-f1-team-title-partner.

"NOAA's Gulfstream IV in the Hangar at Yokota Airforce Base in Japan." 2022. Office of Marine and Aviation Operations, January 10. https://www.omao.noaa.gov/find/media/images/noaas-gulfstream-iv-hangar-yokota-airforce-base-japan.

Noble, Jonathan. 2019. "Ferrari Will Retain F1 Veto as Part of New 2021 Concorde Agreement." *Autosport.* autosport.com/f1/news/147422/ferrari-will-retain-veto-in-new-concorde-agreement.

Noble, Jonathan. 2019. "Ferrari's New Matte Paint a Performance Benefit." *Motorsport.com.* https://us.motorsport.com/f1/news/ferrari-matte-paint-performance-benefit/4338383/.

Noble, Jonathan. 2021. "Gunther Steiner: Haas F1 Concept Inspired by Domenicali." *Motorsport.com.* https://us.motorsport.com/f1/news/steiner-haas-f1-business-model-inspired-by-domenicali/5325509/.

Noble, Jonathan. 2019. "Haas Defends Rich Energy's Aim of Beating Red Bull in Formula 1." *Autosport*. https://www.autosport.com/f1/news/141372/haas-beating-red-bull-is-the-right-ambition.

Noble, Jonathan. 2015. "Haas Formula 1 Squad Buys Marussia Factory but Not the Team." *Autosport*. https://www.autosport.com/f1/news/haas-formula-1-squad-buys-marussia-factory-but-not-the-team-5019509/5019509/.

Noble, Jonathan. 2019. "The Key Battle Facing Rich Energy." *Motorsport.com*. https://www.motorsport.com/f1/news/the-key-battle-facing-rich-energy/4373126/.

Noble, Jonathan. 2009. "Renault Given Two-year Suspended Ban." *Autosport*. https://www.autosport.com/f1/news/-renault-given-two-year-suspended-ban-4433045/4433045/.

Noble, Jonathan. 2019. "Rich Energy Asks Haas to Remove Contested Logo for Canada." *Motorsport.com*. https://www.motorsport.com/f1/news/haas-rich-energy-logo-canada/4454083/.

Noble, Jonathan. 2007. "Super Aguri to Sue SS United." *Autosport*. https://www.autosport.com/f1/news/61700/super-aguri-to-sue-ss-united.

"Obituary: Jean-Pierre Van Rossem." 2018. *Independent.ie*. https://www.independent.ie/world-news/europe/-obituary-jean-pierre-van-rossem-37652550.html.

"OMG Racing Announces New Title Sponsorship with Rich Energy," February 14, 2020. British Super Bike. https://www.britishsuperbike.com/news/omg-racing-announces-new-title-sponsorship-partnership-with-rich-energy/.

"OMG Racing—About," n.d. https://www.omgracing.co.uk/about.

"Organisation | Federation Internationale De L'Automobile." n.d. FIA. https://www.fia.com/organisation.

"Osječka Robna Burza." OSRB. https://osrb.hr/.

"Our Story." LIVINGPROEF. https://www.livingproef.nl/our-story.

Pagliery, Jose. 2016. "Race Car Driver Arrested in Alleged $2 Billion Payday Lending Empire." *CNN Business*. https://money.cnn.com/2016/02/10/news/payday-lending-scott-tucker-arrest/.

Pangarkar, Nitin, and Mohit Agarwal.

2013. "The Wind Behind Red Bull's Wings." *Forbes*. https://www.forbes.com/sites/forbesasia/2013/06/24/the-wind-behind-red-bulls-wings/.

"Parmalat." 2016. Financial Scandals, Scoundrels & Crises. https://www.econcrises.org/2016/11/29/parmalat/.

"Parmalat: 40-year History at Stake—Dec. 23, 2003." 2003. *CNN*. https://www.cnn.com/2003/BUSINESS/12/22/italy.parmalat.sidebar/.

"Parmalat Funds Siphoned by Tanzi." 2003. *BBC News*. http://news.bbc.co.uk/2/hi/business/3355605.stm.

"Part 42—Change of Solicitor—Civil Procedure Rules." n.d. Justice.gov.uk. https://www.justice.gov.uk/courts/procedure-rules/civil/rules/part42.

Partridge, Matthew. 2020. "Great Frauds in History: Jean-Pierre Van Rossem's Money-making Machine." *MoneyWeek*. https://moneyweek.com/investments/-investment-strategy/601415/great-frauds-in-history-jean-pierre-van-rossems-money-making.

Perez, Jerry. 2018. "Show Me the Money: The Finances Behind Indycar, NASCAR, and Formula 1." *The Drive*. https://www.thedrive.com/accelerator/22168/behind-the-shadowy-billion-do llar-payouts-of-f1-nascar-and-indycar.

"Peterwindsor." n.d. YouTube. https://www.youtube.com/channel/UCPwy2q7BNjdLYu1kM_OEJVw.

"Photo of the Day—John Paul, Sr.'s Porsche at the 1978 24 Hours of Le Mans | 24h-lemans.com." 2016. 24 Heures du Mans. https://www.24h-lemans.com/en/news/photo-of-the-day-john-paul-sr-s-porsche-at-the-1978-24-hours-of-le-mans-43873.

"Police Arrested American Oil Financier David Thieme on Allegations." 1981. UPI. https://www.upi.com/Archives/1981/04/14/Police-arrested-American-o il-financier-David-Thieme-on-allegatio ns/2698356072400/.

"Prince Out After Boardroom Tussle." *Autosport*, n.d. https://www.autosport.com/f1/news/6509/prince-out-after-boardroom-tussle.

Pruett, Marshall. 2017. "The Ponzi-Scheming Scumbags of Sports Car Racing That Were on Par with Bernie Madoff." *Road & Track*. https://

www.roadandtrack.com/motorsports/
a32941/sports-car-ponzi-schemes/.

Pruett, Marshall. 2020. "Figueiredo Linked to Investigation Into Embezzlement, Money Laundering." *RACER*. https://racer.com/2020/06/26/-figueiredo-embezzlement-money-laundering/.

Pryson, Mike. 2021. "Uralkali Haas F1 Team to Reveal VF-21 at Bahrain Test." *Autoweek*. https://www.autoweek.com/racing/formula-1/a35769654/uralkali-haas-f1-team-reveal-vf21-bahrain/.

"Q&A." n.d. Rich OMG. https://www.richomg.com/qanda.

"Quantum Still Plotting Lotus Buy-in." 2014. *Yahoo News Singapore*. https://sg.news.yahoo.com/quantum-still-plotting-lotus-buy-072933109.html.

"Red Bull." n.d. Forbes. https://www.forbes.com/companies/red-bull/#36ccfb2861ce.

"Red Bull Energy Drink." n.d. Red Bull CA (EN). https://www.redbull.com/ca-en/energydrink/contact-sponsorship.

"Red Bull Energy Drink—Official Website." n.d. Red Bull. https://www.redbull.com/us-en/energydrink/company-profile.

"Registrirajte SE." RICH d.o.o.—prihod, dobit, zaposleni, analiza, kontakt podaci. http://www.poslovna.hr/(X(1)S(mhcwoppto5azmaaelcmxipju))/lite/rich/1267894/subjekti.aspx?AspxAutoDetectCookieSupport=1.

Rencken, Dieter. 2018. "2018 Formula 1 Team Budgets Revealed: Part Two." *RaceFans*. https://www.racefans.net/2018/12/26/the-cost-of-f1-revealed-how-much-teams-spent-in-2018-part-two/.

Rencken, Dieter, and Keith Collantine. 2018. "Haas-Rich Energy 2019 F1 Deal Came About Quickly—Steiner." *RaceFans*. https://www.racefans.net/2018/10/26/haas-rich-energy-deal-came-about-quickly-steiner/.

"Represent Yourself in Court." n.d. Gov.uk. https://www.gov.uk/represent-yourself-in-court.

Reuters. 2019. "Bahrain: Formula 1 Ignores Rights Commitments." Human Rights Watch. https://www.hrw.org/news/2019/03/22/bahrain-formula-1-ignores-rights-commitments.

Reuters. 2019. "Toro Rosso F1 Team Pushing for Name Change." *ESPN*. https://www.espn.com/f1/story/_/id/27742970/toro-rosso-f1-team-pushing-name-change.

Reuters. 2020. "Mercedes F1 Spent $442 Million in 2019 but Still Made Money." *ESPN*. https://www.espn.com/f1/story/_/id/29823419/mercedes-f1-spent-442-million-2019-made-money.

"Rich Energy." n.d. West Ham United. https://www.whufc.com/teams/women/partners/rich-energy.

"Rich Energy." n.d. Wikipedia. https://en.wikipedia.org/wiki/Rich_Energy.

"Rich Energy (Archived)." Rich Energy, n.d. https://web.archive.org/web/20190123072246/https://richenergy.com/.

"Rich Energy (Archived)." Wikipedia, n.d. https://web.archive.org/web/20210213122656/https://en.wikipedia.org/wiki/Rich_Energy.

"Rich Energy Drink (Archived)." n.d. https://web.archive.org/web/20130616032122/http://richenergydrink.com/.

Rich Energy Drink (Archived). n.d. https://web.archive.org/web/20130620163255/http://richenergydrink.com.ia18.4w.com/?page_id=21.

"Rich Energy Drink Better Business Bureau® Profile." n.d. BBB. https://www.bbb.org/us/ne/lincoln/profile/-food-manufacturer/rich-energy-drink-0714-300172708.

"Rich Energy Haas F1 Team 2019 Livery Unveiled." 2019. Haas F1 Team. https://media.haasf1team.com/files/pdf/FINAL%20070219%20VF-19%20Livery%20Unveil%20Release-475.pdf.

"Rich Energy: Haas Vastly Superior to Rivals." 2019. Planet F1. https://www.planetf1.com/news/rich-energy-haas-vastly-superior-to-rivals/.

Rich Energy US (Archived), n.d. https://web.archive.org/web/20190527144841/https://www.richenergy.us/.

"Rich Energy US." n.d. Rich Energy US—The Sole Distributor Of Rich Energy In The United States. https://www.richenergy.us/.

Richards, Giles. 2014. "Sebastian Vettel Goes to Ferrari for More Than Cash and a Quick Car | Giles Richards." *The Guardian*. https://www.theguardian.com/sport/blog/2014/oct/04/sebastian-vettel-ferrari-red-bull-cash.

Richards, Giles. 2020. "F1 Teams Agree to Introduce Budget Cap from 2021 Onwards." *The Guardian.* https://www.theguardian.com/sport/2020/may/23/-f1-teams-agree-to-introduce-budget-cap-from-2021-onwards.

Robinson, Joshua. 2017. "Liberty Media Names Chase Carey as Formula One CEO, Replacing Bernie Ecclestone." *Wall Street Journal.* https://www.wsj.com/articles/chase-carey-replaces-formula-ones-bernie-ecclestone-as-ceo-1485210949.

Ruhling, Nancy A. 2019. "Buyers in Monte Carlo Have Access to a Billionaires' Playground." Mansion Global. https://www.mansionglobal.com/articles/-buyers-in-monte-carlo-have-access-to-a-billionaires-playground-202155.

Rutherford, Chrissy. "Happy Birthday, Naomi Campbell! See Her Top 10 Moments in Bazaar." *Harper's Bazaar,* March 3, 2021. https://www.harpersbazaar.com/fashion/photography/g2048/naomi-campbell-in-bazaar/?slide=1.

"St. Regis Bangkok." Marriott International. https://www.marriott.com/hotels/hotel-photos/bkkxr-the-st-regis-bangkok/.

Salisbury, Matt. 2007. "Stepney Leaves Ferrari." *Crash.Net.* https://www.crash.net/f1/news/59106/1/ferrari-dismisses-stepney.

Saunders, Nate. 2020. "The Bizarre Haas-Rich Energy Saga Explained." *ESPN.* https://www.espn.com/f1/story/_/id/27221746/the-bizarre-haas-rich-energy-saga-explained.

Saunders, Nate. 2022. "Haas Formula One to Decide on Nikita Mazepin; Drops Uralkali Branding from Car after Russian Invasion of Ukraine." ESPN. February 25. https://www.espn.com/f1/story/_/id/33368180/haas-decide-nikita-mazepin-uralkali-next-week.

Schrader, Stef. 2014. "Bernie Ecclestone Doesn't Like Bloggers Very Much." *Jalopnik.* https://jalopnik.com/bernie-ecclestone-doesnt-like-us-very-much-1660017542.

Schrader, Stef. 2017. "F1 Is Finally Posting Its Most Incredible Moments on YouTube and That Rules." *Jalopnik.* https://jalopnik.com/f1-is-finally-posting-its-most-incredible-moments-on-yo-1794132326.

Schrader, Stef. 2017. "Formula One Starts Acting Like a Modern Racing Series or Something." *Jalopnik.* https://jalopnik.com/formula-one-starts-acting-like-a-modern-racing-series-o-1792784970.

Schrader, Stef. 2017. "The Drug-Running Team Who Got Into Racing with a Bag Full of Cash at Le Mans." *Jalopnik.* https://jalopnik.com/the-drug-running-team-who-got-into-racing-with-a-bag-fu-1821122960.

Scicluna, Tony. n.d. "FIA Stands for Ferrari International Assistance." *Bleacher Report.* https://bleacherreport.com/articles/57410-fia-stands-for-ferrari-international-assistance.

"Sebastian Vettel." n.d. F1. https://www.formula1.com/en/drivers/hall-of-fame/Sebastian_Vettel.html.

Service, Robert. 2015. "The Crater That Keeps Swallowing Up Houses." *Siberian Times.* https://siberiantimes.com/other/others/news/n0388-the-crater-that-keeps-swallowing-up-houses/.

Simmons, Marcus. 2014. "The Short, Dazzling Story of Leyton House in F1: Marching to Civil War." *Motor Sport Magazine.* https://www.motorsportmagazine.com/archive/article/-june-2005/82/marching-to-civil-war.

Skalocky, Stephen. n.d. "Randy Lanier: IndyCar Driver and Drug Smuggler." *Sports Illustrated.* https://www.si.com/longform/true-crime/randy-lanier-indycar-drug-smuggler/index.html.

Smith, Luke. 2019. "Rich Energy Future to Be Decided by Singapore." *Crash.Net.* https://www.crash.net/f1/news/928439/1/rich-energy-future-be-decided-singapore.

Smith, Steven C. 2009. "Racing Rip Job: Pro Drivers Allegedly Burned by Con Man." *Autoweek.* https://www.autoweek.com/racing/more-racing/a2027001/racing-rip-job-pro-drivers-allegedly-burned-con-man/.

Somerfield, Matt. 2020. "Banned: Why Lotus' Twin-chassis Concept Was Outlawed." *Motorsport.com.* https://us.motorsport.com/f1/news/banned-tech-twin-chassis-lotus/4780031/.

"Soprano Ice Hair Removal." Nation Light, n.d. http://nationlight.ca/soprano-ice-platinum/.

Spence, Steve. 2007. "Big Scandal, Big Comedy at the Formula 1 Show." *Car and Driver*. https://www.caranddriver. com/features/a15146433/big-scandal- big-comedy-at-the-formula-1-show/.

Spurgeon, Brad. 1998. "Pollock Engineers the Deals at the Tyrrell Formula One Team: A Young Owner on the Fast Track." *The New York Times*. https:// www.nytimes.com/1998/08/15/sports/- IHT-pollock-engineers-the-deals-at- the-tyrrell-formula-one-team-a.html.

Spurgeon, Brad. 2012. "What's in a Formula One Name?" *The New York Times*. https://www.nytimes.com/2012/03/17/ sports/autoracing/17iht-srf1prix17.html.

"Spurned from F1, Rossi Joins Andretti IndyCar Team." 2016. *Reuters*. https:// www.reuters.com/article/us-motor- indycar-rossi/spurned-from-f1-rossi- joins-andretti-indycar-team-idUSK CN0VW2JL.

Spurring, Quentin. 2007. "McLaren F1 Team Fined $100 Million: Disqualified from 2007 Season." *Autoweek*. https:// www.autoweek.com/news/a2058376/- mclaren-f1-team-fined-100-million- disqualified-2007-season/.

"Staxoweb," n.d. https://staxoweb.com/.

"Steiner: 'Annoying' Electronic Issues Hampering Haas." 2019. F1. https:// www.formula1.com/en/latest/article. steiner-%27annoying%27-electronic- issues-hampering-haas.3VT5p1fCl GzQwDGemrLgH8.html.

"Steiner Fined for Critical Russian GP Radio Message." 2019. F1. https://www. formula1.com/en/latest/article.steiner- fined-for-critical-russian-gp-radio- message.5CuAO9DJR6ejq3or42zznz. html.

"Steiner Saw 'Nothing Encouraging' from Haas in Belgium.'" 2019. F1. https://www.formula1.com/en/ latest/article.steiner-saw-nothing- encouraging-from-haas-in-belgium. 3IoVoRnuYDALq3jKSKBhIl.html.

"Steiner—Low Expectations Numbed Haas's Mexico Disappointment." 2019. F1. https://www.formula1.com/en/ latest/article.steiner-low-expectations- numbed-haass-mexico-disappoint ment.7jIaxhAQgQZUED5ihJ49C8. html.

Stemple, Jonathan. 2020. "Owners of Solar Company That Caused Loss for Buffett Plead Guilty Over Ponzi Scheme." *Reuters*. https://www.reuters.com/ article/usa-crime-dc-solar-fraud- idAFL1N29T1JN.

"Stepney—Not My Fault | F1 News." 2008. *Sky Sports*. https://www.skysports.com/ f1/news/12433/3067476/stepney-not- my-fault.

Straw, Edd. 2020. "The Lost F1 Team That Launched Newey." *Motorsport. com*. https://us.motorsport.com/f1/ news/adrian-newey-leyton-house- march/4809840/?nrt=54.

Sung, Patrick, and Wayne Sterling. 2022. "These Are the Sports That Russia Has Been Suspended From." CNN. March 7. https://www.cnn.com/2022/03/01/ sport/sports-russia-banned-from- football-rugby-spt-intl/.

"Super Aguri Acquisition." n.d. Magma Group. http://magmagroup.co/insight/- case-studies/super-aguri-acquisition/.

"Super Aguri Withdraw from F1 Championship." 2008. *Reuters*. https:// www.reuters.com/article/idIN India-33426520080506.

Sweet, Ken, and Fatima Hussein. 2022. "Sanctions Hit Russian Economy, Although Putin Says Otherwise." Associated Press. April 23. https://apnews. com/article/russia-ukraine-business- europe-economy-dd7bcb1c09b4020a3f 75048c4045fa90.

Sylt, Christian. 2017. "Exclusive: Ferrari's $100 Million F1 Bonus at Risk." *Forbes*. https://www.forbes.com/sites/ csylt/2017/01/21/exclusive-ferraris-100- million-f1-bonus-at-risk/.

Sylt, Christian. 2018. "Haas: The Formula for Reducing F1's Costs." *Forbes*. August 20. https://www.forbes.com/sites/ csylt/2018/08/20/haas-the-formula-for- reducing-f1s-costs/?sh=77eff4552c31.

Sylt, Christian. 2019. "Revealed: Sponsors Fuel Formula One with $30 Billion." *Forbes*. https://www.forbes. com/sites/csylt/2019/05/19/revealed- sponsors-fuel-formula-one-with-30- billion/#4ba8baec2416

Sylt, Christian. 2019. "Revealed: The $285 Million Cost of Winning the F1 Championship." *Forbes*. April 26. https://www.forbes.com/sites/ csylt/2019/04/26/revealed-the-285- million-cost-of-winning-the-f1- championship/?sh=6c97dda223d8.

Sylt, Christian. 2020. "Revealed: The 1,000% Increase in F1 Team Spending."

Forbes. February 9, 2020. https://www.forbes.com/sites/csylt/2020/02/09/-revealed-the-1000-increase-in-f1-team-spending/?sh=77b22713d93e.

Sylt, Christian. 2016. "What Really Fuelled Gene Haas' $1 Billion F1 Bet." *Forbes.* March 25. https://www.forbes.com/sites/csylt/2016/03/25/what-really-fuelled-gene-haas-1-billion-f1-bet/?sh=647bb62b14c6.

Sylt, Christian. 2013. "What's It Cost to Compete in Formula One? An IndyCar Comparison." *NBC Sports' MotorSportsTalk.* https://motorsports.nbcsports.com/2013/05/22/whats-it-cost-to-compete-in-formula-one-an-indycar-comparison/.

Taylor, Louise. 2020. "Founder of Soft Drinks Firm Rich Energy Bids to Buy Sunderland." *Guardian.* https://www.theguardian.com/football/2020/jul/24/-founder-of-soft-drinks-firm-rich-energy-bids-to-buy-sunderland.

"Ten Fascinating Facts About the Very First F1 Race." 2016. F1. https://www.formula1.com/en/latest/features/2016/5/f1-first-race-1950-silverstone.html.

Thomsen, Ian. 1993. "Ligier's De Rouvre: Man of Many Parts." *The New York Times.* https://www.nytimes.com/1993/05/21/sports/IHT-ligiers-de-rouvre-man-of-many-parts.html.

"Toby Sowery." n.d. IndyCar.com. https://www.indycar.com/Series/Indy-Lights/Toby-Sowery.

"Toro Rosso | Formula One." n.d. *Guardian.* https://www.theguardian.com/sport/2007/mar/12/formulaone.motorsports32.

Tran, Mark. 2004. "Red Bull Buys Jaguar F1 Team." *The Guardian.* https://www.theguardian.com/business/2004/nov/15/formulaone.money.

"Tulumarenje: Počinje Party League Croatia Uz Energetski Napitak Rich." 2011. *MojZagreb.info.* https://mojzagreb.info/zagreb/tulumarenje-pocinje-party-league-croatia-uz-energetski-napitak-rich.

"Tyre Issues to Blame Again for Haas's 2019 Chinese Grand Prix Woe." 2019. F1. https://www.formula1.com/en/latest/article.tyre-issues-to-blame-again-for-haas-china-woe.3J9MJC6O0akPEkh5AxAQKj.html.

Ujah, Emma. 2017. "We'll Deliver Electric Cars to Nigerian Market in 2018, Says Prince Ado Ibrahim." *Vanguard News.* https://www.vanguardngr.com/2017/08/-well-deliver-electric-cars-nigerian-market-2018-says-prince-ado-ibrahim/.

UPI. 1982. "$40,000 Swindle Charged to 'Mystery Driver.'" *The Town Talk,* June 26, 1982, 11. https://www.newspapers.com/image/?clipping_id=29781516&fcfToken=eyJhbGciOiJIUzI1NiIsInR5cCI6IkpXVCJ9.eyJmcmVlLXZpZXctctaWQiOjIxNTk3NzAyMywiaWF0IjoxNjQxNTg3OTk2LCJleHAiOjE2NDE2NzQzOTZ9.wb4O8yq3d9-EiBE929hgDK6-PJpee_l9jPzJp6JiMSM.

"Uralkali Announces Partnership with Haas F1 Team." 2021. Press Releases | PJSC Uralkali. https://www.uralkali.com/press_center/press_releases/item43939/.

"US Driver Scott Speed Dropped by Toro Rosso." 2007. *ESPN.* https://www.espn.com/racing/news/story?id=2955466&seriesId=6.

"Used Ferrari for Sale (with Photos)." n.d. CarGurus. https://www.cargurus.com/Cars/l-Used-Ferrari-Enzo-d442.

Valentine, Ian. 2002. "Future Bleak for Arrows F1 Team as Orange Mulls Sponsorship Deal." *Campaign.* https://www.campaignlive.co.uk/article/future-bleak-arrows-f1-team-orange-mulls-sponsorship-deal/150688.

van Wingerden, Joas. 2019. "F1 Pre-season Test Results: Fastest Laps, Full Lap Count." *GPFans.* https://www.gpfans.com/en/articles/4275/f1-pre-season-test-results-fastest-laps-full-lap-count/.

Vaughn, Mark. 2019. "Alexander Rossi Not Holding His Breath Waiting for F1 Call from Ferrari, Mercedes." *Autoweek.* https://www.autoweek.com/racing/indycar/a1719416/alexander-rossi-being-american-f1/.

Vertuno, Jim. "Haas F1 Tussling in Middle of Pack in 2nd Season." *AP News,* October 21, 2017. https://apnews.com/article/f45db47719e844ef8bc6e88dbb891908.

"Wales | History, Geography, Facts, & Points of Interest." 2021. Britannica. https://www.britannica.com/place/Wales.

Wallis, Daniel. 2013. "Venezuela Investigates Sports Stars in Big Currency Scam." *Reuters.* https://www.reuters.

com/article/amp/idUKBRE99H03920
131018?edition-redirect=uk.

Walsworth, Jack. 2015. "Lotus Founder Colin Chapman Dies at Age 54." *Automotive News*. https://www.autonews.com/article/20151215/CCHISTORY/151219934/lotus-founder-colin-chapman-dies-at-age-54.

Warren, Katie. 2019. "15 Wild Facts About Monaco, Where 32% of Residents Are Millionaires." *Business Insider*. https://www.businessinsider.com/mind-blowing-facts-about-monaco-wealth-2019-5.

Watkins, Gary. 2014. "Stand-in Delivers January 2008." *Motor Sport Magazine*. https://www.motorsportmagazine.com/archive/article/january-2008/96/stand-in-delivers.

Watkins, Gary. 2018. "Jean-Pierre Van Rossem, Onyx Formula 1 Team Backer, Dies." *Autosport*. https://www.autosport.com/f1/news/140665/backer-behind-onyx-f1-team-dies.

"'We Didn't Expect It to Be This Big of an Issue'—Steiner Explains Haas Double DNF in Austria." 2020. F1. https://www.formula1.com/en/latest/article.we-didnt-expect-it-to-be-this-big-of-an-issue-steiner-explains-haas-double.6DF2ZPyJu8dW89q2BLJzqh.html.

"'We Have Nothing'—Steiner Admits Haas Can't Wait for 2020 After Difficult USGP." 2019. F1. https://www.formula1.com/en/latest/article.we-have-nothing-steiner-admits-haas-cant-wait-for-2020-after-difficult-home.7jMGGn7a093sJlqfsAkiYP.html.

Weaver, Matt. 2019. "NASCAR Team and Track Sponsor DC Solar Files for Chapter 11 Bankruptcy." *Autoweek*. https://www.autoweek.com/racing/nascar/a1716071/nascar-team-and-track-sponsor-files-chapter-11-bankruptcy/.

Weeks, Jim. 2017. "The Mysterious Nigerian Prince Who Scammed His Way Into Owning an F1 Team." *Vice*. https://www.vice.com/en/article/gvawv7/the-mysterious-nigerian-prince-who-scammed-his-way-into-owning-an-f1-team.

"What Does Business Recovery Actually Mean? Can My Company Be Rescued?" 2021. Real Business Rescue. https://www.realbusinessrescue.co.uk/articles/business-insolvency/what-does-business-recovery-actually-mean-can-my-company-be-rescued.

"What the Teams Said—Race Day in Abu Dhabi." 2019. F1. https://www.formula1.com/en/latest/article.what-the-teams-said-race-day-in-abu-dhabi-2019.1qnfNv0o4bGGsDu8ehcUFQ.html.

"When Did Mazepin Spin?" n.d. When did Mazepin spin? https://whendidmazepinspin.com/.

Whitman, Elizabeth. n.d. "DC Solar Powers Electric Cars in Arizona Parking Lots, NASCAR Races." *Phoenix New Times*. https://www.phoenixnewtimes.com/news/dc-solar-offers-free-power-in-phoenix-parking-lots-and-nascar-races-11071663.

"Why Sergio Perez Took Action Against Force India." 2018. *Eurosport*. https://www.eurosport.com/formula-1/why-sergio-perez-took-action-against-force-india_sto6865773/story.shtml.

"Whyte Bikes: Rich Energy, Haas F1 Team Title Sponsor, Loses Court Case for Copying Whyte Bikes' Stag Logo." May 14, 2019. https://web.archive.org/web/20190516005143/https://whyte.bike/pages/stag.

"William Storey Management," n.d. williamstorey.com.

Williams, Andrew. 2019. "The Rokit IO Pro 3D Is a Strange, Pointless Zombie of a Phone." *Wired UK*. https://www.wired.co.uk/article/rokit-io-pro-3d-review.

"Williams Announce Sale of F1 Team to US Investment Company." 2020. F1. https://www.formula1.com/en/latest/article.breaking-williams-announce-sale-of-f1-team-to-us-investment-company.5hjIdxTo9MOBOlHkmfGjo.html.

"Williams Could Sell F1 Team as Board Announces £13m Loss in 2019 and Split from Title Sponsor." 2020. F1. https://www.formula1.com/en/latest/article.williams-could-sell-f1-team-as-board-announces-gbp13m-loss-in-2019-and-split.455wGjds3WOQf7gdSuqJRf.html.

Williamson, Martin. n.d. "Crashgate Explained | Formula 1 | F1 Features." *ESPN*. http://en.espn.co.uk/f1/motorsport/story/14272.html.

Williamson, Martin. n.d. "Monaco Grand

Prix 1958—Trintignant Wins on Home Soil." *ESPN.* http://en.espn.co.uk/f1/motorsport/story/16050.html.

"Wind Up a Company That Owes You Money." n.d. Gov.uk. https://www.gov.uk/wind-up-a-company-that-owes-you-money.

Winderman, Ira, and Anthony Lednovich. 1986. "Auto Racing Faces Problem of Drug Money Financing." *Sun Sentinel.* https://www.sun-sentinel.com/news/-fl-xpm-1986-03-23-8601180194-story.html.

Wood, Rachel, and Matthew Knight. 2017. "Bernie Ecclestone 'Made Some Enemies ... But He Did a Lot of Good.'" *CNN.* https://www.cnn.com/2017/03/21/motorsport/f1-bernie-ecclestone-maurice-hamilton/index.html.

INDEX

Numbers in **bold italics** indicate illustrations